MANAGEMENT OF HUMAN SERVICE PROGRAMS

FIFTH EDITION

Judith A. Lewis
Governors State University

Thomas R. Packard
San Diego State University

Michael D. Lewis
Executive Director
Educational World Charities, Chicago

BROOKS/COLE
CENGAGE Learning™

Australia • Brazil • Japan • Korea • Mexico • Singapore • Spain • United Kingdom • United States

BROOKS/COLE
CENGAGE Learning™

Management of Human Service Programs,
Fifth Edition

Judith A. Lewis, Thomas R. Packard, and
Michael D. Lewis

Senior Publisher: Linda Schreiber-Ganster

Acquisitions Editor: Seth Dobrin

Assistant Editor: Naomi Dreyer

Editorial Assistant: Suzanna Kincaid

Media Editor: Elizabeth Momb

Program Manager: Tami Strang

Content Project Manager: Greg Johnson,
PreMediaGlobal

Design Director: Rob Hugel

Art Director: Caryl Gorska

Print Buyer: Judy Inouye

Rights Acquisitions Specialist: Roberta Broyer

Production Service: PreMediaGlobal

Text Designer: PreMediaGlobal

Text Researcher: Roberta Broyer

Copy Editor: Maggie Sears

Cover Designer: Caryl Gorska

Cover Image: Dimitri Vervitsiotis/Getty Images

Compositor: PreMediaGlobal

For product information and technology assistance, contact us at
Cengage Learning Customer & Sales Support, 1-800-354-9706.

For permission to use material from this text or product,
submit all requests online at **www.cengage.com/permissions.**
Further permissions questions can be e-mailed to
permissionrequest@cengage.com.

Library of Congress Control Number: 2011930427

Student Edition:
ISBN-13: 978-0-8400-3427-4

ISBN-10: 0-8400-3427-X

Brooks/Cole
20 Davis Drive
Belmont, CA 94002-3098
USA

Cengage Learning is a leading provider of customized learning solutions
with office locations around the globe, including Singapore, the United
Kingdom, Australia, Mexico, Brazil, and Japan. Locate your local office at
www.cengage.com/global.

Cengage Learning products are represented in Canada by
Nelson Education, Ltd.

To learn more about Brooks/Cole, visit **www.cengage.com/brookscole**

Purchase any of our products at your local college store or at our
preferred online store **www.cengagebrain.com.**

Printed in the United States of America
1 2 3 4 5 6 7 15 14 13 12 11

CONTENTS

PREFACE

Human service programs vary widely in terms of the populations they serve, the methods they use, and the specific concerns they address. Overriding these differences, however, is an undeniable commonality of value and purpose. The people who manage and deliver human services do this work because they want to facilitate human development and enhance the quality of life in their communities. Their organizations reflect these goals as well. By and large, the well-being of the clients and consumers is the central focus of any agency.

This focus makes it unlikely that the management models used in the business world could be adopted without modification. Human service organizations have always had their own set of concerns, but the twenty-first century has brought especially difficult challenges. The gap between the haves and have-nots grew exponentially in the first decade of the new century, and the great recession that began in 2007 threw many more families into poverty. These events have placed severe pressure on agencies by causing a rapid growth in the number of people needing services at the same time that the resources for providing assistance have shrunk. The human service organizations that have been most nimble, creative, flexible, and culturally competent are the ones that have been most successful in adapting to these new realities.

The challenges and opportunities facing human service programs provide the context within which managerial functions are carried out. In essence, management is the act of facilitating the creation of a plan; organizing the people and resources needed to carry out the plan; encouraging, supervising, and motivating the workers who perform the component tasks; evaluating the results; and revising plans based on this evaluation. These managerial activities are often carried out by people who define themselves as *managers*, but they are also handled effectively by service providers, community leaders, consumer groups, and people in a variety of other roles. Anyone who cares about a human service program's mission learns that he or she must also care about the way the program is managed.

This book takes the reader along the road toward understanding the purposes and processes of human service management. We begin by addressing some of the management challenges that are unique to human service settings. We examine the environments that have an impact on human service organizations and then move on to explore program planning, organizational design, human resource management, supervision, finances, information systems, program evaluation, leadership, and organizational change. As we delve into these functions, we always go from the theoretical to the practical, including in each chapter both case studies and competency-building activities.

NEW TO THIS EDITION

We recognize that effective human service programs must be nimble in response to rapid change. In each new edition of this book we have included updated material that responds to innovations in managerial practice, to the advent of new technologies, and to challenges brought about by environmental transformations. In this fifth edition, we have also included a number of specific changes, such as the following:

- A case study is introduced in Chapter 1. In each subsequent chapter, we follow the progress of the Grandview Community Center, demonstrating how the concepts we introduce can be applied in real-life practice.
- At the close of each chapter, we provide a competency-building activity. These activities continue from chapter to chapter, allowing readers to create their own hypothetical programs and to develop implementation plans in response to what they have learned. These competency-building activities are included in electronic resource manuals for both faculty and students.
- Discussion questions are now available to students and faculty in their electronic resource manuals.
- We have added new examples of human service efforts drawn from multicultural and international settings.
- Many chapters include lists of relevant Web-based resources that relate to the chapter's content.
- Updated references reflect emerging developments in research and in the field.

These changes are designed to help students and other readers see themselves as people who have the potential to play a managerial role in the multicultural human service organization of the twenty-first century.

ACKNOWLEDGMENTS

First, we would like to thank the reviewers whose comments and suggestions helped us develop the fifth edition: Joe Adamo, Cazenovia College; Brian Aldrich, Winona State University; Bill Culp, Abilene Christian University; Karen Alkema, Bethel College; Robert Amundson, SUNY Ulster; and Galo Alava, Saint Leo University.

Second, our editors at Brooks/Cole Cengage personify excellence in their own work and still manage to be supportive and supremely patient with the authors. We are especially grateful for the help we have received from Seth Dobrin and Greg Johnson. We also appreciate the human service professionals and students who have inspired us with their dedication to their clients and communities. Tom Packard expresses particular appreciation to former students, who asked excellent questions and showed how they assimilated and used this material. Those making specific contributions in this edition include Nicole Bishop and Susan Linn. Consulting clients and research collaborators continue to be helpful, this time including the Academy for Professional Excellence under the direction of Jennifer Tucker-Tatlow, the Child Advocacy Institute at the University of San Diego, and the San Diego Workforce Partnership.

AUTHOR BIOGRAPHIES

Judith A. Lewis retired from Governors State University, where she was a department chair and professor in the College of Health and Human Services. She is a former president of the American Counseling Association (ACA) and the International Association of Marriage and Family Counselors and a board member of Counselors for Social Justice. She is the co-author of two additional texts for Brooks/Cole Cengage, *Substance Abuse Counseling* and *Community Counseling: A Multicultural-Social Justice Perspective.*

Thomas R. Packard teaches administration, macro practice, and social policy in the School of Social Work at San Diego State University and conducts research and consultation projects through the School's Academy for Professional Excellence. He has been an organization development consultant specializing in human service and government organizations, including 6.5 years in the City of San Diego's Organizational Effectiveness Program, which he managed for 1.5 years. He has been the director of two community-based human service organizations and has been a program evaluator for the County of San Diego. He is a Certified Social Work Manager.

Michael D. Lewis, Executive Director, Educational World Charities, Chicago, is a retired Professor of Counseling and Psychology at Governors State University. For more than 35 years he has consulted with national and international corporations with regard to the implementation of their employee assistance programs. He has advised educational institutions around the world in countries as diverse as Israel and Botswana. He has co-authored two other Brooks/Cole texts, *Community Counseling: Empowerment Strategies for a Diverse Society* and *Counseling Programs for Employees in the Workplace.*

FACING THE CHALLENGES OF MANAGEMENT

What do we mean when we talk about human service organizations and the ways in which they should be managed? An organization can be any group of people—large or small—working together toward common goals. In a *human service organization*, however, these goals are always focused on improving the lives of the people and communities being served. Managers and direct service providers work toward the enhancement of human development in many ways and many settings, but their shared focus on human development brings with it a common outlook, a mutual set of problems, and the need for an approach to management that may differ from the business models in the profit-making environment.

TYPES OF HUMAN SERVICE AGENCIES

Human services are most often delivered in the context of the *human service agency*. An agency is a human service organization that is designed specifically to provide services to the community. Examples of human service agencies include (a) community agencies that provide a variety of service to meet the needs of people who live within a specified geographic area; (b) agencies that focus on particular issues or problem areas, such as mental health concerns, substance abuse, or developmental disabilities; (c) population-oriented agencies that meet the service and advocacy needs of a particular cultural group, age group, or gender; (d) career, employment, or rehabilitation agencies that help individuals gain skills and opportunities for positive career growth and economic security; and (e) advocacy organizations that work on behalf of populations that are subject to marginalization and prejudice. Educational institutions are not normally called *agencies*, but they too provide human services to students, families, and communities.

Although human service organizations are commonly described in terms of the kinds of help they provide and the populations they serve, they can also be differentiated on the basis of size. Human service organizations, all of which share a goal of life enhancement, can vary tremendously, from the tiny storefront agency, to the multifaceted community organization, to the statewide public service department. Human service agencies can also be categorized in terms of whether they are non-profit agencies, for-profit organizations, or governmental entities. Most of the examples used in this book are drawn from non-profit organizations, given that they have long played a central role in the human service world. A *non-profit* or *not-for-profit* organization is required to use its revenues for the purpose of carrying out its mission and cannot distribute profits to owners or shareholders. A *for-profit* organization may also have a mission that is focused on service, but its investors expect the revenue that is earned to yield a surplus that can be distributed as profit. A *governmental entity*, or *public agency*, can also be involved in the provision of human services but it does so as an official part of a local, state, or federal government.

The differentiations among human service agencies provide important descriptors, but it is important to be aware of how fluid these differentiations can be. Because human service agencies have people's needs as their first priority, they may change over time as their consumers' needs change. And because human needs do not always divide neatly into categories, an agency will often find it important to broaden programs and implement new helping strategies.

The Harlem Children's Zone (HCZ) provides an excellent example of a community-oriented organization in that it addresses a very clearly delineated neighborhood, but the primary focus of the HCZ has always been children and the search for ways to facilitate their success. In the attempt to help children, the HCZ has steadily moved in the direction of providing services to families and in fact to all members of the community.

> For children to do well, their families have to do well. And for families to do well, their community must do well. That is why HCZ works to strengthen families as well as empowering them to have a positive impact on their children's development. (Harlem Children's Zone, 2009).

Aunt Martha's Youth Service Center, near Chicago, also exemplifies growth and change in response to community needs. Aunt Martha's began as a small drop-in center designed to give young people a welcoming environment for sharing their thoughts and addressing their problems. Over the years, the agency's mission, *to be a caring community resource for children, youth, and families*, has remained intact, but the services have become far more complex.

As was true of the Harlem Children's Zone, the need to enhance the health of families and communities came to the fore. By 2010, Aunt Martha's operated a network of community health centers and had completed its 1,000,000th patient visit (Aunt Martha's Youth Service Center, 2010). What is particularly noteworthy about this organization is its growth from the category of "tiny storefront agency" to the category of large, multifaceted community organization.

Many human service agencies cross categories. Mental health programs that work with recovering patients provide direct mental health services but also carry out education and advocacy. Advocacy organizations created to meet the needs of a particular population expand to deal with issues related to multiple forms of discrimination. Even the distinctions among non-profit, for-profit, and governmental entities have become less clear as agencies work in collaborative networks and as boundaries between public and private financing have begun to blur (Gibelman & Furman, 2008).

THE NEED FOR MANAGERIAL COMPETENCY

Within a human service agency, we often find a number of programs. A *program* is on a smaller scale than a human service agency or institution and might be developed within a larger agency in order to meet specific needs. For instance, a mental health center might have a special program for families of children with mental illness or an agency providing employment services might have a special program for people who have been unemployed for a long period of time.

Especially at the program level, management becomes a major concern not just for agency directors and supervisors but also for the people who see themselves primarily as professional service providers. Human service professionals used to hesitate at the thought of being managers, assuming that they would be cut off from the lifeblood of day-to-day work with clients. Unfortunately, this stereotype led many human service providers to avoid becoming competent in management for fear that they might somehow be turning their backs on their clients or losing their professional identification as helpers. Now, more and more professional helpers have come to recognize the importance of having management skills, even if they have no plan to change their job titles or career goals.

Management can be defined rather simply as the process of (a) making a plan to achieve some end, (b) organizing the people and resources needed to carry out the plan, (c) encouraging the helping workers who will be asked to perform the component tasks, (d) evaluating the results, and then (e) revising plans based on this evaluation. This process can be shared by managers and by people who currently and essentially identify themselves as human service professionals.

Today most people recognize that awareness of managerial functions is important in any human service organization. Many professionals find themselves in supervisory roles because such positions in human service agencies and institutions are normally filled by people with training in the helping professions. Even professionals who spend all their time in direct service delivery know that they should understand how their organizations work so that they can implement new ideas, help improve operations, and influence others to make needed changes.

Everyday incidents tend to remind professional helpers that they must learn how to manage people, programs, and resources, if only to safeguard the humanistic, people-centered orientation that should permeate human services. Many human service workers are being forced to choose either to participate actively in the administration of their own programs or to leave leadership in the hands of others who may have little understanding of the helping process. Many find that their choice is to learn to manage their own programs or lose them altogether.

The following incidents—all typical of the kinds of conflicts professional helpers face every day—speak for themselves.

Keith Michaels

As soon as he had earned his master's degree, Keith Michaels decided to put all his time and energy into the creation of a center that would serve the youth of his community. Now in the fifth year of its existence, that center has grown from a storefront office in which Keith saw a few walk-in clients into a major community center, complete with recreational facilities, a peer counseling project, an ongoing consultation program, a busy staff of individual and group counselors, and a major role in the local youth advocacy movement. Most of the clients, counselors, and community members involved with the center are convinced that the explanation for this growth lies in the fact that the staff has always been close to the community's young people and responsive to their needs. They feel that Keith, with the help of the energetic staff he has recruited, can realize a dream they all share, and they want his promise that he will stay with the center as director.

Keith is hesitant, for the agency no longer "runs itself" the way it used to. There is a need to departmentalize, to organize staff hiring and training, to lay out appropriate plans for further change. Keith is afraid to place the management of the center solely in the hands of a professional administrator because he fears that the community responsiveness that has been a hallmark of the program might be lost. He wants to continue to have an effect on the center's future, but he knows that he will have to learn how to plan, organize, and budget on a larger scale.

Shirley Lane

Shirley Lane has spent several years working in a community agency for developmentally disabled adults. She has developed an approach for working with her clients that she has found highly effective and knows that her approach might be helpful to others. In fact, it would provide a major innovation in the field if research showed it to be as effective as she thinks it is.

Because her approach is so promising, Shirley has consistently been encouraged to submit a proposal for federal funding. Finally, her proposed project is being funded; she will now have the chance to implement a training and research project that can make a significant contribution to the field. She knows, however, that if the project is to be successful, she must develop effectiveness in planning projects, supervising the trainees who will help carry out the project, maintaining the budget, and evaluating the results of interventions. She can meet this challenge only if she can successfully carry out the required managerial functions.

Bill Okita

As the harried director of a small community mental health project, Bill Okita never has enough time. He spends half his time in direct service, working with individuals and groups, and this is an aspect of his job that he would not want to give up. He finds his work with clients to be a positive part of his workday; it is what keeps him going and makes all his efforts worthwhile.

Bill has a small staff of professional service providers, all of whom are highly competent. Perhaps this high level of competence accounts for the dramatic rise in the number of clients. The project now has a waiting list for appointments, which conflicts with Bill's belief that counseling should be readily accessible for community members. Yet the agency's funding does not allow Bill enough financial resources to hire additional counselors. He has to make do with the present staff members, but they are all stretched too thin as professionals.

Bill has just been approached by a local citizens' organization whose members are interested in serving as unpaid volunteer counselors at the center. If they could participate in this way, Bill's time problems would be solved. He would finally have enough personnel available to provide the immediate service that he thinks counselees should have. With the pressure off, he could still devote some of his time to direct services instead of having to spend all his time dealing with pressing administrative problems and fund-raising.

Bill has no doubt that these volunteers could do an effective job of serving clients if he provided training and supervision. It is his own skill in supervising and coordinating their efforts that he questions. In fact, he recently turned down the opportunity to have doctoral-level psychology students complete internships at the center because he was not sure that he could handle their needs. Now, however, the situation is desperate. He needs the help of these volunteers, but he must be able to train, supervise, and coordinate them. If he performs his managerial functions more effectively, he can spend less time on them.

Lillian Sanchez

Lillian Sanchez began her career as an elementary school teacher. She spent many years working with young children and found the work fantastically rewarding. Yet, when she received training as a counselor, she wanted the chance to experience that side of helping, too. She accepted a position as a high school counselor because her city did not employ school counselors at any other level.

That work, too, has been fulfilling. But Lillian has always wished that she could combine the rewards of working with young children with those of working as a counselor. She feels that elementary school is the place where effective counselors should be working, for only at that level might there be a chance to prevent the personal and educational problems her high school clients all seem to be facing.

Suddenly, Lillian has the opportunity of a lifetime. A new elementary school is being built in her area, and the potential principal, a longtime professional colleague, has asked her to join the staff as the district's first elementary school counselor. She will build her own program in the direction she thinks best and perhaps have the chance to consult with other schools in the development of additional programs. Lillian has no doubt that this position would be a dream come true. She has always wanted to counsel at the elementary school level, and now she can create a truly innovative program based on the concept of prevention.

Still, she hesitates. She knows she can counsel the children effectively, but she does not know whether she can build a program where none existed before. She will need to learn how to plan effectively, how to provide leadership for teachers and parents, how to consult beneficially with other counselors, and how to evaluate her efforts. The only way she can have the opportunity to practice her child-counseling skills is to develop administrative skills at the same time.

David Williams

David Williams is one of a group of human service workers conducting a preventive program under the auspices of a child and family service center. In recent years, the financial situation of the center has changed. The agency is being forced to cut back services in some areas to maintain adequate funding for other programs.

David and his colleagues have been called into the executive director's office and told that, as much as she appreciates their fine work, their program might be eliminated within the next year or two. The director recognizes that the preventive program is very popular in the community; calls have been coming in constantly from schools, churches, and recreational centers to request assistance from it. Although she knows that the program is doing something right, she does not know just what it is. She does not know how important it is in comparison with the functions being performed by workers providing direct, clinical services to troubled families.

David and his colleagues now have a real challenge before them. They know that they are helping the community; the informal feedback they have been receiving from young people, parents, and community agencies tells them that. They also know that right now they have no way of proving it, no way of showing that the prevention program is accomplishing something important. They have a short time in which to prove themselves, and they know that their only chance is to plan their program on the basis of goals that the administration agrees are important, to coordinate their efforts with those of other programs, and to develop an accurate evaluation method. If they are going to survive, they need to learn how to carry out these tasks. In short, they need to be able to manage.

Keith Michaels, Shirley Lane, Bill Okita, Lillian Sanchez, and David Williams are all typical human service professionals. They are not necessarily interested in changing their professional identities or in moving up an administrative ladder, but they are interested in improving and enhancing their human service delivery systems. It could be argued that they should not make the professional move they are contemplating. Perhaps Keith should turn over the management of his counseling center to someone whose original training was in business administration. Possibly Lillian should stay at the high school level, where she can spend all her time on direct service, and wait until the program is fully established by someone else before moving into an elementary school situation. Conceivably, David and his fellow human service workers should seek employment at an agency where preventive programs are already appreciated and where they would have no pressure to prove themselves or to sell their program.

If they do make these decisions, however, they should make them freely, based on their evaluation of all the possible options and their values, priorities, and professional judgment. They should not be in the position of having to choose inaction just because they lack the skills needed to bring about change either in their careers or in their programs. This book is intended to provide human service workers and students with basic management knowledge that may help them in their current jobs or prepare them to take on managerial work. Human service organizations will be presented as complex, purposeful organizations with the potential of bettering social conditions and enriching the lives of employees, clients, and community members.

THE PURPOSES OF HUMAN SERVICE PROGRAMS

Human service programs deal with the personal and social development of individuals, families, and communities. Sometimes they enhance this development through the provision of direct services such as education, training, counseling, therapy, or casework. Often they work indirectly, through consultation, advocacy, referral, information dissemination, community development, or social action. The ultimate purpose of these programs, regardless of the methods used, is to enhance the well-being of clients or consumers. In one study addressing excellence in human service organizations (HSOs), Harvey (1998) found that *purpose* was the dimension of excellence that was cited most frequently by survey respondents. According to Harvey, "having a very clear sense of purpose, direction, mission, or vision and a focus on its accomplishments is necessary to achieve excellence in an HSO" (p. 37).

Taylor and Felten (1993) have defined an organization's purpose as the "business mission of the system and its philosophy of human values" (p. 39). They see an organization as having four interactive and interdependent elements. First, an organization is a *transforming agency*, which produces outcomes of value. In the case of human service organizations, people (clients or customers) are typically transformed, from individuals, groups, families, or communities with needs or problems to those with needs met or problems ameliorated. Second, an organization is an *economic agency*, which either produces a profit or, in the case of governmental or not-for-profit agencies, maintains a balanced budget or surplus. Third, an organization is a *mini-society*, with norms and a culture that guide members' behavior and indirectly impact organizational effectiveness. Finally, an organization is a *collection of individuals*, who all come with unique values, beliefs, needs, motivational profiles, expectations, and skills.

The first two elements, concerning *performance* and *fiscal health*, comprise an organization's *mission*: its distinct competencies and reason for existence. The second two elements address organizational *norms* and member *quality of working life* and shape the organization's *philosophy and values. Purpose*, then, is the combination of mission and values: it tells its employees, clients, community, and larger environment why it exists, what it will focus on, and how it intends to treat its staff, clients, and community. Purpose in this sense, when fully articulated and regularly enacted, provides direction, energy, and vision for the organization's employees, who are engaged in a cooperative endeavor to enhance individual and community well-being in some way.

Managers, as leaders of an organization and stewards of its resources, must always maintain focus on purpose, designing systems and behaving in ways consistent with it. Management is a set of systems and processes designed to help employees accomplish organizational and individual goals. In the demanding day-to-day life of a manager, it is important to resist the temptation to focus only on procedure or management needs rather than on organizational results. Management processes and leadership are both essential and should be jointly well executed, and this is a manager's contribution to the success of the organization.

FUNCTIONS OF HUMAN SERVICE MANAGEMENT

Across the categories of human service agencies and programs, the focus should always stay on the organization's ability to bring positive change to individuals and communities. All types of human service programs also share the need to carry out effectively the major components of management. Whether programs provide direct or indirect services and whether they are housed in public or private agencies, they tend to share similar managerial functions. The management of human service programs includes the following major components:

- *Planning:* Developing visions for the future, developing strategy, setting goals and objectives for attaining them, and selecting program models
- *Designing:* Structuring and coordinating the work that needs to be done to carry out plans
- *Developing human resources:* Mobilizing the people needed to make the program work and taking steps to enhance their productivity
- *Supervising:* Enhancing the skills and motivation of service providers
- *Managing finances:* Planning the use of financial resources for reaching goals and controlling expenditures
- *Monitoring:* Tracking progress on program objectives and activities
- *Evaluating:* Comparing program accomplishments with the standards set at the planning stages; using the results as the basis for change

The force that binds together and energizes these processes is *leadership*: working with employees to articulate a vision, manage the external environment, oversee the design of organizational processes, link elements of the system together, create a supportive organizational culture, and manage change. This model is represented in Figure 1.1.

Human service professionals who know how to perform these functions can play important roles in managing their programs. They can make plans to achieve human service goals, organize the people and resources needed to carry out the plans, encourage and assist individuals delivering services, and evaluate the results.

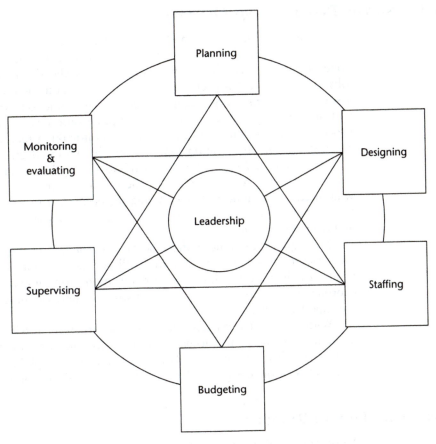

FIGURE 1.1 | A CONCEPTUAL FRAMEWORK FOR HUMAN SERVICE MANAGEMENT

PLANNING

The planning process in human service settings begins with the assessment of community needs and visions of a desired future state, from a perspective that reflects the agency's purpose (mission and values). Planners use a variety of methods to determine what problems and opportunities exist within a given population and, just as important, what community members see as their most pressing priorities. If currently offered services are also analyzed, planners can recognize gaps in the human service system.

This assessment of needs and the identification of community strengths or assets provide the basis for selecting the potential goals of the agency or program. Community members, potential consumers, and service providers, as well as policy makers, must all be involved in setting service goals. Actual programs, or collections of related activities, can be developed on the basis of these goals. Instead of assuming that a given activity should form the heart of a human service program, planners examine alternate methods for achieving the objectives that have been set. Only then can specific plans for service implementation be laid.

DESIGNING THE PROGRAM AND ORGANIZATION

If the planning function helps human service workers determine what should be accomplished, the designing function helps them carry out the plan. Designing is done at three levels: the organization as a whole, the program, and individual jobs. There are two aspects of design. First, structure is the element traditionally associated with the "organizing" function: what functions are in the various units and how the chain of command is set up. Second, design includes organizational processes such as communication and decision-making mechanisms. These are not apparent on the organization chart but are crucial to effective functioning.

Furthermore, *design* is both a noun and a verb. As a noun, it describes structure and processes; as a verb, it is the process for creating the organization—deciding what needs to be done and determining the best structures and processes. Organization design flows from the result of the planning phase: mission, goals, objectives, and overall strategies.

A design, or, as is more often the case, a redesign, of the organization results in the structure and processes that allow all people and units involved to understand what part they are to play in the organization, how ongoing communication and coordination of effort are to occur, and what the lines of authority and responsibility are expected to be.

Within these parameters, the types of structure possible vary tremendously, depending on the goals, needs, resources, size, and environment of the organization. They also vary in accordance with the values, philosophy, and theoretical approaches of the designers. These will be discussed in Chapter 4.

DEVELOPING HUMAN RESOURCES

An organization's plans and design are put into operation by people: human service programs are labor-intensive. A major part of each budget goes toward salaries and benefits for service deliverers and support personnel. The success of services depends on the manager's ability to mobilize valuable human resources so that the immediate and long-term needs of the organization and its clients are met. Especially in times of retrenchment, when financial resources dwindle, human service managers must plan carefully both to bring needed people into the organization and to enhance their development once they have begun to provide services.

The development of human resources involves using the unique contributions that all of the workers of the human service enterprise can make. Special attention needs to be paid to the knowledge and skills that women and people of color bring to the organization (Asamoah, 1995; Bailey, 1995; Healy, Havens, & Pine, 1995). Feminist and transcultural perspectives, as represented by a diverse workforce, enhance the capabilities of human service programs to provide relevant and compatible services to diverse client populations.

Careful recruitment, selection, training, and appraisal processes should be used for both paid employees and volunteers. Hiring practices normally take into account the abilities, experiences, and characteristics of potential human service workers, but managers sometimes forget to consider the organization's unique needs. Job responsibilities and priorities should be defined precisely even before vacancies are advertised.

This analysis should then form the basis for screening applicants and for hiring those candidates whose qualities best fit the actual jobs to be performed. After hiring, the new employee should be fully oriented to the agency in areas ranging from the governance structure and policies and procedures to agency history and organizational culture.

The environment and program activities of human service organizations change so rapidly that ongoing development of staff is essential. The function, formerly known as "personnel and training," has recently been reconceptualized as "strategic human resource management," reflecting the principle that training and development should be guided by the key strategies, priorities, and programmatic needs of the agency. When an agency implements a new program or adopts improved service delivery methods, staff will need appropriate training. As will be discussed later, treating agencies as learning organizations (Senge, 1990) and encouraging lifelong learning on the part of staff are becoming increasingly common principles of staff and organization development. Beginning and advanced training in computer usage will become more necessary as agencies increasingly tap the potentials of the Internet, database management, and other software.

Once people have been hired, performance appraisals should occur regularly. They should be based on objective analyses of the tasks and behaviors that lead to successful job performance. Fair, objective performance appraisals serve dual purposes. They can be used for evaluating individuals and also for identifying areas of needed development in the individual or in the organization. Performance appraisals can point the way toward new behaviors that should be learned and practiced, allowing services to keep pace with client needs.

One way to expand an agency's human resources is to encourage volunteer participation. This approach works as long as recruitment and assignment of volunteer service providers are planned as carefully as is the hiring of professional employees. Volunteers can add significantly to a program's thrust because they provide fresh ideas and strong links to their communities. Community members' participation increases the agency's service delivery capacity, but only if these contributions are respected as highly as those of paid personnel.

SUPERVISING

Supervision involves helping a worker maximize his or her effectiveness in service delivery by providing support and encouragement, helping build skills and competencies, and overseeing the supervisee's work. The nature of the supervisory relationship depends on the supervisor's leadership style, the supervisee's motivation, and the organization's needs. In essence, however, the supervisor's primary task is to ensure that each supervisee (a) views his or her own work as a key component in helping the organization achieve its goals; (b) develops the knowledge, skills, and attitudes necessary for carrying out this work; and (c) remains motivated toward growth.

The supervisor encourages the development of professional excellence in his or her supervisees in the roles of clinical supervisor and educator. In fulfilling all of the functions of the supervisory role, the human service manager provides, as a leader, emotional and psychological support to his or her staff as a means of preventing worker burnout and enhancing motivation and job satisfaction. Educational supervision, in addition, addresses workers' needs for professional growth and development in the provision of job-related services designed to improve client outcomes (Shulman, 1993).

The human service supervisor also fulfills a management, or administrative, function. As such, the supervisor must possess knowledge and skills relevant to the day-to-day direction and control of unit operations—for example, assigning and delegating work, coordinating workers' activities, planning unit goals and objectives, and so on. In addition, the supervisor must have a keen awareness of the agency's broader organizational and administrative concerns, including strategic and tactical planning, structure, staffing, fund-raising, budgeting, and program evaluation.

MANAGING FINANCES

Human service professionals can understand their own programs only if they know how they are budgeted. When they are directing specially funded projects, full-time service providers control the allocation of limited financial resources. Even when their programs make up only parts of total agency structures, human service workers should try to gain access to and understand the financial reports that affect them.

The process of setting and controlling the budget is closely related to planning and evaluation. In fact, a budget is fundamentally a program in fiscal terms. The more closely related the budget is to goals of people who hold a stake in the agency's success, the more effectively it is likely to work.

A budget must be seen as the concrete documentation of the planning process, bringing ideals into reality. An annual budget does not have to be based simply on a slight increment over the previous year's figures. Instead, it can be based on a recognition of program goals and the costs of activities expected to attain those goals. For instance, zero-based budgeting requires that each set of activities be justified in its entirety before resources are allocated. Program budgeting places accountability on programs by allocating resources for the attainment of specific objectives rather than simply to "line items" such as personnel costs or supplies.

Budget making is thus a decision-making process through which allocations are made to one service rather than another. If it is to be closely related to the program development process, human service providers should be involved. At the very least, they need to be aware of how the planning process has been translated into financial terms.

Even when traditional line item budgets are used, planners can ensure that the budget reflects program priorities by following careful procedures for allocating resources to specific activities. The objectives that have been set as part of the initial plan can be analyzed in terms of the activities that need to be performed before the objectives have been met. Each activity can then be broken down in terms of time span, personnel costs, and non-personnel costs until a total cost for the activity has been determined. The costs for these activities can be either budgeted according to program or placed in the context of a line item budget. In either case, the budget that finally sees the light of day is one that has been derived not from assumptions about what items should always be included in a budget but from analyses of program goals and priorities.

Once an effective annual budget is in place, ongoing financial reports help determine whether expenditures and income are as expected or whether significant deviations from what was planned have developed. The human service worker who understands the budget does not need to give it a great deal of attention after the initial stages. Managers, of course, need to pay attention to money matters when there are variances that need to be accounted for or acted on.

Closely related to budgeting is the whole question of funding mechanisms. Public agencies depend for their funding on legislative appropriations as well as other possible sources of revenue. Private, nonprofit agencies tend to depend on some combination of grants, contracts, contributions, and fees paid for services, either by clients or by third parties. For-profit companies operating in the human service field typically are funded by contracts and fees (often paid by third parties) and have the added benefit of using their own capital. The brand of funding can have a major effect on an agency's programs because funding sources vary in terms of long-range predictability and the services they tend to encourage. Program planners and budget makers need to be aware of the agency's major focus and should not lose sight of program goals when new funding possibilities appear. The integrity of agency goals is especially difficult to maintain in times of resource scarcity. At such times, it is most important to recall that budgeting and fund-raising should remain subsidiary to planning.

MONITORING AND EVALUATING

A program must have information systems to enable all staff to keep track of what is being done and accomplished. Such a system is variously referred to as "documentation," "keeping stats," or a "management information system." Such a system should keep track of not only program activities but also the ultimate outcomes, or results, as they relate to clients. Information systems are used both to track organizational activities and progress and to provide data for evaluation. Evaluating a program involves comparing program accomplishments with criteria and standards set at the planning stage. Evaluation is not necessarily a specialized activity carried on only at special times by outside experts descending on an organization. It should be seen as an ongoing self-assessment process in which all human service workers participate.

The agency's information system allows for a constant monitoring of agency activities and provides data for evaluation—an assessment of the effects of services on clients. Human service professionals need to know whether the services being carried out are in accordance with what was planned within a certain time and budget. They also need to know whether the program is meeting its objectives in terms of client change.

When criteria and standards are clear, evaluators can identify the data needed to measure the degree to which objectives have been attained. The next step becomes identifying the source of the data and designing a system for obtaining and reporting information.

If an ongoing information system is in place, evaluations of effort and effectiveness can be implemented either by external consultants or by agency workers. Once evaluation results have been reported, needed program changes can be identified and implemented.

It is difficult to separate evaluation from planning because an effective plan must include an evaluation component, but an effective evaluation must be based on the goals and objectives identified as part of a plan. Most important, human service professionals must be aware of the need to gather appropriate data as part of normal, ongoing program operation. Only then can evaluation gain its rightful place in the management and coordination of all activities. When this takes place, human service workers who already "know" that their services are effective will be able to prove it to others.

HUMAN RELATIONS SKILLS

Management is never a solo performance. It involves the orchestration of complex human elements into a whole that is characterized by harmony rather than discord. In any organization, managers must be able to work effectively with individuals and groups. They must encourage communication, build personal motivation, and form cooperative problem-solving groups. These interpersonal skills are as important in planning and budgeting as in direct supervision.

Effective application of all of the management functions just described requires polished interpersonal skills. If a plan is to be a living document, its formation must involve active participation of the people who will be affected by it, including potential service consumers as well as policy makers, board members, funding sources, managers, and agency employees. The human service professional who is involved in developing any program plan or innovation must be able to encourage and work closely with a variety of individuals and groups, each of whom might have a special priority in mind.

Budgeting requires far greater skill with people than with dollars and cents. Although the budget is closely involved with the planning process, it invariably attracts more conflict than any other planning component. Allocation of scarce resources means that funds are distributed to some programs, services, or individuals at the expense of others. Even when the most rational possible procedures are used to make the necessary decisions, both the processes and the results need to be sold to participants. When more traditional budgeting approaches are used, political processes and the balancing of conflicting interests come to the fore and need to be accepted as realities. No one can build a budget without being in close touch with the needs of funding sources, consumers, and workers.

The balancing of human and organizational needs is also important in creating an agency's structure. Organizing involves dividing and coordinating the efforts of individuals and departments. These tasks can be done successfully only if the manager is sensitive to the needs of the people contributing to the work effort. The degree of centralization or decentralization, of specialization or generalization, of control or independence built into the organization's structure is a function of the needs being met. These needs include both those dictated by the tasks to be performed and those dictated by the human characteristics of the people performing them. Like a plan or a budget, an organizational structure depends as much on interpersonal dynamics as on technical concerns.

Human relations skills interact even more directly and clearly with leadership functions. A key to management is that tasks are performed not just by the manager but by and through the efforts of other people. Motivating, affecting, and supporting others' behaviors require strong interpersonal competency, whether the object of the leadership activity is a supervisee or a local citizen, an individual staff member, or a group participating in a problem-solving meeting.

Finally, human relations skills affect the human service manager's ability to carry out evaluation processes. Not surprisingly, many workers find evaluation threatening. Yet the active participation of all agency employees, at least in data gathering, is necessary to carrying out the evaluation function. If evaluations are to be accurate and if their results are really going to be used as a basis for managerial decisions, cooperative efforts are essential.

The skill of working effectively with individuals and groups runs through the performance of every managerial function, and human service professionals may well find their backgrounds more useful than expected. Professional training can also enhance the development of skills in individual or joint decision making.

DECISION-MAKING SKILLS

Management is, in a very basic sense, a process of making decisions. From deciding whether to spin off a new agency to choosing the location of a water cooler, from selecting a new staff member to considering alternate data forms, the manager is in the position of constantly choosing among alternatives. Deciding, along with communicating, is what a manager actually does with his or her time.

Decision making involves identifying and weighing alternate means for reaching desired ends. In human service settings, the selection of the best means for achieving an objective is often far from clear. Because of the high degree of uncertainty that will always be present in dealing with human needs, completely rational decision making is impossible. Basic values, desired goals, and the wishes of sometimes opposing factions need to be taken into account. In this context, decision-making skill requires sensitivity as much as rationality.

When carrying out the planning function, human service professionals need to decide what approaches to use in assessing needs, how to involve community members and other stakeholders in the goal-setting process, and what reasonable objectives for a program might be. These decisions actually precede the real decision-making challenge: choosing the most effective combination of services to meet the specified objectives. No one administrator or service deliverer makes these decisions alone. Involvement in cooperative decision making, however, is, if anything, more complex than choosing alternatives on the basis of one person's judgment.

Budgeting is also a decision-making activity. Whether working alone or as a member of a planning group, the human service professional must help decide how resources are to be allocated. Especially in times of economic stress, each positive choice can bring with it the need to make a negative decision somewhere else. Choosing to fund one activity means choosing not to fund another.

The decisions that are made as part of designing programs and structuring the organization also have far-reaching implications. In organizing, the manager must weigh the benefits of varying methods of dividing tasks among individuals and departments. The choices made invariably have major effects on the behaviors and productivity of all members of the service delivery team.

In providing leadership for this team, the manager continues to choose among alternate interventions, methods, and targets for change. Each decision affects both the immediate situation and the life of the agency as a whole. Ultimately, evaluation completes the administrative cycle by measuring the effects of past decisions and laying the groundwork for new choices.

LEADERSHIP AND CHANGE MANAGEMENT: KEEPING THE ORGANIZATION RESPONSIVE AND VIBRANT

The managerial functions previously described need to be implemented in order for programs to be effectively maintained. Fortunately for human service managers, the practical, human skills that underlie managerial functions are closely allied with the skills of helping. Social work, counseling, and psychology degree programs, in particular, emphasize effective communication skills such as active listening, giving and receiving feedback, group dynamics and facilitation, and positive regard for all individuals. All these skills are important for managers as they design systems and lead staff in accomplishing organizational goals.

In an era of accountability and limited resources, human service professionals cannot afford the luxury of attending to their own customary activities in isolation from general agency goals and operations. Service providers must know how their activities relate to programs and how these programs, in turn, relate to agency and community priorities. Human service professionals, like everyone with a stake in an agency's continued existence, must be aware of managerial processes that enable them to function on a daily basis (how their check is paid, why they need to keep good client records, why evaluations need to occur). Conveying this information and helping staff come to appreciate the importance of it is a task requiring leadership.

As Figure 1.1 illustrated, leadership is the unifying factor for all management processes. Agency executives and, in fact, managers at all levels need to be leaders who help keep the organization and all staff focused on key organizational outcomes and processes necessary to get there; provide energy, confidence, and optimism regarding meeting the challenges facing human service organizations; and oversee the agency's constant evolution and change so that it remains responsive to community needs and concerns.

In considering the subject of organizational purpose, too, both the technical and leadership functions of management can be seen. The manager addresses the technical system functions through overseeing organizational processes including planning, program and organization design, human resources management and supervision, financial management, and monitoring and evaluation. The manager addresses the social system by providing leadership and vision, articulating key values and ethical standards, ensuring a vibrant organizational culture and high quality of working life, and overseeing constant organizational learning and change.

Change management is a major responsibility for leaders. Chapter 2 will outline some of the powerful external forces affecting human service organizations, pointing out the need for ongoing adaptation and change. As will be seen in Chapter 11, nearly every viable contemporary leadership approach includes change management. Leaders are not always the drivers of change, however, and even when they desire change they sometimes need expertise from an outside source. Organization development, business process reengineering, total quality management, and other change processes are increasingly being used in human service organizations, with both good and disappointing results. Finally, there are techniques for lower-level employees to identify change opportunities and make proposals for improving agency operations. Leadership and change management are the ways that organizational processes and systems are kept up-to-date and responsive so that the agency can be maximally effective and thrive in an increasingly challenging environment.

THE MULTICULTURAL ORGANIZATION

We cannot think of organizational excellence and vibrancy without attending to the vital issue of multiculturalism and diversity. At the center of change-focused leadership is the need to move the organization toward a true commitment in this arena. Effective practitioners across all of the helping professions now recognize that they must be sensitive to cultural differences between themselves and their clients. Less progress has been made, however, in recognizing that multicultural competence is not just an individual characteristic but also a vital organizational characteristic.

> Organizational entities that fail to successfully implement diversity into the very structures of their operations will fail to be relevant to their clients or consumers. In the mental health field, clinics and providers must begin to alter the nature of their service delivery systems to recognize cultural diversity. The development of culturally appropriate mental health delivery systems for a diverse population may require major changes in the very structure of the organization. (Sue & Constantine, 2005, p. 213)

The development of excellence in this area may involve a process along a continuum from a monocultural organization to a nondiscriminatory organization to a multicultural organization (Sue, 1995). In the United States, a *monocultural organization* would be characterized by (a) an exclusion, whether conscious or not, of people from oppressed populations; (b) structures and processes that maintain privileged positions for people from the dominant majority; (c) management based on the values of the dominant culture; and (d) an assumption that employees and clients should adhere to dominant values. A *nondiscriminatory organization* represents a step forward in cultural awareness, but it lacks consistent organizational policies and practices to support it. Multiculturalism and diversity have not yet become true organizational priorities. As an organization moves toward becoming a multicultural *organization*, it demonstrates a valuing of diversity and consistently engages in "envisioning, planning, and problem-solving activities that allow for equal access and opportunities" (Sue, 1995, p. 485). Ideally,

> we define a multicultural organization as committed (action as well as words) to diverse representation throughout all levels, sensitive to maintaining an open, supportive, and responsive environment, working toward and purposefully including elements of diverse cultures in its ongoing operations, carefully monitoring organizational policies and practices for the goals of equal access and opportunity, and authentic in responding to changing policies and practices that block cultural diversity. (Sue & Constantine, 2005, p. 223)

According to Sue and Constantine, certain conditions must exist in order for an organization to become multicultural in outlook. These characteristics include the following:

- "Multicultural commitment must come from the very top levels." (p. 223)
- "Each organization should have a written policy, mission statement, or vision statement that frames the concepts of multiculturalism and diversity into a meaningful operational definition." (p. 223)
- "The organization should have a multicultural and diversity action plan." (p. 224)
- "Multicultural accountability must be built into the system." (p. 224)
- "The organization should create a superordinate or oversight team that is empowered to assess, develop, and monitor the organization's development with respect to the goals of multiculturalism." (p. 224)
- "Organizations must be unafraid to actively solicit feedback from employees related to issues of race, culture, gender, ethnicity, and sexual orientation." (p. 224)
- "Multicultural competence should be infused into evaluation criteria and used for hiring and promotion of employees." (p. 224)
- "Culturally sensitive organizations recognize that mentoring and support networks for employees of color are vital for their success." (p. 224)
- "Active coalition building and networking among minorities and women, for example, should be valued." (p. 224)
- "The organization must be committed to a systematic and long-term plan to educate the entire workforce concerning diversity issues." (p. 224)

Clearly, the kinds of values, commitments, and processes that lead toward the creation of a multicultural organization are also the characteristics of excellence in all organizational endeavors.

FROM THEORY TO PRACTICE

As potential human service managers become more aware of the opportunities and challenges that lie before them, they always benefit from examples, whether these examples raise questions or model effective practices. Throughout the following chapters, we will present cases that illustrate particular ideas or functions. In particular, we will present one ongoing example to which we will return throughout this book: the Grandview Community Center. Box 1.1 provides a history of this human service agency and an introduction to some of the managerial challenges to be explored.

1.1   GRANDVIEW COMMUNITY CENTER

Leona Estrella is the new executive director of the Grandview Community Center (GCC), a human service agency with a long and diverse history. In a small city in the southwestern United States, a local church had founded the GCC in the 1930s. The center's mission was responsive to the needs of the time: serving the many immigrants from the Dust Bowl who had moved to this small, southwestern town during the Great Depression. For many years, the community remained white and working class. Over the past 20 years, however, the population has shifted to a heterogeneous mix of ethnic groups, now predominantly Latino, with a growing number of immigrants from Southeast Asia. The socioeconomic class ranges from lower to lower-middle class. The city in which GCC operates now has approximately 800,000 residents.

Upon her employment at the center, Leona saw an agency that had not necessarily kept up with the pace of change in the environment but that offered valuable services to the community. Her experience with this agency forms the core of this case example, which will continue throughout the following chapters.

The Agency's Work

The agency has four major programs: Counseling Services, In-home Services, Community Development, and Day Care. Counseling services are targeted to children and adults with behavioral health concerns including mental illness and substance abuse. Services by licensed therapists are provided to low income clients, funded by a contract with County Behavioral Health Services to help prevent the need for higher levels of services such as hospitalization. In-home services are provided through a contract with the Public Child Welfare Agency to work with families at risk of child abuse or neglect. Case managers conduct home visits and assist families with parent education, home management skills such as shopping and budgeting, and other services as needed. The Community Development program, which is funded by donations and by two local foundations, works with community members to identify issues that can be addressed through collective action. In recent years, the program has helped community members solve problems such as gang activity at a local park and the need for traffic signals at a busy intersection near a school. The Day Care program receives federal child development funding for subsidized day care for families receiving public assistance.

Managerial History

Until 2 years ago, the agency was run by a minister who had been there for 20 years. He led the agency during a period of moderate but regular program expansion during which time programs such as a day care center, a counseling program, and a welfare advocacy program were implemented. Program administrative functions did not develop as rapidly during this time, and when he retired 2 years ago the board of directors hired an executive director with a Master of Business Administration (MBA) and prior experience as an executive with a corporate foundation that funds not-for-profit organizations.

This new director instituted many administrative reforms, particularly in the areas of budgeting and management information systems, but staff resented his hard-driving style and generally did as little as possible to comply with his initiatives. In fact, all the employees in the counseling program sent a memo to him and the board complaining about his policy change toward short-term counseling only, regardless of need. He responded that there were unit cost problems with long-term counseling but did not act on the memo in any other way. He began the installation of computers for data collection and fiscal management; and although they were installed, they were not used on

(continued)

1.1   GRANDVIEW COMMUNITY CENTER (CONT'D)

a regular basis. When funding source program monitors continued to express concerns about the agency's management and accomplishments (including fiscal controls and progress on objectives), and with staff morale suffering and turnover increasing, the board decided to remove him and hire a new executive. The board consists primarily of local community representatives and other service providers. The board members are committed to the agency and the surrounding community but have not had a major role other than to review reports submitted by the executive.

Leona Estrella's Opportunities and Challenges

Leona had been a program director at another agency and was hired because she had had some administrative experience as well as direct service experience as a Master of Social Work (MSW). The management team she joined consists of a program director for each of the programs and the director of administrative services. The agency occupies four sites in the community, and the main administrative offices are located at the Central site. The Community Development program operates out of Central. The Counseling Program has staff at the East and West sites. Day Care and In-home Services operate at each site.

As a management team, these directors had in the past met every 2 weeks, but the programs had been functioning rather autonomously. At her first meeting, Leona sensed an overall feeling of disorganization. The meeting skipped from topic to topic and there seemed to be no rational decision-making process. She felt that program managers were partly just jockeying for control of scarce resources. Over the past 2 years, the number of clients served by more than one program had grown (for example, many day care clients also receive in-home services). The program directors were used to "running their own shows," although the executive hired 2 years ago made attempts to link the programs through a common computerized information system. He was also successful in bringing in grants and contracts for four new programs. These had been haphazardly subsumed under the existing program managers, in Leona's opinion.

Over the past few years, funding has become increasingly tight, and program managers now find themselves faced with competition from other agencies and also among themselves. Community needs have been changing, and Leona knows from her previous job that agencies face increasing expectations to document program success and value to the community. The agency currently has two major contracts that are due to expire in 8 months, with no clear plan for replacement. Their County Behavioral Health source has recently mandated that the agency demonstrate the use of an evidence-based practice model in the mental health program that it funds.

When Leona began reviewing agency documents, she could not get a clear picture of the programs' accomplishments beyond their scopes of services delivered. Staff records did not clearly show which people were working in which programs, and she had a feeling not all were being scheduled as efficiently as possible. In her initial meetings with staff at all the programs, she sensed disinterest in agency-wide issues and a general lack of positive energy. Staff members were mostly interested in working with their own clients and did not seem to care much about funding, documentation, evaluation, or planning, as long as their own program funding continued.

Leona's decision to implement strategic planning

In this complex and changing environment, and given the internal conditions of the agency, Leona thought that a strategic planning process would help all staff members to develop a clear picture of the challenges facing the agency and to develop plans to thrive in the future.

SUMMARY

This chapter began by pointing out that the goals of a human service organization should always be focused on improving the lives of the people and communities being served. This ideal remains applicable regardless of the category into which a particular agency falls. Among the most common types of human service agencies are (a) community agencies that provide a variety of service to meet the needs of people who live within a specified geographic area; (b) agencies that focus on particular issues or problem areas, such as mental health concerns, substance abuse, or developmental disabilities; (c) population-oriented agencies that meet the service and advocacy needs of a particular cultural group, age group, or gender; (d) career, employment, or rehabilitation agencies that help individuals gain skills and opportunities for positive career growth and economic security; and (e) advocacy organizations that work on behalf of populations that are subject to marginalization and prejudice. Human service organizations can also be differentiated by size and categorized as non-profit, for-profit, or public (governmental) agencies.

Managerial responsibilities fall into the hands not just of professional managers but also of people who view themselves primarily as service providers. Several examples of helping professionals grappling with managerial challenges were provided, and the point was made that managerial proficiency is important for people across varying human service roles. It is important for people with managerial responsibilities, even in the smallest program, to be able to carry out the planning, implementation, and evaluation processes that underlie effect programming.

Finally, this chapter ended by introducing the Grandview Community Center, which will serve as an ongoing case throughout the following chapters.

COMPETENCY-BUILDING ACTIVITY 1.1

CONCEPTUALIZING A NEW HUMAN SERVICE PROGRAM

Begin the process of creating your own hypothetical human service program. As you think about a program that you would want to develop, address the following questions:

1. What kind of need might your program address? Would you be focusing on a particular population or a particular issue or problem? Identify the population or issue you plan to address.

2. As you consider your program, think about what the central mission of this program would be. Write a very brief statement about this central mission.

3. Give your program a name.

Choose a program about which you feel a sense of passion. You will be coming back to your hypothetical program after each chapter so that you can apply what you have learned.

CASE ACTIVITY 1.1 | ### TRANSITIONS INTO MANAGEMENT

Review the situations of the individuals profiled in this chapter: Keith Michaels, Shirley Lane, Bill Okita, Lillian Sanchez, and David Williams. Choose one with which you can identify in some way and answer these questions from their perspective.

1. What prospective changes in role are facing this person?

2. If you were in this situation, what factors would you consider in assessing your career goals and the kinds of activities you would like at work?

3. If you moved further into management, what additional skills and training would you need?

REFERENCES

Asamoah, Y. (1995). Managing the new multicultural work-force. In L. Ginsberg & P. Keys (Eds.), *New management in human services* (2nd ed., pp. 115–127). Washington, DC: NASW Press.

Aunt Martha's Youth Service Center. (2010). *History.* Retrieved September 1, 2010, from http://www.auntmarthas.org/History.aspx

Bailey, D. (1995). Management: Diverse workplaces. In R. Edwards (Ed.), *Encyclopedia of social work* (19th ed., pp. 1659–1663). Washington, DC: NASW Press.

Gibelman, M., & Furman, R. (2008). *Navigating human service organizations* (2nd ed.). Chicago, IL: Lyceum Books, Inc.

Harlem Children's Zone. (2009). *The HCZ project: 100 blocks, one bright future.* Retrieved March 1, 2010, from http://www.hcz.org/about-us/the-hcz-project

Harvey, C. (1998). Defining excellence in human service organizations. *Administration in Social Work, 22*(1), 33–45.

Healy, L., Havens, C., & Pine, B. (1995). Women and social work management. In L. Ginsberg & P. Keys (Eds.), *New management in human services* (2nd ed., pp. 128–150). Washington, DC: NASW.

Rapp, C., & Poertner, J. (1992). *Social administration: A client-centered approach.* New York: Longman.

Senge, P. (1990). *The fifth discipline.* New York: Doubleday Currency.

Shulman, L. (1993). *Interactional supervision.* Washington, DC: NASW Press.

Sue, D. W., & Constantine, M. G. (2005). Effective multicultural consultation and organizational development. In M. G. Constantine & D. W. Sue (Eds.), *Strategies for building multicultural competence in mental health and educational settings* (pp. 212–226). New York: John Wiley & Sons.

Sue, D. W. (1995). Multicultural organizational development. In J. G. Ponterotto, J. M. Cases, L. A. Suzuki, & C. M. Alexander (Eds.), *Handbook of multicultural counseling* (pp. 474–492). Thousand Oaks, CA: Sage.

Taylor, J., & Felten, D. (1993). *Performance by design.* Upper Saddle River, NJ: Prentice Hall.

USEFUL WEB RESOURCES

American Counseling Association. http://www.counseling.org/.

American Public Human Services Association. http://www.aphsa.org/Home/home_news.asp.

National Association of Social Workers. https://www.naswdc.org/.

National Network for Social Work Managers. http://socialworkmanager.org/.

National Organization for Human Services. http://www.nationalhumanservices.org/mc/page.do;jsessionid=DD8E6CE10E087B4B0504AF21E5FABD56.mc1?sitePageId=89929.

National Organization for Human Service Education. www.nationalhumanservices.org/.

National Rehabilitation Association. http://www.nationalrehab.org/cwt/external/wcpages/index.aspx.

U.S. Department of Health and Human Services. http://www.hhs.gov/.

KNOWING THE ENVIRONMENT

CHAPTER 2

Human service programs exist within environments that affect not only their day-to-day operations but also their ability to meet the long-term needs of consumers and communities. Successful efforts—from the smallest, most narrowly focused program to the largest multiservice agency—depend on the degree to which boards, managers, staff, and other stakeholders understand their environments.

In this chapter, we will discuss the environmental contexts of human service organizations. In recognition of the importance of *thinking globally and acting locally*, we review current trends in the larger public arena and then address the impact of these trends on human service management. As we noted in the previous chapter, organizations are purposeful entities that respond to needs and trends in the environment. The ability to scan and understand an agency's current and future environments appropriately will enable boards, staff, and other stakeholders to anticipate and deal proactively with changing conditions. Ideally, the board and staff of the agency will work not only to respond to the environment but also to influence it in return. In order to make the environment more responsive and hospitable to clients, human service managers have come to recognize the importance of advocating on behalf of their consumers.

Agencies must accurately and comprehensively assess their changing environments on an ongoing basis if they are to be successful in appropriately responding to community needs and visions. Historically, the most common technique for this has been the needs assessment. This valuable tool has been augmented in recent years by strength-based approaches, including asset mapping.

This chapter reviews a number of processes that enable the organization to respond effectively to its environment and not only survive but thrive. A general term for this type of activity is boundary spanning or boundary management. One example of boundary management is environmental scanning, a process of identifying trends and issues. Environmental scanning is a key step in strategic planning, presented in the next chapter.

Agencies also manage environmental relations through their involvement in community collaborations, interdisciplinary teams, service linkage agreements, and coalitions. The functions of public relations and marketing can also be very important in helping the agency deliver services in the most responsive ways.

In any successful organization, managers and staff play roles in environmental scanning and ongoing community relations. We must also recognize, however, the key role that is played by the boards that oversee the agency's work in achieving its mission. The members of a board of directors are often the people who provide the strongest connection between an agency and its environment. For that reason, this chapter concludes with an overview of the board's important role.

STAKEHOLDER EXPECTATIONS

The key actors in the human service organization's environment—those who have the most influence on the organization—are now commonly referred to as *stakeholders*. Among the individuals and groups who hold a stake in what the organization does and how it operates are its funding sources, its regulatory bodies, the legal system, other human service organizations, and the organization's clients and constituency groups. Since "environment" does not necessarily refer only to an agency's immediate geographic area, a funding source could be a federal bureau in Washington, DC, the governor's office at the state capital, a private foundation located in another state, or the local United Way. Or, for agencies having diversified funding sources, it could be a combination of all of these funding agencies, each with its own set of funding conditions, reporting procedures, and accountability standards. Thus, in terms of funding sources alone, an agency's environment can acquire complex proportions. Managed care, privatization of government services, and the recent focus on documenting outcomes of service are all reflections of the political context of human service organizations that are requiring major adjustments.

Regulatory bodies such as accrediting councils can also exert considerable external influence on an organization's structure, including its policies and procedures, hiring practices, technology, and so on. Although membership in these standard-setting associations is voluntary, failure to affiliate with one can depreciate an organization's status and power, whereas membership in good standing can increase an organization's prestige and image. Also, the effect of the legal system on organizational practices is a common contemporary phenomenon. Lawsuits and countersuits often result in changes in agency policies.

In addition to these external sources of influence, the human service organization is subject as well to environmental influences from other organizations, especially those competing for political or financial resources; from client groups in need of additional services or dissatisfied with current ones; and from interest groups seeking to impose their own agendas on organizational goals and services.

Finally, expectations for improved customer service are challenging agencies to make improvements in service delivery philosophies and methods. Patients' rights initiatives in mental health and disability services exemplify trends that should improve service delivery.

Managers need both depth perception and peripheral vision when looking at the environment. They need to know what is relevant from the past and need to look ahead into the future. In the present, they need to look "sideways" beyond the daily arena of service delivery programs. For example, the business section of the newspaper may show important trends in finance that an astute manager could turn into an opportunity. The "society" section typically covers local fund-raising events that may give a manager ideas on new places to look for support. Generally, the higher one goes in management, the broader and longer-term the vision needs to be. Even at the service delivery level, however, staff members should be looking at the environment to identify emerging needs and new programs, and to find similar organizations using "best practices" that may be adapted in one's own program.

ANALYSIS OF ENVIRONMENTAL TRENDS

Effective organizations go beyond superficial study of current trends to look for the deeper meaning and future implications of those trends. Only when important trends have been recognized can effective, long-term planning take place. In his book on strategic planning, Bryson (1995) uses the acronym PEST to organize trends in the environment: political, economic, social, and technological factors.

POLITICAL TRENDS

Political trends at national and even international levels have major effects on human service programs, affecting their local environments and challenging their abilities to respond to change. Every era brings new challenges that can sometimes take a human service provider by surprise.

THE CLOSE OF THE TWENTIETH CENTURY The "devolution revolution" (Cooke, Reid, & Edwards, 1997) resulted in heretofore federal responsibilities being shifted to state and local government, also leading to great increases in contracting and other forms of privatization, with increased expectations for innovation and cost savings. Welfare reform and block grants, for example, led to increased interaction across the sectors (government, business, not-for-profit) and new forms of interagency collaboration.

Accountability became an important word in the human services in the 1970s, when the Nixon administration and other conservatives questioned the War on Poverty and other social programs. Subsequently, the "reinventing government" movement (Osborne & Gaebler, 1992), welfare reform, and managed care put renewed emphasis on performance measurement (Martin & Kettner, 1997). This increase in emphasis on outcomes led to concepts like performance- or outcomes-based accountability (Cooke et al., 1997), with human service programs now expected to measure and document outcomes, not just units of services provided. Borrowing parlance from business, agencies needed to show how their services added value, for funding sources, clients, or the public at large.

Another political trend focused on individualism and personal responsibility (Bryson, 1995, p. 89). The welfare reform act of 1996 was a good example: rugged individualism replaced the government entitlement philosophy that had been in effect since the New Deal. Conservatives now expected the philanthropic sector and the faith communities to move in to help the poor and disadvantaged as government support decreased or ended.

THE EARLY TWENTY-FIRST CENTURY This conservative approach to social well-being gained even more traction as the twenty-first century began. At the federal level, public policy focused on tax cuts for people in the highest income brackets and used the need to cut costs as a reason for eating away at the safety net that had always been important for people in poverty. These policies greatly increased the gap between the "haves" and "have-nots" in the American social fabric. Addressing the need to change this perspective, Obama (2006) pointed out the following:

> But over the long term, doing nothing probably means an America very different from the one most of us grew up in. It will mean a nation even more stratified economically and socially than it currently is: one in which an increasingly prosperous knowledge class, living in exclusive enclaves, will be able to purchase whatever they went on the marketplace—private schools, private health care, private security, and private jets—while a growing number of their fellow citizens are consigned to low-paying service jobs, vulnerable to dislocation, pressed to work longer hours, dependent on an underfunded, overburdened, and underperforming public sector for their health care, their retirement, and their children's education. (p. 148)

After 2008, the polarization of political thought came to the forefront of public discourse, with questions about the role of government in protecting citizens' health and welfare at the center of debate. "It's what keeps us locked in 'either/or' thinking: the notion that we can have only big government or no government; the assumption that we must either tolerate forty-six million without health insurance or embrace 'socialized medicine'" (Obama, 2006, p. 40). This either/or thinking moved from political talk to action when fierce opposition came close to derailing the 2010 Affordable Care Act.

IMPACT ON HUMAN SERVICE MANAGEMENT   The political environment has obvious effects on human service programs because (a) their own existence depends on their ability to respond to the winds of political change and (b) the well-being of consumers and clients is always at stake. The political stresses of recent decades highlight the need for human service managers and stakeholders to move from a stance of reaction to a stance of action. The connection between an organization and its environment is a two-way street, which raises the possibility that the environment itself is susceptible to change. In times of political change, advocacy becomes an important human service function (Lewis, Arnold, House, & Toporek, 2002; Mosley, 2010; Ratts, Toporek, & Lewis, 2010). Mosley (2010) suggests that "it is clearly in the best interest of human service organizations to promote policies that facilitate new funding and service opportunities rather than constraining them" (p. 506). People who work in human service settings are usually experienced in advocating on behalf of their organizations. Recent trends have shown, however, that it is just as important to advocate on behalf of the clients, consumers, and communities that are served by the program.

> Advocacy can also be an important tool for human service organizations that are concerned with systematic inequalities in areas such as education, health care, and housing, which serve to limit the opportunities of individual clients. Advocacy work allows organizations to address some of those structural concerns and thus may help organizations more completely meet their missions. When serving clients who face economic difficulties, lack political influence, or experience stigma of different kinds, advocacy by human service organizations has the potential to promote social and economic justice. (Mosley, 2010, p. 506)

Advocacy that is carried out by human service professionals can play a key role in improving environments at three levels: the individual, the system, and the larger public arena (Lewis, Arnold, House, & Toporek, 2002; Ratts, Toporek, & Lewis, 2010).

ECONOMIC TRENDS

The economy, domestically and globally, has its ups and downs, but of one trend we can be sure: we should continue to expect limited public sector resources and growth, which suggests the need for continued productivity improvement and creative service delivery arrangements. Economic development and entrepreneurialism are becoming more prominent than traditional "services" strategies to empower residents of the inner city and others at lower income levels. In spite of these efforts, inequality is increasing, further bifurcating U.S. society.

THE LATE TWENTIETH CENTURY A number of trends that characterized the closing years of the twentieth century have maintained their influences over time. For instance, the increased "marketization" of human services—"the reliance in public policy on natural trade exchange practices (for example, competition, privatization, commercialization, decentralization, and entrepreneurialism)" (Cooke et al., 1997, p. 230)—exacerbated the trend toward increasing inequality. Managed care is another economic force affecting human services, in terms of both quality of service and access to care.

Another economic trend, the increasing globalization of the economy, benefits many of the wealthy but will continue to cause stress and dislocations for residents and workers in the United States. Well-paying blue-collar jobs in the United States are being eliminated in favor of paying lower wages to workers, sometimes including children, in undeveloped countries. Difficult economic conditions in many developing countries add to increased immigration to the United States. With many immigrants able to acquire only unskilled work, often without health benefits, health and social service systems experience strain.

THE EARLY TWENTY-FIRST CENTURY The great recession that began in 2007 placed extreme stress on all human service systems. Of course, human service programs that have missions related specifically to poverty, homelessness, unemployment, and related concerns are accustomed to dealing with the effects of economic downturns. But high unemployment figures and economic stress also bring an influx of new clients to programs that are focused on mental or physical health. It has become increasingly clear that poverty and economic crises are determinants of mental health problems (Hudson, 2005; Knapp, Funk, Curran, Prince, Grigg, & McDaid, 2006; Meyer & Lobao, 2003; Murali & Oyebode, 2004). Murali and Oyebode, for instance, point out that people affected by poverty are "doubly victimized" because they are exposed to more stressors than others but have fewer resources to manage them. People in poverty are also vulnerable to physical health problems. Equating lack of access to equitable health care in terms of social injustice, Levy and Sidel (2006) state that "social injustice leads to increased rates of disease, injury, disability, and premature death because of increased risk factors and decreased medical care and preventive services." Levy and Sidel list a number of health-related effects of poverty, including, for instance, poorer nutrition, greater exposure to unsafe water, increased exposure to infectious disease agents and occupational and environmental hazards, and increased complications of chronic diseases. They also emphasize the inequities in access to health care, including lack of access to diagnostic, therapeutic, and rehabilitative services as well as lack of preventive services.

These data point up the most difficult reality in times of economic distress: greater numbers of people with dire needs facing less robust health and human service programs. "With the shrinking of safety net programs, human service organizations experience increasing demand while coping with declining resources" (Hasenfeld, 2010, p. 2).

SOCIAL TRENDS

Social and organizational complexity is likely to increase, and chaos theory, adapted from the sciences, is being used to make sense of this (Warren, Franklin, & Streeter,

1997). With increases in immigrants from virtually any part of the world, diversity of the workforce, clients, families, and the citizenry will increase. Baby boomers are aging, leading to a search for new ways for the elderly to contribute to society. Young people entering the workforce, in human services and elsewhere, bring with them new values and priorities. They, and in fact all workers, are likely to experience more career changes than in past generations, leading to more job retraining and a greater use of consultants and part-time and contract employees. This situation has implications for agency salary and benefit structures, working environments, and other considerations for the quality of working life.

CULTURAL DIVERSITY The most important social factors affecting the human services involve the rapidly changing demographics in the United States.

> Between 2000 and 2050, the vast majority of America's net population growth will come from racial minorities, particularly Asians and Hispanics, as well as a growing mixed-race population. By the middle of the 21st century, America will have no clear "majority" race. (Kotkin, 2010, p. 1)

This change within the United States is due in part to high birth rates, specifically among Latinos born in the United States (Kotkin, 2010). Immigration is also playing an important role in bringing about increased diversity (Chung, Bemak, Ortiz, & Sandoval-Perez, 2008). Together, these trends will bring this country to the point of becoming "a unique multiracial superpower with deep familial and cultural ties to the rest of the world" (Kotkin, 2010, p. 1).

EFFECTS ON HUMAN SERVICE MANAGEMENT The vibrant, multicultural nature of the population holds great promise for the future, not least for the economic environment (Hinojosa-Ojeda, 2010). As these changes unfold, however, everyone involved in the human services must be diligent to make sure that programs adapt. It is, of course, universally accepted that human service providers must be culturally competent. The increased diversity of the population served requires even more: that all human services programs be designed so that the kinds of services offered fit the cultural values and needs of consumers.

Cultural groups that are marginalized and subject to oppression can present challenges that require not just cultural sensitivity but also focused programming. Consider, for example, the clear needs of immigrant and refugee populations. "Given the politically charged atmosphere that currently exists in the United States regarding immigrants, it is crucial that mental health professionals be aware of the impact that the current sociopolitical environment, immigration policies, pre-migration experiences, post-migration challenges, and various forms of racism and discrimination have on the mental health of immigrant and refugee clients" (Chung et al., 2008, p. 314). The Arab American Community Center for Economic and Social Services (ACCESS) is illustrative of a human service agency that meets the direct-service needs of clients but also attends to community empowerment and advocacy. The ACCESS Mental Health Division provides services to adults, children, and families, but it also includes the Psychosocial Rehabilitation Center for Survivors of Torture, the Partnership for Screening and Advocating for Refugees and Asylum Seekers, the Annual Symposium on Refugees and Survivors of Torture, the Anti-Stigma Initiative Program Countering the September 11th Aftermath, and the Ethnic Minority Empowerment Program (ACCESS Mental Health Division, 2007).

Human service programs that work with marginalized and traumatized populations are not only organized around nontraditional services but must also offer traditional helping services in nontraditional ways. An example of an organization that tries to meet this challenge can be found in the Gaza Community Mental Health Programme.

> The Gaza Strip—one of the most densely populated areas in the world, with two thirds of the population being refugees and 50% being younger than sixteen years— has witnessed extreme forms of violence and suffering…This has made the extent of mental health problems in the Gaza reach unprecedented levels. (Gaza Community Health Programme, 2010a, p. 1)

With poverty, overcrowding, physical health problems, and trauma making human services important, this organization is forced to do its work with extremely meager resources. Although clinical services are provided, outreach methods are important, not only because more people can be reached but also because of the stigma and distrust associated with clinic visits (Celinska, 2009). GCMHP programs, which are especially focused on children and women, include the following (Gaza Community Mental Health Programme, 2010, b):

- Informal home visits are used to meet with extended families and take note of trauma symptoms among a large number of children.
- Outreach methods are used to reach children in schools and, at the same time, train teachers and parents to detect problems and provide help.
- A Women's Empowerment Project provides services in centers located in cities and refugee camps, with residents of refugee camps serving as Community Development Leaders.

The examples of the ACCESS organization and the Gaza Community Mental Health Programme demonstrate that cultural competence must underlie not just service providers but also program planning and management. This fact remains true for programs that are designed for a more general, culturally diverse population.

Consider, for instance, the importance of addressing issues of culture and diversity in the face of community crises. The following principles for cultural competence have been developed by the Substance Abuse and Mental Health Services Administration (2003) and disseminated by the Federal Emergency Management Agency (FEMA) to guide disaster relief efforts: Maintain a current profile of the cultural composition of the community. (Factors include race and ethnicity, age, gender, religion, refugee and immigrant status, housing status, income and poverty levels, percentage of residents living in rural versus urban areas, unemployment rate, languages and dialects spoken, literacy level, number of schools, and number and types of businesses.)

1. Recruit disaster workers who are representative of the community or service area.
2. Provide ongoing cultural competence training to disaster mental health staff.
3. Ensure that services are accessible, appropriate, and equitable.

4. Recognize the role of help-seeking behaviors, customs and traditions, and natural support networks.
5. Involve as "cultural brokers" community leaders and organizations representing diverse cultural groups.
6. Ensure that services and information are culturally and linguistically competent.
7. Assess and evaluate the program's level of cultural competence.

The responsibility to implement these principles lies in the hands of all human service managers and stakeholders.

TECHNOLOGICAL TRENDS

In the human services, technology is almost always assumed to mean "computers." A broader definition is used here: the work rules, tools, equipment, and information used to transform inputs into outputs (goods or services) (Taylor & Felten, 1993, p. 54). The service delivery methods and processes we use to help change people (for example, casework, psychotherapy, and community organizing) are our technologies. This topic will be discussed later in the context of program design, but it is mentioned here because human service organizations are increasingly pressured to change or adopt technologies. For example, managed care policies typically require providers to use short-term models rather than open-ended, long-term treatments, and welfare-to-work programs are precipitating the development of new ways to bring the poor into the workforce.

2.1   ENVIRONMENTAL TRENDS AND THE GRANDVIEW COMMUNITY CENTER (GCC)

In Chapter 1, you were introduced to the Grandview Community Center (GCC). The political, economic, social, and technological trends we have described have very direct and critical effects on Grandview's services.

- The consumers of GCC's services belong to a population that can be described primarily as *have-nots* within a more stratified environment. The human service workers who serve them will find it important to advocate on their behalf.
- The GCC consumers are vulnerable to economic downturns. In difficult times, demand for services will increase while the organization will have fewer resources. Grandview's stakeholders will find it important to seek new ways to do more with less, possibly by entering more community-wide collaborative networks.
- The cultural makeup of the community has changed, making it likely that existing programs and services will need to adapt. Grandview's new clients will have different attitudes and needs in comparison with the less diverse consumer population of the past.
- Grandview Community Center was founded in the 1930s. Since then, the available technology has changed drastically. This pace of change is accelerating, which means managers and service providers might need to grapple with a steep learning curve.

Technological change in agency operations will continue, using techniques such as business process reengineering and total quality management. Further reductions in the ranks of mid-management will affect career development prospects for lower-level workers, while at the same time empowering them in their current jobs. Systems redesign, including services integration and the various forms of interagency collaboration, are also affecting the ways agencies deliver services (O'Looney, 1996).

Finally, of course, information technology and computer use will continue to advance. Human service workers were in the past slow to embrace this trend, in spite of the opportunities to reduce mundane work and have quicker access to more work-related knowledge. Now, a high level of technological sophistication is expected among human service workers at all levels.

FROM THE WORLD TO THE NEIGHBORHOOD: "THINKING GLOBALLY AND ACTING LOCALLY"

The trends we have just reviewed have taken us from the evolving world economy, the World Wide Web, and national political trends to the effects of larger trends at the level of community functioning and agency operations. The wise human service worker or administrator will, in order to function effectively and purposefully, think globally and act locally.

Based on lessons from both business and the not-for-profit sector, organizations that do a better job of assessing and responding to the environment will, other factors being equal, be more likely to thrive. Techniques for doing this include environmental scanning (a component of strategic planning discussed in the next chapter), data collection techniques such as needs assessments and asset mapping, interagency and community collaborations, and managers assuming "boundary-spanning" roles as part of their jobs. Other management processes that help an agency manage its environment include marketing, public relations, coalitions, professional associations, and networks.

NEEDS ASSESSMENT

Human service agencies can be effective only if they allocate resources and respond to expectations based on clear and comprehensive goals. These goals must be responsive to the realities of the given community. Because the services being delivered must be the services that community members require and want, a needs assessment is a common method to inform program selection and design. In this context, a need is defined as "the gap between what is viewed as a necessary level or condition by those responsible for this determination and what actually exists" (Siegel, Attkisson, & Carson, 1995, p. 11). Through a needs assessment, problems in the community can be identified and ways to address them can be sought. The needs assessment might be a broadly based attempt to measure and evaluate the general problems and needs of a total community, as in the instance of a community mental health center or a health agency beginning operation. It might involve a specific measurement of the needs of a narrowly defined target population, as in the case of an existing agency or institution deciding on the efficacy of an innovative service. In either situation, the needs assessment should be comprehensive in the sense that an attempt is made to identify problems, to measure relevant community characteristics, to analyze consumer perceptions of problems and goals, and to determine whether needs are being met by current programs and services.

PROBLEM IDENTIFICATION

Needs assessment involves a recognition that services are being planned in order to bring about some change in the current situation. The process begins with the question of what measurable area of difference exists between the current state of affairs and what is desired. Using a variety of tools and mechanisms, the group conducting a needs assessment tries to determine the extent to which a specific disability, dissatisfaction, or unmet goal exists within the community. Attempts are made to establish the size of the potential target population, the nature and severity of the problems being addressed, and the likelihood that specific kinds of services would be used. In the hope that potential services might be preventive in nature, focus is placed not just on current disabilities but on health-related goals. Interest is centered both on what is and on what can be.

COMMUNITY AND INSTITUTIONAL CHARACTERISTICS

The problems addressed by human service organizations take place within environmental contexts that must be assessed. By taking knowledge of global trends to the level of the immediate community, planners can recognize demographic characteristics of the target population; discover resources available for problem resolution; and isolate social, political, and economic factors that might be causally related to difficulties that consumers experience. A comprehensive needs assessment must identify both problems and the environmental factors that affect them.

ANALYSIS OF CONSUMER PERCEPTIONS

Human service professionals often believe that they can identify the negative or positive conditions that exist in a community. Yet the identification of problem situations is affected by a variety of perceptions, values, experiences, and sociocultural factors. Only members of a given community can decide whether a condition is tolerable or unacceptable, central to the quality of life or tangential. Needs assessment must also take into account potential consumers' perceptions of their own personal needs.

CURRENT PROGRAMS AND SERVICES

Each needs assessment, whether it has been designed to provide a sweeping picture of a total area or to examine the prevalence of a single, concrete problem, must take into account the current efforts being undertaken. Examination of service utilization can help shed light on the prevalence of a specific need. A survey of locally available services can also help to determine whether additional programs are necessary. Analyzing current offerings can be as important as identifying problems because needless duplication of effort can be avoided.

Needs Assessment Instruments and Methods

Most needs assessments utilize a combination of approaches because comprehensiveness requires different tools for the measurement of separate factors. Each of the many types of tools available has the ability to expand or contract, to run the gamut from the narrow and simple to the broad and complex. The human service professional who hopes to be involved in program planning should be aware of the nature of the options available.

SOCIAL INDICATORS Social indicators are quantitative measures of aspects of the community that are thought to correlate with needs for service. A needs assessment based on the use of social indicators normally uses secondary data rather than gathering all of the necessary information specifically for the purpose of the study. The needs assessor decides what kinds of information might be useful for shedding light on the problem of a target group or geographic area. The information is gathered, possibly using a combination of locally gathered data and national statistics. Data that are relevant for needs assessment are found through such sources as census report and other governmental publications, statistics gathered by local or national organizations, needs assessments that have been carried out by local health or planning departments, and a variety of nationally distributed publications.

Some of the aspects of community life that can be measured, at least indirectly, include demographic characteristics, socioeconomic variables, health statistics, educational level, housing, employment patterns, family patterns, local safety issues, and use of leisure and recreational facilities.

SURVEYS OF COMMUNITY MEMBERS When surveys are used, community members are asked directly to provide information concerning their needs and desires. Surveys can be used with a sample of people living in a community or administered to members of a target population. The survey can take the form of a mailed questionnaire, a series of telephone interviews, personal contacts, or online communications. Surveys can be used to gather data concerning any of the needs assessment purposes, including problem identification, measurement of community characteristics, analysis of community member perceptions, and use of current programs and services.

SURVEYS OF LOCAL AGENCIES Survey approaches can also be used to identify the services currently being offered and used in the local community. When surveys are conducted for this purpose, questionnaires asking managers to identify the kinds of services provided, the number and types of consumers served, and other agency characteristics can be sent to known agencies and institutions. This process can have a two-pronged purpose: to gather utilization data that can illuminate client needs and to determine what kinds of resources are currently available within the community. This step helps to prevent duplications of services. Even more importantly, it can point the way toward inter-agency collaborations.

OPEN FORUMS AND MEETINGS The views of community members concerning their own needs and priorities can be determined through community meetings. In such settings, a variety of ideas that would not be heard through other mechanisms might be developed. The forum or meeting approach can run the gamut from small, informal get-togethers to block cub meetings to open hearings. What is important is that many community members be encouraged to voice their views. Moreover, this type of activity might increase the community members' commitment to ongoing participation.

USE OF KEY INFORMANTS The idea behind the use of key informants is that there are people within any community who are well informed about unmet needs and local opinion. Key informants can help with the needs assessment process through meetings, individual interviews, or questionnaires. Their sensitive analyses of the current situations cannot replace more broadly based needs assessments, but they can help to focus the needs assessment on current sentiments within the community.

People who are carrying out needs assessments for the purpose of building effective human service programs must be careful in their selection of key informants. At worst, the people selected might not be representative of the community at large. At best, they can provide an entrée into the community that might not otherwise be available to human service professionals. A good example of this kind of entrée is provided by the IBISS agency, which works very effectively in the *favelas* of Brazil. In a discussion of the organization's first entry into the favelas, Nanko van Buuren, the executive director, said,

> We work in the most violent and socially excluded slums where the government and the police don't enter. These favelas form a state within a state and are ruled by organized crime … You have to understand that these slums are really socially excluded: there are no schools, no health posts, nothing." (Beauchemin, 2006, p. 2)

The IBISS teams were initially able to enter a favela only because they began by establishing a relationship with an association that represented the people living within its environs. Little by little, after that entrée, the organization was able to establish trust where few others had.

NEEDS ASSESSMENT AS AN ONGOING PROCESS

Gilmore and Campbell (2005), in a discussion of the needs assessment process, point out that,

> Health and human service professionals have different reasons for using this process. Some professionals use needs assessments as starting points for program planning. Others use them on a continuing basis with the same populations to detect changing needs over a certain period of time and to adjust services based on those needs. (p. 4)

It should be recognized as well that needs assessment should be an ongoing process not just to study changes within one population but also to recognize how needs within a community alter as the demographics change.

2.2 GCC: THE NEED FOR ONGOING ASSESSMENTS

In your review of the GCC, you noticed that the community changed over time. When GCC first came into existence, it served a primarily white, working-class community. Over time, the community demographics changed; the community is now made up primarily of Latinos, along with immigrants from Southeast Asia. The needs assessment that guided program planning 20 years ago could not be relevant now. This example points out the importance of ongoing assessments of needs and community assets.

DISCOVERING COMMUNITY ASSETS AND STRENGTHS

It is likely that human services organizations will continue to use needs assessments as practical first steps in program planning. As useful as the needs assessment technique is, however, it has a serious limitation when used in isolation. By definition, it focuses on problems or deficiencies in a community or population and does not necessarily consider important factors such as community strengths and assets.

> A growing number of community development leaders argue that the focus on "needs" may itself be problematic. They suggest that needs-focused assessments risk defining an organization, neighborhood, or community by its problems—problems that generally require outside expertise and resources to "fix." (Roehlkepartain, 2008, p. 2)

Asset mapping and Assets-based community development (Kretzmann & McKnight, 1996) provide a broader perspective. According to O'Looney (1996), the mapping of community strengths and capacities is a "first step in learning to build the support structures for self-help, mutual aid, and informal economic development" (p. 248). This provides "a common and comprehensive base of information on which to make decisions" (p. 248), such as where to locate resources and services.

One product of asset mapping can be a database of residents' skills, talents, and willingness to volunteer. Civic associations, families with skills and knowledge to share with others, and goods and services to provide to neighbors can all be identified. Asset mapping must promote a search for multiple resources within the community; meet the needs of diverse social, ethnic, cultural, and interest groups; focus on the grassroots level to uncover hidden resources; involve community residents in the design and implementation of the survey; and "illuminate and enhance the potential for mutual exchange of skills and services" (O'Looney, 1996, pp. 257–258).

Asset mapping illuminates the strengths that are inherent in the community and helps to highlight the importance of strength-based approaches to community assessment. According to Roehlkepartain (2008), strength-based approaches share the following common characteristics:

- Strength-based approaches focus on the capacities or gifts that are present in the community, not what is absent ...
- Strength-based approaches stress local leadership, investment, and control ...

- Strength-based approaches surface both formal, institutional resources (such as programs, facilities, and financial capital) as well as individual, associational, and informal strengths and resources ...
- Strength-based approaches seek to link the strengths and priorities of all partners, including the young people.... This mutual engagement, respect, and commitment yields reciprocal benefits to everyone involved (pp. 3–4).

These positive approaches to community development increase the focus on the community, although not to the exclusion of relevant external forces, and this facilitates the development of relationships among community residents and organizations. This approach to combined assessment is well linked with another emerging technology: the community collaboration.

COMMUNITY COLLABORATIONS

Although service integration and interagency collaboration have a long history in social work, going back at least to the charity organization societies of the nineteenth century, recent attempts at collaboration reach for deeper and more fundamental ways for service providers and community members to interact. Evidence indicates that interagency collaborations can indeed be successful for all involved, but this type of collaboration must be learned and takes time and effort (Mulroy & Shay, 1998). To acknowledge a strengths-based perspective in this context, Bailey and Koney (1996) assert that "all organizational members must recognize and continually acknowledge the valuable resources each brings to the system" (p. 606).

Lewis et al. (in press, pp. 179–181) suggest that well-organized collaborations and networks share several distinct characteristics, including the following:

1. Both those who deliver and those who use services actively plan and evaluate such programs ...
2. Agencies work together in cooperative helping networks.... Without cooperative networks, agencies find themselves simply competing against one another for limited funds ...
3. The network has a coordinating organization that facilitates ongoing planning and includes workers and community members in the process ...
4. The helping network has a mechanism through which it can react to specific issues ...
5. Conventional planning agencies within the helping network are open to broad participation ...
6. Government agencies, social planning agencies, direct service agencies, and community groups maintain on ongoing dialogue ...
7. The rights of consumers, as well as the uniqueness of each agency, are protected at all stages of the planning process.

Models of collaboration are continually evolving in the current dynamic environment. Some basic definitions, examples, and guidelines are offered here to enable the human service manager to assess an agency's local collaboration activities and make decisions regarding how to work within them. Abramson and Rosenthal (1995, p. 1479) offer the following definitions. Collaboration is "a fluid process through which a group of diverse, autonomous actors (organizations or individuals) undertakes a joint initiative, solves shared problems, or otherwise achieves common goals." Interdisciplinary collaboration "describes the process by which the expertise of different categories of professionals is shared and coordinated to resolve the problems of clients." An inter-organizational collaboration "is a group of independent organizations who are committed to working together for specific purposes and tangible outcomes while maintaining their own autonomy; they terminate their collaboration or transform themselves into other forms of organization when that purpose is met." Examples of this type of collaboration include coalitions, networks, strategic alliances, task forces, or partnerships. An even more advanced form of collaboration involves formal merging of funds and staff, sometimes into new organizational entities. This has become known as a "community collaborative" or, as we describe it later, organizationally centered services integration. Collaboration can occur at the service delivery or policy levels.

O'Looney (1996) distinguishes between the "soft," informal process that may be seen as the "spirit" of collaboration, which includes the sharing of goals, values, ideas of fairness, and the experience of joint activity, and the "hard," formal process that he calls service integration. He sees the latter as representing the "fruits of the collaborative social dynamics," which include cross-training and cross-authorization of staff, pooled funds, co-location of services, shared transportation, and job descriptions that include collaboration as a performance requirement (p. 15). O'Looney asserts that collaborations should be undergirded by basic principles or shared values, suggesting that such services be community based, prevention/early intervention oriented, family focused, and culturally sensitive.

Abramson and Rosenthal (1995) note some of the common obstacles to collaboration, including the unequal balance of power among representatives (based on disciplines or the size or status of the organizations); inequities based on differences in color, gender, or culture (for example, male dominance); role competition or turf issues (fighting over limited funds or competition among professional groups); differing value bases; unclear definitions of roles and responsibilities; and inadequate conflict management processes. If these issues are addressed early and explicitly, in a climate of goodwill, collaborations are likely to be successful.

Abramson and Rosenthal suggest key tasks at the different developmental stages of a collaboration to help ensure success. At the formation stage, establishing a common mission, a shared view of problems and tasks, and clear operating ground rules are important. At the implementation stage, it is important to deal with communication difficulties, group dynamics, and interpersonal problems that get in the way of completing products such as a community assessment or a strategic plan. At the maintenance stage, issues or tensions may arise regarding power, leadership, goals, strategies, and follow-through on agreements. Existing norms and ground rules, agreed to upon formation, may be returned to as aids in resolving these problems.

In particular, Abramson and Rosenthal suggest several key roles for leaders, who have particular responsibility for "setting the tone, assessing and managing the group process, keeping the activity on target, and handling administrative details" (p. 1485). Leaders may rotate, or there may be a central core of leaders, but regardless of the formal structure, all leaders must act in the best interests of all participants. Leaders should help develop a positive climate where all can be heard, differences are openly discussed, conflict is proactively managed, and a view of hope and optimism predominates.

BOUNDARY MANAGEMENT: COALITIONS, PROFESSIONAL ASSOCIATIONS, AND NETWORKS

In addition to all of their other responsibilities, managerial leaders, especially those at the upper echelons, need to assume "boundary-spanning" roles that require them to interface with those elements of their organization's task environment, or supra-system, that have a direct bearing on the organization's growth, survival, efficiency, and effectiveness. Knowledge of the environments in which human service organizations are embedded and of the skills required to negotiate balanced exchanges of tangible and intangible goods and services between the organization and its task environment becomes an essential component of the managerial leader's professional armamentarium.

Many direct service staff rarely see their agency executives and wonder where they are during the day. In fact, an effective manager needs to spend much of her or his time actively engaged with aspects of the agency's environments. This includes reading literature on current developments in the field, increasingly via the Internet. Even with these resources, a manager needs to spend a good deal of time outside the agency, in face-to-face meetings with other service providers, funders, community members, advocacy groups, and the news media. A manager may not enjoy traveling to the state capital to meet with legislators or their staff, but such trips, as well as attendance at worthwhile national conferences or meetings of professional associations, can pay off in the future for the agency.

Not only can state-of-the-art information be acquired about successful model programs, new funding sources, or pending legislation, but also personal relationships are built that will be valuable in later collaboration or problem solving. A human service manager should become aware of relevant organizations in his or her field of service and participate in them as appropriate.

PUBLIC RELATIONS

Public relations in general and media relations in particular are important aspects of an agency's interaction with the environment. At the most local level, an agency, especially one providing services that some consider to be controversial or that involve "undesirable" clients, may need to pay extra attention to relationships with local residents and other organizations. Ideally, the agency would have begun to develop relationships with the local community before opening a program there. Sometimes concerns regarding, for example, having ex-offenders or people in recovery living in a neighborhood can be addressed by meeting with residents and introducing the staff and program model. There may be ways to adapt the program or add new services to build community acceptance. Having good relationships with local politicians, community leaders, and relevant local government staff such as zoning administrators should make it easier to solve problems.

On a slightly broader scale, the agency should have a well-thought-out strategy for media relations on an ongoing basis. Cohen (1998) has provided useful suggestions for connecting with local reporters and editors. The agency should learn which editors and reporters handle human service issues and arrange a meeting to be introduced and provide background on the agency and its services. Reporters will then know people to contact when they are preparing a story.

The agency can make available to the media information on new or modified programs and human interest stories illustrating what a program does and what positive effects it has had on the community. News releases, letters to the editor, guest editorials on television or radio, and op-ed articles are effective ways to reach large numbers of citizens.

AGENCY AND ENVIRONMENT: THE DIRECTORIAL ROLE

According to Herman and Heimovics (2005), successful executives "work through their boards to position their organization in its environment" (pp. 163–164). There is little doubt that effective work across the boundaries between an agency and its environment is considerably enhanced by the presence of a flourishing board and by a good working relationship between board and staff. Among the most important roles that boards can perform are defining and advancing the organization's mission, developing the organization's resources, overseeing management, ensuring that organization assessment is carried out, and engaging in "outreach as a bridge and a buffer between the organization and its stakeholders" (Axelrod, 2005, p. 137).

In considering the ways in which a board can act as a "bridge and buffer," Axelrod describes a number of key activities that an organization's board are ideally situated to carry out. These activities include the following (Axelrod, 2005, p. 137):

- Serve as ambassadors to communicate the organization's mission, policies, programs, and services to its various stakeholders.
- Interpret and communicate to the organization the needs of the communities served by the organization.
- Define the organization's position on public policies and serve as advocates.
- Protect the organization from inappropriate intrusions by government and special interests.
- Promote the organization to donors and potential donors.

Clearly, if board members are to communicate accurate information about the organization, they themselves will have to be well informed. If they are to communicate information *from* the community *to* the agency's management, their input must be welcomed by the staff. If they are to promote and advocate for the organization, they must have a clear message that is shared by all stakeholders. These factors serve to highlight the idea that the agency's board and managers must work closely together. It is perhaps for this reason that Axelrod terms the idea of limiting boards strictly to policy an "old bromide" (p. 142). Trying to create and maintain impermeable boundaries between the board's policy domain and the staff's operational expertise is impractical at best. When managers keep board members well informed about the organization's operations, they make it possible for the board to play a significant role in supporting the agency. And when managers are open to the messages that board members bring in their role of conduit from the community, the agency gains input that is valuable to strategic planning process.

SUMMARY

The stakeholders of an effective human service organization know that one of their most important qualities is their understanding of the environment. Human service programs are powerfully affected by environmental factors in the larger public arena. Political, economic, social, and technological changes—even at the national or international level—bring both opportunities and challenges and call for adaptations that might be unexpected. At the local level, human service programs need to be built on an understanding of the needs, the assets, and the strengths of the community being served. This chapter reviewed the connections between human service programs and their environments, moving from a global perspective to the presentation of practical ideas for enhancing the connections between program and environment.

COMPETENCY-BUILDING ACTIVITY 2.1 | KNOWING THE ENVIRONMENT

At the close of Chapter 1, you began the process of developing your own hypothetical program. You began to consider your dreams for this program. You thought about the difference you could make in the lives of a particular population. You gave your program a name.

Now it is time to consider the environment within which your program will exist:

1. What are political, economic, social, and technological factors that would be most likely to affect the clients you will serve?
2. How might you go about assessing the needs and the strengths of your program's community?
3. What factors of culture and diversity would have the greatest effect on your clients and your program?

CASE ACTIVITY 2.1 | MEETING THE NEEDS OF BATTERED WOMEN

Marcia Butler, Angela Ortiz, and Pam Collins worked together at the Department of Human Services (DHS) in a fairly large city. Because they were the only female professionals in their particular branch, they tended to be the ones assigned to work with battered women, and they had all dealt with a number of these situations.

Pam, the youngest and least experienced of the three professionals, often asked Marcia and Angela for advice and support when dealing with difficult problems. One such situation had just presented itself. Pam's client, a very young mother of two who had been severely beaten by her husband on many occasions, had just been referred to DHS for the third

time. Each time Pam worked with her, the same thing happened. Immediate, stopgap measures were taken, wounds were healed and promises made, and the young client returned to the same situation. There was no potential for change as long as this client saw herself as without resources for self-sufficiency. She could not support herself and her children economically, her self-esteem was as battered as her body, and she felt she had no future except with her husband.

Marcia and Angela sympathized with Pam's difficulty in helping this client, but they did not have any answers. Each of them had seen similar situations time and again. Yet, as much as they tried to help, they could see no way out, primarily because of the way services were organized.

Battered women could go to a shelter that had been organized by a nonprofit, private agency, but the shelter provided only short-term (two weeks' or less) refuge for women and their children. No long-term services were offered. Women could receive vocational counseling and training through the employment service and personal counseling through the mental health center. Either of these, however, required that the women enter long-term programs before being able to make drastic life changes. In light of their relationships, most women did not feel safe using such programs within the context of their home situations.

Marcia, Angela, and Pam recognized the need for a more comprehensive program to deal with the needs of battered women in their locality. To be effective, a program would have to combine physical refuge, medical services, personal and family therapy, and vocational counseling. The purpose of such a program would not necessarily be to remove all battered women from their current homes but to work with whole family systems and to ensure that women developed more options for their lives.

Although the general manager of DHS recognized the need for such a program when it was presented to him, he did not see how it could fit into the agency's current plans and appropriations. He made it clear that he did sympathize with the aims of the program and that he would be glad to consider it further if he could see a carefully developed proposal. The proposal would need to include hard data concerning needs as well as specific suggestions concerning pro-

gram activities and funding. He would not consider reallocating funds currently being used by other programs that were already hard-pressed to serve the number of clients needing assistance.

Similarly, community agencies, such as the women's shelter, shared their philosophical support for a more comprehensive program. None of the currently operating programs, however, seemed ready or able to take on the burden of providing additional services.

Marcia, Angela, and Pam began to recognize that they could not help develop this sorely needed program just by mentioning it to others. They would need to become more involved themselves. The program might be brought into being in any of a number of ways, including creation of an alternative community-based agency, application for a grant that might be awarded either to the Department of Human Services or to the women's shelter, or development of a coalition of existing agencies and services. The possibilities needed to be spelled out, and if Marcia, Angela, and Pam did not take the initiative on this, no one else would.

1. If you were in the situation these human service professionals face, would you become involved in seeking a solution? To what extent?
2. What approach to solving the problem seems most promising, given the human service network that exists in the community being discussed here?
3. What steps should Marcia, Angela, and Pam take in developing, and possibly implementing, a comprehensive program?

REFERENCES

Abramson, J., & Rosenthal, B. (1995). Interdisciplinary and interorganizational collaboration. In R. Edwards (Ed.), *The encyclopedia of social work* (19th ed., pp. 1479–1489). Washington, DC: NASW Press.

ACCESS. (2007). *Mental health division*. Retrieved March 20, 2010, from http://www.accesscommunity.org/site/PageServer?pagename=Mental_Health_Division

Axelrod, N. R. (2005). Board leadership and development. In R. D. Herman (Ed.), *The Joosey-bass handbook of nonprofit leadership and management*. (2nd ed., pp. 131–152). San Francisco: Jossey-Bass.

Bailey, D., & Koney, K. (1996). Interorganizational community-based collaboratives: A strategic response

to shape the social work agenda. *Social Work, 41*(6), 602–611.

Beauchemin, E. 2006, 3/10. *Interview with Nanko van Buuren*. Retrieved January 10, 2010, from http://static.rnw.nl/migratie/www.radionetherlands.nl/thenetherlands/underforeignskies/060104ufs-redirected

Bryson, J. (1995). *Strategic planning for public and nonprofit organizations* (rev. ed.). San Francisco: Jossey-Bass.

Celinska, B. (12/17/2009). Personal Communication.

Chung, R. C-Y, Bemak, F., Ortiz, D. P., & Sandoval-Perez, P. A. (2008). Promoting the mental health of immigrants: A multicultural/social justice perspective. *Journal of Counseling & Development, 86*, 310–317.

Cohen, T. (1998). Media relationships and marketing. In R. Edwards, J. Yankey, & M. Altpeter (Eds.), *Skills for effective management of nonprofit organizations* (pp. 98–114). Washington, DC: NASW Press.

Cooke, P., Reid, P., & Edwards, R. (1997). Management: New developments and directions. In R. Edwards (Ed.), *Encyclopedia of social work supplement 1997* (pp. 229–242). Washington, DC: NASW Press.

Gaza Community Mental Health Programme (2010a). *What is GCMHP?* Retrieved January 13, 2010, from http://www.gcmhp.net/

Gaza Community Mental Health Programme (2010b). *Women's empowerment project.* Retrieved January 13, 2010, from http://www.gcmhp.net/File_files/Women/WEP.html

Gilmore, G. D., & Campbell, M. D. (2005). *Needs and capacity assessment strategies for health education and health promotion* (3rd ed.). Sudbury, MA: Jones & Bartlett.

Hasenfeld, Y. (2010). Introduction. In Y. Hasenfeld (Ed.), *Human services as complex organizations* (2nd ed., pp. 1–5). Thousand Oaks, CA: Sage.

Herman, R. D., & Heimovics, D. (2005). Executive leadership. In R. D. Herman (Ed.), *The Jossey-Bass handbook of nonprofit leadership and management* (2nd ed., pp. 153–170). San Francisco: Jossey-Bass.

Hinojosa-Ojeda, R. (2010). *Raising the floor for American workers: The economic benefits of comprehensive immigration reform.* Washington, DC: Center for American Progress, American Immigration Council. Retrieved February 28, 2010, from http://www.americanprogress.org/issues/2010/01/pdf/immigrationeconreport.pdf

Hudson, C. G. (2005). Socioeconomic status and mental illness: Tests of the social causation and selection hypotheses. *American Journal of Orthopsychiatry, 75*(1), 3–18.

Knapp, M., Funk, M., Curran, C., Prince, M., & McDaid, D. (2006). Economic barriers to better mental health practice and policy. *Health Policy and Planning, 21*(3), 157–170.

Kotkin, J. (3/16/2010). *America in 2050—strength in diversity.* Retrieved July 15, 2010, from http://www.newgeography.com/content/001466-america-2050-strength-diversity

Kretzmann, J., & McKnight, J. (1996). Assets-based community development. *National Civic Review, 85*(4), 23–27.

Lewis, J. A., Arnold, M. S., House, R., & Toporek, R. L. (2002). *ACA Advocacy Competencies.* Retrieved May 27, 2010, from http://www.counseling.org/Publications/

Lewis, J. A., Lewis, M. D., Daniels, J. A., & D'Andrea, M. J. (in press). *Community counseling: A multicultural-social justice approach.* Belmont, CA: Brooks/Cole, Cengage Learning.

Martin, L., & Kettner, P. (1997). Performance measurement: The new accountability. *Administration in Social Work, 21*(1), 17–29.

Meyer, K., & Lobao, L. (2003). Economic hardship, religion and mental health during the Midwestern farm crisis. *Journal of Rural Studies.* Retrieved March 1, 2008, from ScienceDirect.

Mosley, J. E. (2010). The policy advocacy role of human service nonprofits. In Y. Hasenfeld (Ed.), *Human services as complex organizations* (2nd ed., pp. 505–531). Thousand Oaks, CA: Sage.

Mulroy, E., & Shay, S. (1998). Motivation and reward in nonprofit interorganizational collaboration in low-income neighborhoods. *Administration in Social Work, 22*(4), 1–17.

Murali, V., & Oyebode, F. (2004). Poverty, social inequality and mental health. *Advances in Psychiatric Treatment, 10*, 216–224.

O'Looney, J. (1996). *Redesigning the work of human services.* Westport, CT: Quorum.

Obama, B. (2006). *The audacity of hope: Thoughts on reclaiming the American dream.* New York: Crown Publishers.

Osborne, D., & Gaebler, T. (1992). *Reinventing government: How the entrepreneurial spirit is transforming the public sector.* Reading, MA: Addison-Wesley.

Ratts, M. J., Toporek, R. L., & Lewis, J. A., (Eds.). (2010). *ACA Advocacy Competencies: A social justice framework for counselors.* Alexandria, VA: American Counseling Association.

Roehlkepartain, E. G. (September, 2008). *Beyond needs assessments: Identifying a community's resources and hopes.* Retrieved July 1, 2010, from http://www.servicelearning.org/instant_info/fact_sheets/cb_facts/beyond_needs_assess

Siegel, L., Attkisson, C., & Carson, L. (1995). Need identification and program planning in the community context. In J. Tropman, J. Erlich, & J. Rothman (Eds.), *Tactics and techniques of community intervention* (3rd ed., pp. 10–34). Itasca, IL: Peacock.

Substance Abuse & Mental Health Services Administration (nd). *Federal Emergency Management Agency crisis counseling assistance and training program guidance, Version 1.1.* Retrieved December 15, 2009, from http://download.ncadi.samhsa.gov/ken/pdf/cmhs/CCP_Program_Guidance_ver1.1.pdf

Taylor, J., & Felten, D. (1993). *Performance by design.* Upper Saddle River, NJ: Prentice Hall.

Tropman, J. (1995). Community needs assessment. In R. Edwards (Ed.), *The encyclopedia of social work* (19th ed., pp. 563–569). Washington, DC: NASW Press.

Warren, K., Franklin, C., & Streeter, C. (1997). Chaos theory and complexity theory. In R. Edwards (Ed.), *Encyclopedia of social work supplement 1997* (pp. 59–68). Washington, DC: NASW Press.

Useful Web Resources

Agency for Health Care Research and Quality. *Data Sources.* http://www.ncrel.org/sdrs/areas/issues/envrnmnt/css/ppt/chap2.htm.

Association of Maternal and Child Health Programs. *Needs Assessment Resources.* http://www.amchp.org/abouttitlev/pages/needsassessmentresources.aspx#data%20resources.

National Consumer Supporter Technical Assistance Center (NCSTAC). *Community Needs Assessment.* http://www.ncstac.org/content/materials/CommunityNeedsAssessment.pdf.

North Central Regional Educational Laboratory. *Conducting a Community Needs Assessment.* http://www.ncrel.org/sdrs/areas/issues/envrnmnt/css/ppt/chap2.htm.

U.S. Department of Health and Human Services. *HHS Gateway to Data and Statistics.* http://www.hhs-stat.net/scripts/fedralagency.cfm.

PLANNING AND PROGRAM DESIGN

Human service managers are always faced with complex challenges and promising opportunities. The degree to which they are successful in meeting challenges and making use of opportunities depends, first and foremost, on planning. An organization's managers and other stakeholders must be able to articulate the organization's reasons for existing, what it will do and how it will operate. The planning processes described in this chapter can provide needed structure and direction for an organization's managers and staff. The important role that planning plays in effective human service management is best understood through real-life applications. The Grandview Community Center, which was introduced in Chapter 1, will serve as an example of how the step-by-step processes of planning can be implemented.

3.1   PLANNING AT GRANDVIEW COMMUNITY CENTER (GCC): THE FIRST DECISION

After getting settled into her new position as executive director of Grandview Community Center (GCC), Leona Estrella concluded that her agency could benefit greatly from going through a formal strategic planning process. She had heard stories about agencies that had developed strategic plans because their boards or funders said they had to, only to have the plans ignored. She wanted to make sure that GCC's efforts in this area would be a meaningful process, leading to a plan that would be helpful and actually implemented. She found a local consultant who had worked with similar community-based organizations and who was able to suggest a useful process.

Several types of planning will be reviewed in this chapter. At the broadest level, *strategic planning* addresses the organization's mission and overall strategies for fulfilling the mission. Strategic planning is sometimes contrasted with *long-range planning*, which assumes that an organization's environment and activities will remain essentially stable over a period of years. Because of the constant changes in HSO organizational environments in recent decades, long-range planning is rarely used except as part of extending the time frame of strategic planning. *Operational planning* outlines plans for implementing the strategic plan and accomplishing annual goals regarding programs and other agency operations. *Program planning*, also known as *program design*, provides detail on service delivery methods and staffing to serve clients and communities. At the same level as program planning, *project planning* is used to implement or modify agency operations such as administrative processes. Many agencies also use *business plans* to detail revenues and expenses needed to put plans into effect (Allison and Kaye, 2005, pp. 7–9). The differences among these plans are outlined in Table 3.1.

At any level, a planning process should attempt to answer the following questions:

- Who should be involved in planning?
- What are the needs, problems, or issues being addressed?
- What outcomes are desired?
- What resources are available to reach goals?
- What constraints should be taken into account?
- What alternate methods could be used to meet the objectives?

- What are the best methods for meeting program objectives?
- What steps need to be carried out to meet each objective?
- How can success be evaluated?

TABLE 3.1 | TYPES OF PLANNING

Strategic planning	Addresses complex and dynamic environmental conditions by outlining the overall direction of the organization
Long-range planning	Assumes that conditions will remain essentially the same, with the organization making minor changes in goals and objectives over time
Operational planning	Provides specific guidance on day-to-day activities necessary to implement the strategic plan
Program planning	Designs service delivery programs to achieve outcomes for clients and communities
Project planning	Provides implementation detail for new or modified administrative projects not related to regular service delivery
Business planning	Provides details on expected revenues and expenses to implement programs and projects

During the planning process, agencies develop viable strategies and clear goals based on assessments of community needs and visions, input from a variety of stakeholders, and consideration of their core competencies. They attempt to reach a broadly based consensus concerning the efficacy of these goals. They translate their mission and strategies into achievable and measurable objectives, and then they use these objectives in program design, resource allocation, and program evaluation. In short, the planning process meets head-on the challenges and opportunities facing human service administrators, service providers, and community members. It enables an agency to respond consciously and proactively to its environment by developing visions of a preferred future and working collaboratively to develop responsive strategies and programs to improve the quality of life in the community.

Of course, organizations are not totally rational. The complications of unexpected events, personality factors, and organizational politics can keep any process from remaining rational. This situation is not necessarily a problem, however. Intuition, insight, creativity, and the adroit management of chaos are valuable aspects of planning and may make crucial differences in outcomes. A well-designed planning process provides participants with a sense of order, control, and focus and can also allow for creativity and adaptation to unforeseen circumstances. And, as Bryson (2004) has asserted, precisely because strategic planning focuses on resolving strategic issues, it goes beyond rational planning and is able to accept and accommodate political decision making.

Another important point is that, according to many strategic thinkers, the planning process used is more important than the actual plan that results, especially if the plan is quickly ignored after being proudly introduced to the agency's board or funders. The planning process enables those involved to develop a shared view of the agency's present, past, and ideal future, which can guide its decision making regardless of the details of a formal plan. Ultimately, both the planning and the plan can be valuable, especially if they augment each other, with the plan providing direction and the process guiding actual implementation.

We will begin this chapter by discussing the broadest level of planning: strategic planning, using a process that has been adapted for governmental and not-for-profit organizations. Strategic planning deals with long-term trends in the environment, important issues facing the organization, and visions for where the organization should be in the future. After developing strategies for the organization to pursue, operational planning occurs: specific programs or projects are developed or modified. This is done by setting goals and then developing specific objectives to achieve them. Management by objectives, a venerable management technique, will be presented as a useful way to identify desired outcomes. Often this involves designing something new, and it will be presented here as the process of program design: choosing an appropriate service delivery technology. Finally, implementation and development of an evaluation plan will be reviewed.

STRATEGIC PLANNING

Strategic planning achieved cliché status in the human services during the 1990s, just as government and the human services embraced other management innovations such as management by objectives, zero-based budgeting, and quality circles in previous decades. The fact that these processes were sometimes treated only as passing fads should not lead one to conclude that they are without value. The value of true strategic thinking continues to be recognized. Although any management technique or principle can be inadequately or improperly used, all can add value if used in the appropriate way in an appropriate situation.

A more common problem is that strategic plans are often developed but not fully used. In the final analysis, the plan itself is not as important as strategic *thinking* and strategic *managing* on a regular basis, but the plan can be a useful tool for thinking and managing. The environmental conditions outlined in the previous chapter clearly require strategic thinking and acting by any human service organization wanting to thrive in the twenty-first century.

Even in government the need for strategic thinking has become apparent in the wake of increased pressures from Congress for accountability, responsiveness, and efficiency. Bryson (2004) and Austin and Solomon (2009) have provided further evidence for the necessity of strategic planning. The value of strategic planning was noted in a recent study of mental health organizations (Singh, 2005), which found that a complete use of strategic planning was correlated highly with superior organizational performance. Bryson has added, however, that there are "bad" times to do strategic planning. If an organization is in the middle of a large crisis such as a huge funding cut, or if an organization does not have basic managerial skills or the commitment of key decision makers to proceed, these situations should be remedied before engaging in strategic planning.

The following discussion is based largely on the work of John Bryson (2004), who created a model that has been used successfully in both governmental and not-for-profit organizations and a book focused specifically on not-for-profit organizations (Allison & Kaye, 2005), augmented by the research of Singh (2005). Bryson defines strategic planning as "a disciplined effort to produce fundamental decisions and actions that shape and guide what an organization is, what it does, and why it does it" (p. 6). Many managers think of strategic planning as something that the board and executive managers do in a one- or two-day annual retreat. In fact, strategic planning is an ongoing process, reflected in strategic management: strategic thinking and strategic acting.

The strategic planning model presented here, adapted slightly from Bryson, consists of eleven stages:

1. Initiate and agree on a strategic planning process.
2. Identify organizational mandates.
3. Identify the organization's stakeholders and analyze their needs and concerns.
4. Clarify organizational vision, mission, and values.
5. Assess the organization's external environment to identify opportunities and challenges.
6. Assess the organization's internal environment to determine strengths and weaknesses.
7. Identify the strategic issues facing the organization.
8. Formulate strategies to manage these issues.
9. Review and adopt the strategic plan or plans.
10. Develop an effective implementation process.
11. Monitor and update the plan on a regular basis.

This process is typically done at an agency-wide level and ideally is then replicated at a smaller scale within each program, with program strategic plans then shared upward with refinements made as necessary to ensure alignment throughout the organization.

Stage 1: Initiate and agree on a strategic planning process. For strategic planning to be successful, several conditions need to be met. First, the organization should have competent leadership, which includes a basic level of overall management competence throughout the organization. If there are weak areas in management functioning, these are likely, in fact, to be strategic issues, because they are likely to threaten the ongoing survival of the organization. Therefore, management weaknesses should be addressed through the use of a consultant to develop both the staff's management skills and the agency's management processes. Strategic planning can also serve as a way to further develop an organization's managerial competence.

Another key condition is the support and commitment of all key decision makers, typically including managers and the governing board. Top leaders must "sponsor" the effort, showing that they will fully support it. The organization must be willing to make the commitment not only to develop a plan but also to implement it. A final important implication is that the strategic plan may require the organization to break out of "business as usual" by doing new things and by approaching the ongoing work of the organization in a new way. Decision makers should understand this point and expect that a new organizational culture, perhaps more dynamic and participative, may evolve.

As an outcome of this step, there should be a work plan: a clearly understood agreement on the purpose of the plan, steps to be taken, the roles of all involved, necessary resource commitments, and the final product (i.e., the plan). Typically a broad-based team is formed to develop the plan. Team members should include the agency's chief executive and some or all of the executive team, and may include representatives from other parts of the organization, including other managers, line staff, and, in the case of not-for-profit organizations, board representation. A person or small group, known informally as "champions," should have overall responsibility for making the process happen.

Stage 2: Identify organizational mandates. Any human service organization has both formal and informal mandates. Formal mandates for government organizations are usually easy to identify. Different units of government are responsible for functions such as protecting children, treating the indigent mentally ill, and providing government benefits such as Temporary Assistance to Needy Families (TANF); these are reflected in legislation, regulations, administrative guidelines, and sometimes court orders. Not-for-profit organizations have formal mandates reflected in their government or foundation grants and contracts and any statements of purpose in the organization's bylaws or charter.

Informal mandates are sometimes harder to discover but may be found by looking at the expectations that the members of the organization's governance bodies bring to their role. For example, elected officials may believe they bring a mandate to make government more accountable or to privatize government services. Agency board members may feel that they need to get the organization to either change or maintain its focus and purpose. Examples would include the use of a feminist philosophy in a battered women's shelter, debates over medical or social models of substance abuse, decisions about the nature of services provided to persons with HIV/AIDS, or approaches to ease the transition for poor people who are coming off TANF.

The strategic planning team should work to identify all key mandates, formal and informal, and also consider whether and how easily they could be changed if necessary. Mandates are then taken as "givens": expectations from outside forces that a strategic plan will need to accommodate. Paradoxically, the identification of mandates can be liberating. A strategic planning team may be surprised at how few or constraining the existing mandates actually are, providing great latitude once the limiting parameters are defined. Sometimes moving into the next step, stakeholder analysis, can provide further detail on what key outsiders expect from the organization.

Stage 3: Identify the organization's stakeholders and analyze their needs and concerns. As discussed in Chapter 2, a stakeholder is an individual, role, group, or organization with a stake in what the agency does. Usually a stakeholder has specific expectations of an organization and standards, at least implied, about how it judges how well the organization is doing. Some stakeholders are very powerful, such as funding sources and regulators, whereas others such as clients and community groups may be important but lacking in formal power. Identifying every stakeholder is neither possible nor necessary, but key stakeholders need to be identified so that their interests and concerns can be addressed by the strategic plan.

The criteria by which each stakeholder assesses the agency should be identified and viewed from the point of view of the stakeholder, not the agency. Once the criteria are clear, assess how well the organization is currently meeting them. This may result in sobering insights, especially if it is determined that the agency is not doing well at meeting the needs of particular stakeholders. This is nevertheless a solid place to begin because it allows strategies to be developed to improve stakeholder relations and it ensures that the agency is under no illusions regarding how well it is doing.

Stage 4: Clarify organizational vision, mission, and values. A powerful way for planners to frame the agency's mission, strategies, goals, and objectives is to develop a vision for the future.

People often enter the human services field or a particular organization based on a personal vision related to addressing social problems or helping people facing challenges to live better, more fulfilled lives. An HSO that can tap into its staff members' personal passions and visions can inspire staff and programs to even higher levels of accomplishment.

Peter Senge (2006, p. 208), in his classic *The Fifth Discipline*, introduced the notion of "governing ideas" for an organization. These include mission, which answers the question "Why do we exist?" *Core values* respond to "How do we want to act?" Finally, *vision* answers the question "What do we want the organization to be?" The first two of these were introduced in Chapter 1 as the elements of organizational purpose. Vision is the element that enables staff to describe the ideal future for the organization and themselves. It is presented here as the foundation of planning processes that include strategic planning, setting goals and objectives, and designing programs.

According to Bryson (2004), an inspirational vision may:

- Focus on a better future;
- Encourage hopes, dreams, and noble ambitions;
- Build on (or reinterpret) the organization's history and culture to appeal to high ideals and common values;
- Clarify purpose and direction;
- State positive outcomes;
- Emphasize the organization's uniqueness and distinctive competence; ...
- Communicate enthusiasm, kindle excitement, and foster commitment and dedication. (p. 235)

An organizational vision is typically a relatively short statement that describes an ideal but realistic or credible future for the organization. Additionally, according to Bryson, an organizational vision should provide "specific and reasonable" guidance to staff, promise that the organization will support members in the pursuit of the vision, be widely circulated, and be used to inform major and minor decisions and actions (p. 226).

As suggested by Senge, an organizational vision should also encompass the personal visions of the members of the organization. In this sense, a vision statement cannot be developed and announced from "on high" but must be developed collaboratively by intensive dialogue among all employees. For a vision to be maximally useful, it should be developed in a highly participatory process, so that everyone's personal visions are reflected in it. Senge (2006) notes that there needs to be alignment between individual visions and the organizational vision to keep everyone focused and working in the same direction.

The visioning process typically occurs in an off-site workshop setting and can include any number of people, from a team to the whole organization. Palmer, Dunford, and Akin (2009, ch. 9) provide detailed guidance on developing an organizational vision.

3.2   ORGANIZATIONAL VISIONING AT GCC

As part of its strategic planning process, GCC held a 2-day workshop for staff and board members. One of the first things participants did was develop a vision statement for the agency:

GCC will be widely recognized as an outstanding human service agency providing the highest quality and most responsive and comprehensive services to enable the people we serve to lead fulfilling lives in a vibrant, supportive, and safe community. We will be widely known for excellence in our programs, staff, and leadership, and for our involvement in our community and advocacy for policies that further social justice in our society.

Along with a vision statement, an organization's mission statement and statement of organizational values provide powerful guidance as to what the organization wants to be and how it operates. Human service organizations are inherently purpose driven, and they often put significant emphasis on the organization's mission and values (recall the conceptual model in Chapter 1). Developing mission statements was another management fad of the 1980s and 1990s for human service organizations, so most agencies probably have an official mission statement that is publicized to some extent. Initiating a strategic planning process is a good time to reassess and update an organization's mission statement to ensure that it is current, relevant, and useful.

A good mission statement should be short, perhaps two sentences. One guideline for length is that it should fit on the back of the agency's business card, where it can be used as a reminder for staff and a statement to those dealing with the organization. A mission statement should answer these questions:

- What basic social needs do we address? (Why do we exist? What is our purpose?)
- What do we do? (What are our primary methods or services? How do we accomplish our purpose?)
- What makes us unique? (What is our niche? How are we different from other similar organizations?)

3.3   A NEW MISSION STATEMENT FOR GCC

The next task at the GCC planning workshop was to review and update the organization's mission statement. Staff agreed that most people rarely thought of the mission statement, and no one could even describe it. After a vigorous, thoughtful dialogue, they agreed on the following as the agency's new mission statement:

The mission of the GCC is to help those in need in our communities to develop and obtain the resources and support they need to lead fulfilling lives. This is accomplished through the provision of a wide range of high-quality community-based social services designed to enhance social and emotional well-being of residents in southeast Adams County.

A statement of organizational values typically consists of a limited number of tight statements describing desired principles of behavior that management and staff are willing to publicize and follow. In this sense, values serve as guidelines for behavior or decision making. They "usually focus on service, quality, people, and work norms" (Allison and Kaye, 2005, p. 108).

Values can also serve as criteria for designing the organization or its programs. For example, organizational values developed by staff of a homeless shelter are widely publicized and addressed in hiring interviews, new employee orientations, staff meetings, and case conferences (Packard, 2001). A values statement should contain no unrealistic expectations, and management should be willing to be held accountable to it. In some agencies, values are displayed along with mission statements in lobbies and offices.

3.4   VALUES FOR GCC

At the planning workshop, GCC staff also brainstormed and developed a set of organizational values that they wanted to use to guide their work behavior and decision making. After small group brainstorming, discussion in the full group, and refinement, they agreed on the following statement:

- We believe that all residents in our community should have opportunities and supports to lead fulfilling lives as productive community members.
- We believe that all services offered should be of the highest quality possible.
- We believe that all clients and staff should always be treated with respect and compassion.
- We believe that staff and clients should be empowered in decision making.
- We believe that staff should always operate with adherence to the agency's ethical standards and the ethics of their professions.
- We believe that we should use the funds and other resources that have been entrusted to us with the utmost efficiency and accountability.

The group decided that after the vision, mission, and values statements were reviewed and approved by the board and staff, the statements would be posted in program waiting rooms, signed by all who helped develop them.

The draft vision, mission, and values statements should be widely circulated throughout the organization for further dialogue, input, and refinement. Through this process, their quality should improve with the application of more minds to the task, and those involved will feel a sense of ownership over the result and be more committed to using the mission and values statements to guide their daily work. The adopted vision, mission, and values should be shared widely and regularly, even before the strategic planning process has been completed. They may be reviewed at agency training events, workshops, or even regular meetings such as case discussions. In this way, they can guide both the strategic planning process and everyday staff behavior in the organization. Many organizations post these statements in agency facilities such as waiting rooms, and put them on agency documents.

Stage 5: Assess the organization's external environment to identify opportunities and challenges (formerly referred to as threats). Doing an *environmental scan* is a useful way to identify opportunities and challenges in the environment. These will, of course, vary from agency to agency, but many items, some of which were mentioned in Chapter 2 as factors affecting human service organizations, will be common to many agencies, at least in general terms. Since boards of directors are likely to have more wide-ranging exposure to current environmental forces than staff that operate in a more limited day-to-day environment, it is especially important to involve the board in this process. This may be done with the whole board or a representative group that is part of the strategic planning team.

Bryson (2004) suggests three categories of factors to be addressed by the environmental analysis: forces and trends in the environment, key resource controllers for the organization, and competitors or collaborators. A useful place to begin the environmental analysis is to conduct a PEST analysis of environmental forces and trends. (As discussed in Chapter 2, PEST refers to political, economic, social, and technological forces or trends.) The planning team can begin by brainstorming factors in each of the categories and then review the organization's key resource controllers, including funders, regulators, and clients. The agency's competitors and collaborators, real and possible, should also be reviewed.

The group should discuss the significance and meaning of each opportunity or challenge. Singh (2005) found that agencies with superior performance used advanced analytical techniques such as scenario planning (assessing possible scenarios that may result depending on how these factors are addressed) to guide analysis and decision making. Possible priorities or suggested action steps can be noted (for example, determining which elements need immediate action, which need monitoring or incorporation into the strategic plan, and which can safely be ignored for the time being). Consistent with the axiom that strategic thinking and management are more important than strategic planning, managers should ensure that the environmental scanning process becomes an ongoing activity for the agency.

Stage 6: Assess the organization's internal environment to determine strengths and weaknesses. After the environmental scan, attention should be focused internally on factors that will eventually be identified as the agency's strengths and weaknesses. As the cliché goes, the agency's greatest resource is its people, so the analysis can begin by looking at the current staff: their knowledge and skills with reference to current programmatic demands and role expectations. Questions here include the following: Do we have staff with the proper competencies or qualifications in all positions? Have our staffing needs changed? Are people properly trained? Are levels of turnover and sick leave within acceptable limits? What is the quality of working life as perceived by employees? Economic resources can then be reviewed: What is the status of current funding? Are program expenditures within the budget? When will grants and contracts end, and what will happen to the programs then? Are foundation funds and donations at expected levels? For government agencies, what are the prospects for changes in the next budget cycle? Have audits been done on schedule, and are identified problems being addressed? Information resources can be assessed by reviewing the management information system to see whether it is providing the data needed to manage and improve program operations. Harder to assess is the organization's culture. Sometimes employee attitude surveys, covered later in the chapter on organizational change, are used to assess the state of the organization's culture.

Even if the organization has never done strategic planning, it is, in fact, guided by strategy, either explicitly or implicitly. If a current strategic plan is not in effect, the organization's present strategies should be articulated so that they can be assessed. Strategy implementation should then be reviewed to see whether activities are on target and what adjustments may be needed, at the levels of both the organization as a whole and individual departments.

Finally, current performance of the organization should be assessed. One discovery here may be that existing information systems do not allow the team to determine what objectives or outcomes are actually being achieved, and this matter may immediately become a strategic issue. Using whatever data or measures exist, the organization's performance over time should be reviewed. Are more or fewer units of service being provided in each program? If effectiveness or efficiency can be measured, how are these figures changing over time? How does each program compare to similar, or competing, programs in the community?

The internal analysis should conclude with the same type of assessment used for the environmental scan: with a discussion of the significance and meaning of each strength and weakness and preliminary thoughts on possible priorities or action steps.

Stage 7: Identify the strategic issues facing the organization. Strategic issues are identified using a strengths, weaknesses, opportunities, and threats (SWOT) analysis. The term SWOC, with *challenges* replacing *threats*, has sometimes been used by those uncomfortable with the term *threats*. This analysis involves assessing how internal strengths and weaknesses interact with environmental opportunities and threats or challenges. Strategic issues can be differentiated from tactical issues with reference to several dimensions. Although identifying strategic issues is by no means an exact science, the following criteria, adapted from Bryson (2004), offer some guidance. Strategic issues tend to be part of the consciousness of the board and executive staff, have long-term implications, affect the entire organization or at least multiple departments, involve significant financial stakes, are likely to require new or modified programs and changes in resource allocations, are sensitive to community or political concerns, and have no obvious way of being addressed.

When an opportunity in the environment can be connected with a strength of the agency, proactive strategies for new programs or initiatives can be developed. The issue is framed as "What should we do to respond to this opportunity?" If a challenge in the environment corresponds with a weakness in the agency, defensive strategies will have to be developed to protect the agency. If there is an opportunity in the environment for which the agency has no distinctive competence (for example, a request for proposals for welfare-to-work programs that is assessed by a child abuse agency), the agency should ignore it or, if it is within the agency's mission, develop the competencies to respond. Finally, environmental challenges in areas where the agency is strong can in some cases be ignored, at least for the time being, but probably should be monitored for later action if conditions change. Priorities should be set to guide the selection of strategies and the development of implementation timelines.

Stage 8: Formulate strategies to manage the issues. Bryson (2004) defines a strategy as "a pattern of purposes, policies, programs, actions, decisions, and resource allocations that defines what an organization is, what it does, and why it does it" (p. 183). Every agency has strategies. For most agencies, these are implicit: continue growing, get new funding sources, keep providing certain services, and so forth. Strategic planning is intended to make strategies both more explicit and, because a thoughtful process is used, more effective.

Strategies can be developed at the overall agency level, at the program level, or for specific functions or processes. There should be a strategy for each strategic issue. Bryson has suggested a five-step process, adapted from the Institute for Cultural Affairs model (Spencer, 1989). The following questions are asked:

1. What are the practical alternatives, dreams, or visions we might pursue to address this strategic issue?...
2. What are the barriers to the realization of these alternatives, dreams, or visions?
3. What major proposals might we pursue to achieve these alternatives, dreams, or visions directly or to overcome the barriers to their realization?
4. What major actions (with existing staff and within existing job descriptions) must be taken within the next year (or two) to implement the major proposals?
5. What specific steps must be taken within the next six months to implement the major proposals, and who is responsible? (Bryson, 2004, pp. 199–200)

After these questions are answered, choices are made from the various options and strategies are selected for action. The team should also consider whether any strategies contradict each other and whether any strategies can be combined or need to be coordinated or sequenced together. After priorities are set, strategies can immediately be turned into action plans, with time lines and responsible people, or a full strategic plan can be prepared. A strategic plan can be valuable because it serves as the history of the thinking and analysis that led to the strategies and may be consulted later for background and insight regarding why particular alternatives were chosen. A plan is also useful to newcomers to the agency or to staff who may not have been involved with the entire planning process. One person, rather than a group, should have major responsibility for actually writing the plan. The plan itself should describe the results of each step of the process. A strategic plan should contain the following elements:

- The background and rationale for doing the plan
- The process used to develop and adopt the plan, including a list of participants
- The organization's mandates
- Key stakeholders and their needs and concerns
- The organization's mission and values
- The environmental analysis
- The organization's analysis of strengths and weaknesses
- The strategic issues identified for action

- Strategies to manage each issue
- The implementation plan
- The plan for monitoring and updating the plan

Stage 9: Review and adopt the strategic plan. The plan should then be shared as widely as possible throughout the organization, ideally at briefing sessions where it can be discussed and the process celebrated. Some organizations may want to send it out for review in draft form for a final round of feedback. The plan in general should not be "news" because employee representatives from all parts of the organization would have been involved in the process, keeping their constituencies informed and getting their reactions and input through the process. Someone should be put in charge of monitoring implementation and ensuring that responsible persons report on their process on a regular, predetermined basis.

Stage 10: Develop an effective implementation process. The keys to successful implementation of the plan are the commitment of all key internal stakeholders and, in fact, to some extent all staff and board members; a detailed action plan that is clear to all and for which responsible persons are assigned; necessary resource commitments (primarily staff time and funding); and clear connections between strategies and daily operations. Especially for an agency new to strategic planning, this process may be a major organizational change (see Chapter 11), requiring a conducive organizational climate (Singh, 2005). If staff members have been involved in the process, the need for and importance of this should be clear, but reminders may help regardless. An agency may want to appoint a strategy implementation team, including some members from the strategic planning team, to oversee implementation and ensure that the process gets the necessary attention and support.

Strategies often involve setting goals, designing new programs, obtaining new funding, or developing or redesigning organizational systems. Examples of the latter would be moving to performance-based budgeting, developing an integrated computerized management information system, or implementing a management development program.

Stage 11: Monitor and update the plan on a regular basis. Bryson (2004, pp. 285–286) offers useful suggestions for monitoring strategy implementation. First, he reminds us to stay focused on what is important: the mission and mandates of the organization. The pressures of day-to-day operations often pull staff into focusing on just following procedures or, at the other extreme, aggressively pushing the plan as an end in itself. Indicators of success or failure should be chosen early, and these should be monitored on an ongoing basis so that adjustments can be made where necessary. The strategy implementation team mentioned earlier can serve as a "review group" to identify strategies or action plans that may need to be modified. The review group and the organization's formal and informal leaders will have to show strong support for the action plans and encourage strategic thinking and management as part of daily work. There should be regularly scheduled sessions with board and staff to review progress and amend the plan as needed.

3.5   A SWOT ANALYSIS TO DEVELOP STRATEGIES FOR GCC

Prior to their strategic planning workshop, staff members at GCC had gathered data on both external and internal factors that could point them to strategic issues facing the organization. For the external analysis, they reviewed demographic and other trends in their county and the communities they served, including local, state, and federal policy changes. Their recent community needs assessment was useful in highlighting possible opportunities. To assess their internal functioning, they examined performance data from all their programs as well as data on their workforce such as staff turnover and the degrees, training, and skills of their current staff.

At the planning session, they looked at how all these factors were connected in order to identify new opportunities for the agency and develop strategies to address emerging problems and challenges. On the opportunity side, they noted several new local funding opportunities to pursue. One of these was the need for a program for teens who were abusing drugs or alcohol and also experiencing mental illness. They identified some administrative issues needing attention, such as improving their management information system to better measure client outcomes, a growing expectation from their county funders. They also realized that they needed to broaden their funding base, so they defined a strategy to create a fund development plan targeting local foundations and philanthropists. They also realized that they needed to broaden membership on their board of directors. Finally, some morale and team-building issues were recognized; and the staff members decided to set a priority on improving team functioning and communication across the agency. The Director of Administrative Services volunteered to draft a strategic plan for further review by staff and the board prior to final adoption. This director was also charged with the lead role in monitoring implementation of the plan.

SELECTION OF GOALS: OPERATIONAL PLANNING

Whereas strategic planning is concerned with the agency as a whole, operational planning focuses on individual programs or projects. Each program or major administrative function of the agency should have an overriding *goal*, the broad expected outcome of a program. For example, a program serving at-risk teenagers may have as a goal to enhance job readiness skills for youth so that they can obtain meaningful employment. For administrative functions, there may be goals related to fundraising, human resources, financial operations, and information systems. Goals need not be measurable but should provide direction and focus.

In each program and administrative function, the people who have a stake in the outcomes should have an opportunity to provide input into the determination of goals and objectives. Only when they have been active participants in setting goals and objectives can staff see their own work in the context of the work of the agency as a whole.

Goals provide the direct link between strategies based on consumer needs and other environmental factors and agency services, which are operationalized through program design. When goals are clear, objectives designed to attain them can more readily be specified. Then, given a specific set of objectives concerning desirable client outcomes, staff can build responsive programs.

3.6	**GCC GOAL FOR A NEW PROGRAM: THE TEEN TRANSITION AND TREATMENT PROGRAM**[1]

Based on the needs assessment that GCC had recently completed, staff decided that they were equipped to address the emerging need for a population of adolescents who were abusing drugs or alcohol and also experiencing mental illness. They decided to apply for funding from the county to develop a program to treat adolescents with co-occurring disorders. Fortunately, the county had already identified this need as a funding priority.

The overall desired outcomes for this program were to eliminate the use of illicit drugs and alcohol among adolescents with co-occurring disorders who are served by this program, help clients develop competency in the skills needed to live without abusing substances, and increase the quality of life among adolescents with co-occurring disorders.

Although staff could not define specific objectives until they had researched the literature to find the best program model, they defined the overall goal for the new program, tentatively named The Teen Transition and Treatment Program, as follows:

> The overall goal of the program is that upon completion of this program, participating adolescents with co-occurring disorders will be substance-free.

[1] The authors express sincere appreciation to Nicole Bishop, who, as an MSW student, designed for a class paper the hypothetical program upon which the Teen Transition Treatment Program referred to throughout much of this book is based (Bishop, 2009).

SPECIFICATION OF OBJECTIVES

Whereas goals are broad statements of the outcomes an agency or program seeks, objectives are specific and measurable statements regarding outcomes. Objectives identify the accomplishments related to a particular goal so that, ideally, if all of the objectives have been reached, the goal will automatically have been attained. Goals are general statements of desired end states. Objectives specify how those end states are to be attained. Objectives are by definition statements of measurable outcomes with a designated time frame. Clear goals and objectives not only guide operations but also form the basis of program evaluation—assessing whether program goals and objectives were met (covered in Chapter 10).

Most of an agency's goals will be for its programs, but there will also be a goal for each administrative or support function, such as finance, human resources, and any other administrative operation. Most of the following discussion will apply to program objectives, the key aspects of a HSO, but some examples of administrative objectives will be provided as well.

Administrative objectives are related to targets ongoing operations or for organizational improvement. For example, "to raise $500,000 by September 1, 2012, for capital improvement" is an administrative objective. So is the following: "to increase the ethnic minority representation on the board of directors from 6 to 12 by the end of the fiscal year." The following discussion will focus on program objectives, but it should be noted that administrative objectives can be developed using the same principles, such as some combination of process and outcome objectives.

Objectives can be categorized into two types: *process* or *activity*, and *outcome*. Historically in HSOs, process objectives have been more common, largely because they are easier to define and measure. Process objectives define program activities to be performed and/or number and types of services to be delivered—for example, "to provide at least one outreach contact to 200 youth in our geographic area during the program year" or "to provide weekly counseling for 12 weeks per family to 20 families per week during the first year of the project." In addition to defining units of service, process objectives can also define *service completions* (Kettner, Moroney, & Martin, 2008). A service completion defines when a client has received the necessary services based on the program model (program models will be discussed later in the chapter). A service completion may mean attending a number of parent education or anger management classes, or completing a series of prenatal care visits.

Outcome objectives refer to the expected impact of program intervention on the recipients of service. One example of an outcome objective is the following: "By the end of the program year, 65 percent of the youth dropouts who have completed the program will have returned to regular school or will have enrolled in an alternative accredited educational program." An objective might also indicate the number of clients completing a program who reach a certain standard in terms of psychological or social functioning, such as a clinical "cut score." Such an objective might read, "At least 60 percent of the couples engaged in marital counseling for six sessions will experience improvement in marital satisfaction, to a score of below 30 on the Index of Marital Satisfaction."

The use of the word "improvement" brings up an important point about objectives. Ideally, an outcome objective should designate a desired quality of life state in some measurable way: having a living-wage job, living independently, having an adequate level of emotional coping. This should be set with consideration of the base level at which the program's clients are currently functioning. In the previous example, if a couple already has a score of below 30, they may not be requesting services from an agency. Ideally, a program would have relevant baseline measures for clients, and the objectives would indicate the state that the clients would ideally reach. Human service organizations designed to serve disadvantaged populations are clearly expected to identify clients with high levels of need, and to help them move to higher levels of functioning. The concept of "creaming" has been used to refer to programs that admit clients who already function at high levels, increasing the prospects for success. This unethical behavior should of course not be allowed. A more common problem with objectives is that they use the word "improve" without reference to an ideal or expected standard. Clients could improve, but not to the extent that they reach a desired level of functioning. For example, a couple could improve from 34 to 31 on the Martial Satisfaction Index but still not be at the expected desirable level. These complexities in setting objectives that are both challenging and realistic often can involve discussions with the program's funding agency to reach agreement.

The objective most revealing of agency effectiveness is the outcome objective. This objective justifies the agency's reason for being, its purported relevance to social needs and problems and to their resolution. It is no longer sufficient for accountability purposes to cite the number of clients served. Such measures of services delivered may be necessary, but they are certainly not sufficient indicators of a program's value to the community.

For objectives to have the utmost utility, they should be stated so that they are SMART:

- **Specific:** clear, concrete, and operational
- **Measurable:** subject to observable verification
- **Achievable:** capable of being accomplished with available resources
- **Realistic:** neither so low as to be meaningless, nor so high as to be out of reach
- **Timely:** have a time frame for completion (e.g., number of clients per month or accomplishment by a certain date)

Moreover, outcome objectives should answer the following questions:

- What is the desired outcome? What behavior, condition, or attribute is expected to change as a result of program effort?
- Who is the target of program efforts? Who is expected to change as a result of program intervention?
- How many of the recipients of service will be expected to achieve desired outcomes? That is, among the target population, what is the degree or extent of positive effect anticipated?
- When are desired outcomes expected? By the end of the program year? After three counseling sessions?

Regardless of how they are worded, outcome objectives must address the *what, who, how many,* and *when* dimensions of program activity.

MANAGEMENT BY OBJECTIVES

Management by objectives (MBO) is a way of managing the efforts of people in an organization and ensuring active involvement and coherence in the planning process. In addition to the criteria for objectives listed, MBO requires identification of the person or unit responsible for achievement of the objective.

Objectives for programs or individuals are determined within the context of overall goals. The objectives to which all stakeholders have agreed are used as the basis for planning the work of each member of the organization. Each individual, in concert with his or her supervisor, decides on the part he or she will play in meeting organizational objectives, and this agreement provides the basis on which the individual's work will be evaluated.

PROGRAM DESIGN

With a guiding vision, a well-thought-out strategy, and a clear goal in mind, those responsible for planning services and programs can identify possible alternatives, specify any constraints that affect decision making, and determine the services most likely to be feasible, efficient, and effective for meeting consumer needs. Even though objectives follow directly from program goals, the flow of the planning process often goes from an overall goal statement, often to start a new program, to the examination of possible interventions. Until the specific intervention model is chosen and designed, it will not be possible to write precise objectives.

3.7 OBJECTIVES FOR THE TEEN TRANSITION AND TREATMENT PROGRAM

Staff members working on the design of the new program knew that a set of specific program objectives would need to be developed to guide staff toward successful accomplishment of the program's overall goal. They had also learned from their strategic planning consultant that designing of a new program should be based on the principles of the emerging field of evidence-based practice. Knowing the specific elements of a chosen program can guide the development of specific objectives for outcomes and service activities. The objectives here were actually not developed until the evidence-based practice search described later was completed, but they are shown here to better demonstrate the flow between goals and objectives.

Staff developed four outcome objectives and three process objectives for this program. The process objectives are:

1. All participants (adolescents with co-occurring disorders) will attend at least 10 of 12 scheduled weekly individual counseling sessions.
2. All participants will attend at least 10 of 12 scheduled weekly psycho-educational group therapy sessions.
3. The program will maintain a minimum case load of 50 clients.

The outcome objectives are in three areas: knowledge, behavioral, and behavioral/affective. (Details on the measurement of objectives will be covered in Chapter 9.)

1. Upon completion of the program, 80 percent of clients will demonstrate skills competency on topics covered in group sessions as evidenced by a score of 70 percent or higher on the skills competency post-test (knowledge objective).
2. Upon completion of the program, 80 percent of clients will completely discontinue use of illicit drugs as evidenced by a urine analysis at 12 weeks (behavioral objective).
3. Sixty percent of clients will be clean of drugs as evidenced by a urine analysis conducted 6 months after completion of the program (behavioral objective).
4. Upon completion of the program, 80 percent of clients will have a quality of life scores at or above the midpoint of the Moderate functioning levels for the three components of the Child and Adolescent Measurement System (CAMS) (behavioral/affective objective).

Therefore, before writing specific objectives, time should be spent searching for the best program model, using principles of *evidence-based practice* (EBP). The EBP process described below is often used by a practitioner at an individual client level. The process here is slightly different: the design of a program that will provide services to a group of clients with similar conditions. This has been called *evidence-based programming* (Briggs and McBeath, 2009): choosing an evidence-based intervention for implementation as an entire program, rather than leaving the use of EBPs as a method to be used by an individual worker.

This is a process of program design: conceptualizing a program to achieve outcomes to meet identified needs, including resources needed and service delivery methods.

IDENTIFYING AND SELECTING ALTERNATIVES: EVIDENCE-BASED PRACTICE AND EVIDENCE-BASED PROGRAMMING

Choosing an appropriate service delivery method, or technology, is a key step in the planning process. This use of the term *technology* does not mean computers, as is commonly assumed in our field. Rather, it refers to the transformation process—in our case, changing people or communities. Sandfort (2010) offers a simple definition: "Organizational technology is the process used to transform inputs into outputs" (p. 269). Particularly relevant for the human services is the notion that "resources" include people and information. This is in essence the program design process: selecting methods and determining needed staff capabilities to achieve objectives for a particular client population.

In many agencies, staff design a new program using methods with which they are familiar and that are often inadequately conceptualized (for example, "casework" or "short-term counseling"). With increasing pressure for agencies to demonstrate successful outcomes, more attention must be paid to the selection of service methods. Poertner and Rapp (2007) use the term "theory of helping" to emphasize that any method used should be based on theory and ideally have evidence of effectiveness in the form of research results or promising pilot demonstrations. In its most basic form, the theory of helping looks at what the expectations of the client and worker are in achieving predetermined goals and objectives. More specifically, Kettner, Moroney, and Martin (2008) use a process for developing a "program hypothesis" (pp. 98–111) that provides a basis for program design. They start by identifying a condition that represents a social problem, such as infant mortality. A specific needs assessment may show data related to infant mortality, such as identifying low birth weight as a major risk factor. A program hypothesis may suggest that identifying high-risk pregnant women, recruiting them into a program, and providing appropriate services should reduce premature births and infant mortality. This thinking should be based on at least a preliminary understanding of current research and practice in this problem area, and it will need to be refined through a thorough search for the best program model.

The consideration of alternative models should begin with a search to locate those with demonstrated success, known as *best practices*. Not a precisely defined term, best practices are generally considered to be programs that have been proven through research or evaluation to be the best examples in a particular field. Relevant factors include specific services provided, the *mix* of multiple services, service *dosage* (amounts of services provided), and staff characteristics (e.g., degrees, licensing). The search for best practices often uses *benchmarking*: "a system that compares the organization's practices with those of others doing similar things but who are deemed to be doing it better" (Murray, 2010, p. 447).

A commonly used criterion for best practices is evidence-based practice, defined as "the integration of the best research evidence with clinical expertise and client values in making practice decisions" (McNeese & Thyer, 2004). Cournoyer

(2004) has noted that the terms *evidence-based* and *empirically based* are often used interchangeably, with the former being used more in medicine and the latter becoming more widely used in psychology and social work. The process outlined here is a brief summary of the thorough coverage provided by Cournoyer to find an "ethical and effective program" (p. 32).

The first step is *questioning*: formulating a question based on the designated target population and the desired outcome. Finding the best answer to the question will point to a viable program model that the agency can adopt (or adapt).

The second step, *searching*, "involves seeking, locating, documenting, and compiling information needed" (p. 49) to answer the practice question. A search can begin at a broad, general level, using a standard Internet search engine with relevant keyword. It will probably be necessary to dig deeper, using databases in the fields under consideration. Many sources are provided by Cournoyer, and a few are listed at the end of this chapter. Student interns in fields such as social work or faculty in professional programs at a local university can be valuable aids for this process. Many of the best sources will be in professional journals, which are available to students and faculty through a university library's online subscriptions. Other valuable sources can be current research-based books, federal government publications, and the websites of research centers and professional organizations.

After useful references have been identified, *analyzing* of these sources will enable the agency researcher to identify the most promising program models. The source of the evidence and its quality will be key factors. *Primary sources* are valuable because they are reports by the people who actually conducted the research under consideration. *Secondary sources*, which summarize primary research, can be valuable as well because they typically include a range of primary sources that can then be perused individually.

A more important distinction contrasts *research-based* and *authority-based* sources. According to Cournoyer (2004, p. 123), "Professors, practitioners, directors of agencies, advocacy organizations, professional organizations, clients, and consumer groups are authorities that frequently share information in the form of opinions, assertions, claims, or arguments." These can be considered as legitimate sources, but they should be carefully evaluated in terms of their content, and with consideration to the particular interests they represent. Research-based sources, in contrast, present findings from quantitative and/or qualitative studies, which are a stronger source on which to design a new program.

Within research studies, there is a continuum of standards, from most to least rigorous:

- Meta-analyses: comparing findings across similar studies
- Randomized controlled trials: random assignment of clients to treatment and control conditions
- Quasi-experimental studies: treatment and control groups without random assignment
- Case-control and cohort studies: following one group of subjects over time
- Pre-experimental studies, such as post-test only studies
- Surveys such as self-report questionnaires or interviews
- Qualitative studies performed without statistical analysis

After enough high-quality evidence has been gathered, *synthesizing* involves summarizing and critiquing the findings, and recommendations for application to the program goal under consideration. A final factor to consider when deciding on a program model is *transportability* (Roberts-DeGennaro, 2010). Program planners will need to see if any adjustments in the EBP need to be made for adaptation to the local conditions of the agency. For example, an evidence-based program may have shown experimental success with native-born clients but may not have been fully tested with immigrant populations. If an agency is serving a population with cultural or other demographic characteristics that are different from the EBP, local adjustments, such as building in cultural competency, will need to be made to the model.

Broad staff participation should be involved in selecting the criteria that will be used and assessing alternatives. Particularly relevant will be the criteria of possible funding sources, funding availability, and program costs. In particular, the qualifications of required staff members and their salaries, the other necessary resources (facilities, equipment, staff training), and other program elements with costs attached need to be considered with reference to the amount of service to be provided (for example, numbers of clients) and the funds available.

Depending on the situation and the resources available, the decision-making procedure might be as complex as a cost-effectiveness analysis or as simple as the use of an individual rating system. At its most basic level, decision making includes some procedure for considering alternative solutions in terms of the criteria selected. The outcome of the process should be selection of a service model that is appropriate to the goal, acceptable to stakeholders, and economically feasible. Each alternative should be assessed in terms of the following questions:

- Does this service fit agency or program strategy, goals, and priorities?
- Is there documented evidence of the success of the model (e.g., evidence-based practice)?
- Are available or potential resources adequate for service provision?
- Can the service be accepted by community members and consumers?
- Can the service be delivered by available or potentially available service providers?
- Does the service meet the policy constraints within which the agency or program must work?
- Do the potential benefits of the service appear to outweigh the estimated costs?
- Can we measure service effectiveness?
- Can we develop an implementation plan?
- Are serious risks involved in implementing the service?

Any service methods being considered should be described and critiqued using a logic model (described next) to help ensure that methods chosen have realistic prospects for being successful. When this decision-making process has been completed, the procedures of program design and planning for actual implementation become reasonably uncomplicated.

The final steps of the EBP process, *applying* and evaluating, occur through program design, implementation, and evaluation. Ideally, applying will be aided by the availability of evidence-based practice manuals or detailed protocols that define criteria for full implementation of the program. These should be incorporated into the design of the new program. In addition to formal descriptions of the program in program procedures, new job descriptions, staff training, additions or changes to facilities, and changes to the information system will probably be necessary. These systems, and evaluating the new program, will be covered in later chapters.

3.8   SEARCHING FOR EVIDENCE FOR THE DESIGN OF THE TEEN TRANSITION AND TREATMENT PROGRAM

GCC was fortunate to have a social work intern named Nicole who could be assigned the task of searching for the best evidence-based model for its new program. Nicole began with the practice question that the planning team had developed:

> "What programs are the most effective in treating co-occurring disorders among adolescents? More specifically, what programs are the most effective in decreasing or eliminating the use of illicit substances and alcohol among adolescents and the most effective in decreasing negative behaviors and outcomes associated with co-occurring disorders?

Nicole's first step was to begin an online search through her university's library to identify relevant practice intervention strategies and to look through journal articles in order to identify the most effective treatment modality. She found relevant articles that reported success using Cognitive Behavioral Therapy (CBT) with adolescents (Suveg, Sood, Comer, & Kendall, 2009; Eskin, Ertekin, & Demir, 2007). A third study (Malouff, Thorsteinsson, & Schutte, 2007) was especially valuable because it was a meta-analysis—the highest level of evidence—of 31 studies. She then searched other EBP sites, and at the SAMSA *National Registry of Evidence Based Programs and Practices* (SAMSA, 2010, August 3) she used the Advanced Search tab to find an evidence-based model intervention, using the keywords *topic* (co-occurring disorders) and *age* (13–17). The search results included 11 evidence-based programs for the criteria specified, and from this list she chose one as the best practice: Chestnut Health Systems—Bloomington Outpatient (OP) and Intensive Outpatient (IOP) Treatment Model.

After Nicole shared her report with staff, they decided to adapt this program model. They noted several transportability issues that they could easily address. First, their target population had a different ethnic composition, which would require different cultural competency considerations. Also, their program was smaller in size, and it did not have school-based staff; but these could be addressed in their program design. The team then began detailing the design, setting objectives and developing a logic model.

CONCEPTUALIZING THE PROGRAM: THE LOGIC MODEL

One very useful tool for describing a new program is the *logic model*. Program logic models provide detail on all of the elements that will be necessary to fully implement a program as designed.

The elements of a program (Kettner, Moroney, & Martin, 2008) are as follows:

- Inputs—raw materials and resources, including clients, staff, facilities, and equipment
- Throughputs—the service delivery or "conversion process," or how the client's condition is intended to change; includes service definitions and tasks (activities) and the method of intervention (the technology employed and the ways services are delivered)

- Outputs—the products, such as units of service provided or service completions (e.g., completion of a 28-day treatment program)
- Intermediate Outcomes—changes in client condition at service completion (e.g., improved job skills)
- Final or Ultimate Outcomes—the actual changes in the client's quality of life (e.g., self-sufficiency, employment)

For example, planners can begin by assessing the characteristics of people targeted for entry into the program, including their demographics, histories, strengths, needs, and problems. It may also be useful to assess the communities in which these potential clients reside in order to identify community assets and strengths that can be brought to bear in the program design. Other key inputs are staff members and their characteristics. The EBP program model should designate the qualifications and criteria of staff implementing the intervention. Other inputs include the physical facilities, supplies, training resources, and equipment needed to implement the program. This may also include, for home-based services, staff vehicles or funding for staff mileage. Programs requiring ancillary staff, such as consultants or staff from other agencies or schools should note these as inputs.

3.9   DESIGN AND LOGIC MODEL OF THE TEEN TRANSITION AND TREATMENT PROGRAM

To *adapt* the EBP model chosen for this program, GCC staff determined that they would need four staff members: two full-time counselors, one half-time clinical supervisor, and one half-time administrative assistant. Based on past client referral sources, they expected that schools or the juvenile system would refer clients to the agency. The first activity for clients would be an initial screening/evaluation conducted by one of the therapists using the Global Appraisal of Individual Needs–Short Screener (GAIN–SS), which screens for behavioral health disorders, including substance abuse. In her research, Nicole found that this was used in the program model they were adapting, and had good validity (McDonnell, Comtois, Voss, Morgan, & Ries, 2009, p. 159).

The next activity would be for the client and therapist to discuss the treatment plan and then schedule 12 individual sessions. The therapist and client would also pick one of the two time slots for the client to attend weekly group sessions. Since individual and group therapy were to occur concurrently, the client would complete the program in 12 weeks. After program completion, the client would take the group post-test to demonstrate mastery of the material covered in the groups. The client would also take the CAMS during the last individual therapy session. Immediately after completion of these two activities, the client would give a urine sample for a urine analysis. The client would again be asked to give a urine sample at 6 months after program completion.

The activities, including both individual and group therapy, would occur at offices within one of the agency's existing facilities. Staff also noted that the therapists would need to communicate effectively and frequently with parents, teachers, and other community members. At least one of the therapists would need to be bilingual in English and Spanish. One complication would be the "rolling" and open nature of the psycho-educational groups. Both therapists would facilitate one group per week, with

(continued)

<table>
<tr><td colspan="2">

3.9 DESIGN AND LOGIC MODEL OF THE TEEN TRANSITION AND TREATMENT PROGRAM (*CONT'D*)

</td></tr>
<tr><td colspan="2">

two groups operating at any given time. Because clients need to start group therapy early in their treatment process, groups would be getting new members on a regular basis. Given that this change in group participants could affect the group dynamics, facilitators would need to pay special attention to this aspect of group process.

The program logic model staff members developed can be seen in Figure 3.1.

</td></tr>
</table>

Throughputs describe the theory of helping: what technology (job training, interview training, and so forth) or activities would be part of the service delivery. This should include specifications of the evidence-based program model in terms of types and amounts of service.

INPUTS	THROUGHPUTS (Activities)	OUTPUTS	OUTCOMES
Client: Adolescents with co-occurring disorders • Characteristics: Low socioeconomic status, adolescents, mostly Hispanic and Caucasian, co-occurring mental disorder and substance abuse diagnosis Staff: • Two dual recovery counselors (licensed and certified) • One 0.5 FTE admin assistant • One 0.5 FTE supervisor Other Resources: • In-kind donation of facilities (3 offices and work space for admin assistant) • Teachers and other school-based staff	• Individual counseling • Psycho-educational/ group therapy sessions lasting 40 minutes covering 6 topics • Each topic will be covered in 2 sessions; group sessions will be planned for and prepared by dual recovery counselors • Group topics include relapse prevention, life skills, self-esteem, family issues, recovery lifestyle, and recreations/leisure • Groups will build the skills adolescents need to live without abusing substances • Individual therapy will focus more on mental health issues and clinical interventions • Cognitive Behavioral therapeutic approach, Rogerian model, and systems theory in individual counseling	• 12 individual counseling sessions and 12 group therapy sessions occurring concurrently every week for 12 weeks • Clients complete psycho-educational group process (12 sessions) • Program maintains a case load of 50 clients	• Intermediate: Upon completion of psycho-educational groups, clients demonstrate competency of topics covered in group • Clients will be substance-free at 12 weeks (completion of program) • Clients will be substance-free 6 months after completion of program • Final: Client increased quality of life, decreased occurrence of internalizing and externalizing behaviors, and increased social competence

FIGURE 3.1 | LOGIC MODEL FOR THE TEEN TRANSITION AND TREATMENT PROGRAM

Outputs designate the units of services that are expected to be delivered and service completions: clients completing the full complement of required services. Outputs in the logic model also include outcomes. *Intermediate outcomes* describe the quality of life conditions of clients upon successful completion of the program. *Final outcomes* describe former client conditions at a future time, such as at a 6-month follow up assessment (Kettner, Moroney, & Martin, 2008). In a youth employment program, intermediate outcomes could include new knowledge or skills, perhaps linked with employment opportunities, and final outcomes may include youth remaining employed in living wage jobs.

A *flowchart* can be used to outline specific steps to be taken in a service delivery process. This is especially useful for programs with multiple services or interrelationships among services. Standard flowcharting uses symbols for individual steps, with an oval indicating beginning and ending steps, rectangles for individual steps, diamonds for decisions, and lines with arrows connecting each symbol, with arrows indicating direction. For the purposes of using a flowchart to describe a service delivery process, these conventions need not be followed, but every step of the process should be clear to all who are using it. Figure 3.2 shows the service phase of an interdepartmental collaboration called "Parents and Children Together," or PACT. This program is a collaboration between two county departments in which parents of child protective service clients are referred to a special unit that includes Behavioral Health (mental health and substance abuse) staff who provide services to augment child protective services activities. As can be seen in the flowchart, Department of Social Services staff members assess a family that has been referred for child abuse or neglect and eventually refer the client to a Behavioral Health Mental Health Rehabilitation Technician (MHRT). Subsequent steps include a clinical assessment by a clinician and referral to a treatment team. In this flowchart, the circle in the middle indicates ongoing services provided throughout the process, leading eventually to family reunification (FR) or family maintenance (FM).

DEVELOPING AN IMPLEMENTATION PLAN

Once objectives and general methods or services to be used have been identified, the planners must begin to lay out a program of action that can provide for the implementation of new or changed services. Plan implementation may also be used for administrative or organizational goals, such as the design of an agency diversity program or planning a move into a new building.

Implementation procedures depend on clarity, and some kind of formal or informal document should be in the hands of those responsible for carrying out any aspect of the plan. Each general goal statement should have its own list of objectives because achieving all objectives will lead to goal attainment. Each objective, in turn, should have a specified program or set of activities to meet the objectives. Each service or project depends for its achievement on an organized set of implementation activities. In short, there must be a plan for implementing the plan. This should include designation of the planning team membership, including those with relevant knowledge of and interest in the program or project; a list of activities necessary, individuals responsible at each step, a timeline, and a list of necessary resources (e.g., staff time, funds, supplies). The plan should be flexible enough to meet unexpected situations, but it should also provide clear and concrete statements concerning individual responsibilities and time frames for completing actions.

In most human service situations, simple time lines with milestones for task completion are adequate for illustrating projected implementation activities. For

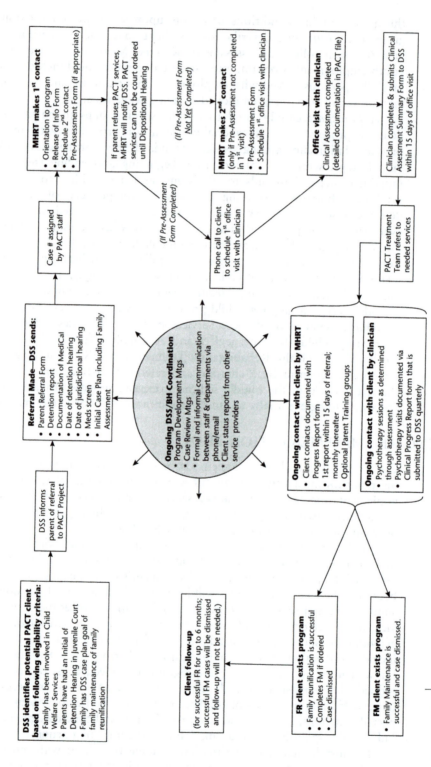

FIGURE 3.2 | PACT SERVICE DELIVERY FLOW CHART—BEHAVIORAL HEALTH STAFF

Source: Evaluation Committee, PACT Project. Used with permission from the Imperial County Departments of Social Services and Behavioral Health, County of Imperial, El Centro, CA.

example, a program for providing newly designed counseling services to young people recruited from the community could not actually begin until counselors were hired and trained, clients were recruited, and clients and counselors were oriented to the program. The time line would need to specify the number of days or weeks needed for recruiting, interviewing, and selecting counselors; for designing the counselor training program; for implementing the counselor training program; for planning client recruitment; for carrying out client recruitment; for screening potential clients; for implementing an orientation session; and so on. The implementation plan would need to specify exactly what procedures would be carried out and by whom. The timeline for the Teen Transition and Treatment Program is shown in Figure 3.3.

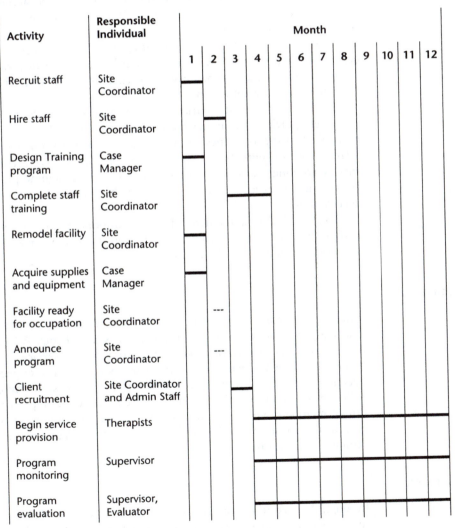

FIGURE 3.3 | TIMELINE FOR THE TEEN TRANSITION AND TREATMENT PROGRAM

DEVELOPING AN EVALUATION PLAN

At the same time that the initial planning is being implemented, planners should consider the methods that will be used to evaluate the success of the services to be delivered. The objectives identified as part of the planning process also provide the basis for evaluating program outputs and outcomes. Thus, evaluation criteria have, at this point, been identified. If the planners also use this opportunity to plan for gathering relevant data on an ongoing basis, effective data collection and evaluation will be quite manageable. (Chapter 10 provides a detailed discussion of evaluation.)

MARKETING

The notion of HSOs doing marketing has come to be accepted as an important aspect of agency functioning (Lauffer, 2009). Developing a marketing plan often follows the development of a strategic plan, which typically includes plans to initiate new programs. Although marketing is often conducted through an agency's central offices, it is discussed briefly here because staff in program operations may be involved in marketing processes, especially as it relates to the design of programs that their publics want and need.

Many people equate marketing with sales when in fact they are very different processes, particularly in the human services. Some human service organizations, particularly for-profit ones or not-for-profit agencies on fee-for-service contracts, actively solicit clients, but of course many programs serve involuntary or hostile clients. Marketing takes on a different flavor when designing programs for substance abusers or domestic violence perpetrators, but marketing principles can be valuable nevertheless.

Lauffer (2009) summarizes the key components of marketing using "five Ps": publics, product, price, place, and promotion. These "five Ps" can structure the development of a marketing plan.

PUBLICS

Input publics consist of those who provide resources, primarily funding sources. Throughput publics are staff. Output publics are clients. All of these groups need to be treated as important stakeholders, and agency services and processes should be designed in ways that respond to their key concerns or expectations. This matter becomes particularly complicated, of course, in the case of involuntary clients. In a child abuse situation, protection of the child and perhaps the mother and other family members will be of utmost importance, but attention will also need to be paid to the abuser and relevant funding, policy, or legislative expectations, such as family reunification.

PRODUCT

Product, the second P, consists of the program's services. From a marketing perspective, it is important that services are in fact seen as a valuable product—something that clients, funders, or referring agencies will want to use. A useful marketing concept in this regard is the notion of the market *segment* or *niche*. An agency will determine a niche (for example, an area of unmet need or an opportunity for a new service) in a community and design a program to fill it. For example, a community may have several programs for sex offenders but none for juvenile sex offenders. After a needs assessment, it may be determined that a program in this niche would be a valuable addition to the spectrum of services in a community.

Determining a program's niche can be aided by analyzing unmet needs in service delivery. What services are other providers offering? What services should be offered but are not? In any case, it is important for a program to assess what service gaps exist and offer services that will truly respond to important unmet needs. The analysis might include listing programs within a defined target area to determine which ones provide services similar to those provided by one's own organization. For each agency, additional lists are developed, often put in the form of a matrix with each agency occupying a separate row. The lists, displayed in columns, describe for each program its primary services related to the service area being assessed (for example, support services for seniors), the program, staff characteristics (master's degree, bachelor's degree, and so forth), geographic location, and fees, if any. Additional columns list the market share (the percentage of eligible clients being served) and the market segment (the specific characteristics of clients served) for each program. This information is then used to identify service gaps: the percentage of the market share and the segment that is not being served. Gaps can become niches to be filled by a new or expanded program.

PRICE

Price is of course relevant in terms of the cost to clients for service, which may range from nothing to sliding-scale fees to reimbursements from funders or insurance companies. There are also psychic costs to clients: will there be embarrassment or inconvenience factors to overcome? A client decision to come to an agency may be based partly on the client's weighing of the benefits and the costs. Price is also relevant in the context of grant or contract amounts. Unit costs for services may need to be outlined in the agency's funding proposal. It will be increasingly necessary for an agency to be "competitive," offering funders or clients a valued service at the best cost. The challenge for the agency when negotiating the grant or contract funding amount and scope of services will be to ensure that quality services and desired outcomes can be delivered for the agreed-on cost. Sometimes donations to the agency or foundation funds are used to offset other agency costs to keep service delivery costs to clients or government funders as low as possible.

PLACE

The fourth P, place, is relevant in the preceding analysis. An agency may see from the analysis that services are missing in a particular geographic area. Strategically, the agency needs to decide what the geographic scope of its new, expanded, or reconfigured program should be. This feature may be defined from a funder's perspective, using identified geographic areas or responding to a request for proposals for programs in a certain area. Place also considers the location of services with respect to client accessibility and convenience. Public transportation routes, parking, and other factors of access need to be considered. Another aspect of place involves days and hours of operation of the program, which should be set based on when clients need the services to be available (for example, evenings or weekends).

PROMOTION

Finally, promotion involves putting all the other Ps together and "selling" the program's services to its various publics. Focus is first placed on the identified market segment, which may have been chosen based on geography, specific type of service, or client demographics. Market "positioning" then involves orchestrating the way the program or services are presented to the various publics. This is partly a public relations effort: shaping the agency's or program's image through media relations, advertising, brochures, networking, or other public relations activities. More fundamentally, however, the concern should be for addressing the real needs of the various publics, making sure that the services will add value to the lives of clients and the community, will respond to funder and referring agency staff expectations, and will ensure a high quality of working life for agency staff.

SUMMARY

A vision of a preferred future can play a key role in focusing energy and commitment. Strategic planning is a way of developing organizational responses to an assessment of the agency's mission and mandates, stakeholder expectations, opportunities and challenges in the environment, and internal strengths and weaknesses. Strategies are developed and then operationalized through goals and action plans. Then, a program needs to be designed using best practices and evidence-based practice research. Implementation and evaluation are where the vision comes to life and results are assessed. Before we look at how the multiple programs of an agency are put together, we will review some useful theoretical perspectives that can provide guidance in the design of human service organizations.

COMPETENCY-BUILDING ACTIVITY 3.1

PLANNING

After reading Chapter 1, you began the process of creating your own hypothetical human service program. Now that you have a greater understanding of planning and program design, you are ready to answer the following questions:

1. What should be the mission and primary goal for this program?

2. Give some examples of specific, measurable objectives that would help meet the goal you have identified.

3. What are some activities or services that would be helpful in meeting objectives?

Save your work so that you can use the same hypothetical agency as a basis for later activities.

| CASE ACTIVITY 3.1 | THE MODEL COLLEGE COUNSELING CENTER |

The counseling center of Hillsboro University had been a model of excellence in its early years. It was one of the few such centers offering long-term therapy for students who desired higher degrees of self-awareness. Only in cases of serious psychiatric crisis were students referred to outside agencies. The director of the counseling center prided himself on the fact that, with the highly qualified and credentialed staff of counselors he had hired, Hillsboro students could have all their mental health needs met within the boundaries of their peaceful, tree-lined campus.

In the past several years, however, changes had begun to take place. The number of clients presenting themselves for services at the counseling center had dropped so drastically that the center's staff—all licensed psychologists or clinical social workers—had time to spare. Waiting lists for appointments had never been long, but now the reception area was ominously quiet. This situation was surprising because any indicator that could possibly measure aspects of mental health among students showed that problems did exist. Disciplinary measures for drug and alcohol abuse had increased; the dropout rate at final exam time was as high as ever; and complaints from local police officers and residents showed that students were, indeed, "letting off steam" in the late hours.

In light of the situation, the university's vice president for student affairs, Mary Belmont, initiated a series of discussions with Simon Young, the counseling center director. Vice President Belmont's contention was that the counseling center no longer met the needs of Hillsboro students.

She pointed out, "We simply don't have the kinds of students we used to. The students we have now are not here to find themselves. They're not interested in spending long hours delving into their reason for being. These young people are practical. They want help with immediate decisions, help with time management, help in developing methods for dealing with stress. They are not going to spend long periods of time in a therapist's office. Something has to change."

"But that's exactly my point," Young responded. "These students do have problems, and they're not dealing with them. They think it's not important to delve into their reasons for being, but it is important.

They think they can solve their problems with a quick how-to session, but they can't. A good proportion of these students do need therapy—at least as many as needed it five years ago. What we have to do is get those dormitory house parents, student advisers, and professors to start referring students to the center so they can get what they need."

"We're not going to do that, Simon. We don't know what these students need unless we ask them. What I'd like to suggest is that we involve the members of your counseling staff, and then some other members of the university community, and try to implement some planning about what steps should be taken. We can't afford to be paying high salaries for clinicians to be sitting in their offices waiting for someone to remember they're there."

"Now I understand what you're really saying, Mary. It's getting near budget time again. You're not concerned about what these students need. You're concerned about the money being spent on the counseling center, and you're trying to cut costs. I wouldn't mind it so much if you'd just be straight about it. Just remember this: When you hired me as counseling center director, you told me I'd have a free hand to build a quality center. You said that was what you wanted, and that's what you got. If you don't want that anymore, just tell me."

"Simon, I don't want that anymore."

"Then you'll have my resignation on your desk in the morning. I don't know whether the staff will join me or not."

"Simon, just wait a minute. You had some ideas about what kinds of things you wanted to accomplish with young people. You had some goals in mind, and, for a long time, you met them. Now times are changing. Why is it so impossible to consider using different methods to reach students? Why not use decision-making kits that students can use on their own? Why not go into the dorms with life planning workshops? Why not train peer counselors to work with the students who live off campus?"

"Because, Mary, you're talking about a bunch of fads. They may save money on professional salaries, but in no way do they accomplish the same ends. These are shortcuts that don't reach the places we're trying to go. What good are they? Maybe I was hasty in talking about my resignation, but I have to tell you that I'm going to support my staff, no matter what it takes. I won't have you firing experienced therapists left and right just to bring in a bunch of kids or pieces of paper that you think can fix people up."

"I'm not suggesting that. What I am suggesting is that the plans you made when you started this counseling center were solid, and your methods worked. But you can't stay married to your methods."

"These aren't my methods, which I just invented. These are the methods that clinicians learn as part of their professional training. They fit accepted professional standards."

"Look, Simon, I understand that. Just give me a commitment that you'll try to explore this further.

We won't take any action until we've thought it through."

1. What are the real issues at stake in the conflict between Mary Belmont and Simon Young?
2. Do you see one of these two differing viewpoints as being essentially correct in terms of your own values? Would you be able to present an argument justifying the opposite viewpoint?
3. If you were to design a planning process like the one suggested by the university vice president, what steps would you follow? Who should be involved in the planning process?
4. Is there any way that the use of planning processes at an earlier date might have prevented the conflict described in this case?

REFERENCES

Allison, M., & Kaye, J. (2005). *Strategic planning for nonprofit organizations* (2nd ed.). New York: Wiley.

Austin, M. & Solomon, J. (2009). Managing the planning process. In R. Patti (Ed.), *The handbook of human services management* (2nd ed., pp. 321–337). Thousand Oaks, CA: Sage Publications.

Bishop, N. (2009). *Program Plan Paper*. Unpublished Manuscript, School of Social Work, San Diego State University, San Diego, CA.

Briggs, H. & McBeath, B. (2009). Evidence-based management: Origins, challenges, and implications for social work administration. *Administration in Social Work, 33* (3), 242–261.

Bryson, J. (2004). *Strategic planning for public and nonprofit organizations: A guide for strengthening and sustaining organizational achievement* (3rd ed.). San Francisco: Jossey-Bass.

Cournoyer, B. R. (2004). *The evidence-based social work skills book*. New York: Pearson.

Eskin, M., Ertekin, K., & Demir, H. (2007). Efficacy of a problem-solving therapy for depression and suicide potential in adolescents and young adults. *Cognitive Therapy and Research, 32*(2), 227–245.

Kettner, P., Moroney, R., & Martin, L. (2008). *Designing and managing programs* (3rd ed.). Thousand Oaks, CA: Sage.

Lauffer, A. (2009). Confronting fundraising challenges. In R. Patti (Ed.), *The handbook of human services management* (2nd ed., pp. 351–372). Thousand Oaks, CA: Sage Publications.

Malouff, J. M., Thorsteinsson E. B., & Schutte, N. S. (2007). The efficacy of problem solving therapy in reducing mental and physical health problems: A meta-analysis. *Clinical Psychology Review, 27*(1), 46–57.

McDonell, M. G., Comtois, K. A., Voss, W. D., Morgan, A. H., & Ries, R. K. (2009). Global appraisal of individual needs short screener (GSS): Psychometric properties and performance as a screening measure in adolescents. *American Journal of Drug and Alcohol Abuse, 35*(3), 157–160.

McNeese, C., & Thyer, B. (2004). Evidence-based practice and social work. *Journal of Evidence-Based Social Work, 1*(1), 7–25.

Murray, V. (2010). Assessing nonprofit organization effectiveness. In Renz, D. (Ed.). *The Jossey-Bass handbook of nonprofit leadership and management* (3rd ed., pp. 431–458). San Francisco: Jossey-Bass.

Packard, T. (2001). Building commitment through mission and values: The case of a homeless shelter. *Administration in Social Work, 25*(3), 35–52.

Palmer, I., Dunford, R., and Akin, G. (2009). *Managing organizational change: A multiple perspectives approach.* New York: McGraw-Hill Irwin.

Poertner J. & Rapp, C. (2007). *Textbook of social administration: The consumer-centered approach.* New York: The Haworth Press.

Roberts-DeGennaro, M. (2010). Using an Evidence-Based Program Planning Model in a Macro Practice Course, *Journal of Teaching in Social Work, 30*(1), 6–63.

SAMSA (2010). *SAMSA (Substance Abuse and Mental Health Service Administration) National Registry of Evidence-Based Programs and Practices.* Retrieved August 2, 2010, from http://www.nrepp.samhsa.gov/AdvancedSearch.aspx

Sandfort, J. (2010). Human service organizational technology: Improving understanding and advancing research. In Y. Hasenfeld (Ed.), *Human services as complex organizations* (2nd ed., pp. 269–290). Thousand Oaks, CA: Sage Publications.

Senge, P. (2006). *The fifth discipline: The art & practice of the learning organization.* New York: Currency.

Singh, K. (2005). *The impact of strategic planning processes variation on superior organizational performance in nonprofit human service organizations providing mental health services*. (Doctoral dissertation, Columbia University).

Spencer, L. (1989). *Winning through participation*. Dubuque, IA: Kendall/Hunt.

Suveg, C., Sood, E., Comer, J. S., & Kendall, P. C. (2009). Changes in emotional regulation following cognitive-behavioral therapy for anxious youth. *Journal of Clinical Child and Adolescent Psychology, 38*(3), 390–401.

Useful Web Resources

California Evidence-Based Clearinghouse for Child Welfare. http://www.cachildwelfareclearinghouse.org.

Campbell Collaboration. http://www.campbellcollaboration.org.

Cochrane Collaboration. www.cochrane.org.

Evidence-Based Associates. http://www.evidencebasedassociates.com/.

Guide to Community Preventive Services. http://www.thecommunityguide.org.

Homeless Resource Center. http://homeless.samhsa.org.

National Clearinghouse for Alcohol & Drug Information. http://www.health.org.

National Clearinghouse on Child Abuse and Neglect. http://www.childwelfare.gov/can/.

National Clearinghouse on Families and Youth. http://www.ncfy.com.

National Registry of Evidence Based Programs and Practices. http://nrepp.samhsa.gov.

OJJDP Model Programs Guide www.ojjdp.gov/mpg/.

Promising Practices Network on Children, Families, and Communities. www.promisingpractices.net.

Research in Practice for Adults. http://www.ripfa.org.uk.

SAMHSA National Clearinghouse for Alcohol and Drug Information. http://ncadi.samhsa.gov/.

SAMHSA Co-Occurring Center for Excellence. http://www.coce.samhsa.gov.

Social Programs that Work: Coalition for Evidence-Based Policy. http://www.evidencebasedprograms.org/static/.

Striving to Reduce Youth Violence Everywhere. http://www.safeyouth.gov/Pages/Home.aspx.

US Agency for Healthcare Research & Quality (AHRQ). http://www.ahrq.gov.

Washington University Alcohol and Drug Abuse Institute. http://adai.washington.edu/ebp/matrix.pdf.

4 CHAPTER | APPLYING ORGANIZATIONAL THEORIES

Chapter 1 presented a definition of the term *organization*, suggesting that an organization can be any group of people—large or small—working together toward common goals. This definition seems simple on the surface, but its components can be complex, especially when the entity in question is a human service organization. Consider, for example, the question of what *people* can be considered to be part of the organization. Although managers and other employees are clearly members of the organization, can we appropriately leave out the clients who are served by the agency? Not only are they affected by the organization; they also affect it in return. The same is true of the community members, policy makers, funders, and others who are stakeholders in the organization's success. Consider also the concept of *common goals*. Human service organizations have in common a general mission of improving the lives of the people they serve, but whether organizations can accomplish this mission depends on their ability to offer services that are effective in helping clients and communities. Complexity arises again when we realize that "the definition and measurement of service effectiveness is ... indeterminate, ambiguous, and multidimensional" and remains a "contested terrain" (Hasenfeld, 2009, p. 56).

Although some believe that organizations, by their very nature, have "clearly defined, demarcated, and defended boundaries" (Pfeffer, 1997, p. 9), this assumption is questionable in the case of human service organizations, which are particularly subject to external control. Hasenfeld (2010) suggests that human service organizations "must constantly seek and maintain legitimacy for what they do" (p. 14). This dependence on external approval from multiple sources affects not just the goals of the organization but also the specific technologies that are used to meet those goals.

> Technologies ascend in importance as they gain greater legitimacy in the institutional environment. They do so not only because of their demonstrated efficacy, which in itself is a negotiated process, but also because they are supported by politically powerful interest groups that influence the discourse, the knowledge, and the cultural symbols that reinforce the merits and moral benefits of the technologies. (Hasenfeld, 2010, pp. 16–17)

All of these issues lead toward great complexity. Human service agencies, unlike many other organizations, "have to cope with a turbulent environment, grapple with service design and management issues that are highly value-laden, lack clear and unambiguous end-states, and manage staff and clients who cannot be readily controlled" (Hasenfeld, 2009, p. 56).

Given the intricacy of human service organizations, the development and implementation of organizational theory is challenging. "In management practice, theories describe how organizations and the people within them function, how organizations maintain themselves, how power and resources are distributed in organizations, and how organizations interact with the surrounding environment" (Hardina, Middleton, Montana, & Simpson, 2007). Although "theories provide a lens through which to view the organizational environment" (Kirst-Ashman & Hull, 2009, p. 119), they are not merely descriptive. In many cases, they are also prescriptive, studying what organizations do but also providing direction about what organizations should do. Organizational theories reflect the interests, assumptions, and perceptions of theory builders.

This chapter is intended to provide a core of knowledge about organizational theories currently being articulated and used, so that a manager can consciously and thoughtfully choose the use of an appropriate theory to enhance his or her effectiveness in an organizational context. The array of organizational theories has changed over time, so this chapter begins with a historical overview going back a century.

Few human service workers maintain clear awareness of the practical differences dividing organizational theorists. Although all thinkers in the field of organizational theory seek the "best" answers to the basic questions, they seldom agree about what those best answers really are. The designers of an organization are faced with a myriad of choices. They can build structures that are highly centralized and specialized or systems based on widespread decision-making responsibility and participation. They can departmentalize the organization's activities by joining all the people who perform a specific function, or they can build teams of people with differing but complementary skills. They can use traditional, hierarchical designs or experiment with task forces, committees, or even leaderless groups. The organization's form has major implications for the way its functions will be performed.

CLASSICAL THEORIES

Three prominent classical theories of organization originated in the nineteenth century. Sociologist Max Weber articulated theoretical principles of the ideal bureaucracy. Industrial engineer Frederick Taylor developed scientific management guidelines for the "best way" to supervise workers in a factory. Henri Fayol developed a set of management principles that are still influential today.

BUREAUCRACY

The earliest major thinker to formulate the concept of an ideal organization was Max Weber, who saw the "rational legal bureaucracy" as the efficient organization in its pure form (Gerth & Mills, 1958). Weber's ideal structure included high degrees of specialization and impersonality, authority based on comprehensive rules rather than on social relationships, clear and centralized hierarchies of authority and responsibility, prescribed systems of rules and procedures, hiring and promotion based solely on technical ability, and extensive use of written documentation.

Weber saw this pure system as a historical trend that would meet the needs posed by the increasing size of organizations and at the same time replace unfairness and uncertainty with rationality and clarity. Perrow (1986) summarizes the key elements of the rational-legal bureaucracy this way:

1. Equal treatment for all employees
2. Reliance on expertise, skills, and experience relevant to the position
3. No extra organizational prerogatives of the position; that is, the position is seen as belonging to the organization, not the person. The employee cannot use it for personal ends.
4. Specific standards of work and output
5. Extensive record keeping dealing with the work and output

6. Establishment and enforcement of rules and regulations that serve the interests of the organization
7. Recognition that rules and regulations bind managers as well as employees; thus employees can hold management to the terms of the employment contract (p. 3)

Speed, precision, and reduction of friction were associated with the ideal bureaucracy because in this organization everyone would have a clear awareness of both his or her and others' functions. All aspects of the organization's work would be regulated. The repetitiveness of the work would bring with it both steadiness and high quality. Personal enmity and constant questioning would be replaced by rationality and regularity.

One of the most common criticisms of an organization, unit, procedure, or manager is that it or he or she is "too bureaucratic." On the other hand, Perrow (1986) asserts that "many of the 'sins' of bureaucracy really reveal the failure to bureaucratize sufficiently" (p. 5). Other complaints in a bureaucracy are that a person (usually a manager) is not qualified or that someone is receiving preferential treatment—both violations of the principles of bureaucracy. Clearly, one of the failures of modern human service organizations, particularly public sector ones, is that they have sometimes enthusiastically and single-mindedly misapplied bureaucratic thinking, and even Weber was "extremely critical of the way bureaucracy destroys spontaneity" (Gortner, Mahler, & Nicholson, 1997, p. 5).

Ultimately, most would admit that bureaucracy, as it was first articulated by Weber, might provide some useful principles. It is also true that bureaucracy alone is insufficient to fully guide modern managerial behavior, and the subsequent movements discussed later, starting with the human relations movement, do not replace bureaucracy but add to it. Bureaucratic thinking provides a foundation for personnel practices that many workers appreciate: clear job roles and performance expectations, fair treatment, and due process; but later models would need to add principles recognizing that individuals and situations also must be addressed with appreciation for their differences.

Although Weber's approach was philosophical, the ideals of clearly defined objectives, specialization, hierarchical chains of command, and responsibility commensurate with authority are also basic to the thinking of early management scientists such as Taylor (1911) and practitioners such as Fayol (1949). Taylor in particular has been vilified as much as bureaucracy has, but he also provided principles that are still useful.

SCIENTIFIC MANAGEMENT

Frederick Taylor, the founder of the scientific management school of organizational theory, focused on the assembly line: the core work processes of the organization. As an industrial engineer, Taylor mainly consulted in the steel industry at the turn of the twentieth century. He believed that engineers could study a work process such as loading steel onto railway cars and determine the "one best method" for the task to be done. Workers were then trained on exactly how to do their job and repeated it over and over through their shift. He used time and motion studies to observe workers and identify wasteful steps or movements.

Perhaps his best-known quote describes job requirements for one who loads pig iron (a 92-pound piece of steel): "One of the very first requirements for a man who is fit to handle pig-iron ... is that he shall be so stupid ... that he more nearly resembles in his mental make-up the ox than any other type" (1912 hearings, cited in Sashkin, 1981, p. 208). "Taylorism" has come to refer to managers who assume their employees are stupid and need to be told what to do in excruciating detail, assuming that the manager is always right. In fact, Taylor was a complex person who believed that bosses should be "servants of the workmen" (Weisbord, 1987, p. 34) and that workers should share in the profits of the organization.

Taylor's main legacies today are work analysis methods used by industrial engineers (sometimes in human service settings) and profit-sharing plans for workers in industry. As was the case with bureaucracy, some principles such as scientifically analyzing the work to be performed and rewarding workers based on their performance are valuable and can be seen today in the quality movement and organizational reward systems.

UNIVERSAL MANAGEMENT PRINCIPLES

The final theorist of the classical school is Henri Fayol, a French contemporary of Weber and Taylor whose views became known as the universal principles school. He conceptualized the five basic functions of management (planning, organizing, commanding, coordinating, and controlling) and developed a set of principles for the design of an organization (Bowditch, Buono, & Stewart, 2008):

1. Division of work—Specialization of tasks and control of the number of people under each worker or manager improves effectiveness and efficiency.
2. Authority and responsibility—The person in authority has the right to give orders and the power to obtain obedience; responsibility emerges directly from authority.
3. Unity of command—No person should have more than one boss.
4. Remuneration—Pay should be fair and satisfactory to the employer and employee; no one should be under- or over-rewarded.
5. Esprit de corps—Morale and good feelings about the organization are enhanced by effective face-to-face communication and group cohesiveness.

Fayol also talked about the *gangplank*, a figurative bridge that enabled individuals at the same level but in different units or departments to talk directly to each other rather than using the chain of command (Sashkin, 1981). The term *gangplank* is, of course, pejorative in current language usage, but the concept of making connections across units or departments is valued today, possibly more than it ever has before. Effective managers are aware that having separate, unconnected *silos* for each department bodes poorly for organizational efficiency and effectiveness.

PROFESSIONAL BUREAUCRACIES

Two particular characteristics of bureaucracy, centralization ("the degree to which decision making authority is confined to the top echelons of the bureau or assigned to the lower echelon offices and officials" [Gortner et al., 1997, p. 95]) and formalization ("the extent to which an organization relies on rules and standardized procedures to direct the behavior of members" [Bowditch, Buono, & Stewart, 2008, p. 286]), have caused problems in organizations doing nonroutine work, including human service organizations. Professional employees want decision making to be decentralized and formal rules to be lessened, giving them more autonomy. Employees who have professional training can make all the decisions covered by their professional codes, but they do not necessarily take agency goals, or even changing client needs, into account. On the other hand, a centralized bureaucracy cannot be successfully implemented because the presence of a large number of professionals confounds the hierarchy and eliminates unquestioning subservience to agency-wide objectives.

An adaptation of bureaucracy has emerged to deal with these problems: the "professional bureaucracy" (Mintzberg, 1979, 1993). Like the traditional bureaucracy, this type of organization depends on the regularity of the tasks to be performed, standardization, and stability. The tasks to be performed in the professional bureaucracy, however, are too technical and complex to be dictated by managers. Instead, authority is based on professional expertise, so the regularity of the bureaucracy is combined with a high degree of decentralization. Each professional worker controls his or her own technology in terms of professional standards and training, even though some of the skills used may be repetitive. "The professional bureaucracy emphasizes authority of a professional nature—the power of expertise" (12manage, 2005, p. 2)

> Change in the professional bureaucracy does not sweep in from new administrators taking office to announce major reforms. Rather, change seeps in by the slow process of changing the Professionals: changing who can enter the profession, what they learn in its professional schools (norms as well as skills and knowledge), and thereafter how willing they are to upgrade their skills.

In a professional bureaucracy, conflict can occur between professional judgments and agency policies, especially in a public sector agency with many rules, sometimes from outside the organization based on federal or state laws and regulations. As a principle of organization design, professionals in such settings sometimes need to advocate for the use of decision-making models such as the human resources approach to enable them to use their professional judgment with individual cases. A complication of this model occurs when multiple professions operate within the same organization, such as a hospital, where there may be disagreements among various professionals involved with a case.

CLASSICAL THEORIES IN TODAY'S HUMAN SERVICE ORGANIZATIONS

With classical management theories still prevalent in so many settings, we need to ask how relevant or useful they are for human service programs and agencies. A human service agency designed on the basis of classical principles would be organized so that all employees, including professionals, paraprofessionals, and clerical workers, perform regular, specialized tasks. A counselor or social worker assigned to perform individual counseling with adolescents might spend all of his or her time in this activity, while other specialists might conduct group sessions or work with parents. Although the degree of specialization would depend on the agency's size and resources, each task would relate to the basic goals of the program as a whole. The activities to be performed in the interests of meeting these goals would have been identified first, and then competent individuals would have been selected and trained to carry them out. It would be understood that the resources and jobs involved in the program would belong not to individuals but to the agency, with replacement of individual workers being possible without disruption in the flow of work. (Agency activities would not change, for example, because a behaviorist was replaced by an Adlerian or because a social worker was replaced by a psychologist.) Each worker would report to one supervisor or director, who would have the authority and responsibility to carry out policies chosen by the ultimate authority (in the case of a human service agency, ultimate authority is usually delegated to an executive director by a board of directors). Each human service professional—like every other worker—would understand the precise limits of his or her function. All similar clients would receive similar services.

The major contribution that classical theories offer to human service programs is in the area of unity of effort, with the idea that all of an organization's activities should relate to its general goals. Human service organizations could benefit from increased rationality in the planning process because one of the weaknesses of human service programs has been the tendency of professionals to perform the functions that are comfortable for them rather than those that can best meet the client-oriented goals of the agency or institution. The idea that a program or agency should have a clearly defined set of objectives that should be met through the coordinated efforts of all workers is one that could enhance the efficiency and effectiveness of helping professionals. Even the bureaucratic ideal of "impersonality" could have something to offer because, as Perrow (1986) points out, it involves the purging of "particularism" and discrimination or favoritism in hiring and service delivery.

The strengths of the classical approach are counteracted by its weaknesses, at least in human service programs. The major problems in applying classical management principles to the helping services lie in the insistence on specialization and centralized hierarchies of authority. Human service professionals tend to see themselves as having responsibility not just to their agencies or institutions but to their clients and professional colleagues as well. They are not easily able to conform to a system that expects them to obey orders that may conflict with their professional standards or their views of their clients' best interests. The use of very specialized, routine work patterns may be of little value in dealing with humans and their unique problems. The worker who gains a "habitual and virtuoso-like mastery" of his or her subject may overlook the differing needs of individuals being served, with the result that agency rules gain in ascendancy while consumer rights are lost.

Human service agencies are beginning to come to grips with the fact that creative approaches are needed to deal with the problem of increasing client needs coinciding with decreasing agency resources. Unfortunately, what bureaucracies may offer in terms of rationality is lost in terms of creativity. Proponents of the human relations approach address many of these weaknesses.

HUMAN RELATIONS APPROACHES

The origins of the human relations approach to organization are usually traced to Elton Mayo. Mayo and his colleagues were involved in Western Electric's Hawthorne plant experiments in the 1920s and 1930s. These studies were undertaken to determine whether changes in the physical work environment affected worker productivity. In essence, they were designed to test some of the postulates of scientific management, specifically those having to do with the effects of illumination, fatigue, and production quotas on worker performance. The underlying purpose of the Hawthorne studies was to find means of increasing organizational efficiency. Small experimental and control groups of workers were identified and placed in separate rooms, where their work was closely observed and recorded by members of the research team. Environmental conditions for the experimental group were altered in both a positive and a negative direction; that is, the lights were turned up and down, rest periods were increased and decreased, and quotas were raised and lowered. Yet the group's productivity continued to increase steadily until it leveled off at a rate unaffected by environmental manipulations (Perrow, 1986).

Finding little support for the hypothesis that variations in environmental conditions (except for the extremely negative, such as almost total darkness) affect productivity, the researchers attributed major experimental results to social phenomena theretofore given slight importance by theorists. Mayo's conclusions included the following (Accel-Team, 2005):

- Work is a group activity.
- The social world of the adult is primarily patterned about work activity.
- The need for recognition, security and sense of belonging is more important in determining workers' morale and productivity than the physical conditions under which he works.
- A complaint is not necessarily an objective recital of facts; it is commonly a symptom manifesting disturbance of an individual's status position.
- The worker is a person whose attitudes and effectiveness are conditioned by social demands from both inside and outside the work plant.
- Informal groups within the workplace exercise strong social controls over the work habits and attitudes of the individual worker.
- Group collaboration does not occur by accident; it must be planned and developed. If group collaboration is achieved the human relations within a work plant may reach a cohesion which resists disruption (that might otherwise be brought about through technological change).

At least two of these factors continue to have an impact on today's organizational practices: (a) the existence and influence of the informal group within the formal organization and (b) what later became known as the "Hawthorne effect." Both of these findings have implications for today's human service manager. The first has to do with issues of control; the second, with coordination—two important elements of organizational structure.

With respect to the informal group, the Hawthorne researchers found that the relationships formed among the members of the test groups appeared to meet certain social and psychological needs for affiliation that in turn led to enhanced group productivity. Moreover, findings indicated that informal group members established their own production rates based on their collective perception of survival within the organization rather than on quotas imposed by management. That is, the informal group determined at what point under-productivity might lead to being fired and over-productivity might lead to being laid off. Fortunately, and perhaps coincidentally, the Hawthorne subjects established a production rate that was within their managers' zone of acceptance (Perrow, 1986).

The Hawthorne experiments served more to illuminate the importance of the human element in organizational life than to demonstrate the importance of illumination on organizational productivity. Dimensions of worker motivation beyond fear and greed were introduced as valid managerial areas of concern and study.

The human relations approach to organization assumes that the bureaucratic view of human beings is too narrow to be useful in real-life organizations, and it has added immeasurably to views of organizational behavior and management practice. Nevertheless, the human relations school as developed following the Hawthorne studies was later seen to be incomplete as well. This conclusion required further thinking about how to address the human dimension to make organizations more effective.

Before we leave the human relations school, we will visit yet another contemporary of both the classical theorists and the Hawthorne experimenters. Mary Parker Follett was a hugely influential consultant to industry until her death in 1933 and subsequently in her writings (Graham, 1995). Of interest to human service managers, Follett had a 25-year career as a social work manager in Boston before becoming famous as a speaker and writer focusing on the business sector (Syers, 1995, p. 2585). Her thinking predated and influenced such current concepts as participatory management and empowerment, total quality management, conflict management, and leadership (Selber & Austin, 1997). Some of these concepts will be discussed later, but one of her insights is particularly relevant to the transition from the human relations movement begun in the 1920s to a more advanced view articulated by writers including Argyris, McGregor, and Likert.

According to Child (1995), the human relations approach articulated by Mayo and others in fact supported the classical notion of managerial control, whereas Follett believed in substantive worker participation in decision making. In his words, the human relations view "ascribed a privileged rationality to managers that legitimated their authority and was naturally attractive to members of the management movement working on their behalf" (p. 88). The later developments in the human relations school are, in fact, substantively different from the earlier version. This distinction was made by Miles (1965, 1975) as he assessed different types of employee participation in decision making. He defined his approach as the human resources model, which implied more fully using the skills and talents of workers than the human relations model of the Hawthorne studies.

THE HUMAN RESOURCES MODEL

An early humanistic psychologist, Argyris (1957) pointed out that workers are motivated by many factors other than economics, including desires for growth and independence. To Argyris, the organizational forms mandated by the classical theorists make for immature, dependent, and passive employees with little control over their work and thwart more mature employees capable of autonomy and independence. The purpose of the human resources approach is to develop organizational forms that build on the worker's strength and motivation.

McGregor (1960) distinguished between managers adhering to Theory X and those adhering to Theory Y. He did not say that either of these theories is correct. He did say that each is based on assumptions that, if recognized, would have major implications for organizing activities.

McGregor's Theory X manager assumes that people dislike work, lack interest in organizational objectives, and want to avoid responsibility. The natural result of this situation is that managers must base their organizations on the need to control; to supervise closely; and to use reward, punishment, and active persuasion to force employees to do their jobs. In contrast, the manager who adheres to Theory Y assumes that people enjoy working, desire responsibility, have innate capacities for creativity, and have the potential to work toward organizational objectives with a minimum of direction. The implication of these assumptions is that work can be organized in such a way that personnel at all levels have the opportunity to do creative, self-directed, and responsible jobs.

The organizational implications of McGregor's model are clear. Theory X managers would use high degrees of specialization, clear lines of authority, narrow spans of control, and centralized decision making. Theory Y managers would use less specialization, less control, and more delegation of decision making and responsibility. The organization would be decentralized so that workers' natural creativity could be channeled effectively.

Likert (1967) examined a number of specific organizational variables, including leadership, motivation, communication, decision making, goal setting, and control. He divided organizations into four basic types, based on how they deal with these organizational variables: System 1 (exploitive authoritative), System 2 (benevolent authoritative), System 3 (consultative), and System 4 (participative group). Likert's System 1 organizations are characterized by leaders who distrust their subordinates, decision-making processes that are concentrated at the top of the organizational hierarchy, and communication that is almost exclusively downward, from supervisor to supervisees. Control and power are centralized in top management so that others feel little concern for the organization's overall goals. System 2 organizations also centralize power in the hands of the few at the top of the hierarchy but add an increased degree of communication. More trust is placed in subordinates, but it is condescending in nature. System 3 increases communication; employees have the opportunity to give input, although all major decisions are still made at the top of the management hierarchy. System 4, the opposite of System 1, is characterized by leaders who have complete confidence in workers, motivation that is based on responsibility and participation as well as on economic rewards, communication among all organization members, extensive interaction, decentralized decision making, wide acceptance of organizational goals, and widespread responsibility for control.

Likert (1967, p. 46) said that most managers recognize System 4 as theoretically superior to the others. He pointed out that if clear plans, high goals, and technical competence are present in an organization, System 4 will be superior.

The key to its superiority lies in a structure based on group decision making and on the relationship of each group in an organization to every other group through common members or linking pins.

How would an organization based on the thinking of Mayo, Follett, Argyris, McGregor, and Likert differ from a bureaucratic agency? If a human service program were organized in accordance with a human relations or human resources approach, it would be characterized by greater freedom of action, both for human service professionals and for their coworkers. Instead of departmentalizing the agency by function, the organization might divide work according to purpose or population being served. An interdisciplinary task force, including various helping professionals, paraprofessionals, community members, and consumers, might work together to solve a specific problem. Such a group might design a program to improve the agency's services to court-referred juveniles or troubled families. It might provide outreach services to displaced homemakers or school-age drug users. It might educate the community concerning mental health or stress management.

The task force itself might be permanent or ad hoc, but this organizational structure would allow each person to participate actively in planning and decision making while decreasing the prevalence of routine, specialized activities. Less attention would be directed toward authority and control, and greater emphasis would be placed on the flow of information from person to person and group to group. In the case of a large agency, people would identify with their own projects and feel responsible for their success. In the case of a small agency or a program within a larger institution, all staff members would participate in setting objectives and choosing evaluation methods for the program as a whole. Although a hierarchy of authority might exist, decision-making powers would not be limited to those at the highest levels, and the boundaries between jobs and specializations would not be clear-cut. Structure would be seen as a changing force rather than a constant factor.

A strength of the human resources school for human service agencies is its consistency with the approach of helping professionals. Human service workers tend to favor increasing self-responsibility and options for their clients, and they generally prefer that their supervisors give them high levels of autonomy, as the human resources school prescribes.

The human resources–based organization also has a greater allowance for change than does the bureaucratic structure. Although bureaucracies are efficient for dealing with routine tasks, they do not allow for the creative responses to change that a more fluid environment can make. The human service field needs new approaches to help clients deal with a continually changing world. Professionals who have the opportunity to create and the freedom to innovate might provide better service than their highly specialized colleagues.

Of course, the human resources theories do not provide easy answers. Creating an organization based on concepts of democracy and independence is, if anything, a more complex task than developing a more traditional structure. Although people might have innate capacities for growth and creativity, they have not necessarily had the chance to develop these capacities in schools and work settings that still tend toward Theory X. The Theory Y manager must carefully create structures that can encourage workers to learn how to function without close supervision and at the same time provide effective training and leadership.

A final note is that human service organizations are often closely related to larger systems, and a structure that differs greatly from those used by others is often misunderstood. A System 4 counseling department, for example, within a System 1 school or a System 4 community agency attempting to deal with a System 1 city government faces conflicts that might seem surprising.

OPEN SYSTEMS THEORY

Systems can be thought of as sets of elements that interact with one another so that a change in any one of those elements brings about a corresponding alteration in other elements. Open systems take in and export energy through interfaces with the environment so that units within the system are also affected by changes in other systems. Open systems theorists recognize that rationality within organizations is limited by both internal factors, such as organization members' characteristics, and external factors, such as changes in the supply of available people and materials.

What are the characteristics of a system? As defined by Accel-Team (2005, p. 6):

- A system is defined by its properties.
- A system is a physical and/or conceptual entity composed of interrelated and interacting parts existing in an environment with which it may also interact.
- The system has a preferred state.
- The parts of the system may in turn be systems themselves.

Theoretically, there could be *closed systems* that do not interact with their environments. In fact, however, all systems are affected by their environments. An *open system* has a two-way interaction with the environment, affecting the environment and being affected by it in return. Any organization, as a system, would fall somewhere on the continuum between a closed and an open system.

The fact that the system has a preferred state means that it tries to maintain itself in a stable, steady state, or *homeostasis*. The system reacts to change by making adaptations in ways that bring it back to its homeostasis without changing its essential character. Systems vary in their ability to carry out this adaptation.

An adaptive system is one that is capable of responding to changes in the condition of the environment or to contingencies imposed by the environment. A non-adaptive system does not react to its environment.

- A perfectly adaptive system can respond to any change or contingency in the environment.
- All systems lie somewhere between non-adaptive and perfectly adaptive systems.
- In order to continue existing, any open system in a dynamic environment must adapt (Accel-Team, 2005, p. 8)

Managers who view their organizations from the systems perspective tend to see the organization more as a process than as a structure. They know that structural changes both affect and are affected by changes in all the other components of the organization. They know, too, that the goals and activities they choose will be influenced by environmental factors that are often beyond their control.

The ideas offered by systems theory might well be more important to human service agencies than to private sector firms because environmental effects on both the program as a whole and individual clients must be considered. Human service professionals using these ideas would develop structures indicating the relationships between the agency and other systems as well as those within the agency. Methods of coordination with community groups, funding sources, government agencies, other helping agencies, educational institutions, professional organizations, and a variety of other systems would need to be identified. In addition, organizational strategies would take into account the progress of individual clients through the system. Methods would be developed for linking clients with various services, following up on clients as they move into other systems, and communicating with referring agencies as new clients are accepted. These methods would be built into the organizational structure, with communication to outside agencies planned as carefully as communication within the program itself.

A major strength of the systems approach is the encouragement it gives to human service professionals to think of themselves as part of a network that, as a totality, can serve the individual client in a coordinated way. This does not mean that human service administrators should allow their programs to be buffeted about by external systems, all making conflicting demands. The other organizational approaches, including the classical management approach, provide some benefits as well, for they can help agencies in their attempts to clarify basic program goals and to find ways to develop unity of effort in reaching those goals.

Most of the organizational theories and principles that have emerged over the last half-century operate under the assumption that all formal organizations are in fact open systems that respond to the environments around them. Organizations have to devise new ways of addressing emerging community needs and goals, competition from other organizations, and a workforce with changing expectations regarding the quality of working life. Organizations must also recognize the need for flexibility in applying the perspectives that adapt best to their own missions and environments.

CONTINGENCY THEORIES

No one form of organization is appropriate for all types of settings. In fact, principles from many or all of the theories discussed here may be useful in a given human service organization. Several researchers have indicated that organizational technologies (tasks), environments, and even sizes affect strategy, which should help determine structure. Different organizations bring with them the needs for different structures. Determination of the most efficient and productive type of structure in a given situation depends on the specific contingencies being faced.

The contingency theories—unlike the traditional, human relations, and human resources approaches—recognize that there is no "one best way" to structure all organizations. Rather, a number of "contingency" factors have differential effects on organizations and should be considered in designing structure.

Contingency theories are, in effect, systems theories in the sense that they recognize the effect of the organization's external environment on its internal structure. The contingency perspective, in other words, accounts for the importance of the interaction between the organization and the outside world—a world that provides it with the sanctions (legitimacy, societal acceptance, political support), energy (money, technological advances, human resources), and raw materials (microchips, steel, human beings) to meet its goals. Just as individuals are affected by their environment—its climatic fluctuations, the quality of its atmosphere—so are organizations subject to their environments. Adaptation to new environmental conditions is accomplished, as was reviewed in Chapter 3, through the design and implementation of new programs. Organizational adaptation at a larger scale is accomplished through designing or, more typically, redesigning the organization. This reflects Chandler's (1962) principle that structure follows strategy: once members of the organization decide where they want to go, the best structure and organizational processes are developed to enable the organization as a system to implement its programs and thrive in a complex environment.

The work of Lawrence and Lorsch (1967) provides particular insight into organizational needs in varying situations. Lawrence and Lorsch identify four organizational features that vary with the degree of environmental certainty: (1) reliance on formal rules and communication, (2) time horizon, (3) diffuse or concentrated goals, and (4) relationship- or task-oriented interpersonal styles. They stress that effective organizations have a good "fit" with their environment. An organization with a stable environment can use formal rules, a short time horizon, traditional communication channels, and task-oriented management. An organization with an unstable environment needs more points of contact with the external world so that changes can be recognized promptly. Such an organization also requires a longer time orientation and a more complex communication pattern. Formal rules and hierarchies would interfere with the needed information flow, so it would be inappropriate to rely on them.

Burns and Stalker (1994) distinguish between what they term mechanistic and organic forms of organization. The mechanistic form, comparable to the classical type of structure, depends on formal authority, specialization, and structured channels of communication. The organic form is highly flexible and informal, with communication channels based not on the hierarchical chain of command but on the need to solve immediate problems by consulting the person with the needed data. In studying a number of British firms, Burns and Stalker found that the organic style seems most appropriate for firms such as electronics companies facing rapid technological change and the need to solve novel problems. The mechanistic form is productive for firms needing efficiency in dealing with very stable conditions.

The contingency theorists make clear that an effective organization can run the gamut from a traditional bureaucracy to a highly organic, constantly changing structure. Which structure is appropriate depends on the organization's needs. At its most basic level the contingency approach offers administrators a method for clarifying their ideas about organization.

If human service managers were to use contingency theory to determine the best ways to structure the work of their programs or agencies, they would, as a first step, identify the most salient characteristics of their services and settings. They would need to determine whether their environments were characterized more by rapid change or by stability over time, recognizing that agencies dealing with shifting populations or subject to changes in funding cannot afford to use slow-moving, unwieldy organizational structures. Moreover, human service managers and service providers must consider their perceptions regarding the intrinsic nature of their work. Human service workers who view themselves as technicians offering consistent services to a wide range of clients might be able to use mechanistic organizational structures, but such designs would be inappropriate for professionals attempting to deliver multifaceted services based on client and community needs.

4.1   ORGANIZATIONAL THEORY AT GRANDVIEW COMMUNITY CENTER

A review of the development of Grandview Community Center (GCC) shows the impact of organizational theory on a human service organization. The staff of Grandview reacted negatively when the previous director came in and tried to implement bureaucratic structures and technological changes that were foreign to Grandview's culture. This attempt at organizational change lasted only 2 years.

When GCC current director took over, she implemented changes that reflected a different philosophy. Her first goal was to begin a process of strategic planning, but the most important feature of her tenure might have been her interest in building broad involvement in the process. The center's move from an uncomfortable director-staff relationship to an era of collaboration with a new director in place reflects not just personal differences but also differences in organizational theory.

ORGANIZATIONAL APPROACHES FOR TWENTY-FIRST CENTURY HUMAN SERVICES

Today's human service organizations tend to be larger, more complex, and subject to greater external controls than has been true in the past. Some agencies cope with these realities by implementing more bureaucratic controls. At the same time, however, an important counter-trend can be seen. Across the helping professions, services to consumers are increasingly characterized by (a) a focus on client empowerment; (b) an emphasis on clients' strengths, rather than their deficits; (c) a recognition that service providers should carry out advocacy on behalf of clients who belong to oppressed or marginalized groups; and (d) a philosophy oriented to social justice (Lewis, Lewis, Daniels, & D'Andrea, 2011; Lewis, Toporek, & Ratts, 2010; Nelson & Prilleltensky, 2005; Sowers & Rowe, 2006; Toporek, Gerstein, Fouad, Roysircar, & Israel, 2006). With services to individual consumers becoming more client centered, human service managers are faced with a pressing question: How can a human service program or agency be organized in a way that provides an appropriate context for this kind of work?

ALTERNATIVE AGENCIES OF THE LATE TWENTIETH CENTURY

The 1960s brought the advent of small, nonbureaucratic, not-for-profit organizations known as alternative programs or street agencies. These agencies developed as an alternative to traditional bureaucracies, which were seen as ignoring or oppressing particular people in need. They were usually started by small groups of committed individuals who ran their programs on very small budgets, initially with little or no government funding and often using donated facilities, furniture, and equipment. According to Perlmutter (1995, pp. 204–205), these programs typically had the following characteristics:

1. They were deeply committed to social change.
2. They were reluctant to acknowledge the reality and legitimacy of formal authority and power.
3. They were designed to meet the needs of special populations not being serviced by existing agencies.
4. Their services were often exploratory or innovative.
5. Staff were deeply committed ideologically to clients, were closely identified with them, or were former clients.
6. Small size of the agency was valued.
7. Agencies were usually in a marginal economic position.

The people who originated and ran these agencies used democratic or consensus decision making, eschewing authoritarian directors and trying to avoid power differentials among clients and service providers.

As these programs progressed over time, some acquired government funding and entered the mainstream, a few stayed small and true to the original philosophies on which they had been created, and many died. Today, in an era of multimillion-dollar budgets, professional staffs, and expensive facilities, it is hard to believe that the philosophy underlying the alternative agency can live on. In fact, however, empowerment-focused attitudes and the theories that support them are central to the study of organizations.

CRITICAL AND FEMINIST THEORIES

"If the aim of human service administration is to improve and protect the well-being of clients, it must critically examine its own ideology" (Hasenfeld, 2009, p. 72). Critical theory addresses this issue by calling into question virtually all of the assumptions and values that underlie mainstream organizations.

> The central goal of critical theory in organizational studies is to create societies and workplaces that are free from domination and where all members have equal opportunity to contribute to the production of systems that meet human needs and lead to the progressive development of all. Given that power is a key variable in defining the structure, processes, services, and worker-client relations of human service organizations, the emancipatory focus of the critical perspective becomes particularly salient. For example, a trusting client-worker relationship—a necessary condition of effective services—is predicated on some degree of power balance between clients and workers. (Hasenfeld, 2010, pp. 46–47)

Feminist organizational theory, which is based on the notion that "organizations replicate the oppression of women found in society by establishing hierarchical decision-making structures in which one or a few top decision-makers control what happens in the organization" (Hardina, Middleton, Montana, & Simpson, 2007, p. 34), has been an important source of critical analysis. The contributions of feminist viewpoints go beyond issues of gender, providing intellectual leadership for the creation of nonhierarchical organizations of all kinds. In practical terms, however, feminism has been particularly important in the development of agencies and programs that respond to the needs of women.

Many of the small alternative agencies of the late twentieth century were women's programs that came into being in response to the difficulties women had in receiving services that were sensitive to their needs. Among the concerns these kinds of organizations addressed were women's health concerns, including reproductive health; victimization by violent partners; and rape crises. Recognizing that women were often re-victimized by organizations that were not cognizant of women's rights, the people who designed these alternative programs avoided hierarchy in favor of equality.

In the twenty-first-century environment, it is often difficult to maintain organizations that are small and underfunded. Adaptations are made, however, especially through the mechanisms of networking and collaboration. The Illinois Coalition Against Sexual Assault (ICASA) provides a good example of this kind of adaptation.

> The Illinois Coalition Against Sexual Assault is a not-for-profit corporation of 34 community-based crisis centers working together to end sexual violence. Each center provides 24-hour crisis services, counseling and advocacy for victims of sexual assault and conducts educational programs in Illinois communities (Illinois Coalition Against Sexual Assault, Spring, 2009).

The coalition model makes it possible to combine the personal and egalitarian relationships of the small agency with the resources that a larger organization can access.

The ICASA example also highlights the efficacy of the social movement service organization, which combines human services provision with advocacy efforts (Meyer, 2010). The coalition makes it possible to carry out educational and advocacy-oriented activities that might be beyond the scope of what a small agency could do on its own.

> The purpose of the Illinois Coalition Against Sexual Assault (ICASA) is to end sexual violence and to alleviate the suffering of sexual assault victims. This work is inseparable from ICASA's commitment to eliminate oppression in all its forms. To accomplish these goals, ICASA advocates for public policy that prevents sexual violence, guarantees sensitivity to victims, and promotes social justice. ICASA uses the power of public education to change beliefs and attitudes about the causes and consequences of sexual violence and the devastation of oppression. Through community programs that provide advocacy, counseling and education, ICASA works for a safe, free and just society (Illinois Coalition Against Sexual Assault, Spring, 2009).

In a social movement service organization, the connection between the direct-service and social-change aspects of the agency is very direct. When working with oppressed populations, service providers soon learn that meeting their clients' needs involves not just amelioration of presenting problems but also prevention of these problems through social change and empowerment.

HUMAN SERVICE ORGANIZATIONS AND EMPOWERMENT

Hardina et al. (2007) suggest that an "empowering approach" to social service management is characterized by the following basic principles:

1. Empowerment-oriented organizations create formal structures to support the participation of clients in organizational decision-making ...
2. Empowerment-oriented organizations create partnerships with program beneficiaries in which all parties (clients, staff, and board members) are equal participants ...
3. The purpose of client involvement in service delivery is to decrease personal feelings of powerlessness and to improve the quality of, and access to, services ...
4. Empowerment-oriented organizations explicitly develop policies, programs, and procedures that can be used to bridge cultural, ethnic, gender, and other demographic barriers to effective service delivery ...
5. Empowerment-oriented organizations have top managers who are ideologically committed to the empowerment of both staff members and program beneficiaries ...
6. Empowerment-oriented organizations engage in specific strategies to increase the psychological empowerment and motivation of workers ...
7. Empowerment-oriented organizations promote the use of team building and collaboration among staff members ...
8. Empowerment-oriented organizations encourage staff to advocate for improvements in services and policies ...
9. Empowerment-oriented management approaches can only produce effective outcomes when a consistent funding base is available to maintain the organization ...
10. Empowerment-oriented organizations involve clients, community constituency groups, and staff members in ongoing evaluation of services and program renewal ...
11. Empowerment-oriented organizations act to increase their own political power as well as the political influence of program beneficiaries ...
12. Empowerment-oriented organizations acknowledge the limitations of participatory management approaches and take proactive measures to balance inclusion in decision-making with tasks associated with organizational maintenance ... (pp. 12–16)

These principles are especially important if the organization's consumers are drawn from populations that are marginalized and disempowered. Of course it is important to meet the urgent needs of people who face multiple sources of oppression and multiple traumas. It may be even more important, however, to make sure that help is provided in a way that is respectful and empowering. Diaz-LaPlante (2010) describes an experience of building community mental health program in Haiti after a major earthquake brought untold devastation. Under the assumption that "mental health is a human right," Diaz-LaPlante and her colleagues sought to build a responsive, community-based mental health program that would be seen as desirable and important by people who had no words for "mental health" in their Creole language. Participating together in focus groups and interviews, Haitians from the community of Jeremie and their international visitors began the work of creating a program in which power would be shared and activities would be based on the Haitian culture. One important outcome of this process was the recognition that "sustainable livelihood is needed for mental health." Because of this learning, the mental health interventions in Jeremie and neighboring communities include farming projects and housing for women.

The mental health program is part of the Haitian Connection (2010), which works to carry out the following mission:

> The Haitian Connection—Koneksyon Ayiti has been established as a compassionate response to the poverty and misery that so many Haitians face. We are committed to the creative energy and inherent worth of each individual. We foster self-help and grassroots development by building shelter for the most vulnerable in society—women and children, by promoting mental health and by strengthening the educational infrastructure.

Programs like this make clear that the human service programs of the twenty-first century can benefit from organizational theories that (a) adhere to the empowerment strategies that are implicit in direct services and (b) avoid the assumption that corporate models can be applied to human services without appropriate adaptations.

SUMMARY

Organizational theory is used to explain, and sometimes guide, the way organizations work. The classical models of bureaucracy, scientific management, and human relations as well as more current approaches such as the human resources models of Likert, McGregor, and Argyris and systems theory all have relevance today. Human service managers do use theory, consciously or unconsciously, and they are likely to be more effective if they are thoughtful about their own theoretical beliefs and apply them consciously. Being aware of a variety of theoretical frameworks helps human service professionals know that, as they seek to organize their programs, they do have choices. The theories discussed here should offer guidance to those who are designing or redesigning an agency so that all the various components will work effectively and efficiently together.

| COMPETENCY-BUILDING ACTIVITY 4.1 | ORGANIZATIONAL THEORIES |

Chapter 4 discussed several approaches to organizational design, including (a) classical, bureaucratic theories; (b) human resources approaches; (c) contingency theories; (d) open systems theory; and (e) empowerment-oriented theories.

1. Do you find some of these theories more helpful than others?

2. What theories do you see being used, explicitly or implicitly, in an organization with which you are familiar? Are these the appropriate theories to be used? If not, which ones would be better?

3. In the human service program you have been designing, which theory would you be most likely to use?

| THE COMMUNITY CAREER CENTER

The Community Career Center (CCC) was initiated several years ago by a group of professionals who had become impatient with the impersonality and red tape that overwhelmed their work in public agencies. All four of the center's founders had previously worked for departments of human resources or vocational rehabilitation, and their experiences had led them to think that there must be better ways to deal with clients' career development needs.

A few basic concepts had been part of the center's orientation since it had first begun operation under Department of Labor and fee-based funding. First, the founders felt that one counselor should work with the total scope of a client's career needs, linking him or her with training programs, with educational institutions, with other needed services, and, finally, with jobs. They also believed in using training formats to deal with the kinds of needs many clients shared. From its unassuming start, the center had provided training programs dealing with midlife career change, retirement planning, job-hunting skills, self-assessment, and a variety of other topics. These programs were offered to members of the general public, such as women reentering the job market, and to local institutions and businesses.

At first, the founders of the center provided most of the services themselves. If they felt that a particular training format had exciting possibilities or if they were invited to design something special for a local group, they would provide workshops and group sessions. In the meantime, each of the four also carried a caseload of clients to whom they were dedicated. They saw themselves as counselors, advocates, and placement specialists for their own clients, and their success exceeded even their own idealistic expectations.

Last year, the center's management began to get out of hand. Its size had mushroomed, and so had its funding. Local businesses had proven so supportive, especially in contracting training programs, that the initial Department of Labor contract provided only a small percentage of the agency's total funding. Each training program was self-supporting, and the number of individual clients kept growing. To keep pace, the center had had to hire additional staff members to provide services, so there were now a number of trainers and counselors who had not been in on the original planning. Little by little, the original four founders had become frustrated. Instead of spending all their time with clients and trainees, they were becoming involved in keeping books, planning repetitive services, and supervising staff members. This supervision especially bothered them. New staff members somehow did not understand the concept of being dedicated to their clients. These counselors did their work, but they were not bubbling over with creativity. They were not seeking new challenges, coming up with new ideas, or making that extra effort that made the difference. The original founders, who did have that urge for creativity, were unable to use it. They had become managers, and they did not like it.

Their solution was to bring in a business manager, a recent MBA who knew how to organize and control a growing firm. The center's founders breathed a collective sigh of relief when management concerns were taken out of their hands. They gave their new manager a free hand and were pleased with the way he took control of the budgets and financial reports. The new organizational structure that he created also seemed to make sense. He divided the center into departments, including the training department, where programs were designed and implemented; the marketing department, which had responsibility for selling the training programs to industrial and other organizations; the counseling department, which provided direct services to clients; the job development department, which canvassed the community for placement possibilities for clients; and the business department, which took care of administrative concerns, including personnel.

This approach seemed to work for a while. The newer staff members, in particular, seemed pleased with the increased clarity of their job descriptions. They were no longer badgered with instructions to "be creative." They knew what their responsibilities were and could carry them out. The center's founders—still the board of directors of the agency—were pleased to have management responsibilities taken out of their hands. Now they could be creative again.

Yet that sense of renewed creativity had not taken hold. Somehow the agency's new organization did not allow for it. Now in its fifth year of existence, the Community Career Center was in jeopardy, not because it had failed but because it had succeeded. Two of the four board members wanted to resign and spin off a new smaller, more responsive agency. Monica Shannon and Paul Ramirez did not really want to make this move, but they could see no way to carry out what they believed to be their mission through an organization as unwieldy as the CCC had become.

At the most volatile meeting ever held at the center, the board of directors cleared the air. Shannon, one of the two original members who had decided to leave, spoke first.

"Look," she exclaimed, "our original idea was to have an agency that would be responsive to our clients' career needs. We would stick with an individual, be an ombudsman, help meet all this one client's needs. Now we have a department for counseling and another department for finding jobs. What happened to the idea that got us started in the first place?"

"And what about the training component?" Ramirez chimed in. "The idea was to meet community needs by designing special sessions, not to keep repeating the same program all the time to make it easier for the marketing department. Everything we do lately is to please the marketers, to make it easier for them to sell. But what have they got to sell? We've got the tail wagging the dog."

"Now, wait a minute," Mark Morgenstein responded. "We've got a big organization here. We can't expect everything to be the same as it was. Growth and change was supposed to be one of our big aims, too."

"And you were the ones who got the most excited about bringing in a manager to take the business responsibilities out of your hands," Colleen Morgan pointed out. "You can't have everything."

"I'll tell you one thing," Shannon said. "We may be a large organization now, but we accomplished more in a day when the four of us began than that whole gang of bureaucrats we've got here now accomplishes in a month. That's what we've got here now: a bureaucracy. Why did we ever bother leaving the Department of Human Resources? We've got a duplication right here."

1. Would you describe the Community Career Center's current organization as a bureaucracy? How does it compare with the structure that the agency had at first?

2. The agency grew in size over the years. What organizational theories should guide the organization at this stage?

3. At this point, do you think Monica Shannon and Paul Ramirez are right in wanting to leave the organization? What options do they have?

REFERENCES

12manage.com (2005). *Organizational configurations: Mintzberg.* Retrieved September, 2005, from http://www.12manage.com/methods_mintzberg_configurations.html

Accel-Team. (2005). *Elton Mayo: Findings.* Retrieved September, 2005, from http://www.accel-team.com/human_relations/hrels_01_mayo.html

Accel-Team. (2005). *Open systems approach to OD.* Retrieved September, 2005, from http://www.accel-team.com/ltzpubz_10mxAT1005/atPDF_06_openSystems.pdf

Ammons, D. (1998). Benchmarking performance. In S. Condrey (Ed.), *Handbook of human resource management in government* (pp. 391–409). San Francisco: Jossey-Bass.

Argyris, C. (1957). *Personality and organization.* New York: Harper & Row.

Bombyk, M. (1995). Progressive social work. In R. Edwards (Ed.), *Encyclopedia of social work* (19th ed., pp. 1933–1942). Washington, DC: NASW Press.

Bowditch, J., Buono, A., & Stewart, M. (2008). *A primer on organizational behavior* (7th ed.). New York: Wiley.

Bryson, J. (1995). *Strategic planning for public and nonprofit organizations.* San Francisco: Jossey-Bass.

Burns, T., & Stalker, G. (1994). *The management of innovation* (rev. ed.). New York: Oxford University Press.

Chandler, A. (1962). *Strategy and structure: Chapters in the history of the industrial enterprise.* Cambridge, MA: MIT Press.

Child, J. (1995). Follett: Constructive conflict. In P. Graham (Ed.), *Mary Parker Follett: Prophet of management* (pp. 87–95). Boston: Harvard Business School Press.

Cohen, B., & Austin, M. (1994). Organizational learning and change in a public child welfare agency. *Administration in Social Work, 18*(1), 1–18.

Cooke, R. A., & Rousseau, D. M. (1988). Behavioral norms and expectations: A quantitative approach to the assessment of organizational culture. *Group and Organization Studies, 13*(3), 245–273.

Diaz-LaPlante, J. (2010, July 16). *Disaster, Community Readiness, and Recovery: Contributions from Community Psychology: Community Mental Health Program.* Paper presented at the Psychologists for Social Responsibility 2010 Conference, Brookline, MA.

Fayol, H. (1949). *General and industrial management.* London: Sir Isaac Pitman.

Fischer, F., & Sirianni, C. (1984). Organization and bureaucracy: A critical introduction. In F. Fischer & C. Sirianni (Eds.), *Critical studies in organization and bureaucracy* (pp. 3–20). Philadelphia: Temple University Press.

Gerth, H. H., & Mills, C. W. (Eds.). (1958). *From Max Weber: Essays in sociology.* New York: Oxford University Press.

Gilson, S. (1997). The YWCA women's advocacy program: A case study of domestic violence and sexual assault services. *Journal of Community Practice, 4*(4), 1–26.

Gortner, H., Mahler, J., & Nicholson, J. (1997). *Organization theory: A public perspective* (2nd ed.). Fort Worth, TX: Harcourt Brace College Publishers.

Graham, P. (Ed.). (1995). *Mary Parker Follett: Prophet of management.* Boston: Harvard Business School Press.

Gummer, B., & McCallion, P. (Eds.). (1995). *Total quality management.* Albany, NY: Professional Development Program of Rockefeller College.

Haitian Connection. (2010). *Mission.* Retrieved December 1, 2010, from http://www.haitianconnection.org/index.htm

Hammer, M., & Champy, J. (1993). *Reengineering the corporation.* New York: HarperBusiness.

Hardina, D., Middleton, J., Montana, S., & Simpson, R. A. (2007). *An empowering approach to managing social service organizations.* New York: Springer Publishing Co.

Harvey, C. (1998). Defining excellence in human service organizations. *Administration in Social Work, 22*(1), 33–45.

Hasenfeld, Y. (2009). Human services administration and organizational theory. In R. J. Patti (Ed.), *The handbook of human services management* (pp. 53–80). Thousand Oaks, CA: Sage.

Hasenfeld, Y. (2010). The attributes of human service organizations. In Y. Hasenfeld (Ed.), *Human services as complex organizations* (2nd ed., pp. 9–32). Thousand Oaks, CA: Sage.

Hawkins, F., & Gunther, J. (1998). Managing for quality. In R. Edwards, J. Yankey, & M. Altpeter (Eds.), *Skills for effective management of nonprofit organizations* (pp. 525–554). Washington, DC: NASW Press.

Holleb, G., & Abrams, W. (1975). *Alternatives in community mental health.* Boston: Beacon.

Illinois Coalition Against Sexual Assault. (2009, Spring). *Coalition commentary.* Retrieved December 1, 2010, from http://www.icasa.org/docs/commentary/ii%20spring%202009.pdf

Katz, D., & Kahn, R. L. (1978). *The social psychology of organizations* (2nd ed.). New York: Wiley.

Keys, P. (1995a). Japanese quality management techniques. In L. Ginsberg & P. Keys (Eds.), *New management in human services* (2nd ed., pp. 162–170). Washington, DC: NASW Press.

Keys, P. (1995b). Quality management. In R. Edwards (Ed.), *The encyclopedia of social work* (19th ed., pp. 2019–2025). Washington, DC: NASW Press.

Kirst-Ashman, K. K., & Hull, G. H. (2009). *Generalist practice with organizations and communities* (4th ed.). Belmont, CA: Brooks/Cole Cengage Learning.

Kurtz, P. (1998). A case study of a network as a learning organization. *Administration in Social Work, 22*(2), 57–73.

Lawrence, P. R., & Lorsch, J. (1967). *Organization and environment.* Cambridge, MA: Harvard University Press.

Lewis, J. A., Toporek, R. L., & Ratts, M. J. (2010). Advocacy and social justice: Entering the mainstream of the counseling profession. In M. J. Ratts, R. L. Toporek, & J. A. Lewis (Eds.), *ACA Advocacy Competencies: A social justice framework for counselors* (pp. 239–244). Alexandria, VA: American Counseling Association.

Lewis, J. A., Lewis, M. D., Daniels, J. A., & D'Andrea, M. J. (2011). *Community counseling: A multicultural-social justice perspective.* Belmont, CA: Brooks/Cole Cengage Learning.

Likert, R. (1967). *The human organization: Its management and value.* New York: McGraw-Hill.

Mangier, M. (1999, July 24). Japanese firms use bullying to thin their ranks. *Los Angeles Times,* Section 1, pp. 1, 11.

McGregor, D. (1960). *The human side of enterprise.* New York: McGraw-Hill.

Micklethwait, J., & Wooldridge, A. (1997). *The witch doctors: Making sense of the management gurus.* New York: Times Books.

Miles, R. (1965). Human relations or human resources? *Harvard Business Review, 9*(43), 148–152.

Miles, R. (1975). *Theories of management: Implications for organizational behavior and development.* New York: McGraw Hill.

Mintzberg, H. (1979). *The structuring of organizations.* Upper Saddle River, NJ: Prentice Hall.

National Assembly of National Voluntary Health and Social Welfare Organizations. (1989). *A study in excellence: Management in the nonprofit human services.* Washington, DC: Author.

Nelson, G., & Prilleltensky, I. (2005). *Community psychology: In pursuit of liberation and well-being.* New York: Palgrave MacMillan.

Osborne, D., & Gaebler, T. (1992). *Reinventing government: How the entrepreneurial spirit is transforming the public sector.* Reading, MA: Addison-Wesley.

Osborne, D., & Plastrik, P. (1997). *Banishing bureaucracy: The five strategies for reinventing government.* Reading, MA: Addison-Wesley.

Ouchi, W. G. (1982). *Theory Z: How American business can meet the Japanese challenge.* New York: Avon.

Perlmutter, F. (Ed.). (1988). *Alternative social agencies: Administrative strategies.* New York: Haworth.

Perlmutter, F. (1995). Administering alternative social programs. In L. Ginsberg & P. Keys (Eds.), *New management in human services* (2nd ed., pp. 203–218). Washington, DC: NASW Press.

Perrow, C. (1986). *Complex organizations: A critical essay* (3rd ed.). New York: Random House.

Peters, T. J., & Waterman, R. H., Jr. (1982). *In search of excellence.* New York: Harper & Row.

Sashkin, M. (1981). An overview of ten organizational and management theorists. In J. Jones & W. Pfeiffer (Eds.), *The 1981 annual handbook for group facilitators* (pp. 206–221). San Diego, CA: University Associates.

Schein, E. (1992). *Organizational culture and leadership* (2nd ed.). San Francisco: Jossey-Bass.

Schmidt, W., & Finnegan, J. (1992). *The race without a finish line: America's quest for total quality.* San Francisco: Jossey-Bass.

Selber, K., & Austin, D. (1997). Mary Parker Follett: Epilogue to or return of a social work management pioneer? *Administration in Social Work, 21*(1), 1–15.

Sowers, K. M., & Rowe, W. S. (2006). *Social work practice and social justice: From local to global perspectives.* Belmont, CA: Cengage Learning.

Syers, M. (1995). Follett, Mary Parker (1868–1933). In R. Edwards (Ed.), *The encyclopedia of social work* (19th ed., p. 2585). Washington, DC: NASW Press.

Taylor, F. W. (1911). Principles of scientific management. New York: Harper & Row.

Taylor, J., & Felten, D. (1993). *Performance by design.* Upper Saddle River, NJ: Prentice Hall.

Toporek, R. L., Gerstein, L. H., Fouad, N. A., Roysircar, G., & Israel, T. (2006). *Handbook for social justice in counseling psychology: Leadership, vision and action.* Thousand Oaks, CA: Sage.

Trice, H. M., & Beyer, J. M. (1993). *The cultures of work organizations.* Upper Saddle River, NJ: Prentice Hall.

Walton, R. (1975). Criteria for quality of working life. In L. Davis & A. Cherns (Eds.), *The quality of working life: Volume 1: Problems, prospects, and the state of the art* (pp. 91–118). New York: Free Press.

Weisbord, M. (1987). *Productive workplaces.* San Francisco: Jossey-Bass.

Zell, D. (1997). *Changing by design: Organizational innovation at Hewlett-Packard.* Ithaca, NY: ILR Press.

CREATING ORGANIZATIONAL DESIGNS

Human service managers and service providers must often seek answers to questions like the following: Should service providers in an agency be divided according to specialization? Should an agency's services be departmentalized according to the type of client served or according to the type of activity that is performed? How can we make sure that information flows smoothly among individuals and units?

As was noted in Chapter 3, planning involves assessing an agency's environment, developing strategies, and setting goals and objectives. Programs are then designed to enable the accomplishment of the desired end results. Managers must also figure out how all the programs and functions should fit together and operate, and this step is the province of organization design. As Burton, DeSanctis, and Obel (2006) point out,

> The structural components of organization design include goals, strategies, and structure [and] the human components include work processes, people, coordination and control, and incentive mechanisms. Together, these components provide a holistic approach to the organization design challenges (pp. 3–4).

In Chapter 4, we reviewed some of the most influential organizational theories as they apply to the design and functioning of organizations. The next step is to create a design that will lead toward an effectively functioning agency. At the same time, it is important to remember that creating an organizational design is not a one-time event but a process that must be revisited frequently over time.

DIMENSIONS OF ORGANIZATION DESIGN

Senge (2006) notes the importance of design by using the analogy of a ship. His point is that, when asked how they would see their role as leader if their organization were an ocean liner, people most often see themselves as captains, navigators, helmsmen, engineers, or social directors. Seldom do they show an awareness of how important the role of designer must be.

> No one has a more sweeping influence on the ship than the designer. What good does it do for the captain to say, "Turn starboard thirty degrees," when the designer has built a rudder that will turn only to port, or that takes six hours to turn to starboard? It's fruitless to be the leader in an organization that is poorly designed" (Senge, 2006).

Organization design has two components: structure and process. *Organizational structure* is what people usually think of when describing an organization: how departments and other functions are organized and who reports to whom. *Organizational processes* (Robey and Sales, 1994) are key activities that occur within the structure, including coordination among functions, organizational communication processes, control systems, decision making. After both of these components are reviewed, a process for designing the organization will be presented.

Organization design is both a noun and a verb. As a noun, it describes the structure and key processes (such as communication and decision making) of the organization. As a verb, it is the process used to select the most appropriate structures and processes for the organization, given its environment, size, programs, and strategies. Once initial planning has been completed, an organizational structure and related processes are needed to carry out the strategies, goals, objectives, and programs that have been selected. This involves seeking the best possible answers to the following questions:

- What activities need to be performed to implement the programs that have been selected as part of the planning process?
- How can the necessary activities be divided so that individuals or groups can be assigned responsibility for performing them?
- Once activities have been grouped into specific jobs, what kind of authority and responsibility should be assigned to each position?
- How should the different programs and units of the agency be organized with reference to each other?
- How and by whom should decisions be made?
- How specialized should roles and jobs be?
- Who should control the nature and quality of the work being performed?
- How can communication and coordination among members of the organization be facilitated?
- How can coordination and communication with the external social environment be facilitated?

The answers to these questions bring with them the ability to describe and chart interlocking roles that in turn form a structure and processes for communication, coordination, and decision making. The result of the entire process is the creation of an organization, or a social unit that has been purposefully designed to meet a set of goals through a regular series of planned and coordinated activities.

The nature of the design that is finally chosen varies tremendously, based on the goals, needs, size, environment, technology, age, and resources of the organization, as well as on the theoretical orientations of the people engaged in the design process, as discussed in Chapter 4.

CRITERIA FOR THE DESIGN OF AN ORGANIZATION

The human service professional's philosophical approach toward organization design will affect every decision that he or she makes as a structure is developed. Regardless of theoretical orientation, however, each designer must decide how to identify key processes and individual roles within the organization, how to divide activities among groups or departments, and how to coordinate efforts both within the organization and at interfaces with the environment.

In many human service organizations, organization redesign is approached simply as restructuring: moving around boxes on the organizational chart without thoughtful consideration of strategy, technology parameters and options, and effects on processes such as decision making. This restructuring is typically done by the agency's top managers, occasionally with consultant help and more rarely with the input of other managers. According to Mohr (1989), traditional approaches to organization redesign rarely deliver promised improvements because they:

- are not based on a detailed operational analysis of actual, current work practices,

- have not meaningfully involved those persons closest to the operational process (i.e., workers and line managers),
- focus on solving only today's—or even yesterday's—problems rather than creating an organization capable of flexibly responding to tomorrow's challenges,
- do not have the necessary commitment and support of those at lower levels, which are required for successful implementation,
- are based on the false assumption that modifying only authority/reporting relationships will be sufficient for obtaining intended results,
- use analytic perspectives that make the "designers" prisoners of their own histories, cultures, and traditions, and
- stem from a constraint orientation emphasizing all that cannot be changed, rather than from an inventive/creative orientation central to effective organizational change. (p. 208)

These problems have been addressed in current models of organization redesign that use an explicit analysis and design process and that have high involvement of workers from all levels of the hierarchy. Any design or redesign process needs top-level sanction and support, known as sponsorship, and a champion responsible for making things happen on a daily basis. Often two groups are set up to do the design (more typically, a redesign of an existing organization). A steering committee, consisting of representatives of key stakeholder groups including executive and middle management, supervisors and line staff from different programs, support staff, and representatives from employee organizations, provides overall guidance and policy direction for the effort. A design team, similarly constituted with a representative group, focusing more on the lower levels of the organization, will do the detailed analysis and make recommendations for a new design to the steering committee. Ultimately, final decisions are usually made by the organization's executive management and governing board, although if the process is well done, recommendations should be mostly approved as submitted.

The following design process (based on Taylor & Felten, 1993) can be used by the steering committee and the design team, with the bulk of the day-to-day tasks performed by the design team. Steps 1 and 2 would already have been accomplished during the strategic planning process.

1. Review the organization's purpose and strategic directions. Consult the agency's strategic plan for answers to such questions as: What needs and opportunities need to be addressed? What are the overall strategies and goals? What specific objectives need to be accomplished?
2. Determine the best service delivery technologies.
3. Allocate staff roles and determine the most appropriate decision-making and communication processes.
4. Determine the most appropriate organizational structure.
5. Ensure that the entire system, including service delivery programs, structure, staff roles, and organizational processes are all aligned, or "fit" together.

In the 1990s, a specific form of redesign, *reengineering*, or *business process reengineering*, reached fad status in the business and government sectors in the United States, in spite of evidence that many such efforts fail (Hammer & Champy, 1993).

Reengineering has been defined as "a fundamental rethinking and radical redesign of business processes to achieve dramatic improvements in critical contemporary measures of performance such as cost, quality service, and speed" (Hammer & Champy, 1993, p. 32).

Reengineering typically involves a thorough examination of the whole organization, focusing on structures and processes. The current organization is assessed, and a new, ideal organization is proposed that eliminates all processes that do not add value for customers. Through the 1990s it came to be seen as a euphemism for downsizing, but reengineering experts asserted that they are not equivalent processes, although a common result of reengineering is the elimination of management layers and positions. Some of the concerns related to reengineering were discussed in Chapter 4. Because it typically requires the use of an outside consultant who can suggest a complete process, we will provide only a brief outline here.

The reengineering process typically begins with the organization developing a vision of a preferred future, identifying change opportunities, forming reengineering teams, and focusing resources. At the next stage, the current processes are assessed, often known as defining the current business model: the way the process identified for reengineering is done at present. After choosing processes that seem to be good opportunities for reengineering, benchmarking and identifying best practices can locate organizations whose practices can be used as standards and goals. Sometimes the organization conducts a gap analysis to show the differences between the current state and the ideal state (sometimes known as the future business model), which is based on benchmarks and the organization's vision. Next, reengineering teams solicit input from customers and employees and redesign existing processes by eliminating steps that do not add value to the product or service. This stage usually includes getting rid of the "silo mentality" of many organizations in which staff from different functions or units do not communicate or work well together. Often management positions are seen as not adding value but rather slowing things down, and positions can be eliminated. This is where reengineering got its reputation as a euphemism for downsizing. When positions are eliminated, an organization should do everything possible to retain employees in still-needed positions. After viable proposals for change are approved, the organization needs to transition to the new designs and systems. Monitoring continues to see whether changes are having the intended effects and to identify other change opportunities. Even if an agency does not conduct a formal reengineering process, some of its techniques may be used.

Although the specifics of a design cannot be predetermined, the following list outlines design criteria to suggest how an effective organization should operate (e.g., Daft, 2010; Kettner, 2002; O'Looney, 1996).

1. Ensure that the design is in alignment with the strategic plan. Structures and processes should facilitate implementation of strategies, programs, and action plans.
2. Organize around outcomes, not tasks. Have one person perform as many steps in a process as possible, or have this done by a team whose members work closely together.

3. Keep in mind the client's perspective. How will the client experience the organization? Clients should have as simple an experience as possible. If a client needs multiple services within the agency, have a case manager who can coordinate the work of different staff who will be involved and be certain that the client does not fall between the cracks.

4. Ensure clarity of individual roles and reporting relationships. It is important that individuals have a clear idea of expectations and know to whom they are accountable. This does not mean that a bureaucratic structure must be followed. Even in a strongly decentralized decision-making structure such as Likert's System 4, participants do know what role they can expect to play, what kind of decision-making power they have, and how subsystems interact within the organization.

5. Maximize the ability of staff to act autonomously, within broad policy guidelines. If agency staff members are trained professionals, they will not normally need close supervision and should be able to operate with a minimum amount of bureaucratic oversight.

6. Minimize the number of layers in the hierarchy and the number of support staff so that several managers will not need to get involved in decisions that line staff can make. Keep the structure as simple as possible.

7. Ensure that the various functions coordinate and communicate well with each other and outside agencies. The effective human service organization needs to emphasize coordination, both within the agency and between the agency and its environment. All employees need ready access to the information that is necessary for them to do their jobs.

8. Build a structure that allows for responsiveness to the need for change. Human service agencies need to combine some degree of clarity of structure, communication, and decision making with the kind of flexibility that can bring needed adaptations to changing client needs. One key to dealing with this issue is the management philosophy leaders use. Participative styles such as System 4 enable an organization to respond quickly to new needs and situations.

9. Create a culture of teamwork, trust, and support. In such a climate, communication can be open and effective, and workers will be able to do their work in a state of high morale.

Design criteria such as those just discussed will ultimately result in organizational structures of units, roles, and responsibilities as well as decision-making and communication processes. The final sections of this chapter will review common models that organization designers can consider and adapt.

ORGANIZATIONAL STRUCTURES

Organizational structures can range from a simple structure in a very small agency in which one supervisor can oversee all activities to complex forms such as a matrix in which workers may have more than one supervisor. The most common structures are the functional and divisional forms.

FUNCTIONAL STRUCTURES

Functional structures are very common, particularly in bureaucratic agencies. *Functional departmentation* involves grouping together all personnel who share common functions or procedures, such as personnel, finance, information systems, administrative support, and so forth. Service delivery units may also be structured by function. For example, a welfare-to-work program might have units for skills training, child care, and job placement. Sometimes divisions are made based on funding requirements that originate in the laws or regulations that created the programs.

This type of departmentation is usually considered efficient because functions are routinized and duplication of effort is avoided. A weakness of the functional form might be that individuals tend to be so aware of their own departments that they lose sight of the common purpose of the organization as a whole. Power and authority can become overly centralized in the hands of the few top managers who are able to see the "big picture." A major disadvantage of the functional model is that it often treats a client in a fragmented way: client needs may span multiple programs, requiring a transfer of a client to a new worker at each stage in the service delivery process.

DIVISIONAL STRUCTURES

The problem of fragmentation can be mitigated to some extent by a divisional structure. In this model, the agency is organized by program, process, client, or geographic area (Kettner, 2002). *Program departmentation* involves grouping services based on a particular population or problem, such as teen pregnancy or drug counseling. This is appropriate when services require staff with specialized knowledge or skill. *Process departmentation* can be used when different skills are needed at different points in service delivery. For example, a child protective services division may have units for court intervention, permanency planning, and adoptions. *Customer or client departmentation* involves all the workers dealing with a specific category or segment of the public being grouped together, such as children and adult units in a psychiatric hospital. *Geographic departmentation* involves decentralizing operations of a large agency so that smaller organizations are duplicated in each of several geographic areas. Its strength is that individual workers can closely identify with the outcome of their work in terms of the creation of goods or services rather than becoming involved strictly in means or methods. When agencies divide by geographic location, using small, community-based agencies rather than centralized offices, they tend to increase the active participation of both service deliverers and consumers. Effective coordination and sharing of resources among such outreach branches are important because duplication of effort is as uneconomical in the human service agency as it is in the production-oriented firm. For small organizations, however, the duplication of effort involved in re-creating functions across divisional lines can be costly.

An example of functional and divisional structures in local government is a redesign through a merger of a department of social services and a department of health services. Social Services had divisions organized by functions, including Income Maintenance, Employment and Training Services, and Child Protective Services. Health Services included Mental Health, Drug and Alcohol Services, and Community Health. Because many clients received services from more than one program, it was decided to move to a divisional structure based on geography. In the new model, there are regional managers in all sections of the county who each have responsibility for all programs in the region. Every client has a case manager who facilitates the client's receiving services from other professionals. A welfare client needing job development, income maintenance, child protective services, and substance abuse treatment, for example, would be treated in a comprehensive manner so that she or he would not need to drive to multiple locations to meet with different workers for each need.

MATRIX STRUCTURES

A more complex structure can be seen in the matrix, which blends functional and divisional forms. Organizations using this structure are functionally divided but use teams or task forces for projects that require the work of several specialists. Each project has its own manager, and personnel receive temporary assignments to work with special projects. The strength of this structure is that it uses the positive aspects of both of the other types of departmentation. It tends to be complex and require strong human relations skills on the part of managers who must share authority with others, but it allows for rapid reorganization in response to immediate needs for change.

LINKING AND COORDINATING MECHANISMS

All but the smallest human service organizations will have several functions that, because of their unique needs, are differentiated from each other. In social service settings, agencies are often divided between counseling services and income maintenance services, and differing organizational structures might be appropriate for each. Similarly, counseling departments housed within traditional academic institutions might develop methods of coordinating efforts that previously had been seen to have little in common. Functions need to be integrated so that the organization as a whole can function well.

The simplest integrating mechanisms are bureaucratic: a hierarchical command and communication system (direct supervision) and the use of rules, regulations, plans, and schedules (Gortner et al., 1997, p. 97). Other formal integrating mechanisms include staff meetings, task forces, and memos. A valuable integrating mechanism is an integrator role, which may be formal, such as a liaison position, or informal, in which an individual can serve as an internal boundary spanner, communicating with different groups in the organization to ensure that they work well together. Project organizations have multifunctional teams as in a matrix but are more temporary (for example, a project team formed to start an agency facility in a new community). Team-based organizations (such as multidisciplinary mental health teams) are more permanent than project organizations. The matrix is the most complex and formal way to ensure high levels of integration.

Managers also need to ensure that the organization has mechanisms for coordinating with its environment. The concepts of networking and linkage are especially useful for the coordination function. Networking involves a recognition that human services are part of a helping network that includes mental health facilities, educational institutions, rehabilitation settings, and a wide variety of specialized agencies. In the interests of efficient use of resources as well as effective delivery of services, the efforts of these services should be coordinated.

Networking combines the creativity and flexibility of individual organizations with a broader utilization of resources involving other organizations. As a coordinating technique, networking is appropriate both for coalitions of small, independent agencies and for subdivisions of large, complex service organizations.

Closely related to the concept of networking is the idea of linkage. Effective coordination requires that consumers, as well as providers, of services recognize the connections among departments and among separate agencies. Organizing for linkage involves developing procedures that overcome fragmentation in service delivery so that individual clients do not become lost in a tangle of agencies and programs. Linkage efforts can include special coordinating departments, interface task forces among agencies, or client advocates.

Structural arrangements are represented visually using organizational charts, which we will now review. They do not tell the whole story, however. They do not show how decisions get made or how different roles and units communicate with each other.

ORGANIZATIONAL CHARTS

Most organizations use organizational charts to clarify the chain of command, to show differentiation across functions or divisions, and to illustrate the expected flow of communication. Of course, an organizational chart alone does not explain functions in great detail but instead provides an overview showing how each part of the organization is expected to interact with the others and with the entity as a whole. The Grandview organizational chart provides an example for analysis.

5.1	GRANDVIEW COMMUNITY CENTER'S ORGANIZATIONAL CHART

Grandview Community Center's organizational chart points up the agency's vision at one point in time. The primary focus of the agency is clearly on functions, with counseling, in-home services, community development, and day care providing the primary structural components. The geographical components, Grandview North, South, East, and West, are subsumed under the functions. Notice, too, that at this point in the center's development, the administrative structure is relatively simple.

As the agency grows over time, it is likely that the administrative structure will become more complex. It is also possible that the organization might change from a functional emphasis to a divisional structure. Suppose each of the neighborhood centers were to grow. Suppose, too, that the centers, which were created to be more accessible and responsive to their own neighborhoods, were to go in slightly different

(continued)

5.1   GRANDVIEW COMMUNITY CENTER'S ORGANIZATIONAL CHART (*CONT'D*)

directions in terms of the kinds of services provided. In that case, the organizational chart might change, showing the geographical centers as the primary structural components with the appropriate functions subsumed under these divisions.

These conjectures suggest that organizational charts must be subject to regular review as the organization's context and values change over time.

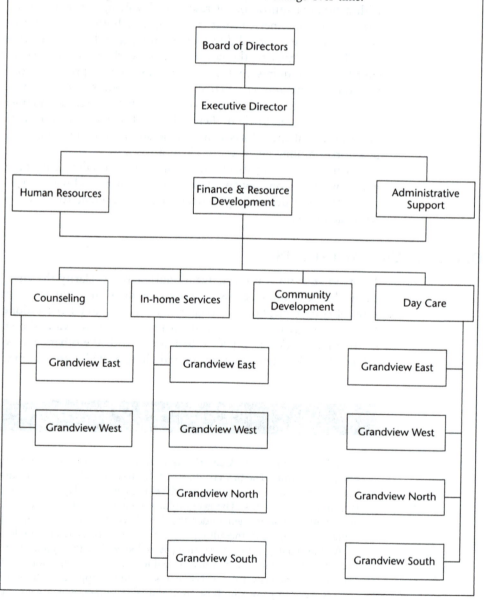

In general, as small, traditionally structured agencies grow, changes tend to involve the addition both of more vertical levels and of more horizontal specializations. Vertically, growth would bring the placement of directors in charge of smaller programs, with supervisory levels added between directors and staff members. Horizontally, new programs would be added as funds become available, and specialties such as training director and personnel director might be added.

NON-HIERARCHICAL ORGANIZATIONS

Organizational charts, even for the smallest of agencies, tend to show a hierarchy of power and authority, with the board of directors at the top and the executive director and other administrators next, followed by departmental or program supervisors. Consider, however, the feminist and other empowerment-oriented organizations that were discussed in Chapter 4. The central tenets of the organizational theories underlying these entities involved a rejection of hierarchy, not only among managers and employees but also among clients. In fact, adherents of these theories would say that traditional human service organizations leave out clients or consumers altogether in their organizational charts and would, in a more accurate view, place clients and consumers at the bottom of the hierarchy.

These agencies, being purposefully nonhierarchical, would have an altogether different type of chart, which would be horizontal rather than vertical. But horizontal charts are not necessarily appropriate only for very small organizations. Consider the ideas that Sadove, chair chief of Saks, Inc., expressed in a 2010 interview carried out by Bryant (May, 2010, p. BU2):

> I ... found so many examples where people were working in silos. To me it was just obvious that if people worked together you would get a better result than if you were working independently. The first 10 years of my career I found that getting people to think differently, and moving from what I call a vertical organization to a horizontal organization, was transformational.

In a very large organization, it would be unlikely to have a purely horizontal organizational chart. Clearly, there would be some levels of authority, but with very of these levels and more equality across departments. In small human service programs, however, it is still possible to avoid differentiations based on power and authority and to illustrate equality by flat, or even circular, charts.

KEY ORGANIZATIONAL PROCESSES: DECISION MAKING, COMMUNICATIONS, AND ORGANIZATIONAL CULTURE

An organizational chart cannot show how decisions are made or how communications occur. These factors deserve at least as much attention as do structural considerations, which often dominate discussions of "reorganization."

Decision-making processes at the broadest level can be grounded in management theories discussed earlier. In a highly centralized organization, most decisions will be made at the top, as proposed in scientific management or as reflected in

McGregor's Theory X or Likert's System 1. In decentralized, professional organizations, human resources models such as Theory Y and System 4 are more appropriate. In such a system, a worker has a large amount of autonomy to make decisions in her or his area of responsibility, whether it be regarding services to clients or management of a program. Of course, contingency theory suggests that there is no one best way, but individual supervisors and their teams should discuss explicitly which decisions should be made by which roles in the organization. Perhaps the most commonly cited problem in organizations is "poor communication." Because communication is so fundamental, communication processes and mechanisms in organizations, paradoxically, are often neglected. We will review here some communication mechanisms that should receive specific attention when designing an organization. These range from the grapevine and rumors at the informal level to communication roles to, at the formal level, newsletters and memos.

The grapevine and rumors should be recognized, both because some studies have shown that the grapevine is up to 75 percent accurate (Bowditch, Buono, & Stewart, 2008, p. 131) and because rumors often begin because accurate and timely information has not been forthcoming from reliable formal sources. This situation points to the importance of effectively using formal mechanisms such as newsletters, videos, websites, memos, and meetings to keep employees informed. The use of rituals and ceremonies, which will be discussed later in the context of organizational culture, are powerful ways for leaders to communicate using symbolism as well as facts.

An untapped resource for communication is the use of staff in communication roles. Liaisons were mentioned briefly earlier as integrating functions in the organization. Their main responsibility is to serve as links between different groups and coordinate their joint work. Liaisons need to have the same characteristics as gatekeepers and also be able to generate respect and trust from the different groups with which they are working. The linking pin role Likert identified is an example of a formal liaison: an individual who has membership in two or more groups and serves as a communication link between them. Boundary spanners are liaisons who interact with the environment. They may be upper-level managers who meet with external groups as part of their jobs, intake workers or others who interact with other agencies as part of their job, or employees who serve as members of external task forces or coalitions. Liaisons and boundary spanners are key roles, and individuals who can fill them should be identified and sanctioned by the organization.

Informal communication roles such as gatekeepers and opinion leaders should also be acknowledged when assessing organizational communication patterns. Gatekeepers are individuals who control the flow of information as part of their job (Bowditch, Buono, & Stuart, 2008, p. 133). They are often secretaries or administrative assistants who have access to large amounts of information and can decide what information to pass on to whom. An effective gatekeeper needs to be aware of managers' information needs, know when information is needed, and assess the quality of information being shared. Opinion leaders are able to informally influence other members of the organization. They are usually influential only in specified areas. Managers can share information with opinion leaders to get initial feedback and reactions before making formal announcements and can attempt to influence opinion leaders to share particular information or preferences with others in the organization.

Decision making and communication processes are key aspects of organization design. At a broader level, additional aspects of organizational culture are relevant to the design process because they help shape how programs and subsystems in the organization operate. Organizational culture can be seen as

> the *shared pattern* of beliefs, assumptions, and expectations held by organizational members, and their characteristic way of perceiving the organization's artifacts and environment, and its norms, roles, and values as they exist outside the individual. (Bowditch, Buono, & Stuart, 2008, p. 320, italics in original)

These are reflected in several "interpretive frameworks" described by Bowditch, Buono, & Stewart (2008, pp. 326–328). First, organizational values provide guidelines for how people should behave in the organization. Next, managerial culture is reflected in dominant leadership styles and management philosophies, such as authoritarian or participative approaches. Organizational heroes "represent what the company stands for and reinforce the values of the culture by underscoring that success is attainable, acting as a role model for others." Organizational myths and stories and organizational taboos, rites, and rituals such as awards ceremonies are very useful for passing on belief systems and for shaping beliefs and values. Finally, cultural symbols reflected in the organization's physical layout, furniture, logos, and elsewhere provide clues as to what is rewarded and who has the most power. Organizational leaders have a particular responsibility in creating a culture that is consistent with the agency's strategic plan and facilitates accomplishment of goals and effective agency functioning.

SUMMARY

We began this discussion by noting the importance of design in creating an effective organization. Organization design can be a noun or a verb. As a verb, staff can engage in a process to determine how the parts of an organization should be organized and operate together. An organization should be designed, or, more commonly, redesigned, based on contingencies such as the nature of the clients and services, the environment, and the organization's size. A process that involves staff will be more likely to result in a design that will both respond effectively to client needs and provide a high quality of working life for staff.

The result of this process is organization design as a noun: a description of the structures and processes such as decision making, communication, and organizational culture in use. In recent years, the more common functional structures are often being replaced with divisional structures oriented to client or geographic considerations. Of course, a structure means very little until people are inserted into it. We will now look at the various human resources functions necessary for an agency to hire, train, evaluate, and develop its staff.

| COMPETENCY-BUILDING ACTIVITY 5.1 | DESIGNING THE PROGRAM |

In previous competency building activities, you began the process of creating your own hypothetical human service program. Now, you should be ready to decide how to organize your program by addressing the following questions:

1. How should the organization's work be departmentalized?

2. How should work be divided among departments and individuals? Draw an organizational chart that you could use to describe the agency's design.

3. How would you make sure that the work of various individuals and groups was effectively coordinated?

| CASE ACTIVITY 5.1 | THE UMBRELLA ORGANIZATION |

The roots of the Atlantis Community Mental Health Center (ACMHC) were in its inpatient, outpatient, and emergency services. Although, in keeping with the federal mandate, consultation and education services had always been included, emphasis had never been placed on preventive, community-based interventions until a recent major upheaval.

In response to an evaluation report showing that many groups within its highly diverse geographic area were not being reached through traditional services, the board and administrative staff of the ACMHC decided to add several new service components. The new programs were to include an outreach program for families, a drug and alcoholism program, a crisis intervention team, and several storefront outposts that would encourage using the service by members of the minority community.

The ACMHC's funding sources were uniformly in favor of this approach but would provide funding only if a major organizational change were made. The funding sources recognized that many of the proposed services were already being offered on a smaller scale by tiny, community-based agencies scattered throughout the area. Each of these small agencies had worked independently for years, often with unknowing duplication of the services of other organizations. This new thrust of the ACMHC was recognized as a possible vehicle for a more efficient approach to human services than had been possible before. It was suggested that the human service network of Atlantis develop more effective linkages, with each agency maintaining a degree of autonomy but with the organizations joining for the sharing of resources. The mental health center would act as the umbrella organization, offering community outreach services through existing local agencies rather than duplicating these services with the development of new programs.

Because of the obvious financial benefits to be gained through this cooperative endeavor, the mental health center and a number of community agencies made the commitment to developing a new organizational structure. A subcommittee, including a number of agency and center service deliverers, as well as funders and community members, was charged with the responsibility of drafting a suggested structure, to which the various member agencies could respond. Of course, representatives of differing organizations brought divergent viewpoints to the meeting.

Hilary Johnson, the ACMHC's program officer, represented a major source of funding for the organization. Her primary concern was that services be effectively delivered at Atlantis without needless duplication of effort and without the usual endless competition among agencies for limited funds. She knew that all of the agencies involved provided greatly needed services, but she also knew that these services could be provided more efficiently through greater coordination. She thought it would be possible to centralize the work of these agencies to accomplish common goals and to divide resources equitably among programs.

Caroline Brown, Juan Casel, and Evelyn Mays were all staff members of small, community-based agencies. Each of them brought to the meeting a high degree of concern for maintaining the nature of his or her own agency. They knew that their agencies' strengths lay in their responsiveness to local needs and in the fact that their programs had been developed by community members. They had always resisted pressures to expand, recognizing that the smaller agency can sometimes maintain a degree of responsiveness and flexibility that a large organization cannot duplicate. They knew that fiscal realities meant they had to become part of a larger entity, but they also realized that there would be dangers involved in losing their own identities. They could not duplicate the center's lack of accessibility; they understood that if that happened, they would go under.

Similarly, Nick Chan and Sally Allen, representing local citizens' groups, recognized that maintaining accessibility would be important. They knew that many of their neighbors resisted using the services of the center but felt more comfortable in their dealings with the smaller agencies in their immediate neighborhoods. They knew that the creative and open atmosphere of the small agencies needed to be maintained. Chan and Allen also realized, however, that the service consumers would be the losers if more efficient use of funds did not begin to take place.

Nelson Richards, director of the ACMHC, was most interested in the degree of centralization that could be accomplished. Although he would have preferred unilateral expansion of services on the part of the center, he recognized that some major benefits could be gained from using the center as an umbrella organization. He could see great possibilities for the sharing of resources. For instance, each agency could become part of the management information system so that the flow of clients from agency to agency would be enhanced. Common budgeting could mean a significant increase in the funding available for the center as a whole. Such activities as staff training, personnel, and purchasing could be centralized, so each agency would gain greatly in efficiency. Planning could be broadly based, and purchases could be made in money-saving quantities. Looking at it from a more humanistic standpoint, services to consumers would be improved, and no client would ever again be able to "fall between the cracks" because of lack of information or lack of comprehensiveness.

Melvin Hammond was also in favor of a high degree of centralization but for a different reason. As a human service consultant called in by the state funding agency, he knew that the best resource utilization would involve having one central agency to act as fiscal agent for funds. He recognized, however, that the direction this agency would take would depend to a great extent on the kind of organizational structure they developed. One possibility would be to departmentalize the new, enlarged organization by type of service, with all direct service providers in one department, all outreach specialists in another, and all community organizers in still another. A different alternative would be to divide the organization according to population served, with all drug abuse program personnel working in one department, all family service professionals in another, and so on. To Hammond, the important aspect of the organization was that workers should identify themselves with Atlantis rather than with their former agencies.

Each of these individuals had organizational priorities that differed. Yet the committee would need to decide on an organizational structure that would please everyone, at least to a degree, and that would work.

1. What are the major organizational issues involved here?
2. What do you see as the primary alternatives for the organizational structure? What would be the implications of varying approaches to departmentalization?
3. If you were asked to give input to the committee, what organizational structure would you suggest? Why?
4. What processes would you suggest to ensure effective coordination, decision making, and communication among the various programs?

REFERENCES

Bowditch, J., Buono, A. , & Stewart, M. (2008). *A primer on organizational behavior* (7th ed.). Hoboken, NJ: John Wiley & Sons.

Bryant, A. (2010, May 30). For the chief of Saks, it's culture that drives results. *New York Times*, p. BU2.

Burton, R. M., DeSanctis, G., & Obel, B. (2006). *Organizational design: A step-by-step approach*. New York: Cambridge University Press.

Daft, R. (2010. *Organization theory and design* (10th ed.). Cincinnati, OH: South-Western Cengage Learning.

Gibelman, M. (2000). Structural and fiscal characteristics of social service agencies, in R. Patti (Ed.), *The handbook of social welfare management* (pp. 113–131). Thousand Oaks, CA: Sage Publications.

Gortner, H., Mahler, J., & Nicholson, J. (1997). *Organization theory: A public perspective* (2nd ed.). Fort Worth, TX: Harcourt Brace College Publishers.

Hammer, M., & Champy, J. (1993). *Reengineering the corporation*. New York: HarperBusiness.

Kettner, P. (2002). *Human service organizations*. Boston: Allyn and Bacon.

Mohr, B. (1989). High-performing organizations from an open sociotechnical systems perspective. In W. Sikes, A. Drexler, & J. Gant (Eds.), *The emerging practice of organization development* (pp. 199–211). Alexandria, VA: NTL Institute.

O'Looney, J. (1996). *Redesigning the work of human services*. Westport, CT: Quorum.

Robey, D., & Sales, C. (1994). *Designing organizations* (4th ed.). Homewood, IL: Irwin.

Senge, P. (2006). *The fifth discipline: The art and practice of the learning organization* (2nd ed.). New York: Doubleday Currency.

Taylor, J., & Felten, D. (1993). *Performance by design*. Upper Saddle River, NJ: Prentice Hall.

USEFUL WEB RESOURCES

Association for Community Organization and Social Administration. http://acosa.org/.

How to Develop an Organizational Chart. http://www.ehow.com/how_6080763_develop-organizational-chart.html.

National Council of Nonprofits. http://www.councilofnonprofits.org/.

National Network for Social Work Managers. http://www.socialworkmanager.org.

U.S. Small Business Administration. http://www.sba.gov/.

Developing and Managing Human Resources

Human service agencies are labor-intensive organizations. After the environment has been assessed, strategies developed, programs designed, and structure chosen, the organization is brought to life by the team of people who are charged with bringing its goals to fruition. Human resource development plays an important role in ensuring that employees feel that they have a stake in the organization's success and that the organization, in turn, values their contributions.

> When you ask people what it is like being part of a great team, what is most striking is the meaningfulness of the experience. People talk about being part of something larger than themselves, of being connected, of being generative. It becomes quite clear that, for many, their experiences as part of truly great teams stand out as singular periods of life lived to the fullest. (Senge, 2006, p. 13)

Effective human resource development provides a context for a broad vision, encompassing the needs of the organization as a whole. It also uses a long-term perspective in planning, attempting to deal with both immediate needs and future requirements. Developing and managing human resources focuses on addressing the goals and needs of the organization as a whole, but it must also provide for the fair and just treatment of employees. The Society for Human Resource Management includes in its code of ethics a set of guidelines intended to "create and sustain an environment that encourages all individuals and the organization to reach their fullest potential in a positive and productive manner" (Society for Human Resource Management, 2005). These guidelines include the following:

1. Respect the uniqueness and intrinsic worth of every individual.
2. Treat people with dignity, respect, and compassion to foster a trusting work environment free of harassment, intimidation, and unlawful discrimination.
3. Ensure that everyone has the opportunity to develop their skills and new competencies.
4. Assure an environment of inclusiveness and a commitment to diversity in the organizations we serve.
5. Develop, administer, and advocate policies and procedures that foster fair, consistent, and equitable treatment for all.
6. Regardless of personal interests, support decisions made by our organizations that are both ethical and legal.
7. Act in a responsible manner and practice sound management in the country(ies) in which the organizations we serve operate.

The idea that the needs of the organization and the needs of its employees can be complementary fits well into the culture of a human service agency.

In order to meet their human resource needs, human service managers must deal effectively with a number of related issues, including the following:

- Designing jobs that will enable program objectives to be accomplished and workers to use all of their training knowledge, skills, and creativity.
- Developing effective and efficient methods for hiring, appraising, and rewarding agency employees.
- Providing training and development to enhance the staff's effectiveness.
- Making serious efforts to increase the inclusiveness and diversity of the workforce.

- Maintaining a commitment to equal employment opportunity, even in the face of cutbacks.
- Expanding human resources by encouraging the participation of volunteers.
- Protecting valuable human resources by taking steps to prevent burnout and improve the quality of working life.

Each of these steps plays an important part in the effective development of human resources.

JOB DESIGN

Program design, which was discussed in Chapter 3, results in a clearly articulated set of activities to be performed by staff in order to accomplish organizational objectives. The next step is to design the specific jobs that fit into the program design. Two considerations are implicit here: (1) the job needs to allow for the accomplishment of program objectives and satisfy the expectations of key stakeholders, including clients, and (2) the job should have built into it elements that will provide a high-quality working life for the employee.

The first consideration is addressed initially through a program design with clear expectations for the provision of particular services. This should result in a general set of staff positions needed to implement the program. Depending on the size and complexity of the organization, this set of positions might include jobs in management, supervision, service provision, and support. The specific characteristics of each position can be listed once a careful analysis has been completed. At that point, the job analysis describes the key aspects of the job and differentiates it from other positions. Once this process has been completed, stakeholders will have a clear picture of the work activities, job performance standards, context, and competencies that are inherent in the job.

A key component of the job analysis is the creation of task statements that are clearly related to the expectations of a position. Someone who reads these task statements should come away with a good sense of how the job relates to program objectives. This is most likely to happen if managers and staff members have collaborated in the development process.

The second aspect of job design is concerned with the employee's quality of working life. It is widely recognized now that the quality of work life means more than the individual's job. It also relates to the degree to which the organization supports the employee's ability to balance his or her work and personal life. According to the Council of Economic Advisers (March, 2010), this balance is enhanced when workers have flexibility, which can involve control over when they work, where they work, and how many hours they work. In situations where increased flexibility is possible, workers can be evaluated based not on their work schedules but on the results they achieve.

> Perhaps the ultimate form of workplace flexibility is the evaluation of employees based on what they produce rather than the number of hours they work. This management practice, called "results-only work environment" (or ROWE), allows for flexibility along multiple dimensions because it permits workers to choose when, where, and for how long they work, as long as they are sufficiently productive. (Council of Economic Advisers, March, 2010, p. 12)

Within the organization as a whole, a positive quality of work life can be seen when employees find their work stimulating, believe that their efforts are meaningful, and see the end results of their endeavors. The quality of the work environment is also related to the degree to which employees are committed to the organization's goals while also being empowered to make decisions about how they will carry out their day-to-day activities.

In the human service context, job design can make the difference between staff members who feel powerless and disconnected from the outcomes of their work and staff members who feel that they are doing something meaningful and exhilarating. Suppose, for example, that a designer in a child protective service bureau could decide between two options: (a) to require that workers hand off a case when it moves from one stage to another (for example, intake to court intervention) or (b) to charge one worker with the responsibility for following a case from intake to resolution. Although the "hand-off" option allows staff members to gain expertise in one specialization, the casework approach makes it more likely that workers will be able to develop relationships with clients and see the positive effects of their interventions. In general, an enriched and motivating job for a human services worker would allow that employee to perform a variety of tasks, work with the client holistically, see that the work is important to the client and society, have the freedom to make professional decisions without excessive bureaucratic control, and see the results of work with the client.

HIRING PRACTICES

Hiring consists of recruitment and selection. When recruitment is effective, the person or team involved in hiring has a reasonable number of qualified applicants to consider. The selection process can then focus on assessing the job applicants and making good hiring decisions.

RECRUITMENT

The first step of recruitment should already be done: defining the job through the job description, which should include necessary knowledge, skills, and aptitudes. These are typically listed using the job title, classification, and description of duties, with minimum requirements in terms of educational degrees, any licensing or certification, and years of related job experience included. Work hours, location, and any particular requirements (such as a driver's license and availability of a personal car to use for field visits) should also be clearly noted. There must be a clearly demonstrated connection between each requirement and the work to be performed. The salary range, employment benefits, and the agency's equal employment and diversity values and policy should be included as well. The starting date, application procedures, and closing date for applications should be listed.

INTERVIEWING AND SELECTION

In the spirit of team management and to bring a wide range of screening and assessment expertise to the hiring process, others beyond the supervisor of the position should be involved. For example, a committee may be used to act in an advisory capacity or play a role in screening or selection. Staff can be involved in all phases of the process, from developing criteria to hiring.

Selection processes work most effectively when information about job openings is widely disseminated. Wide dissemination helps ensure fairness for potential applicants, but it also assists the agency by expanding the pool of available individuals. In addition to newspapers, employment agencies, employee referrals, recruiting firms, professional journals, and association newsletters, also beneficial are university departments and placement centers, local community organizations, and special interest newspapers and newsletters. Tapping into these resources can enhance the diversity of the applicant pool by reaching people who might not be contacted by some traditional sources. Announcements for jobs tell the community your agency is hiring and is particularly interested in hiring its members. This approach may demonstrate an interest in becoming more inclusive of segments of the community historically underrepresented in particular jobs or fields.

Once the group of applicants has been narrowed down to the finalists, interviews can be conducted. The screening process can ensure that potential staff members are drawn from a pool of people who hold appropriate qualifications in terms of education, licensure, and experience. It is important, however, to assess the more subtle characteristics and attitudes that determine whether the individual and the organization are a good fit. Not only for direct service providers but also for other members of a human service organization, the answers to the following questions are important:

- How likely is it that this individual will treat clients and consumers with unflinching respect?
- Is the individual's philosophy and theory of helping congruent with the agency's general approach?
- Does the individual demonstrate not just an acceptance of but also a true appreciation for multiculturalism and diversity?
- Does the individual bring a spirit of creativity and flexibility to the problem-solving process?
- Is the individual enthusiastic about this particular organization's mission and goals?
- Has the individual demonstrated a facility for acting as part of a truly collaborative team?

A résumé alone is unlikely to provide the answers to these questions. Reference letters do help, but there is no substitute for an in-depth interview.

Normally, an interview involves a structured set of job-related questions asked in the same way to all candidates. Questions are open-ended and followed by probes as needed. They enable applicants to describe how they have performed relevant duties or handled situations in the past and to explain how they would do so in a future work situation. Role-plays, done in the same way for all candidates, are often used to see how a candidate might respond to a case or a management team problem.

Armstrong and Mitchell (2008) recommend the use of behavioral interviews, which ask job applicants to give specific examples of past performance. The interviewer can focus questions on the behaviors that are most relevant to the organization's priorities. Among the kinds of questions that might be included in a behavioral interview are the following:

- Can you think of a time when you found that coworkers were treating clients less respectfully than you might have liked? How did you handle it?
- Talk about a time when you found it difficult to communicate with a client whose culture was very different from your own. How did you go about reaching across these differences to build a good connection?
- Give an example of a work-related problem that you found particularly difficult? How did you go about reaching a resolution?
- Talk about an experience when you had a particularly good relationship among the members of a team of work. What do you think it was that made this team function so effectively? How would you try to duplicate that experience?

These kinds of questions might meet the general needs of human service organizations, but the behavioral interview can also focus more narrowly on the precise needs of the job being filled.

After all interviews have been completed, the team must systematically assess all relevant information about the candidates, from the résumés and screening forms to interview notes and feedback from all staff who met all the candidates. Hiring decisions should be made quickly. This process is another aspect of public relations. Good candidates can be lost because of delays in the decision-making process. The person accepted should receive a letter of confirmation with relevant details. After the offer is accepted, applicants who are passed over deserve the courtesy of being notified and thanked for their interest.

ORIENTATION

Orienting a new employee begins with some very concrete and practical actions. Managers make sure that everything is ready for the person to begin working on the first day, from a clean and well-stocked office to all relevant paperwork ready to be filled out. On the employee's first day, they try to make sure that she or he feels welcomed into the organization. They reintroduce the new hire to those met during interviewing, and introduce her or him to other staff. Relevant materials (for example, program descriptions, strategic plans, funded grant or contract proposals, the most recent annual report, information system forms, policies and procedures) are ready to be read and the agency's performance appraisal system and instruments are shared with the employee in some detail.

It is important, however, to move quickly from details to the big picture, focusing on the organization's culture and making sure that the new employee understands the mission of the agency and the goals of his or her own program.

> Too often ... orientation programs focus on administrative details and lack a clear statement of how the job contributes to the company's overall success. The key is to articulate your company's vision, mission, and values in words and actions. (Armstrong & Mitchell, 2008, Chap 3, Sec 4, Para 2)

The long-term success of the employee-organization relationship may well depend on a fruitful orientation process.

Orientation is, indeed, a process—not just a one-time event. If we assume that orientation to the organization's mission and culture is at the heart of a successful orientation, we must also assume that *re-orientation* must play a role in the ongoing life of an agency. Any organization's mission and culture change over time. When an organization's mission, strategic plan, or preferred methodologies are altered, a re-orientation must take place, especially if employees have not been deeply involved in the process. Consider, for example, a difficult time in the history of Grandview Community Center.

6.1   GRANDVIEW COMMUNITY CENTER: CHANGE FROM THE TOP

Before Grandview Community Center's current executive director came on board, a previous director instituted a number of reforms. These reforms included not only administrative changes in budgeting and management information systems but also alterations in how services would be provided. With the center's employees resisting all of these changes, both employee morale and the organization's progress were negatively affected. This crisis led the board to replace the director.

This story of an unsuccessful change from the top highlights the importance of orientation as an ongoing process. Ideally, the employees should have been involved from the beginning if such radical changes were contemplated. But even if the director believed that these changes were imperative to the health of the organization, he should at least have spent time and energy on the process of orienting the employees before the changes had become irrevocable. The employees' acceptance of the mission and loyalty to the organization might have been saved.

PROMOTION

Many of the principles already discussed can be used or easily adapted for promotion decisions. Assessment centers, discussed in the next section, may also be used as part of the evaluation process. In many governmental organizations, promotional opportunities (except at the executive level) are typically available only to current employees. In most not-for-profit agencies, promotional opportunities are treated as new hiring opportunities with the exception that the organization's current employees may apply.

Promotion from within has obvious benefits in offering career growth opportunities to employees, and more is known about candidates with a work history at the agency. One perceived disadvantage is that if a current employee is not selected, the hiring staff will need to provide very specific feedback regarding reasons for his or her not being selected and perhaps deal with feelings about this decision that may affect future performance. If criteria are clear to and accepted by all applicants, this possible outcome may not be a problem.

A new hire into a supervisory position has the advantage of bringing a fresh perspective and new ideas and will be less susceptible to the "that's the way we have always done it" syndrome. A disadvantage is created, however, if the new hire has brought her or his own "that's the way we have always done it" view from the previous setting. Any transition issues can be handled through discussions with one's supervisor (see the next chapter) and team members.

STAFF TRAINING

Effective use of limited human resources requires that human service workers receive ongoing training to meet the changing needs of community and clients. The basic steps to be followed in implementing training programs are the same whether the focus is on an individual or a group, on immediate needs or long-term plans.

Assessing Training and Development Needs

For the sake of both appropriate use of resources and participant motivation, training programs must be based on careful assessment of real needs. The assessment might be based on new programs or organizational strategies, existing problems in service delivery, suggestions of employees or supervisors, or the results of an assessment center.

At the most comprehensive level, Van Wart (1998, p. 279) has suggested the use of an organizational needs analysis consisting of seven elements:

1. Ethics assessment or audits look for gaps between stated values and organizational performance;
2. Mission, values, vision, and planning statement reviews use formal documents to identify possible gaps and needs;
3. Customer and citizen assessments provide data on emerging needs;
4. Employee assessments reveal employee opinions and values;
5. Performance assessments identify gaps between stated and actual performance;
6. Benchmarking involves looking for best practices elsewhere and using them as standards; and
7. Quality assessments review customer satisfaction, employee involvement and development, continual learning and improvement, prevention over inspection, and supplier partnerships.

These steps are not normally all done at once. An organization should focus on those areas that seem to need attention.

The second level of assessment is a departmental needs analysis, for which two approaches are available: the performance gap approach and the comprehensive approach (Van Wart, 1998). The performance gap approach works best when there is an obvious need area and typically begins with a "pre-analysis" during which a training advisory group considers whether training will be the right answer. In the data collection phase, focus groups, interviews, questionnaires, or surveys can be used to get feedback on training needs and options. The analysis phase involves looking at the gap between the needs of the job and current skills, knowledge, and abilities of employees. It should be noted that a gap may be based on factors beyond the employee (poor management, excessive job demands, and the like), and training may not be the answer. In either the comprehensive approach or the departmental analysis, recommendations for training or other interventions are made to administrative decision makers. A third level of analysis—individual training needs—can also be done as a part of supervision and performance appraisal.

The assessment center concept was pioneered by industries attempting to assess potential managers or executives. It is both a process (a set of activities) and a place (typically an off-site setting such as a hotel or community center with conference rooms) (Swanson, 1998). A group of middle-management personnel might be brought together in an assessment center to examine their skills in leadership, organizing, decision making, human relations, or other factors considered relevant for managerial performance. Behavior samples are gleaned from a combination of in-basket exercises, leaderless group discussions, simulations, individual presentations, objective tests, management-style instruments, and interviews (Swanson, 1998).

Centers use multiple methods of assessment and multiple assessors, each of whom has been trained to make judgments based on observations of performance. Assessors' independent evaluations are combined to make final assessments of participants using pooled data. Assessment center methods can be adapted to the needs of human service agencies and used to assess service deliverers as well as managers. When such analyses have been completed, even small agencies can use some of the assessment center ideas by building opportunities for objective behavioral appraisals into the selection process and performance appraisal system.

Once learning needs are identified, they need to be prioritized by the training advisory committee, managers, supervisors, and the learners themselves so that the most pressingly felt needs can be imminently addressed. Without an adequate assessment effort, subsequent training/development programs may miss their mark, affecting agency performance.

DEVELOPING TRAINING OBJECTIVES

All of these approaches to staff development and training lead to the same point. Once learning needs have been clearly identified, they can be stated in terms of objectives. In some way, it is expected that trainees will be different after the educational intervention. Their behavior will be changed because they will have developed new skills, gained new knowledge, or learned new attitudes. The specific nature of the desired change should be clearly stated before the training program is designed.

DESIGNING THE TRAINING PROGRAM

The design of the training program depends on the objectives being met and the resources available. In most work settings, training can run the gamut from on-the-job instruction and coaching to specially designed workshops for groups, ongoing classroom teaching, individualized programmed instruction, use of audiovisual media, laboratory training, conferences, and online learning. Within the confines of the workshop format, which is used very commonly in human service settings, methods can involve lectures or panel discussions, case conferences, demonstrations, use of media, discussions, structured experiences, role playing, exercises, or simulations. The nature of the activity selected must take into account the availability of both human and inanimate resources, and the program design must be based on the learning objectives that have been set. Knowledge acquisition objectives can sometimes be met through essentially passive learning, such as reading, watching videos, listening to lectures, or using programmed materials, but changes in skill level or attitudes require more active learning.

Either skill acquisition or attitude change depends on learners' active involvement and should use principles of adult learning such as emphasizing immediate usefulness, responding to learners' concerns, building on experience, using media to match learners' styles, offering immediate feedback, and providing opportunities for reflection (Rapp & Poertner, 1992). Well-designed online offerings provide the kind of active involvement and flexibility that fits these principles as well as presenting opportunities for virtual teamwork (Zach & Agosto, December, 2009; Loh & Smyth, June, 2010). Given these characteristics, it is likely that online courses and webinars will replace in-person workshops in the future.

IMPLEMENTING THE TRAINING PROGRAM

If the training methods selected are appropriate to the objectives that have been set, the likelihood of effectiveness is enhanced. It is still important to remember, however, that intervention methods should be appropriate to adult learners' needs. Their motivation depends on their ability to recognize the importance of the training program to their own work effectiveness. They must have been actively involved in selecting training goals. At the same time, they should be assured that the skills and knowledge they are gaining will be recognized and reinforced in the context of their post-training work. The training program to avoid is one that has little connection with the ongoing work of the agency and its employees. The one to use extensively is the type that seems a natural outgrowth of the needs that have been identified through the appraisal process and are recognized by all involved.

EVALUATING TRAINING

Evaluation of training is useful in several ways: it shows the ultimate effects on job performance, it identifies additional training or development needs, and it provides feedback on the usefulness of various training activities and methods. Criteria for training evaluation exist on several levels (Goldstein, 1993). The reaction level assesses what trainees thought of the program. Measuring learning involves looking at what principles, facts, techniques, or attitudes were learned. Behavior measures regard changes in job performance. Finally, results criteria assess effects on organizational objectives such as costs, turnover, error rates, and morale. Unfortunately, the criteria of most interest—behavior and results—are the hardest to measure. Trainee reactions are commonly measured with an anonymous questionnaire. Learning can often be measured with an instrument (for example, reactions to a case that are subjected to content analysis), ideally in a pretest-posttest format. Behavior on the job can be measured by observation by an evaluator or the supervisor, and results can sometimes be assessed using the agency's management information system. Care must be taken to ensure that results are related to the training and not other variables. At a minimum, training events should be evaluated with reaction forms, and ideally results (based on training objectives) should be assessed.

PERFORMANCE APPRAISAL

Every organization has some kind of performance appraisal system. Whether the system is formal or informal, explicit or implicit, objective or subjective, the organization uses some method to evaluate the way employees do their jobs. This process can have a major influence on the effectiveness of the organization as a whole.

The performance appraisal should not be looked at in isolation and thought about only a few weeks before the employee's hiring anniversary date, when most policy and procedures manuals say the review should be done. Performance appraisal flows logically from a clearly defined job with clear standards and expectations and is based on the supervisor having worked closely with the subordinate over the previous rating period (see the next chapter). According to Millar (1998), "a good performance evaluation system should meet three criteria: it should be valid, reliable, and practical" (p. 222). This means that it should measure what it is supposed to measure, give consistent appraisals to all individuals, be acceptable to all staff, and be relatively easy to use.

Despite their limitations, performance appraisals serve several functions, each of which is important to the management of human resources. These functions boil down to two major purposes, which might seem to be in opposition to each other: judgmental and developmental (Daley, 1998, p. 369). Both are concerned with the employee's performance, but whereas developmental purposes focus on the growth of the employee and enhancing her or his skills, judgmental purposes focus on compliance with organizational expectations and often on related rewards or punishments. One way of addressing this dilemma is to have multiple appraisals that allow for more focused evaluations over time. Another way to mitigate the inherent dilemmas of performance appraisals is to ensure that they are clearly based on the job itself: the job analysis discussed earlier (Daley, 1998, p. 376). The assessment should be concerned only with two factors: behavior and results (Daley, 1998, pp. 371–372), or what the employee has done with reference to job criteria and what the employee has accomplished with reference to stated objectives over the course of the rating period.

A further strategy to ensure that the appraisal process is seen as fair and useful is to involve the subordinate in both the development of performance criteria and the appraisal process. (Criteria development will be addressed later in the sections on behaviorally anchored rating scales and management by objectives.) Involving the subordinate in the appraisal process is a notable advance over the traditional approach of having the supervisor doing all the assessing and rating. Supervisors and other staff who will be asked to implement the appraisal program need to receive ongoing training so that they can use rating mechanisms fairly and confidently. If supervisors and employees agree that the strengths and weaknesses being measured are the ones that matter, appraisal can provide guidelines for meeting the training and development needs of human service workers.

The process should, of course, be participative: the agency's system should be designed by a representative group of employees, and criteria for a specific job should be developed by the subordinate, the supervisor, and ideally others who know the subordinate's work. Generally an appraisal is done annually, and the best time seems to be the anniversary of the employee's beginning employment, if timely information on the employee's accomplishments and all relevant behaviors is available.

After the instrument is designed, it should be completed by evaluators in advance of the performance appraisal session. Results should be reviewed at the session, with a focus on development for the future, collaboration, mutual support, and fairness. The session should end with a joint assessment of the subordinate's strengths and accomplishments for the year and specific action plans for correcting problem areas and advancing further growth and development.

APPRAISAL MECHANISMS

Any appraisal system depends on the use of some kind of mechanism to form the basis of rating employee performance. The best appraisal mechanisms come closest to evaluating the behaviors that actually distinguish between successful and unsuccessful job performance. Any mechanisms used should be based on objective criteria that have been established through analysis of the jobs being performed. Although this point may seem obvious, arbitrary and subjective performance measures are still too frequently used in human service organizations. The nature of many commonly used evaluation techniques makes unreliability and rater bias common. For example, every human service worker has used evaluation systems based on rating scales. Usually, a list of characteristics is presented, and the assessor is asked to rate the employee on each quality listed. Ratings are usually on three-, four-, or five-point scales, from "excellent" to "poor" or "needs improvement," with gradations in between. Such ratings are usually vague, subjective, unreliable, and ultimately not helpful in improving employee performance. Another historically common system, rating and comparing employees, has similar weaknesses. Performance tests (for example, rating videotapes of worker performance) have been less common but equally limited. Assessment centers, mentioned earlier, can be useful here if they are well designed.

The most objective approaches are behaviorally anchored rating scales (BARS) and the uses of management by objectives (MBO). These should therefore be the key elements of a rating system. The final form used should have the employee's role, the time period, all job standards, BARS and MBO factors and ratings, narrative by the supervisor, and any action plans for further development. Overall ratings should be based on a compilation from all raters, weighted if necessary using a formula agreed to in advance. Both the employee and supervisor should sign the form, which is typically reviewed and signed by the supervisor's supervisor and filed to be referred to during the next rating period if necessary.

BEHAVIORALLY ANCHORED RATING SCALES

Five major steps are used in developing behaviorally anchored rating scales, or BARS. First, people who are familiar with the job list specific kinds of incidents that would illustrate effective or ineffective performance, referring to all dimensions of the job articulated in the job analysis. These incidents are then clustered into groups or performance dimensions. For each performance dimension, five to seven behaviors are developed to represent performance levels ranging from clearly deficient to outstanding. Typically the midpoint is the basic expectation for the position. Once incidents and performance dimensions have been selected, the incidents are scaled and a final instrument is developed. The incidents that have been selected now serve as "behavioral anchors" that translate important performance dimensions into concrete, behavioral, measurable terms. An example can be seen in the Box 6.1.

BOX 6.1	**BEHAVIORAL DIMENSIONS: IDENTIFYING AND ASSESSING CLIENT PROBLEMS**

This dimension considers your ability to identify and assess problems. Are you able to collect information and prioritize the presenting problems? Can you see how these problems interfere with client functioning?

7—This person has a superior ability to collect data and identify significant client problems. He or she can expertly see how the problems interfere with client functioning.

6—This person has an excellent ability to collect data and identify client problems. He or she can skillfully see how the problems interfere with client functioning.

5—This person has advanced ability to collect data and identify significant client problems. He or she can readily see how the problems interfere with client functioning.

4—This person has ability to collect data and identify significant client problems. He or she can see how the problems interfere with client functioning.

3—This person has some ability to collect data and identify client problems. He or she can see, to some extent, how the problems interfere with client functioning.

2—This person has deficiency collecting data and identifying client problems. He or she has difficulty appreciating how the problems interfere with client functioning.

1—This person is unable to collect data and identify client problems. He or she cannot see how the problems interfere with client functioning.

Source: Copyright 1998, National Association of Social Workers, Inc., Skills for Effective Management of Nonprofit Organizations. Reprinted with permission.

A possible shortcoming of this approach is that many people must spend long hours developing the instrument, and some human service managers might not want to devote a great deal of time and energy to performance appraisal. Once such an instrument has been developed, however, it will save time and effort by streamlining evaluation. In the long run, more time will be wasted by using inaccurate measures that take supervisors' time but do not provide real assistance in decision making.

MANAGEMENT BY OBJECTIVES

Management by Objectives, or MBO, is a commonly used mechanism to identify outcomes of service activities and other tasks such as special projects. Based on the strategic plan, objectives are set at the program level and then at lower levels, with involvement by those who will be responsible for their accomplishment. MBO is also valuable as an element of performance appraisal.

As in the case of BARS, this process is based on the employee's job tasks. At the beginning of the annual cycle (or when new activities need to begin), the employee and supervisor meet to select 4 to 5 (up to 8 or 10, based on particular employee assignments) major responsibilities for which the employee will be accountable over the year (rating period), and these are written as objectives. Objectives by definition are measurable and have a time frame. Ideally they should be stated in terms of outcomes: accomplishments that have clear benefits to clients or the organization (for example, ensuring that a percentage of a worker's clients are living independently by the end of treatment). There may also be process objectives, which are activities taken to reach outcomes, such as attending a training event. Standards can be based on historical results from past years or on grant or contract requirements. They should be both challenging, so that the employee will need to stretch, and realistic, so that achievement is possible. It should be agreed to in advance whether 100 percent accomplishment is expected (BARS levels may be used for this, with the basic expectation at the midpoint). All objectives should be reviewed together, with analysis, if necessary, to ensure that they are achievable by the employee in the reporting period with resources available and given existing organizational and environmental conditions. If some objectives are more crucial than others, they may all be weighted.

CRITICAL INCIDENT TECHNIQUES

Supervisor logs of important incidents demonstrating employees' strengths or weaknesses provide solid data that can be used to give feedback to employees. Such incidents should refer specifically to job-related criteria and be described specifically enough to enable later recall by the employee and supervisor. Supervisors using this method do need training to be as objective as possible in selecting and recording incidents. A halo effect can occur, with supervisors finding negative or positive incidents that support their overall impressions of certain employees. Critical incident summaries should be used only as an adjunct to more thorough systems such as BARS and MBO.

VALUING DIVERSITY

The dominant formal organizations—business, government, and not-for-profit—in the United States have gone through three broad periods regarding ethnic and gender demographics of employees. In the first period, organizations were owned, managed, and largely staffed by white males. This history of discrimination does not need to be recounted here, except to note that the history of such organizations sometimes still affects aspects of organizational life. The second period dates from the beginnings of the civil rights movement in the 1950s to the affirmative action backlash that began in the 1980s. The third period of paradox and complexity began in the 1980s and is characterized by continuing conflicts over affirmative action, recurring documentation of discrimination in the workplace, greater attention to groups beyond the initial civil rights emphasis on African Americans and other people of color (sexual harassment and the glass ceiling; people with disabilities, gay, lesbian, bisexual, and transgender individuals; and aging workers) and the current interest in the value of diverse and inclusive workforces.

In the new millennium, agencies need to go beyond earlier support of affirmative action to a strategic commitment to valuing, creating, and sustaining a diverse workforce because it is consistent with the values and policies of human service professionals such as social workers and because such agencies will, all other things being equal, be more effective and responsive to community needs and visions. Equal employment opportunity has often been viewed as "a means to prevent discrimination in the workplace on the basis of race, color, religion, gender, national origin, age, and physical and mental abilities" (Riccucci, 1998, p. 166). Now, however, attention is paid to employment discrimination across a number of additional areas of diversity, such as sexual orientation, immigration status, marital status, and disability.

Diversity in this larger context represents a philosophy of valuing and working to create a workforce that includes qualified and committed workers from all sectors of society. This concept amounts to a change of organizational culture, from one in which homogeneity and conformity may be the norms to one in which differences are valued and capitalized on, teams are common, and collaboration is a preferred method for dealing with conflict. According to Hyde (1998), this "mainstream" model of diversity makes three assumptions. First, the rationale for diversity is improved organizational performance. In fact, there is increasing evidence for the "business case" for diversity: that a diverse workforce makes better decisions (Guy & Newman, 1998, p. 88). Second, "diversity is conceptualized as all-inclusive, broadened beyond race and gender to encompass national origin, age, disability, sexual orientation, education, marital/parental status, functional specialty, religion, and leadership style as dimensions of diversity" (Hyde, 1998, p. 20). Third, diversity is both a goal and a process to be managed.

FEDERAL LEGISLATION

Diversity and discrimination are also addressed through legislation and executive orders in areas including equal employment opportunity and affirmative action. Equal employment opportunity laws require that organizations eradicate discriminatory conditions. Attention to these laws is very important for human service organizations of all types and sizes.

> Because of their tax-exempt status and because they often depend on government contracts, social service organizations must carefully and systematically examine all their employment policies. They cannot operate to the detriment of any people on the grounds of race, color, religion, national origin, sex, age, or status as a person with a disability, disabled veteran, or veteran of the Vietnam era. These organizations should also prevent and eliminate biases related to gay, lesbian, bisexual, or transgendered employees. (Pecora, 2009, p. 263)

Some of the key pieces of legislation affecting equal employment include Title VII of the Civil Rights Act of 1964, the Equal Employment Opportunity

Act of 1972, the Americans with Disabilities Act of 1990, the Civil Rights Act of 1991, the Family and Medical Leave Act of 1993, and the Lily Ledbetter Equal Pay Act of 2009. Since state laws and case law are changing in this area, a proactive manager keeps up-to-date on relevant laws and government policies in the agency's jurisdiction.

ENFORCEMENT OF FEDERAL LEGISLATION

The Civil Rights Act of 1964, along with its later amendments, is enforced by the Equal Employment Opportunity Commission (EEOC), which maintains offices in a number of cities. An individual who believes that he or she has been a victim of employment discrimination can file a charge with the EEOC. After an investigation of the charges, the commission can seek a conciliation agreement with the employer. If no settlement is reached and if the EEOC decides that the employer is in violation, a suit can be filed by the commission (if the employer is a private company) or by the U.S. attorney general (if the employer is a public agency). If the EEOC does not bring suit, a "right to sue" letter is provided for the individual, who is then free to sue privately.

If the employer is found to have engaged in discriminatory practices, the company may be required to make up for losses suffered by the employee or applicant, often involving payment of back wages. If systematic discrimination has taken place, the employer might need to develop organization-wide remedies, including affirmative action programs.

AFFIRMATIVE ACTION

Affirmative action programs are designed to remedy discriminatory patterns that have existed in the past. An organization, recognizing that past inequities have brought about an underrepresentation of women and minorities in the workforce, can develop a set of goals for hiring and promoting groups that have been the victims of past discrimination. It should be emphasized here that goals are not the same as quotas. Opponents of affirmative action often criticize the use of quotas, which are in fact rare and are "generally set by courts after a finding of employment discrimination" (Riccucci, 1998, p. 173). Goals are flexible indicators of a desired level of employment for certain groups (protected classes, usually based on race, ethnicity, gender, disability, or age) and take into account both the specific problems of the organization and the presence of the protected class of workers in the available labor force.

Affirmative action plans are usually based on surveys of the local labor market and the employer's own workforce. If inequities are found, the employer develops goals, usually in terms of time guidelines, and decides on the methods to be used in reaching them. The goals might affect either the percentage of targeted groups in the company's total workforce or the number of women and minorities in managerial or professional positions.

In the 1990s, affirmative action laws were increasingly challenged and repealed. Any human services manager should become familiar with current laws and regulations at the state and federal levels.

DIVERSITY IMPLICATIONS FOR HUMAN RESOURCE DEVELOPMENT

It is important that human service managers work toward achieving a diverse workforce, while maintaining an awareness of the basic intent of equal employment legislation and affirmative action. The spirit of equal opportunity recognizes that changes in human resource management practices must occur if equity in the workplace is to grow. These changes can take place only if people involved in hiring and appraising employees take time to think through the methods they are using. A great deal of discrimination happens not because decision makers purposely exclude women and minorities but because unexamined practices result in unintentional exclusion. Unfortunately, however, these unexamined practices are often the products of institutionalized sexism, racism, and other forms of discrimination. It is therefore incumbent on human service managers to reassess the organization's employment policies and practices to divest it of any possible vestiges of outmoded perspectives on the place of women and minorities in today's human service enterprise.

Concerns regarding discrimination and diversity can be addressed to a degree through fair and effective personnel policies such as those discussed earlier in this chapter. In addition, human service managers cannot afford to be aloof with respect to the controversies surrounding equal opportunity and affirmative action policies and practices. They must realize that the gains made over the years in equal employment and affirmative action programs have been outcomes of arduous and contentious sociopolitical processes and that maintenance of achievement in these areas also requires sociopolitical strategies and clear commitments on the part of agencies and their managers.

Diversity initiatives are becoming increasingly common as one way to address these issues. In one study of diversity efforts in human service organizations, Hyde (1998) found that diversity efforts had three interrelated goals: "to create a welcoming place, to develop culturally competent staff, and to formulate critical analyses and take action" (p. 24). Diversity training involved "integrating diversity into the organization's daily activities, relationship-building, and consciousness-raising" (p. 26). In addition to providing cultural awareness training, agencies engaged in outreach and retention activities and in some cases addressed power dynamics in the agency. The fact that numerous barriers were identified suggests that this is an area of great challenge for agencies and will require strong leadership and a major commitment of resources over time.

Although some managers find it difficult to intensify commitments to diversity and inclusion and maintain their commitments to affirmative action in the face of economic adversity, equal employment opportunity must be maintained. In the private sector, fairness in hiring, appraising, and promoting diverse workers is often seen almost entirely as a benefit for the employees themselves. In human service agencies, the presence of diverse service providers and managers is also of major importance for clients. A human service program is limited in its effectiveness if the makeup of its professional staff differs significantly from that of its clientele. A diverse workforce affects the agency's services as much as it benefits the target group of employees.

People involved in making decisions about the allocation of human resources need to understand exactly how the intent and effects of their practices can either make the organization more effective and responsive or perpetuate discrimination against people of color, women, and others. Beyond this, managers and supervisors must be aware of the federal and state legislation and guidelines governing fair employment practices. In human service agencies, which are often too small to maintain separate personnel departments, equal employment opportunity must be understood by everyone with decision-making power.

In addition to serious and proactive efforts at compliance with relevant laws and policies, agency leaders need to be assertive in establishing a new organizational culture of inclusiveness and policies and practices that value diversity and advance it within the organization. An organizational culture that values teams and cross-functional collaboration and that works to avoid competition as a conflict management mode will be more welcoming for diverse employees and also create a better work environment for all. Evaluating and rewarding managers for diversity efforts, redesigning jobs to support team functioning, and mentoring underrepresented employees will help advance diversity goals. Mor-Baran and Chemin (1998) have suggested that the dimension of inclusion-exclusion perceptions of employees can be used to assess how supportive an organization's culture is to diversity. Specific activities for responding to and enhancing diversity are detailed elsewhere for the areas of aging workers (West, 1998), advancement of women as managers (Chernesky, 1998), sexual harassment (Hoyman & Stein, 1998), management of a multicultural workforce (Asamoah, 1995), sexual orientation (Appleby, 1998), and general diversity issues (Daly, 1998).

ENCOURAGING VOLUNTEER PARTICIPATION

The use of volunteers in administering and providing social services enjoys a long and fruitful history dating back to the 1880s, when volunteer community leaders served on the boards and as the "friendly visitors" of the Charity Organization Societies and as social advocates in the settlement house movement. The patterns of volunteering have changed, however: volunteers are likely to be involved in more than one cause (Dunn, 1995), and the roles volunteers fill have been changing. Perlmutter and Cnaan (1993) found that many volunteers were involved not only in direct practice but also in administration, advocacy, and policy. Well-planned and competently administered volunteer programs are well worth the effort to both agency and clients.

The use of volunteer human service deliverers must be as carefully planned as the hiring of paid employees. Determining the need for and the organization's readiness for volunteers is the first step (Dunn, 1995). Dunn has suggested the following questions as part of this assessment:

- What is to be achieved through a volunteer program?
- Is there a legitimate need for a volunteer staff?
- How committed are the board of directors and upper-level management to establishing and monitoring a volunteer program?
- Can the work be divided into jobs, some of which can be performed by part-time volunteers? (p. 2485)

Other questions that should be asked would ensure that potential volunteers are available, that there are resources for training and supervision, and that staff would be supportive of a volunteer program. A volunteer program then should be planned as any other program, using processes similar to those for paid staff regarding the development of job descriptions, recruitment, orientation, training, supervision, evaluation, and rewards and recognition (Dunn, 1995).

WORK-RELATED STRESS

The development of human resources must take into account the fact that agency employees are valuable and that steps must be taken to protect them, to the degree possible, from the impact of work-related stress. Some individuals may be more vulnerable than others to stress-related problems, but managers should pay particular attention to the working conditions that affect all employees.

Maslach and Leiter (1997) have divided the stress-creating characteristics of workplaces into the categories of work overload, a lack of control, insufficient rewards (from money to joy), a breakdown in community, the absence of fairness (trust, openness, and respect), and conflicting values. These environmental characteristics fall under the human service manager's area of control.

Stress has an adverse impact on worker productivity and therefore on organizational effectiveness. Human service agencies cannot afford the loss in productivity involved when an active, enthusiastic professional burns out. This process can never be completely prevented because individual, as well as organizational, characteristics affect susceptibility. Still, the organizational structure and climate of the agency can be improved in a purposeful manner.

One approach is to change the way jobs are structured. Many human service professionals find it stressful to work continually at a single type of service, often without feedback or collegial interaction. Changes might be as simple as assigning more varied types of clients to each service deliverer or, of course, lowering caseloads. Flextime, part-time work, job sharing, and increased use of volunteers can provide some relief from inherently demanding jobs. Creating opportunities for new program development and new career options for staff can help. Adaptations must depend on the unique problems of a specific organization, but the key factor is to find ways to modify routine patterns and to increase the rewards that participation in human service delivery can provide.

Attention should also be paid to the supervisory relationships that each human service professional has the opportunity to form. New professionals often need support, information, and some degree of structure because they tend to be concerned about their own competence. Supervisors can help human service workers make the transition from newcomers to self-sustaining, confident professionals if they devote energy to establishing strong relationships and if they understand their own importance as role models. Supervisors, too, can burn out, and they need feedback, support, and interaction in their own work lives.

The organization as a whole can also provide a more or less stressful work environment depending on whether all organizational members share a sense of excitement and strong purpose and clear goals and objectives. Human service professionals, paraprofessionals, and volunteers can often withstand very demanding work if they feel they are participating in an effort that will lead to major accomplishments. Clarity of purpose in an agency and a commitment to ongoing learning and development of staff and the organization can help in providing such a supportive climate.

To address the underlying causes of stress-related problems, a participative management philosophy will maximize staff autonomy and allow creative and innovative ideas to flourish. Also in this vein would be strategies for ongoing organizational improvement such as the use of problem-solving groups and other organizational change activities. These organizational strategies for stress prevention and remediation are a major responsibility of managers who have the power to ensure that staff members are not in situations where they feel overloaded and powerless. At the individual level, staff development interventions such as in-service training, especially on subjects such as time management, and peer support groups for problem solving and resource exchange can provide symptomatic relief from burnout but do not address underlying causes. This is also true for the provision of counseling for employees that can help meet staffs' emotional needs, usually offered through employee assistance programs, to which we now turn.

EMPLOYEE ASSISTANCE PROGRAMS

In any organization, most employees want to be productive. Unfortunately, a number of factors can stand in the way, causing job performance to deteriorate and productivity to decline. These influences—all correlated highly with absenteeism, loss of motivation, and errors—include both job-related stress and personal concerns. Alcoholism, drug dependency, emotional problems, family conflicts, interpersonal difficulties, and legal and financial issues are all personal matters. They become the concern of the organization, however, when they affect on-the-job behavior.

Many organizations provide employee assistance programs (EAPs) for workers experiencing such problems (Van Den Bergh, 1995). EAPs typically offer direct services including counseling and referrals as well as crisis management services after incidents such as workplace or client violence. Indirect services include lectures or workshops on subjects to enhance employee well-being, supervisor training, and employee problem-solving task forces.

There is now clear evidence that EAPs can both improve productivity and lower costs (Van Den Bergh, 1995). Human service agencies are faced with increasing challenges along with level or declining resources. They cannot afford to lose the productivity of their most valuable resource: the people who make the programs work. Employee assistance programs and burnout prevention strategies can help mitigate the effects of these pressures, and effective practices in the areas of hiring, training, and appraising staff can have a major effect on creating an environment conducive to effective and satisfying work.

SUMMARY

For programs to function properly, they must have well-designed jobs that allow workers to use their skills and talents fully. Staff members need to be carefully selected, and an ongoing training program should be available to ensure that they remain responsive to program and job needs. An agency needs a good performance appraisal system to provide feedback and ensure that employees are meeting expectations. The value of a diverse workforce is becoming increasingly clear, and an agency should give deliberate attention to creating a welcoming and inclusive environment for all staff and clients. The use of volunteers, stress prevention, and employee assistance programs are ways of ensuring that staff can function effectively in the challenging human services environment. A key factor in pulling these processes together is the supervisory relationship, the subject of the next chapter.

COMPETENCY-BUILDING ACTIVITY 6.1 | JOBS

By now, you have a good sense of the way your hypothetical program will work. As you completed the previous chapter, you designed an organizational chart to fit your program's mission. Now it is time to consider the kinds of jobs that will fit your organization. Identify several of the key jobs that will make your program work. Identify the jobs and address these questions for each:

1. How will this job fit into the organization as a whole?

2. What will be the most important activities that the person holding this job will carry out?

3. If you were planning to hire a person for this job, consider the following questions: (a) What would be the primary qualifications that you would look for? (b) How would you assess whether the job candidates possess these qualifications? (c) What would be the key questions you would ask in an interview situation? (d) What answers would you be seeking?

CASE ACTIVITY 6.1 | DIRECTOR OF TRAINING

When the Atlantis Community Mental Health Center became an umbrella organization, the traditional services normally offered by the center were combined, for the first time, with the more nontraditional approaches favored by the small grassroots agencies in the community. ACMHC now included both "the center" and the "neighborhood outposts" that had formerly been independent agencies.

This drastic change in the organization brought with it the need for new approaches to training. Nelson Richards, director of the center, recognized this need. His response was to hire Ellis Shore, a mental health professional with experience in university teaching, to design and implement a comprehensive training program.

Richards's directive to his new training director was clear. The skills of the paraprofessionals in the outposts were to be upgraded. Richards felt that the service deliverers in the community-based agencies lacked the background and education that he would expect of professional helpers. These people were now working under the Atlantis name, so they would have to provide professional-level services. He would leave the methods up to Shore, but the mental health skills of the community agency workers would need to be enhanced.

Shore began this work with great enthusiasm. He created, almost single-handedly, a series of workshops designed to develop trainee competencies in individual, family, and group therapy. He also developed a complex schedule that would allow the workshops to be provided on-site at each of the neighborhood centers. Knowing that he could not provide all the training himself, he involved several mental health professionals who had been employed by the center before the creation of the umbrella organization. He asked these professionals to serve as cotrainers and made sure to include people with varying therapeutic orientations, from psychodynamic to behavioral to existential.

Shore and his co-trainers agreed that the workshops he had designed would upgrade trainees' skills if they became actively involved in the process. Use of the outposts as training sites would mean that participation would be so convenient for agency workers that attendance could be purely voluntary.

With high expectations, the training director and his co-trainers began the first series of workshops. At the first workshop, 20 participants appeared. Although only 12 remained for the whole day, Shore was relatively pleased with the turnout. At the second workshop, only 10 paraprofessionals attended. The third drew only 6.

Shore, in frustration, confronted Isabel Phillips with this evidence of lack of motivation among agency workers. Phillips, who had administered one of the more successful of the city's community-based agencies and who was now coordinator of the outreach program, was in touch with the paraprofessionals in the neighborhood centers. She would know how to get these service providers more actively involved.

"Isabel, I've been given the authority to make these workshops compulsory," Shore pointed out, "but I really don't want to do that if I can avoid it. How can I light a fire under these people? You know them. Why aren't they motivated?"

"As a matter of fact, you're right," Phillips responded. "I do know these people, and what I know about them is that they're the most motivated people you're ever going to see in your life. Every one of them has put in more hours in a week than you can imagine for pay that hardly puts them over the poverty level. They do it because they believe in what they're doing and because they know how much they're needed. When you say they're not 'motivated,' I have a hard time picturing what you're talking about."

"Well, what I'm talking about is the fact that they're not showing up for these workshops, which they know are encouraged by the director, which they know they have released time for, and which they don't even have to step outside doors of their agencies

to get to. Now, if these folks are so concerned about their work, something just doesn't fit."

"You're right, Ellis. Something doesn't fit, but the thing that doesn't fit is your training program. What makes you think they need upgrading in their therapeutic skills?"

"Isabel, are you kidding? That's what I was hired to do. When Richards gave me the job, he told me that he didn't care what methods I used, but that the skills of the paraprofessionals in the outreach programs had to be upgraded. That was the word he used: upgraded."

"Well, let me tell you something about Richards. He's completely out of touch with the community. He's always been out of touch. He doesn't know what the people need from the agencies, and he doesn't know what kind of training the workers need. They don't do therapy in those agencies. They don't have the luxury of sitting in their offices dealing with one person at a time for months on end. They're out there in the streets, getting people organized and helping them deal with real, concrete problems. In fact, has it ever occurred to you that you just might be designing all these beautiful training interventions for the wrong people? The folks in my agencies know what they're doing. It's the people in the center who need training. They don't know how to do anything but therapy, and the community isn't buying it. If you want to make a training contribution, why don't you hire yourself some paraprofessionals as cotrainers, go up to the center, and provide some on-site training on how to close the gap between the center and its so-called consumers? From what I hear, business isn't exactly booming in that big granite building uptown."

1. If you were Ellis Shore, what steps might you take to develop a more comprehensive and appropriate training program?
2. What special leadership issues might be involved in a decentralized agency such as the ACMHC?

REFERENCES

Appleby, G. (1998). Social work practice with gay men and lesbians within organizations. In G. Mallon (Ed.), *Foundations of social work practice with gay and lesbian persons.* New York: Harrington Park.

Armstrong, S., & Mitchell, B. (2008). *The essential HR handbook.* Franklin Lakes, NJ: The Career Press. (Kindle). Retrieved from Amazon.com.

Asamoah, Y. (1995). Managing the new multicultural workplace. In L. Ginsberg & P. Keys (Eds.), *New management in human services* (2nd ed., pp. 115–127). Washington, DC: NASW Press.

Chernesky, R. (1998). Advancing women in the managerial ranks. In R. Edwards, J. Yankey, & M. Altpeter (Eds.),

Skills for effective management of nonprofit organizations (pp. 200–218). Washington, DC: NASW Press.

Council of Economic Advisors. (March, 2010). *Work-life balance and the economics of workplace flexibility*. Executive Office of the President. Retrieved February 5, 2011, from http://www.whitehouse.gov/files/documents/100331-cea-economics-workplace-flexibility.pdf

Daly, A. (Ed.). (1998). *Workplace diversity issues and perspectives*. Washington, DC: NASW Press.

Daley, D. (1998). Designing effective performance appraisal systems. In S. Condrey (Ed.), *Handbook of human resource management in government* (pp. 368–385). San Francisco: Jossey-Bass.

Dunn, P. (1995). Volunteer management. In R. Edwards (Ed.), *The encyclopedia of social work* (19th ed., pp. 2483–2490). Washington, DC: NASW Press.

Foster, M. (1998). Effective job analysis methods. In S. Condrey (Ed.), *Handbook of human resource management in government* (pp. 322–348). San Francisco: Jossey-Bass.

Goldstein, I. (1993). *Training in organizations*. Pacific Grove, CA: Brooks/Cole.

Guy, M., & Newman, M. (1998). Toward diversity in the workplace. In S. Condrey (Ed.), *Handbook of human resource management in government* (pp. 75–92). San Francisco: Jossey-Bass.

Hoyman, M., & Stein, L. (1998). Sexual harassment in the workplace. In S. Condrey (Ed.), *Handbook of human resource management in government* (pp. 183–198). San Francisco: Jossey-Bass.

Hyde, C. (1998). A model for diversity training in human service agencies. *Administration in Social Work, 22*(4), 19–33.

Kaman, V. S., & Bentson, C. (1988). Roleplay simulations for employee selection: Design and implementation. *Public Personnel Management Journal, 17*(1), 1–8.

Lawrence, S. (1987, September). Has the push for workers' rights shaped social change? *Personnel Journal,* pp. 74–91.

Loh, J., & Smyth, R. (June, 2010). Understanding students' online learning experiences in virtual teams. *MERLOT Journal of Online Learning & Teaching, 6*(2), 335–342.

Millar, K. (1998). Evaluating employee performance. In R. Edwards, J. Yankey, & M. Altpeter (Eds.), *Skills for effective management of nonprofit organizations* (pp. 219–243). Washington, DC: NASW Press.

Mor-Baran, M., & Chemin, D. (1998). A tool to expand organizational understanding of workforce diversity: Exploring a measure of inclusion-exclusion. *Administration in Social Work, 22*(1), 47–64.

Professional Assessment Resources Center. (2005). *HR profession defined*. Retrieved September 2005, from http://www.cchra-ccarh.ca/parc/en/section_2/ss21e.asp

Pecora, P. (1998). Recruiting and selecting effective employees. In R. Edwards, J. Yankey, & M. Altpeter (Eds.), *Skills for effective management of nonprofit organizations* (pp. 155–184). Washington, DC: NASW Press.

Pecora, P. J. (2009). Managing human resources: Administrative issues. In R. J. Patti (Ed.), *The handbook of human services management* (2nd ed., pp. 255–282). Thousand Oaks, CA: Sage.

Perlmutter, F., & Cnaan, R. (1993). Challenging human service organizations to redefine volunteer roles. *Administration in Social Work, 17*(4), 77–95.

Rapp, C., & Poertner, J. (1992). *Social administration: A client-centered approach*. New York: Longman.

Riccucci, N. (1998). A practical guide to affirmative action. In S. Condrey (Ed.), *Handbook of human resource management in government* (pp. 165–182). San Francisco: Jossey-Bass.

Sager, J. (1995). Change levers for improving organizational performance and staff morale. In J. Rothman, J. Erlich, J. Tropman, & F. Cox (Eds.), *Strategies of community intervention* (5th ed., pp. 401–415). Itasca, IL: Peacock.

Senge, P. M. (2006). *The fifth discipline: The art and practice of the learning organization* (2nd ed.). New York: Currency Doubleday.

Society for Human Resource Management. (2005). *Code of ethical and professional standards in human resource management*. Retrieved September 2005, from http://www.shrm.org/ethics/code-of-ethics.asp

Swanson, C. (1998). A practical guide to conducting assessment centers. In S. Condrey (Ed.), *Handbook of human resource management in government* (pp. 349–367). San Francisco: Jossey-Bass.

U.S. Department of Health & Human Services. (1998). *Summary of findings and proposed action plan: Quality of Work Life Conference*. Retrieved October 2005, from http://www.hhs.gov/ohr/qwl/resources/actionplan.htm

Van Den Bergh, N. (1995). Employee assistance programs. In R. Edwards (Ed.), *The encyclopedia of social work* (19th ed., pp. 842–849). Washington, DC: NASW Press.

Van Wart, M. (1998). Organizational investment in employee development. In S. Condrey (Ed.), *Handbook of human resource management in government* (pp. 276–297). San Francisco: Jossey-Bass.

West, J. (1998). Managing an aging workforce: Trends, issues, and strategies. In S. Condrey (Ed.), *Handbook of human resource management in government* (pp. 93–115). San Francisco: Jossey-Bass.

Zach, L., & Agosto, D. E. (December, 2009). Using the online learning environment to do real-life collaboration and knowledge-sharing skills: A theoretical discussion and framework for online course design. *MERLOT Journal of Online Learning & Teaching, 5*(4), 590–599.

Useful Web Resources

National Association of Social Workers. http://socialworkers.org/.

Society for Human Resource Management. http://www.shrm.org/Pages/default.aspx.

Society for Organizational Learning. http://www.solonline.org/aboutsol/.

U.S. Equal Employment Opportunity Commission. http://www.eeoc.gov/.

7 CHAPTER | BUILDING SUPERVISORY RELATIONSHIPS

The supervisor who oversees the work of other staff members is a key link between organizational expectations and the provision of services. Most human service professionals find themselves playing at least limited supervisory roles throughout their careers. Some carry out supervision in the context of a managerial role, but many supervise the work of a limited number of direct-service staff.

The distinction between managerial and professional supervision may be less important to supervisory effectiveness than the quality of the relationships that the individual supervisor is able to create. A model for supervision should be broad enough to accommodate the subtle role differences within the supervisory relationship. Such an all-encompassing model must take into account issues related to the supervisee's motivation, the supervisor's relational style, the relevance of power and authority, and the special problems inherent in human service settings.

SUPERVISORY ROLES

Today's human service supervisor must fulfill several roles and functions to ensure efficient and effective services to clients. First and foremost, the supervisor, by virtue of the position, is an organizational leader. In this role, supervisors possess positional authority that allows them to facilitate supervisees' motivation and activity toward the accomplishment of organizational goals and objectives. This general purpose of supervision is accomplished through the supervisor's assumption of three corollary roles and functions: manager, mediator, and mentor. Together with and anchored by the leadership component, these dimensions bring to fruition a dynamic model of human services supervision.

As a manager, the human service supervisor must develop knowledge and skills in the areas of planning, budgeting, organizing, developing human resources, and evaluating programs. In today's world of organizational accountability, the administrative, or managerial, function of supervision has attained significant importance. The supervisor is responsible not only for his or her own performance but ultimately for the performance of his or her supervisees as well. In fact, supervisory performance is usually measured in terms of the performance of the supervisor's unit or team of supervisees. The supervisor is accountable to the organization and has an important role to play in ensuring positive outcomes for the agency's clients.

As a mediator, the human service supervisor is at the nexus between the two primary technologies found in the human service organization: the technologies of administration and direct practice. It is where the two technologies meet that service goals are operationalized into functional service objectives. It is the responsibility of the supervisor to mediate between and articulate the two technologies in a manner that satisfies the requirements of both in the efficient and effective delivery of services. As a mediator, the supervisor is the link between administration and direct services, between policy formulation and policy implementation. A critical function of the mediator role involves the facilitation of successful relationships within the supervisor's own group and between the group members and people in other units of the organization. When necessary, the supervisor may serve as a mediator between supervisees and the organization's environment, including clients and other service providers. This role requires considerable skills in decision making and conflict management as well as sensitivity to the needs of clients, staff, and the organization. It also leads at times to the supervisor feeling that he or she is "caught in the middle."

In addition to fulfilling the roles and executing the functions of leader, manager, and mediator, the human service supervisor also assumes the role and function of mentor to his or her supervisees. As leader, the supervisor is concerned with the morale, productivity, and job satisfaction of subordinates, including their integration into the agency and their identification with agency mission, goals, and objectives. As manager, the supervisor must deal with the day-to-day administrative tasks of planning, coordination, and evaluation. As mediator, the supervisor attends to the negotiation of relationships among staff members and between staff and other internal and external organizational units. As mentor, the supervisor's main responsibility is the professional growth and development of his or her supervisees.

It is in the mentor role that the supervisor has the best opportunity to provide individual emotional and psychological support to subordinates as well as to impart knowledge and help develop skills to enhance service delivery. This important role and function reflects the supervisor's commitment to professional values and ethics in service to clients and to the assurance that those values and ethics are reflected in the supervisees' practice. In this capacity, the supervisor differentially socializes the supervisees to such professional norms as fostering client self-determination, being nonjudgmental and objective, and protecting the confidentiality of case information. As mentor, the supervisor also helps workers develop self-awareness of their own feelings and responses to clients and the various issues that clients present.

THE SUPERVISORY PROCESS

Across supervisory roles and settings, a supervisor's key tasks are likely to include the following:

- Providing encouragement and support for the supervisee
- Building motivation
- Increasing the mutuality of individual and organizational goals
- Enhancing the supervisee's competence in service delivery
- Carrying out ongoing assessments of the supervisee's success in fulfilling his or her responsibilities
- Providing prompt and objective feedback designed to enhance the supervisee's professional development

Of course, the nature of the supervisory relationship depends on the specific situation, especially on the supervisee's needs and developmental level. It is unrealistic to think that one supervisor could form the same kind of relationship with each of his or her supervisees. In fact, the relationship with each supervisee changes over time as the supervisee grows in competence and independence.

In the context of a collaborative interaction, the supervisor and supervisee should select both the objectives toward which the individual is expected to strive and the goals of the supervisory process itself. It is important to have clarity concerning both the supervisee's work objectives and the supervisor's role in providing support and assistance.

It is helpful to think of the supervisee's needs in terms of the Hersey, Blanchard, and Johnson (2007) situational leadership model, which emphasizes the concept of readiness. Readiness encompasses the degree of willingness and ability the individual demonstrates. Willingness is "a combination of the varying degrees of confidence, commitment, and motivation" (Hersey et al., 2007, p. 476), whereas "ability is determined by the amount of knowledge, experience, and demonstrated skill the follower brings to the task" (p. 477). Both willingness and ability are clearly relevant to the supervisory process. The supervision needs of a "high-readiness" supervisee can be expected to differ significantly from those of an individual who needs active assistance either in the development of ability to perform or in the enhancement of willingness to learn.

In human service settings, the equivalent of the less "ready" worker is simply one who does not have a fully developed set of goals, methods, and motivations for carrying out specific tasks that relate to client needs or organizational mission. The major factor is not the supervisee's length of time on the job or years of training but rather his or her readiness to function independently. A specific supervisee may need additional task supervision to gain competence in a new area, or he or she may simply prefer a close working relationship with the supervisor. Whether the level of readiness is defined in terms of abilities or personal needs, the supervisor's goal should be to help the worker move steadily toward increased autonomy. A supportive supervisory relationship can form the basis for moving the individual from a stance of dependence to one of independence.

Throughout the supervision process, the supervisor and supervisee work together to specify objectives, clarify the criteria against which progress will be measured, and identify movement from one stage to the next. The supervisor must also specify his or her own contributions to the relationship, ensuring that the degree of personal support and task-oriented training needed will be offered. The supervisory contract involves recognizing both the supervisee's work objectives and the supervisor's contribution toward meeting them. As the worker becomes increasingly competent, the relationship may move away from a high task orientation to a more supportive interaction and, finally, to increased delegation and autonomy.

Skilled supervision is needed in the joint selection of goals in the attempt to find commonality between the supervisee's individual needs and the agency's or program's mission. When dealing with a professionally competent supervisee, the supervisor should place a high priority on seeking a set of goals and objectives that are acceptable to both parties of the supervisory dyad. These goals must be based on a recognition of changing client needs, with both supervisor and supervisee attempting to determine what amount and kinds of services the specific worker can reasonably be expected to provide. The degree to which additional training or support is needed should also be specified. Most important, the supervisor should accept that, once agreement about goals and objectives has been reached, the mature supervisee should be allowed to work in an autonomous fashion.

Yet autonomy does not mean isolation. Throughout the supervisory process, the relationship between supervisor and supervisee remains important. Although the need for active intervention may lessen, the supervisory dyad thrives in an atmosphere of trust and supportiveness. The supervisee in a human service setting is learning not just to perform tasks but to use the self as an instrument for helping others. That process implies a need for continual growth and nondefensiveness. In human service organizations, workers should be, and usually are, motivated by high needs for achievement and effectiveness. Their continued motivation—whether they are professionals, paraprofessionals, or volunteers—depends on the degree to which their jobs can be enriched and the degree of involvement they feel in the ongoing work of the program.

CLINICAL SUPERVISION

When helping supervisees explore their interactions with clients, the supervisor is carrying out *clinical supervision*. This aspect of supervision is, of course, appropriate only in situations when the supervisor has appropriate clinical expertise along with supervisory skill. The American Board of Examiners in Clinical Social Work (2004, p. 3) specifies four separate domains of clinical supervision:

- *Clinical supervision of direct practice* refers to activities in which the supervisor guides and educates the clinical social worker supervisee in assessment, treatment/intervention, identification and resolution of ethical issues, and evaluation of client interventions.
- *Clinical supervision of treatment-team collaboration* refers to client-oriented activities in which the supervisor guides and educates the clinical social worker supervisee in interacting with other professionals in the service environment, influencing policies and procedures in the professional environment, and affecting political systems whose policies have an impact on client treatment/interventions.
- *Clinical supervision of continued learning* refers to activities in which the supervisor guides and educates the clinical social worker supervisee to develop the skills required for life-long continued professional learning.
- *Clinical supervision of job management* refers to activities in which the supervisor guides and educates the clinical social worker supervisee in work-related issues that frame the clinical work: record-keeping, fees, handling of phone calls and missed sessions, timeliness, report-writing, caseload management, and resolution of ethical issues.

This conceptualization makes it clear that although clinical supervision differs from administrative supervision, it still takes place in and must attend to the larger organizational environment.

The need to straddle the gap between the individual's professional practice and the exigencies of the environment is always a key component in supervision. The climate of the supervisor-supervisee relationship tends to change, however, when the focus turns to specific client needs rather than administrative concerns.

The purpose of clinical supervisors is to help practitioners develop skills, overcome obstacles, increase competency, and practice ethically with clients. It is historically a teaching, training, mentoring, and monitoring position with an emphasis on developing and maintaining competence. The focus in clinical supervision is on the individual supervisee's activities with clients. The vehicle for supervision is the review of client cases and the offer of suggestions and corrective feedback for improvement. (Campbell, 2006, p. 5)

According to Falander and Shafranske (2004), clinical supervision, when effective, rests on three pillars: the relationship, the process of inquiry, and the educational praxis. The supervisory *relationship* allows for the development of an alliance that is at the heart of a successful supervisory experience. The process of *inquiry* enhances the supervisee's understanding of the therapeutic process and awareness of his or her professional responsibilities. *Educational praxis* "provides multiple learning strategies, including instruction, observation, and role playing, tailored to enhance the supervisee's knowledge and to develop his or her technical skills."

THE RELATIONSHIP IN CLINICAL SUPERVISION

A longstanding set of standards for counseling supervisors (Association for Counselor Education and Supervision, 1990) helps to clarify the competencies underlying successful clinical supervision, stating that the counseling supervisor:

1. Demonstrates knowledge of individual differences with respect to gender, race, ethnicity, culture and age and understands the importance of these characteristics in supervisory relationships;
2. Is sensitive to the counselor's personal and professional needs;
3. Expects counselors to own the consequences of their actions;
4. Is sensitive to the evaluative nature of supervision and effectively responds to the counselor's anxiety relative to performance evaluation;
5. Conducts self-evaluations, as appropriate, as a means of modeling professional growth;
6. Provides facilitative conditions (empathy, concreteness, respect, congruence, genuineness, and immediacy);
7. Establishes a mutually trusting relationship with the counselor;
8. Provides an appropriate balance of challenge and support; and
9. Elicits counselor thoughts and feelings during counseling or consultation sessions, and responds in a manner that enhances the supervision process (pp. 30–31).

This conceptualization of the work of the competent clinical supervisor's work clearly assumes that it is possible to have a supervisory relationship that is built on the same facilitative dimensions and helping skills that are implicit in successful work with clients. These standards also recognize, however, that the strong evaluative dimension of supervision has obvious effects on the mutuality of the relationship. Supervisors are always faced with the question of how they can build trusting relationships with supervisees even in the face of a clear power differential. Although anxieties about evaluation cannot always be overcome, it is helpful if the supervisor addresses this issue directly in the early stages of supervision and returns to it on a regular basis. In fact, Durham and Glosoff (2010) suggest that power issues, when addressed directly, can even be used as a means for helping supervisees consider their own interactions with clients.

Use issues of power inherent in most supervisory relationships to help supervisees explore their own issues of power, oppression, and privilege. Empowering supervisees to voice their opinions and understand their own knowledge and expertise and building on their strengths are critical factors to modeling what we hope they do with their clients. (p. 145)

Effective clinical supervisors also find it helpful to keep the focus of the supervision on client well-being. Although supervisees are encouraged to carry out careful self-analysis, the ultimate purpose of this process is to make a difference in clients' lives.

CASE SUPERVISION

Reviewing the supervisee's current cases tends to be at the heart of most clinical supervision. Members of the helping professions often tend to think about supervision in terms of the processes they experienced in their training programs. In training programs, however, there are opportunities to go into depth on a very small number of cases, to view videos or listen to audio tapes, and to role play in a group setting. In the day-to-day world of a human service organization, however, using a variety of strategies may seem like a luxury. Supervisees often have very large client loads, making it difficult to focus for very long on just one case, and the use of video with actual clients is complex at best. Given these exigencies, supervisors and supervisees tend to focus on conceptualizing specific cases and making concrete plans for working with clients. It is possible, however, to enhance the supervisory process so that supervisees develop in positive directions and clients benefit. Consider the following pragmatic guidelines, which are realistic for a complex and fast-moving agency environment.

- *Adhere to a regular schedule of supervisory meetings.* In the face of competing demands, supervision might not always seem to be the best use of time for either the supervisor or the supervisee. The success of the supervisee and of the organization as a whole depends on good supervision, however, so these meetings should be seen as a high priority. When a schedule of supervisory meetings is not maintained, the supervisions tend to occur in response to client crises and the development of the supervisory relationship is sacrificed.
- *Focus on a range of clients and clinical issues.* The combination of time constraints and large case loads tends to lead toward supervisory meetings that are focused only on the most difficult issues and problematic clients. Ideally, supervision should attend to the development of the supervisee's competence, rather than a concentrating on a few examples of less competent practice. Placing the focus on a wider range of clients and issues makes it possible to start a meeting with a discussion of recent successes, as Campbell (2006) suggests, rather than keeping all of the emphasis on problems.
- *Gather evaluative information in a broader context, rather than depending solely on the case consultation.* Campbell (2006) suggests that the supervisor try to obtain additional information about the supervisee's work with clients rather than depending solely on the case consultation. One of the points that Campbell makes is that the clinical supervisor might face liability issues if it can be demonstrated that monitoring and evaluation were based on limited or biased data. In any human service organization, people in supervisory

positions have access to clients' records and can often identify problems that have not arisen in the narrow context of the case consultation.

- *Provide case supervision that attends to client advocacy as well as direct services.* Members of the helping professions are expected to be competent advocates as well as direct service providers (Schneider & Lester, 2001; Ratts, Toporek, & Lewis, 2010). Despite this fact, clinical supervision in many settings tends to address the activities that go on within supervisees' offices at the expense of activities that involve helping clients indirectly by affecting their environments. Supervisors should, in fact, keep tabs on their supervisees' advocacy-related actions and work to enhance the competence levels of their staff members. Even when working on a direct-service case, supervisors should make sure that the environmental factors affecting the client are discussed. In reviewing a case, the supervisor can often enhance a supervisee's critical consciousness by raising questions about the degree to which a client's concerns are affected by social, political, economic, and cultural factors and about the possibilities for bringing about change through advocacy on behalf of the client.

CLINICAL SUPERVISION FROM A MULTICULTURAL PERSPECTIVE

It would be difficult for a supervisor to help practitioners work effectively with clients and systems without a high degree of multicultural competence. Multicultural competence always involves self-interrogation as well as knowledge and awareness about the cultural factors affecting others, and this is no less true for the supervisory relationship.

> Supervisors need to assess racial and cultural identity attitudes of both themselves and their supervisees. Of critical importance is identifying from the outset of the supervisory relationship the areas of convergence and divergence supervisors share with their supervisees regarding racial and cultural issues. Supervisors need to be aware of and acknowledge their areas of tensions or bias and prepare how to negotiate with each supervisee the unique resolutions of these tensions or biases. (Miville, Rosa, & Constantine, 2005, p. 197)

Just as helping professionals must bring to the surface the cultural factors affecting their relationships with clients, so must supervisors make sure that they are fully conscious of cultural issues affecting the supervisory dyad.

Multicultural competence includes, of course, knowledge as well as awareness. Supervisors have a responsibility to make sure that they, themselves, are knowledgeable about multiculturalism, especially in regard to the communities their agencies serve. Beyond this, they are also responsible for assessing and enhancing their supervisees' knowledge in this important arena.

> Anxiety in multicultural supervision may stem not only from biases but also from lack of knowledge about and experience in working with culturally different people. Targeting the racial-cultural knowledge base for dealing with the specific client load of the supervisee (or of the agency in which the supervision takes place) is an excellent place to begin. (Miville et al., 2005, p. 198)

Supervision takes place within an environmental context, so it is important for supervisors to be multiculturally competent not just in the one-to-one supervisory relationship but also in the daily life of the organization.

Activities beyond the supervision dyad increase the supportive context in which multicultural supervision occurs. Being involved as a multicultural or social justice leader ... provides a clear message to supervisees about the importance of being multiculturally competent. (Miville et al., 2005, p. 198)

7.1   SUPERVISORY ISSUES AT GRANDVIEW COMMUNITY CENTER

Many of the things we learned about Grandview Community Center (GCC) in earlier chapters have implications for supervisory processes.

- We know that the communities and clients the center serves have changed over the years, with GCC now serving a much more diverse clientele than was true in its earlier years. This fact highlights the urgency of having multiculturally competent supervisors who are able to enhance their supervisees' effectiveness in working with clients and community members.
- We know that Executive Director Estrella decided to embark on a strategic planning project in part because she found that many members of the center's staff were focused on their own particular areas and did not have a strong sense of the mission and goals of the organization. Of course, one of the purposes of supervision is to encourage supervisees to view their own work in the context of the agency's overall mission. Supervision that connects individual and organizational goals can provide continual support for the sense of unity that the executive director is seeking.
- We learned from the center's organizational chart that (a) the organization does not have many administrative levels in which supervision would be carried out; (b) the center's work is divided by functional programs; and (c) the organization is also divided geographically. With the supervision role carried out primarily by the executive director and the program coordinators, conscious effort is required to maintain effective and regular supervision in the separate programs and communities. Good supervision tends to provide a means for implementing the organization's mission and, at the same time, helping service providers to meet needs that might differ between one neighborhood and another.

THEORIES OF MOTIVATION

Supervision requires an understanding of the complex needs that affect individual performance. These needs have been categorized and explained in a number of ways. At the broadest level, motivation theories are grouped as content theories, which have specific motivating factors, and process theories, which are content-free and describe the ways in which needs, behaviors, and rewards may interact. We will first review the three most common content theories of motivation, followed by a discussion of the most popular process theory: expectancy theory.

CONTENT THEORIES

The mid-twentieth century brought to light a number of content theories that are still widely used. These theories include Maslow's hierarchy of needs, Herzberg's Motivation/Hygiene Theory, and McClelland's Needs Theory.

MASLOW'S HIERARCHY OF NEEDS Maslow's (1954) hierarchy of needs is familiar to human service professionals in the context of personality theory. This concept is also important in the study of motivation in the workplace.

According to Maslow, human needs can be identified in terms of a hierarchy, with higher needs coming to the fore after lower needs have been met. The hierarchy of needs includes, from lowest to highest, (1) physiological needs, at the level of basic survival; (2) needs for safety and security; (3) needs for belonging, love, and social interaction; (4) esteem and status needs; and (5) self-actualization needs. Maslow's notion is that the lower needs dominate until they have been reasonably satisfied. When the lower needs have been met, the human being becomes increasingly motivated to satisfy higher needs. Finally, the search for self-actualization, or the realization of individual potential, can begin.

This idea has strong implications for work-related motivation because leadership must involve the identification of those needs that will form the basis for employee performance. Traditionally, attempts to motivate workers were oriented toward the use of economic rewards and the giving or withholding of job security. This process recognized only the lower-order needs.

Maslow's theory makes it clear that once these lower-order needs have been met, they no longer serve as motivators. When economic needs have been met and when some degree of security has been achieved, workers will tend to seek ways to meet higher-level needs through their work. When that point has been reached, the supervisee can best be motivated if some method is used to help him or her strive toward self-actualization. The worker at this level can be motivated only if the job itself allows for some degree of creativity, autonomy, and growth toward increased competence. It should also be remembered that if an agency is going through funding cuts or if there are real threats to security such as possibilities of client violence, higher-order needs will be replaced in prominence by lower-level ones until concerns related to basic needs are resolved.

HERZBERG'S MOTIVATOR/HYGIENE THEORY The notion of differing sets of motivating needs is enhanced in the work of Herzberg (1975), who makes a clear distinction between the factors related to job dissatisfaction and those involved in producing job satisfaction and motivation. The factors that relate to job dissatisfaction, what Herzberg calls maintenance factors, involve such aspects of the work environment as the fairness of company policies, the quality of supervision, relationships with supervisors and coworkers, salary, job security, and working conditions. These are not motivating factors; their presence or absence determines whether the worker will be dissatisfied with the work setting. The motivator factors relate to the job itself and involve the ability of the specific job to offer the worker opportunities to accomplish something significant, receive recognition for accomplishments, grow and develop, gain increased responsibility, and advance.

According to Herzberg, the maintenance factors simply trigger the worker's pain avoidance behavior, and the motivator factors relate to the need for growth and advancement. These growth factors are intrinsic to the nature of the job and relate to job satisfaction. Attention to hygiene factors is insufficient to motivate workers. The only way supervisees can be effectively motivated is through attention to the degree to which their work provides chances for growth, development, and increased responsibility. Herzberg's notion is to use the concept of job enrichment, building into each job the maximum opportunity for challenge and advancement (see the discussion of job design in Chapter 6).

MCCLELLAND'S NEEDS THEORY McClelland (1965) suggests that three distinct motivators can impel individuals in the work setting: the need for achievement, the need for power, and the need for affiliation. Although workers may possess all these needs to some degree, each individual is most strongly motivated by one. Thus, the achievement-motivated person values personal success and views it in terms of his or her ability to achieve measurable accomplishments. The individual who is motivated by achievement needs sets individual goals that are ambitious but clearly attainable and seeks frequent feedback concerning his or her competence and success. The person motivated by affiliation needs is most concerned with interpersonal relationships and is most effective in a setting offering supportiveness and opportunities for positive interactions. The power-motivated worker, being primarily concerned with influencing others, is most highly motivated in a setting giving him or her the opportunity to meet this need.

McClelland also makes an important distinction between two types of power. Personalized power involves the worker acting to enhance her or his own power and influence without regard to larger organizational goals, and it is generally seen as dysfunctional. Socialized power is manifested through an attempt to influence others for the good of the organization as a whole; it is seen as a legitimate and valuable motivator.

This approach to motivation has several implications for supervision. First, it makes clear that people with differing motivational sets have contrasting supervision needs. The affiliation-motivated worker is likely to respond to a relationship-oriented style, but an achievement-motivated person can be most effective when he or she has been delegated tasks that allow for individual performance. A power-oriented worker can be put in a position of leadership such as chairing a task force, in which this person will have opportunities to influence others to accomplish desired tasks.

A second implication for supervision is that achievement motivation, which may be closely related to high performance on the job, can be developed. In many work settings, training modalities and job redesign have been used to increase individuals' achievement motivation, and this approach might work in human service settings. In fields such as counseling and social work, an emphasis has historically been placed on affiliation—building relationships—with less attention to achievement. In counseling, for example, the client is seen as responsible for achieving change and the worker acting as a catalyst. Power dynamics in the past were typically seen as distasteful, with some exceptions in family therapy and radical therapy approaches articulated beginning in the 1970s. McClelland's model offers an opportunity for workers and supervisors to give greater attention to achievement of results, ranging from more adaptive behavior by a person with a mental illness to a welfare recipient getting a job. This model can also validate the appropriate use of power or influence to help create change.

PROCESS THEORIES: EXPECTANCY THEORY

Expectancy theory is a general model of motivation developed by Vroom (1964). Bowditch, Buono, and Stewart (2008) have summarized its key elements:

> (1) an effort-performance expectation that increased effort will lead to good performance (expectancy); (2) a performance-outcome perception that good performance will lead to certain outcomes or rewards (instrumentality); and (3) the value or attractiveness of a given reward or outcome to an individual (valence). (p. 82)

An employee's effort is affected by the perceived value of the reward, the likelihood that effort will lead to the reward, and organizational factors such as the job context. Effort does not automatically lead to performance, however. It is moderated by the employee's abilities and traits and her or his role perceptions: work may not be performed if the employee feels an activity "is not my job." Performance may result in intrinsic rewards such as a feeling of accomplishment and extrinsic rewards such as praise or perhaps an extra day off (lack of performance may ultimately lead to no rewards, such as being fired).

The implications for supervisors are several. First, the supervisor should understand the employee's perceptions and abilities: what rewards are valued, what the employee's role conception is and views regarding equity, and whether effort does lead to rewards. The manager can then intervene by showing how effort leads to results and that results will in fact be rewarded in ways the employee appreciates. The employee's role can be clarified, and additional training can be provided to enhance abilities if needed. As a process theory, this model allows for vast individual differences in terms of motivating factors: particular content (rewards) can be applied based on individual employee needs and values.

APPLYING THEORIES OF MOTIVATION

We will now review some supervision techniques that can be used to apply motivation theories toward worker performance. These include management by objectives, organizational behavior modification, reward systems, and the use of power and influence.

MANAGEMENT BY OBJECTIVES AS A MOTIVATOR

Although Management by Objectives (MBO) may be thought of primarily as a planning and a performance appraisal tool, it also has strong implications for individual motivation. When an organization uses MBO, overall goals are developed through the agency's planning process. Objectives are then set so that each department or work unit has a set of objectives designed to work toward the general goals of the organization. Individuals participate with their immediate supervisors in setting objectives for their own participation in the overall design. These objectives then form the basis on which their performance is evaluated.

The use of MBO has been questioned, but it can improve productivity; in fact, the way in which it is implemented, rather than the technique itself, is the usual source of problems (Bowditch, Buono, & Stewart, 2008). Several principles should be applied to maximize the effectiveness of the process. First, objectives should be developed mutually by the worker and supervisor, not imposed from above. If a worker feels pressured to set particular objectives, she or he is likely to comply only as much as possible to avoid negative consequences. Also, according to Bowditch, Buono, and Stewart (2008):

> If it is to be successful, MBO should be characterized by (1) an active give-and-take between managers [or supervisors] and their subordinates; (2) a high level of face-to-face communication; (3) top management support and involvement; (4) flexibility in setting goals; (5) attention to implementation details (e.g., communication of its importance; MBO-related training; sufficient time frame; monitoring); (6) a high degree of fit with the specific needs of the organization; and (7) an organizational culture and climate that supports openness and sharing. (p. 86)

The agreement that forms the basis of MBO can be broadened to involve a mutual understanding of the kinds of outcome rewards that might be attached to successful meeting of objectives, as well as the degree of support needed to "clear the path" to success.

ORGANIZATIONAL BEHAVIOR MODIFICATION

Many in the human services have viewed behavior modification with skepticism or aversion. In fact, however, even a person-centered therapist nodding earnestly and saying, "Tell me more," is using behavior modification. As is the case of many techniques, behavior modification is not inherently bad or good, effective or ineffective. Organizational behavior modification (OBM) is, of course, not universally necessary, but it can be a useful element of some supervisory relationships. Even if the organization does not comprehensively apply the model, OBM principles may be useful to a supervisor and worker as they discuss, for example, how the worker can best be rewarded.

Luthans and Kreitner (1975) suggest that OBM can provide a system through which positive reinforcement, or reward, is made contingent on improvements in work-related performance. The supervisor and supervisee would work together to define specific target behaviors. The individual's interests, concerns, and abilities would be taken into account as reinforcers for specific behaviors that were selected. As the individual's work effectiveness improved, he or she would receive positive reinforcers. The supervisor would also try to make the work environment favorable for skill development. Ideally, as the supervisee became more effective and confident, he or she would have complete control over the reinforcement schedule, with little outside help needed. The behavior modification approach might be used more directly with new or inexperienced workers or with those grappling with a specific difficulty. Experienced professionals can more easily monitor and reward their own behavior.

Once again, Bowditch, Buono, and Stewart (2008) offer useful guidance. They suggest that in successful OBM programs, managers "(1) reward people with what they value; (2) explicitly link the reward with the desired behavior; (3) appropriately fit the magnitude of the reward with the magnitude of the behavior; (4) reward better performers more than average performers; and (5) give meaningful feedback and the reward after the performance" (p. 89).

REWARD SYSTEMS

Rewards are a key element of all models of motivation. We will review here examples of the types of rewards available to supervisors. The broadest categories of rewards are intrinsic and extrinsic. Extrinsic rewards include direct compensation (basic salary, overtime and holiday premiums, and performance bonuses), indirect compensation (health, pension, and other benefits), and nonfinancial compensation (desirable work assignments and office furnishings such as a computer). Intrinsic rewards are those at the higher levels of Maslow's hierarchy and are almost unlimited, including opportunities for participation in decision making or personal growth, interesting work, autonomy, and a feeling of accomplishment.

Because supervisors often have no control over some rewards, such as pay levels or intrinsic feelings of satisfaction felt by the employee, they must work with the subordinate to discuss what available rewards are desirable and how and under what conditions they may be given. For example, the supervisor may be able to recommend that the employee be moved up a step in pay grade or receive a bonus for exceptional work on a special project. The supervisor may also have some control over assignment of office space or equipment such as computers and accessories. The supervisor can usually provide rewards in the form of interesting work assignments or training opportunities, and, of course, recognition in the form of praise and symbolic rewards such as token gifts is possible. If an agency has employee- or team-of-the-month awards, a supervisor can nominate staff. Supervisors should remain up-to-date on what an employee would feel rewarded by and be alert for opportunities to reward whenever appropriate.

Some rewards such as praise may be given independent of agency systems; many rewards should be an explicit part of the agency's personnel policies. This would include pay scales, criteria and standards for advancement, the use of merit pay or bonuses, and perhaps employee-of-the-month awards. Any effective reward system should meet these requirements (Orsburn, 1994):

1. They must be visible and understandable to the people.
2. They must be perceived as being consistent and fair.
3. They must be aimed at the appropriate target (individual or team).
4. They must dispense a valued reinforcer (money, praise, status, etc.).

Recent developments in formal reward systems, including merit pay (Gabris, 1998) and team-based rewards (Orsburn, Moran, Musselwhite, & Zenger, 1990), may be options for some organizations. Administrators designing such systems will need to consult specialized sources (see, for example, Siegel, 1998) for guidance to ensure that any system chosen is appropriate and well designed. Even within limited or traditional agency systems, an individual supervisor can use dialogue and creativity with a subordinate to develop meaningful and useful rewards.

POWER AND INFLUENCE

Helping professionals sometimes view power (the ability to control others), influence (the ability to persuade others), authority (formalized power or influence), and their uses with distaste or ambivalence, but it must be admitted that human service workers do use power and influence in their work, in enforcing require-ments of clients or trying to persuade coworkers (Gummer, 1990). It therefore behooves human service workers to be comfortable with the appropriate use of power and influence and to use power tactics to enhance organizational performance.

The use of power in the supervisory relationship is an example. Fortunately, if a subordinate wants to succeed in a job or profession, the supervisor does have the power to influence behavior. In fact, some supervisors are more influential than others, depending on the kind and amount of power they hold in the organiza-tional context. The interactions among power, authority, and leadership are com-plex, and they can have significant effects on the supervisory process.

An individual's power to direct or influence others comes from a variety of sources. Most observers of power relationships still find useful the categories French and Raven (1959) suggested: coercive power; legitimate, or positional, power; expert power; reward power; and referent power. Hersey, Blanchard, and Johnson (2007) add to this list information power and connection power. In a supervisory situation, the use of coercive power is based on the supervisor's ability to control punishments, such as poor job assignments, low compensation, or disci-plinary action. Legitimate, or positional, power involves acceptance of the supervi-sor's right to influence the supervisee's work by virtue of his or her official position in a hierarchical organization. Expert power depends on the supervisees respect for the expertise and knowledge that the specific supervisor brings to the work setting. Reward power finds its source in the supervisor's ability to provide positive rewards as incentives for defined behaviors. Referent power depends not on the external trappings of power but on the personal relationship between supervisor and supervisee and on the degree to which the supervisee respects and identifies with the supervisor. Information power draws on the supervisor's access to valu-able information: a supervisor who has "inside information" or knowledge of upcoming developments before others may be more highly valued by staff. Connec-tion power becomes a reality when the supervisor is perceived as having close con-tact with other influential people.

The supervisee must perceive a supervisor's power as real if the relationship itself is to prove influential. Some supervisees will respond to position power alone, however, and others will respond only to other types of power such as expertise. Supervisors do want to influence supervisees' behavior, attitudes, and effectiveness, and the supervisory relationship is the vehicle through which this process takes place. The form of the relationship must take into account the source of supervisory power. If supervisees are inexperienced, insecure, or at the beginning of the training process, they might at first respond to supervisors who clearly con-trol the rewards and punishments that the system has to offer. More experienced and professional human service workers tend to gain only from supervisory rela-tionships based on their respect for the expertise of a supervisor who is willing to maintain an egalitarian affiliation. Ideally, the supervisory relationship can develop and change over time, as the supervisee is actively encouraged to take increasing control over his or her learning.

In human service settings, issues of power are often especially difficult because supervisors tend to be wary of over-controlling others' efforts. Professionals want to be mentors but might feel uncomfortable about evaluating and influencing other workers' progress toward effectiveness. The supervisory relationship must recognize the existence of power while taking into account the unique aspects of the human service environment.

PARTICIPATIVE DECISION MAKING AS A SUPERVISION APPROACH

Because human service workers are often motivated by idealistic needs, they tend to work most effectively toward goals in which they feel a sense of ownership. Given that their work entails personal involvement as well as task completion, they must be committed to what they are doing. The human services, almost by definition, do not lend themselves to mechanistic task performance.

The nature of human service organizations also lends itself to collegial and democratic approaches to management. The goals toward which human service organizations work are often complex and certainly are subject to a variety of interpretations. At the same time, many possible methods can be used to serve client needs. If an attempt is to be made to work toward client goals rather than to emphasize performance of accustomed services, the ideas of many people are needed. Workers who are very familiar with client needs can help reach innovative solutions to long-standing problems.

People in human service settings tend to realize that everyone who will be affected by a decision should have a part in making it. All of the people whose commitment will be needed in carrying out a new solution should be involved in the problem-solving process. All of the people whose individual objectives will lead to the meeting of organizational goals should be part of the goal-setting process.

Participative Decision Making (PDM) and participative management have evolved as generic terms for involving employees in greater decision making, based on the human resources theories of Likert, McGregor, and others, as reviewed in Chapter 4. PDM is defined here as "actual staff involvement, whether formal or informal, direct or indirect, in decision processes regarding issues affecting the structure, funding, staffing, or programming" of the organization (Ramsdell, 1994, p. 58). PDM is not an either/or factor but is on a continuum from no involvement in the decision to "complete control or veto power over the decision" (Ramsdell, 1994, p. 58). In one test of the use of PDM, Packard (1989) found that child protective services units whose supervisors were seen as more participative had higher performance and job satisfaction than those with less PDM. Interestingly, Packard (1993) also discovered that these supervisors felt that workers were capable of much more PDM than they were currently allowed, suggesting that this is an underused approach.

To respond to this opportunity, Shera and Page (1995) suggest strategies for employee empowerment that allow greater PDM: at the organizational level, this can happen through a culture of shared leadership and meeting chairing, team problem solving and decision making, and flexible job designs. Effective communication, rewarding employee initiative, mutual (two-way) feedback, and employee development can enhance empowerment. Shera and Page add that the agency's service delivery technology (for example, focusing on client outcomes) and information sharing through computers can be empowering. Bowditch, Buono, and Stewart (2008) suggest that empowerment depends on employees' knowledge of organizational expectations, awareness that they will be rewarded for their contributions, possession of appropriate knowledge and skills, and the power to make relevant decisions. The facts that human service workers are likely to want more PDM, that supervisors and managers believe they are capable of more PDM (Packard, 1993), and that there is growing evidence of the effectiveness of PDM with skilled and motivated workers (Pine & Healy, 2007) suggest that supervisors should look for opportunities to increase their use of PDM.

PDM is often used in group settings, such as a team of a supervisor and her or his subordinates. Human service professionals are often very familiar with principles of group dynamics, but they may have difficulty applying them when they serve in supervisory capacities in their own agency settings. A few basic guidelines can help in the process.

First, when a group of colleagues is expected to make a decision, develop a plan, or solve a problem, be sure to clarify beforehand what constraints might be present. Groups in human service settings often spend endless hours developing novel solutions only to learn later that their ideas cannot be implemented because of budgetary constraints, little-known federal regulations, specifics in the agency's bylaws, or opposition of a powerful board member. After this happens several times, workers' commitment to involve themselves in agency governance lessens, and a low degree of energy is available to the task.

Second, clarify the purpose of a meeting or task force. Sometimes there is misunderstanding concerning the purpose of a procedure, whether it involves a face-to-face meeting, a series of task force projects, or individual interviews and questionnaires. The people who are asked to give input need to know whether the process they are involved in is meant to provide useful advice to a problem solver or whether they, as a group, will be asked to solve the problem or submit the plan of action. A meeting, like an agency plan, must be seen as a means to some specific end.

Third, clarify the procedures to be used. Just as participants must be aware of the goals toward which they are working, they must also be privy to the process being used. Clarity concerning procedural questions is especially important in human service settings, in which clear-cut guidelines are often lacking and participants can be expected to be reasonably expert in using a variety of processes. Many human service workers know how to use such approaches as brainstorming and priority setting with clients but fail to use such useful tools in the context of their own meetings.

Fourth, pay attention to process variables. A major concern in democratic supervision is the blending of concern for task with concern for people or relationships. As workers join in a mutual search for effective solutions, they need to stop and check the process of their own interactions. This awareness of human interactions is an important part of the leadership process and one that cannot be left to chance.

Fifth, choose carefully who is to be involved in each problem-solving process. The human service professional as leader often makes the error of involving too many or too few people in a problem-solving or planning process. It is well worth the time spent to identify, as specifically as possible, who will be affected by a particular decision and then to involve all the people listed in the decision-making process. At the same time, there is a need to recognize the differences between major and minor problems and to use human resources wisely. A large number of people, including volunteers, should be involved in setting broad agency goals; a small number of people should strive to set the specific objectives of one individual or work unit. A large number of people should be involved in seeking the solution to a major problem; a small number should work actively on the elimination of a minor annoyance.

In the long run, it is up to the supervisor to recognize that human service workers bring a variety of needs and motivations to the work setting and that they can meet those needs most effectively if they are actively involved in controlling the quality of their own work lives.

CHALLENGES IN SUPERVISION

Inevitable problems and challenges in supervising staff can typically be handled using techniques already discussed. However, even though a supervisor does everything "right," sometimes disciplinary action is necessary. The agency should have a fair and clearly outlined progressive discipline procedure in its personnel manual, and the supervisor should ensure that the worker is aware of the process and that it is followed precisely if it is needed.

Weinbach and Taylor (2011, pp. 257–260) outline a useful progressive discipline process through which a problem may be addressed as early as possible, using the appropriate level of intervention. If work performance is below expectations, the worker should receive fair and objective feedback as soon as possible. This action is often enough to get performance on track again. If the employee does not respond to such efforts, a verbal reprimand ("a direct, private, and confidential communication of the staff member's shortcomings") (Weinbach and Taylor, 2011, p. 258) may be necessary. A common occurrence in organizations should be avoided: giving a group reprimand at a staff meeting when only one worker is at fault. Comments such as "Staff should stop being rude to clients" leave all wondering whether they are doing anything wrong and inevitably lower morale. If verbal reprimands are not effective, a written reprimand, with a copy for the employee's personnel file, may be needed. This should list specific behaviors that need to be changed, the expected behavior, and a time line. At this point, and before all subsequent steps, the supervisor's manager should be informed and consulted. If necessary, a next step may be a behavioral contract indicating specific steps to be taken to remedy the performance problems.

Some organizations have additional procedures such as provisions for suspensions without pay. Transfers of staff may be warranted in particular circumstances, such as personality or other situational factors, but should not be used to move problem employees with no prospect of a behavior change.

Termination of a worker is the next step and normally occurs only for unsatisfactory performance that has not been corrected despite explicit attempts or for gross misconduct, such as sexual involvement with a client. Termination for gross misconduct can normally occur "on the spot," without using progressive discipline, but agency procedures and standards still need to be followed.

Rivas (1998) and Weinbach and Taylor (2008) both offer useful guidelines for handling termination. At the termination interview, the supervisor needs to be not only fair and considerate but also absolutely clear that the employee is being terminated and that the decision is not negotiable. The reasons for the termination should at this point not be surprises, and they should be stated clearly in behaviorally specific terms. If the agency has an appeal or grievance procedure, the worker should be made aware of it. Of course, the worker should be treated with dignity and respect, and support in the form of suggestions for new employment, education, or behavior change may be offered. An exit interview may be offered, in which mutual feedback and a debriefing of the worker's experience at the agency can be reviewed. The supervisor should also take any necessary steps to prevent or minimize disruption to the workplace by addressing any organizational climate issues that emerge.

MAKING THE TRANSITION TO THE SUPERVISORY ROLE

Many new supervisors find the transition from practitioner to manager and motivator of others difficult to make. Managerial functions can be carried out effectively by human service professionals if their clinical training is supplemented by the development of leadership skills.

Yet the transition from service provider to supervisor is by no means easy. The professional must move from the position of being nonjudgmental with clients to one of being an evaluator of workers, from a stance of encouraging clients to take total responsibility for their own goals to one of motivating other human service workers to strive toward the meeting of mutually accepted objectives. These sometimes subtle differences often lead to ineffective supervision, with the individual either placing total focus on relationship behavior at the expense of the tasks to be performed or, recognizing that accustomed behaviors are not workable in this new situation, focusing total attention on the task in an authoritarian style. These difficulties in finding a comfortable leadership style are exacerbated by the problems inherent in human service organizations: the facts that appraisal of the quality of work is difficult and that those being supervised are often professionals who themselves have little interest in conforming to organizationally defined expectations.

A number of other transitional issues are involved in moving from direct practitioner to supervisor, not the least of which is the shift in both position and occupation, requiring new sets of skills and knowledge and involving greater responsibilities and authority. According to Kadushin (1985), the supervisor "has responsibility to the supervisees for administration, education, and support, and ultimate responsibility for service to the client." Additionally, he or she "assumes greater responsibility for policy formulation in the agency and community-agency relationships," and, "instead of being responsible for a caseload, the supervisor is now responsible for a number of caseloads" (p. 299).

Adaptation to the exercise of authority is another issue facing the new supervisor. The principle of client self-determination, so protected and promoted in direct practice, does not enjoy the same prominence in the supervisor-supervisee relationship. As an employee of the agency, the worker is subject to the organization's policies and procedures and its administrative directives, commonly implemented by the supervisor. The worker's freedom of choice is usually limited to complying with those policies, procedures, and directives or selecting to work elsewhere. By the same token, the supervisor has no choice but to enforce administrative dicta if the supervisor wishes to remain in that position. This is not to say that workers cannot and should not be allowed to participate in decision making. What it does mean is that in some cases workers will not accept administrative decisions and that it is the supervisor's responsibility to exercise the authority inherent in the position to ensure that these decisions are carried out. The new supervisor must therefore learn to live with the consequences of sometimes enforcing unpopular decisions.

Another transitional issue is one of either partially or completely giving up the satisfaction of direct therapeutic contact with clients in favor of nontherapeutic contact with supervisees. In his or her new role and occupation, the supervisor learns to derive satisfaction from serving clients through others and from helping workers grow and develop professionally.

The shift from worker to supervisor thus entails several changes in perspectives and behaviors, in allegiances and responsibilities.

> In accepting the transition, the new supervisors face the complex processes of developing a clear conception of what the new position entails behaviorally and attitudinally; they have to divest themselves of old behaviors and attitudes appropriate to the direct service worker's position and learn and commit themselves to behavior and attitudes appropriate to the new position; they have to emotionally accept a changed image of themselves and a changed relationship with former peers and newly acquired colleagues. (Kadushin, 1985, p. 306)

Transition involves change, and change can be painful. Change, however, can also offer the opportunity for personal development and self-actualization, and it is in this latter dimension that the neophyte supervisor can find solace and encouragement.

SUMMARY

Many human service professionals find themselves in supervisory positions at some point in their careers. In this important role, they work closely with supervisees to help them play their parts in assisting clients and accomplishing the organization's mission. Across all supervisory roles, supervisors provide encouragement, build motivation, increase the mutuality of individual and organizational goals, enhance confidence, carry out ongoing assessments, and provide supervisees with fair and prompt feedback. In clinical supervision, the specific focus is on increasing supervisees' success in their interactions with clients, with particular emphasis placed on multicultural competence. Because motivation is at the heart of the supervisee's professional development, supervisors understand and are able to apply the principles of motivation within a climate of participative decision making.

| COMPETENCY-BUILDING ACTIVITY 7.1 | SUPERVISION |

In your most recent competency-building activities, you designed an organizational chart for your hypothetical program or agency and then went on to identify some of the jobs that would need to be created in order to carry out your mission. Now, it is time to consider your organization's supervisory needs.

1. As you examine your organizational chart, see whether you have a clear way to identify the key supervisory roles that need to be played. Do you have a clear picture of what the supervisory relationships might be in your organization? Identify the supervisory pairs that would carry out general and clinical supervision.

2. In the previous chapter, you developed some ideas about a particular job that would need to be filled. Once this job is filled, what would be the most important issues that a supervisor would need to address?

CASE ACTIVITY 7.1 | THE TOKEN ECONOMY

Having worked as a therapist for a number of years, Jim Forrest had developed a high level of expertise in dealing with problems related to substance abuse. His work had included jobs in several settings, including a short-term detoxification program in a hospital, a community-based methadone treatment center, and a community mental health outpatient program.

Although his work with clients had always been satisfying, two things continued to trouble him. One major issue for Forrest was that his experience had convinced him that his clients' milieu was more important than any other aspect of treatment. Although one-to-one counseling could be helpful, it was always less important than the reinforcement clients got for various behaviors in their immediate social environments.

The other aspect of his work that tended to trouble him was the question of management. As a professional therapist, he had grown impatient with the pressure on him to stick to specific time lines and methods regardless of his clients' needs. In each agency, managers tended to create methods of operation based more on business principles and treatment costs than on the effects of various treatment modalities. Forrest felt that given the chance to do what he felt was best for his clients, he could work both effectively and efficiently.

Forrest finally had the chance to try out his ideas when he was invited by a former colleague to take on a job as head of a newly funded detoxification program being set up in one wing of the local community mental health center. The program had been funded to provide short-term services, and two of the therapists from the previous, smaller program were to remain on staff. With this exception, Jim would be free to develop the program in whatever way he saw fit. Funding was sufficient to provide for the hiring of a staff of four more professional therapists and eight paraprofessionals.

Forrest began interviewing potential employees, telling each of them the same thing. The program would be based on use of a token economy, meaning that clients would receive concrete and specific reinforcements for behaviors that were consistent with responsible, adult conduct. Every staff member would need to be involved in recording and reinforcing

appropriate client behaviors, for only then would the clients begin to learn new ways of dealing with their environment. Beyond this "bottom line" of commitment to the token economy as a treatment modality, professionals would be free to set their own hours and work with clients according to their best interests. Newcomers would be more closely supervised at first. Later they, too, might have the kind of freedom already granted to the experienced professionals.

Most of the new workers started in at their tasks with a high degree of enthusiasm. It was like a dream come true, and after a few weeks, Forrest began to think that he was already seeing results in terms of client change. A few problems, however, were beginning to surface.

First, Hugh Schmidt, one of the two therapists who had already been employed at the center, began to complain to anyone who would listen about the idea of the token economy. Schmidt believed that long-term therapy, insight, and intrapsychic change were the only ways to deal with substance abusers. Changes in behavior could not get at the root cause of the problem, and the token economy could change only concrete behavior, not attitudes. He continued to work with clients in the same way he always had, but the token economy was constantly being sabotaged.

Another member of the professional staff was troubled not by the token economy but by the freedom Forrest allowed the employees. Carol Cooke pointed out that although the staff members had been enthusiastic at first, they would not maintain a high level of commitment unless they were aware of the rules and regulations governing their own behaviors. Forrest scoffed at these concerns until one Friday afternoon when he had to make a presentation at an out-of-town conference. When he realized he had forgotten something, he called the office. Not one of the professional staff members was there.

The problems Forrest had begun to face were minor, but they started to make him think. Could he maintain a central focus in the program if every member of the professional staff were not necessarily committed to it? Could he trust the professional staff in the way he had always wished to be trusted? The challenges began to seem a little more difficult than he had expected.

1. What do you think of Jim Forrest's approach to the position of program administration? What are his strengths and weaknesses in dealing with his new leadership position?
2. If you were Forrest, what would you do about the problem Hugh Schmidt's attitude poses? Is it necessary for the staff to work as a closely knit team, or is there room for a great deal of variation?
3. What would you do about the problem Carol Cooke poses? Do employees—even trained professionals—need clearer behavioral guidelines than Forrest provided?
4. Do you think Forrest has the potential to be more effective than the business-oriented professional managers he had encountered before?

REFERENCES

Akin, G., & Weil, M. (1981, October). The prior question: How do supervisors learn to supervise? *Social Casework*, 62, 472–479.

American Board of Examiners in Clinical Social Work. (2004). *Position statement: Clinical supervision: A practice specialty of clinical social work*. Retrieved October 1, 2005, from http://www.abecsw.org/docs/superfinal.pdf.

Association for Counselor Education and Supervision. (1990). Standards for counseling supervisors. *Journal of Counseling & Development*, 69, 30–32.

Bowditch, J., Buono, A., & Stewart, M. (2008). *A primer on organizational behavior* (7th ed.). New York: Wiley.

Campbell, J. M. (2006). *Essentials of clinical supervision.* New York: Wiley.

Durham, J. C. & Glosoff, H. L. (2010). From passion to action: Integrating the ACA Advocacy Competencies and social justice into counselor education and supervision. In M. J. Ratts, R. L. Toporek, & J. A. Lewis (Eds.), *ACA Advocacy Competencies: A social justice framework for counselors* (pp. 139–150). Alexandria, VA: American Counseling Association.

Falender, C. A., & Shafranske, E. P. (2004). *Clinical supervision: A competency-based approach.* Washington, DC: American Psychological Association.

Fiedler, F. E. (1967). A theory of leadership effectiveness. New York: McGraw-Hill.

French, J. R. P., & Raven, B. (1959). The bases of social power. In D. Cartwright (Ed.), *Studies in social power*. Ann Arbor: University of Michigan Press.

Gabris, G. (1998). Merit pay mania. In S. Condrey (Ed.), *Handbook of human resource management in government* (pp. 627–657). San Francisco: Jossey-Bass.

Gummer, B. (1990). *The politics of social administration*. Upper Saddle River, NJ: Prentice Hall.

Hersey, P., Blanchard, K., & Johnson, D. (2007). *Management of organizational behavior: Leading human resources* (9th ed.). Upper Saddle River, NJ: Prentice Hall.

Herzberg, F. (1975). One more time: How do you motivate employees? In Harvard Business Review (Ed.), *On management*. New York: Harper & Row.

Kadushin, A. (1985). *Supervision in social work* (2nd ed.). New York: Columbia University Press.

Luthans, F., & Kreitner, R. (1975). *Organizational behavior modification*. Glenview, IL: Scott, Foresman.

Maslow, A. H. (1954). *Motivation and personality*. New York: Harper & Row.

McClelland, D. (1965). Achievement motivation can be developed. *Harvard Business Review*, 43, 6–24.

Miville, M. L., Rosa, D., & Constantine, M. G. (2005). Building multicultural competence in clinical supervision. In M. G. Constantine & D. W. Sue (Eds.), *Strategies for building multicultural competence in mental health and educational settings* (pp. 199–211). New York: John Wiley & Sons.

Morse, J. J., & Lorsch, J. W. (1975). Beyond Theory Y. In Harvard Business Review (Ed.), *On management*. New York: Harper & Row.

Orsburn, J. (1994). Recommendations regarding a competency-based reward system. Unpublished manuscript.

Orsburn, J., Moran, L., Musselwhite, E., & Zenger, J. (1990). *Self-directed work teams: The new American challenge*. Homewood, IL: Business One Irwin.

Packard, T. (1989). Participation in decision making, performance, and job satisfaction in a social work bureaucracy. *Administration in Social Work*, 13(1), 59–73.

Packard, T. (1993). Managers' and workers' views of the dimensions of participation in organizational decision making. *Administration in Social Work*, 13(1), 59–73.

Pine, B., & Healy, L. (2007). New leadership for the human services: Involving and empowering staff through participatory management. In J. Aldgate, L. Healy, B. Malcolm, B. Pine, W. Rose, & J. Sedens (Eds.), *Enhancing social work management: Theory and best practice from the UK and USA* (pp. 35–55). Philadelphia: Jessica Kingsley Publishers.

Pine, B., Warsh, R., & Maluccio, A. (1998). Participatory management in a public child welfare agency: A key to effective change. *Administration in Social Work*, 22(1), 19–32.

Ramsdell, P. (1994). Staff participation in organizational decision-making: An empirical study. *Administration in Social Work*, 18(4), 51–71.

Ratts, M. J., Toporek, R. L., & Lewis, J. A. (Eds.). (2010). *ACA Advocacy Competencies: A social justice framework for counselors*. Alexandria, VA: American Counseling Association.

Rivas, R. (1998). Dismissing problem employees. In R. Edwards, J. Yankey, & M. Altpeter (Eds.), *Skills for effective management of nonprofit organizations* (pp. 262–278). Washington, DC: NASW Press.

Schneider, R. L., & Lester, L. (2001). *Social work advocacy: A new framework for action*. Belmont, CA: Brooks/Cole.

Shera, W., & Page, J. (1995). Creating more effective human service organizations through strategies of empowerment. *Administration in Social Work*, 19(4), 1–15.

Shulman, L. (1993). *Interactional supervision*. Washington, DC: NASW Press.

Siegel, G. (1998). Designing and creating an effective compensation plan. In S. Condrey (Ed.), *Handbook of human resource management in government* (pp. 608–629). San Francisco: Jossey-Bass.

Vroom, V. H. (1964). *Work and motivation*. New York: Wiley.

Weinbach, R. & Taylor, L. (2011). *The social worker as manager: A practical guide to success* (6th ed.). Boston: Allyn & Bacon.

USEFUL WEB RESOURCES

American Board of Examiners in Clinical Social Work. http://www.abecsw.org/.

Association for Counselor Education and Supervision (A Division of the American Counseling Association). http://www.acesonline.net/.

Association of Psychology Postdoctoral and Internship Centers. http://www.appic.org/.

Child Life Council Clinical Supervision Statement. http://www.childlife.org/files/ClinicalSupervisionPS08.pdf.

National Association of Social Workers. http://www.naswdc.org/.

U.S. Dept. of Health & Human Services. Child Welfare Information Gateway. Clinical Supervision. http://www.childwelfare.gov/management/mgmt_supervision/clinical/.

Managing Finances to Meet Program Goals

CHAPTER **8**

Budgeting and fund-raising are probably seen by most human service workers, and perhaps even by many mangers, as the least appealing aspects of their work. Nevertheless, of course, acquiring, effectively using, and accounting for funds are essential aspects of providing valuable services to clients and communities. Fortunately for both managers and staff, the basic processes of financial management can be readily understood with exposure to only a few key concepts and processes. The focus in this chapter will be on financial management at the program level, in the context of a whole agency. Additionally, the focus here is on financial management in not-for-profit organizations. Many of these concepts and processes also apply in government organizations, but those organizations have unique characteristics that warrant specific financial management systems. These are addressed in public administration books (e.g., Wang, 2010).

A program exists to meet needs or address social problems, which are identified through a needs assessment and addressed through strategies that ultimately are reflected in the design and implementation of a program. A budget is fundamentally a program reflected in fiscal terms. Just as the previous two chapters showed the importance of people—the staff who work with clients and the community and those who support direct service providers—this chapter highlights the importance of additional resources, such as facilities, supplies, and equipment, that are reflected in the budget.

The budget itself is simply a projection of operational plans, usually for a one-year time span, with the plans stated in terms of the acquisition and allocation of dollars for varying functions or activities. As a decision-making tool, the budget helps transform goals into service realities. Proficient use of this tool requires expertise on the part of the human service manager not only in budgeting but in other aspects of financial management as well.

Although the human service administrator does not need to be an accountant, he or she is responsible for the total management and operations of the agency. Other agency staff members, such as program and project directors and supervisors, are often called on to write a budget for their program or unit or to serve on a budgeting committee. Therefore, it is incumbent on the administrator, supervisor, or project leader to have some working knowledge of financial management.

Any manager or staff member in a human service program that receives government funds, foundation grants, or charitable contributions is a steward of the resources of others. This stewardship implies the best possible use of these scarce resources. Having a well-thought-out strategic plan to respond to pressing social and community needs; using well-designed and proven service delivery methods; and having trained, competent, and motivated staff are part of this stewardship, as is the responsible use of funds. This includes thorough planning on how to acquire funds, allocate funds through a budgeting process, and making and accounting for the expenditures as planned (reflected in ongoing financial reports). In this chapter, we will cover these core processes, including fund-raising, writing proposals, and using financial reports and controls.

| 8.1 | FINANCES AT GRANDVIEW COMMUNITY CENTER |

Shortly after Leona took over at Grandview Community Center (GCC), she concluded that she would need to pay significant attention to finances, from acquiring funds to clearly tracking and documenting expenditures. A contract with County Behavioral Health Services funds the Counseling Services Program. In-home services are provided through a contract with the Public Child Welfare Agency to work with families at risk of child abuse or neglect. Donations and two local foundations fund the Community Development Program. The Day Care Program receives federal child development funding. Because their funding source program monitors had expressed concerns about the agency's fiscal controls and because funding had become increasingly tight, Leona knew she would need to make some significant improvements to the agency's financial management systems. She arranged an external audit by a CPA who specialized in not-for-profit organizations. That audit would show where the agency's accounting systems needed to be improved. While the audit was occurring, Leona worked with each program manager to make sure expenses were clearly planned for and within the programs' budgets. She also reviewed the status of current grants, contracts, and fund-raising plans to get a realistic picture of each program's current and future revenues.

GCC's new Teen Transition and Treatment Program will be used here to illustrate the budgeting process. As was discussed in Chapter 3, this new program was based on an evidence-based best practice. This model required that all direct service staff have clinical licenses, be certified (e.g., Certified Alcohol and Drug Counselor), or be working toward licensure or certification. The objectives stated that the program would have an ongoing caseload of 50 clients. Program staff decided that clinicians could each carry a caseload of 13 clients, so they budgeted four full-time clinicians to serve 50 clients at a time. Using current costs in the agency's existing programs as guidelines, they determined costs for the line items in this new program. The final budget can be seen in Table 8.1.

THE FINANCIAL MANAGEMENT PROCESS

After a program is designed, including plans for staffing and usage of other resources such as facilities and supplies, a budget for its accomplishment is prepared. Budgeting is actually only one part of a larger process of *financial management*.

There are three major stages in the financial management process (Mayers, 2004, p. 22):

- **Resource acquisition** focuses on the future and includes planning/budgeting, writing proposals for grants or contracts, and other fund development including fees and donations.
- **Resource disposition** focuses on the present and includes control/budgeting, allocating, and investing.
- **Resource reporting** looks at the past and includes accounting, financial reporting, and evaluation.

These steps, with the exception of the advanced concept of investing, will be addressed in this chapter. Consistent with the scope of this book, our discussion will focus on budgeting at the *program* level. In all but the smallest human service organization, the *agency* budget will have separate budgets for multiple programs. Program budgeting will be briefly mentioned in the following sections.

RESOURCE ACQUISITION

A program budget may be looked at in two ways. First, a program has a *revenue* budget that indicates the various funding sources for a program and the amount of funds contributed by each source. In a simple program, there may be only one source, such as a government contract or a foundation grant. However, some programs have multiple sources, such as a grant that is supplemented by donation or fee income. Here, in discussing the development of a budget, we will assume that a program has only one revenue source.

The second type of budget for a program is an *expense* budget, which lists exactly how the funds will be spent. The processes of acquiring funds and planning how to expend funds are inextricably linked. We will first discuss expense budgets, assuming that the new program idea came from the strategic plan and funds are not yet available. Because a funding source will want to know what will happen to funds if they are provided, developing an expenditure budget for a new program often precedes soliciting funds to implement it. After discussing budget development, we will review how to locate a funding source and develop revenue for the program.

ESTIMATING EXPENDITURES

Acquiring resources for a program typically begins with planning, such as the strategic planning described in Chapter 3. Implementation of the strategic plan eventually gets to the stage of acquisition and allocation of funds to implement the plan. At the program level, this consists of the design of a program for which funding can then be solicited. The program model (that is, the services to be provided, staff needed and their qualifications, required facilities, and other resources) and the program objectives (service outcomes expected, numbers and types of clients, projected units of service and activities) become the basis for estimating expenditures. Projected expenditures are first developed using two basic formats: line item budgeting and program budgeting.

Line item budgeting, the simplest format, involves listing total projected expenditures in functional groupings, typically including such categories as personnel (salary and fringe benefits), and nonpersonnel, including consultant costs, equipment, supplies, travel, capital outlay, and other expenses. Each of these categories is a line item in the budget. In Table 8.1 we will show the budget of the new Teen Transition and Treatment Program as an example.

A line item budget obviously says nothing about how resources will be specifically applied to the accomplishment of particular objectives, except perhaps on the broadest level. Therefore, line item budgets typically are useful only if they are incorporated into program budgets.

A *program budget* replaces such line items as personnel costs, travel, and postage with program groupings such as, in the case of the Grandview Community Center, Counseling Services, In-home Services, Community Development, and Day

Care. Program budgets also typically have agency administrative functions, and occasionally fund-raising, as separate categories. These are sometimes referred to as *functional* budgets (Ezell, 2009), with the functions of programs, management, and fund-raising. The program budget ties resources to specific sets of activities. This approach facilitates the budgeting process being tied closely to planning and evaluation. When resources are related to programs, the programs themselves are considered accountable for achieving objectives that lead to accomplishment of the agency's overall goals. Assessing performance in this way is sometimes referred to as performance budgeting (Ezell, 2009). Thus, program, or performance, budgeting facilitates analysis to determine which programs are effective in terms of outcomes achieved and efficient in terms of resources consumed in pursuit of objectives.

Table 8.1	Line Item Budget for the Teen Transition and Treatment Program, July 1, 2012, to June 30, 2013. Adapted from Bishop (2009).

Line Item	Amount
Personnel	
Program Director (1 FTE)	$60,000
Licensed therapists (4 FTE @ $55,000/year)	220,000
Office Manager (1 FTE)	30,000
Personnel positions subtotal	310,000
Fringe benefits (20% of Personnel positions subtotal)	62,000
Personnel Total	$372,000
Nonpersonnel	
Program Supplies	$1,000
Office Supplies	560
Office Furniture	3,880
Telephone	1,600
Printing	$60
Postage	1,000
Software	2,000
Computers, other equipment	6,000
Rent @ $1,200/month	14,440
Evaluation Consultant	2,000
Local travel @ $0.50/mile x 400 miles/month	2,400
Nonpersonnel Total	$34,940
Total (Personnel and Nonpersonnel)	$406,940
Agency Indirect @ 10% of program costs	40,694
TOTAL PROGRAM	$447,634

An entire agency's budget can be represented comprehensively with all line items in the left column and columns for each program, listing their projected expenditures in line items. Program managers will not typically need to be involved in this level of budget formatting, but they should have a basic understanding of all the programs in the agency.

We will discuss here how to develop a line item budget for a specific program. That is, we will determine how many of what kinds of staff will be needed to accomplish program objectives using the designated service delivery method and what nonpersonnel expenditures, from rent and telephones to mileage and training, will be needed as well.

Budgets need to be developed under two circumstances. First, in the preparation of a proposal for the funding of a new program, a budget needs to be developed to determine what funds will be needed and how they will be spent on staff, facilities, equipment, training, and other program needs. Second, budgets for ongoing programs are typically updated every fiscal year. The fiscal year for many human service programs begins on July 1 and ends on June 30, the common cycle used for government agencies. The major exception is that the federal government uses an October 1–September 30 fiscal year. Budget preparation should begin several months in advance of the start of the new fiscal year, with the specific timetable determined by the deadlines of funders and the agency's board.

Even if a program is new, the agency will have established line item formats into which budget numbers for the new program can be inserted. The agency will also have job roles with qualifications and salary ranges and knowledge of facilities expenses, travel expense rates, and other nonpersonnel costs to use as starting points and guidelines. Existing agency spreadsheet formats will be particularly useful for computations such as fringe benefits.

CREATING THE ANNUAL BUDGET

As noted, line item budgets have two major categories: personnel and nonpersonnel. Personnel costs include salaries and benefits for all paid staff. Nonpersonnel costs include everything else, as can be seen in the budget in Table 8.1. Note that in the budget example, pay for a consultant is included as Nonpersonnel. This is because consultants are not considered to be staff, do not receive fringe benefits such as health insurance, and do not have deductions for Social Security and other benefits.

These are some of the questions that can be asked to determine budget amounts:

- What are the qualifications (and salary rates) of staff needed to deliver services and provide support?
- How many staff of each classification will we need to accomplish program objectives?
- What kind of facility will be needed, where should it be located, and what should the hours of operation be?
- What supplies and equipment will be needed?

- What travel will be required?
- What training will need to be offered to staff?
- What consultants will need to be used (staff development, management information systems, and so on)?

As has been emphasized previously, budget needs depend on the objectives that have been developed as part of the planning process. By closely scrutinizing their implementation plans, budget makers can come close to estimating precisely what the budgetary needs of various activities might be.

We now give an example of the development of the budget for a new program, such as would be described in a proposal for funding submitted to a governmental or foundation funding source (Table 8.1). We use the Grandview Community Center's new Teen Transition and Treatment Program as an example (adapted from Bishop, 2009).

When reviewing the table, it is best to begin with personnel expenditures because they are the essential component of the service delivery process and because they will in all likelihood be the largest line item.

Staff allocations are listed in full-time equivalent (FTE) positions. A staff position allocated for a year at 100 percent time would be 1.0 FTE. In our example, four therapists are included on one line item, for 4 FTE staff. The budget planner also needs to determine other costs of the program, including office and program supplies, printing, postage, and telephone.

With all of this information taken into account, the planner can make a reasonably accurate estimate of the cost of operating the program. These estimated costs can then be integrated into the amounts budgeted for the agency's line item budget as a totality (that is, specifying the total personnel costs for the agency by adding together the salary expenditures for this and all other agency programs). Whether these planning data are used to develop program budgets or are subsequently translated into line item terms, the same kinds of procedures can be followed. The only major factor involved is that the agency's budget must fit the reality of its planned activities. If plans include carefully designed implementation strategies, the creation of a budget simply means translating activities into monetary terms.

Tremendous variation is possible in the forms that budget documents, once completed, can take. The agency will need to use the formats the funding source provided. In our example, we have a line item budget for a county-funded program. The agency is asking for $447,634 from the funding source. This includes $406,940 of direct program costs. Additionally, *indirect costs* (Kettner, Moroney, & Martin, 2008), sometimes known as administrative costs, overhead, or organizational and maintenance costs, are included to help pay the project's share in the total overhead of the agency housing the program. Indirect costs are those not directly related to program operations. A funder may have specific definitions of indirect costs or overhead (that is, what line items are "allowable" for billing to the funder). If guidelines are provided, they should, of course, be followed.

Usually, the budget of all of the agency's central office would be considered an administrative or indirect cost. An exception would be if the agency executive spends a percentage of her or his time providing programmatic or clinical supervision to the program, in which case that amount could be charged as a program rather than administrative cost. The amount of indirect costs can vary tremendously, depending on the agreements worked out between the agency and the funding source, but it is usually computed as a percentage of total direct (program) costs. In this instance, the government funder has agreed to pay for overhead at 10 percent of the total direct costs: $40,640. Thus, the total cost of the program, including direct and indirect costs, would be $447,634.

The form a budget takes and the information included depend on the funder's and the agency's requirements. The agency must meet the guidelines of the funding source. In this example, the requirements are relatively simple. In many instances, agencies are required to provide matching funds (sometimes known as cost sharing), either in money or in "in-kind" contributions. Examples of in-kind contributions include office space provided to the program by the agency or volunteer time. Cash matches are usually from the agency's unrestricted funds (for example, donations or fees) that are not paid by another government grant or contract. When adding a match, include another column, showing local contributions, in the budget. In our example, the funding source has not required a match, so the additional column is not needed.

As is the case with overhead rates, make sure the funder's definitions of acceptable match items are followed. In addition to following all the funder's requirements and definitions, remember that budget format follows need, and the most important factor to consider is whether the items and figures are readily understandable to the people who need to make decisions regarding allocations, expenditures, reports, or accountability.

RESOURCE DEVELOPMENT

The next step is to acquire funds for the program. In actual practice, new program planning and resource acquisition are often intermingled, as in the case of the announcement of a new funding opportunity that has its own specifications. An agency may then write a funding proposal that addresses the priorities of a prospective funder and meets community needs identified by the agency.

Once financial needs have been defined through the budgeting process, resources must be acquired. For government agencies such as school districts or local governments, there are standardized processes for acquiring resources. In the case of not-for-profit human service agencies, this is done through the writing of proposals for grants or contracts and through other fund development activities. While not-for-profit human services have been increasingly relying on grants and contracts from government or foundations, other funding sources include fees (including third-party payments), gifts, and donations. The nature of an agency's funding has major implications for the planning and budgeting processes as well as for the way the agency's accountability is perceived. *Fund development* is the term used to describe the efforts agencies make to solicit and acquire resources from their environments to provide needed community services. Funding—that is, the acquisition of funds—is the result of an agency's direct and/or indirect efforts at fund development. Examples of direct fund development by the agency are proposal writing (applying for grants or contracts through the submission of written proposals to funding sources for the provision of particular human services) and arranging donations through annual funds, capital campaigns, special events, and other sources.

GRANTS AND CONTRACTS

Grants and contracts can come from either public funding sources, such as federal agencies, or private foundations. Grants and contracts differ in terms of the degree of control and specificity on the part of the funding agent. A *grant* is a sum of money provided for the achievement of a set of objectives through the recipient's activities. A *contract* is similar but usually lays out the specifics of activities to be performed even before the recipient of the funds is selected. To initiate the process of funding a grant or contract, a funding source will release a *request for proposals* (RFP) that spells out a need and goals to be addressed, preferred or required methodologies, budget limits, and other requirements. Federal funding availability is announced through the *Catalogue of Federal Domestic Assistance* (https://www.cfda.gov/) and the *Commerce Business Daily* (http://www.cbdweb.com). More specific information is available at websites for individual programs, usually in the Department of Health and Human Services (http://www.hhs.gov/grants/). A proactive human service manager will also check state and local announcements for new governmental funding opportunities and will monitor relevant private foundations.

Foundations small and large are very active in offering grants to human service organizations. Some of the Web links at the end of the chapter provide access to more detailed information on foundations.

The use of contracting—or, more specifically, purchase of service contracting—has increased in recent years, for reasons including increased privatization of government functions and higher demands for accountability that are more easily achieved through contracts than grants. Although increased accountability cannot be denied as a legitimate goal, problems have emerged related to this funding mechanism. Recent government funding cuts often result in increased workloads and declining quality of services as agencies try to cope with "doing more with less." This situation has important implications for agency strategy development and may lead to strategies to stop taking contracts that result in low salaries and service quality. This concern can be addressed through good management, from dynamic and insightful strategic planning to evidence-based program design, efficient use of resources, and, as discussed in the next two chapters, information systems and evaluation designs that can clearly show program impact, including efficiency and effectiveness, on social problems.

Historically, contracts have been *cost reimbursement* contracts, in which the agency is reimbursed for actual allowable expenses (from the original budget) when services are provided (Martin, 2001). More recently, *performance contracts*, or *performance-based contracts* (Taylor & Shaver, 2010), have become increasingly common. Under performance-based contracting, the agency is not given a fixed sum based on the budget but is only paid (reimbursed) when specific performance targets are reached. Performance to be reimbursed can include outputs (such as the number of home-delivered meals provided) or outcomes (such as the number of clients placed in jobs at a specified wage). This method has some notable advantages as well as disadvantages such as potential cash flow problems due to reimbursement procedures and goal displacement in which staff focus exclusively on reimbursable performance elements when additional services may be appropriate.

The growing use of managed care in contracting has particular relevance for human service agencies providing behavioral health—specifically mental health and substance abuse—services. For example, a local government agency "that has previously contracted directly with local nonprofit agencies for community mental health services now may provide a fixed sum of money to a 'managed care organization' that will be responsible for managing the mental health services for a specified number of clients" (Smith, 2010, p. 562).

WRITING PROPOSALS FOR GRANTS OR CONTRACTS

Any project that is eventually funded must meet priorities set by the funding agency. Thus, when a human service agency submits a proposal or application for funding to a government funding agency or a foundation, the proposal will be considered first in terms of its appropriateness to the funding organization's priorities and guidelines. If the proposal does not fit funding priorities, it will be eliminated without consideration, regardless of its merits. If the proposal does have potential for helping meet the funding program's goals, it will be considered, in most instances, on the basis of answers to the following questions:

- How well does the applicant demonstrate that there is a real need for the proposed project?
- How clear and attainable are the project's objectives?
- Does the proposal spell out a plan of action that suits project goals and objectives? Is the program model supported by research and best practices?
- Is the applying agency likely to be able to carry out the proposed project and meet the specified goals within the suggested time frame?
- Is the budget clearly thought out and appropriate for the scope of the project?
- Are plans for evaluation and dissemination well documented, feasible, and appropriate?

The questions potential funding agents ask bear obvious similarities to those human service planners ask in the context of budget preparation. Careful planning and goal clarity are valued in the process of awarding grants and contracts. This factor provides one of the major strengths of the project grant as a funding mechanism for human services. There is a potential for tying resource allocation and goal accomplishment together through this type of funding.

Obviously, writing a proposal is not strictly, or even primarily, a financial matter: it involves needs assessments, sound strategy development and program design, consideration of staffing issues, and the development of information systems and evaluation methods. Because it leads, if funded, to an agreement to manage resources, proposal writing is included in this discussion of financial management. Excellent guidance on writing proposals is now widely available (see, for example, Brody, 2005, Ch. 15; Browning, 2008; Carlson & O'Neal-McElrath, 2008;

Coley & Scheinberg, 2008; Grobman, 2008; Henry, 2006; and Web resources at the end of this chapter), so only some general guidelines will be offered here.

First, any proposal should be firmly grounded in the agency's strategic plan, which will ensure that the agency has the capacities to implement it if funded and that it fits within the agency's mission. The need for funding often encourages human service planners to take on projects that would not ordinarily fit the scope of their agency, interfering with efforts to maintain the integrity of their mission. Agencies are easily tempted to submit proposals for grants or contracts that look attractive but do not fit the agency's mission, distinct competencies, strategic plan, or market niche. When this happens repeatedly, agency administrators, service providers, and consumers suddenly find that the very nature of the agency's program thrust has inadvertently been changed. Administrators and boards must use good judgment, restraint, and discretion in choosing which grant or contract to respond to. In this context, it is challenging to keep in mind a clear picture of the agency's primary mission.

Second, a human service manager should have good, ongoing, and up-to-date knowledge of the range of funding possibilities in the agency's arena, including federal, state, and local government sources; national and local foundations; United Ways and local religious or civic organizations; and perhaps corporate sources.

Proposals typically originate as a concept evolving from a need or opportunity identified in the strategic plan or as a response to an RFP, and our remaining suggestions have to do with responding to an RFP by writing a proposal. The format and requirements in the RFP should be followed precisely (do not be afraid to call the funder's contact person for clarification), but the following are common elements of a good proposal.

The proposal often begins with a cover letter and an executive summary or abstract. The narrative section typically includes a statement of need, a description of the organization's capabilities, a budget including staffing patterns and job descriptions, a project time line, and data collection and evaluation plans. In the midst of this is the "heart" of the proposal: the project design and description, including specific goals and objectives to be achieved. Sometimes plans are outlined for the future of the program after the grant or contract has ended. Often letters of support, agency forms, organization charts, and time lines are included in an appendix.

A number of almost unavoidable problems are associated with grants and contracts when they form the agency's fiscal base. Most immediately apparent is the uncertainty of funding. Grants are designed for the support of short-term projects, and although ongoing support is often possible, it is not built into the official funding process. Contracts, although often renewable, are usually for short time periods such as one year. An agency that depends solely on grants or contracts for its survival is unable to make long-range plans easily because of the lack of a financial base. Any vibrant and dynamic agency should not rely on only grants or contracts for funding. Other sources not only provide "unrestricted" funds that can be used for purposes not funded by grants or contracts but also enhance the agency's relationships with different segments of the community. We will look briefly at a few additional funding sources: fees, planned giving, and other contributions.

FEES

Many human service agencies charge direct fees for services rendered. When these fees are charged to individual clients, they are often based on sliding scales, with individuals paying differing amounts depending on their financial status. Frequently, fees are paid not by consumers themselves but by outside organizations or third parties. Third-party payments can come from insurance companies, Medicaid, public agencies purchasing services for clients, or other sources.

Sometimes third parties can have the same effect on agency practices as other funding sources might have. For example, an insurance company might pay for counseling services only if they are provided by licensed therapists, despite the fact that other trained professionals normally provide such services in a particular agency. Such "strings" attached to payments can place restrictions on an agency's activities. With this exception, however, fees for service tend to have the same effect on budgeting whether they are paid by consumers or outside organizations.

A rarely noted problem faced by agencies that depend on fees for a significant percentage of their fiscal base is the tendency to emphasize direct services at the expense of alternate activities, such as community education, consultation, and advocacy. Although grants or appropriations might provide some support for such indirect services, fees are most closely associated with such traditional treatment modalities as individual counseling or therapy. Fee-based human service agencies have difficulty moving into innovative service areas when their funding depends almost completely on the number of individuals personally served. This is true not only when fees are charged to consumers but also when agencies receive contracts from public organizations to provide treatment for a specific number of clients.

Another implication of the use of fees as a funding base is the inherent difficulty in predicting income. Planners must be able to estimate very accurately the number of clients likely to be served in a given time period, with estimations becoming even more complex if sliding scales mean that not all clients will generate the same amount of revenue. Some agencies can use a flexible form of budgeting, but this works only if service costs are highly variable. (For example, if a training program uses part-time trainers on a consultant basis, hires them only when enough trainees are enrolled, and rents temporary facilities at the same time, then each training implementation can have its own budget.) Normally, however, human service agencies have fixed costs, especially personnel costs, that must be met; so revenues must be predicted with a high degree of accuracy when the yearly budget is developed. Mayers (2004, pp. 152–155) offers useful guidelines for setting fees and implementing this system, such as pricing based on cost or the market, and ensuring that the system is fair and equitable.

CONTRIBUTIONS AND PLANNED GIVING

Contributions to an agency's operating budget can run the gamut from $5 donations by individuals to multimillion-dollar endowments. The process of fundraising can mean anything from sending out direct mailings to knocking on the doors of corporate offices to mounting campaigns for special-purpose funds.

Agencies that depend on large contributions for their fiscal bases often use the services of professional fund-raising or development specialists as well as encouraging the fund-raising efforts of board members. Regardless of the size of the fund-raising operation, however, human service professionals and administrators are likely to be affected, at least indirectly.

As is the case with proposal writing, many useful resources regarding fund development are available (for example, Benefield & Edwards, 2006; Brody, 2005; Fogal, 2010; Grobman, 2008; Worth, 2009). In fact, many principles for writing effective proposals apply here as well. Fund development activities should be part of the agency's strategic plan and should be coordinated with the acquisition of funds from other sources (grants, contracts, fees). Indeed, the agency's planned giving program should be a major component of the strategic plan.

Fund development involves knowing the environment: identifying a donor base and conducting prospect research, which can range from clients to national corporations and foundations. Amounts of donations can range from very large "principal gifts" to much smaller and greater in number "annual gifts" (Worth, 2009). Prospective donors may then be conceptualized at the center of the "donor-giving triangle" (Benefield & Edwards, 2006), which consists of motivation, capacity, and opportunity.

Mechanisms for obtaining funds may include capital campaigns (for example, to buy a building for the agency), cultivation of major gifts from wealthy individuals or organizations, planned giving (endowments and bequests), annual fund campaigns for support of ongoing operations, and special events such as dinners.

A growing trend toward greater entrepreneurial thinking in human service organizations that relates to agency strategy development, program development, and fund-raising includes *social entrepreneurship* and *social enterprise* strategies (Helm, 2010; Nash, 2010; Worth, 2009). These strategies include greater use of business practices such as market-driven thinking, innovation, more fee-based programming, and nonprofit or for-profit subsidiaries as business ventures. For example, DC Central Kitchen "prepares meals for shelters and other institutions serving the homeless in Washington, D.C. It employs homeless men and women in its kitchen and offers training programs in the culinary arts to prepare them for careers on the food industry" (Worth, 2009, p. 275).

A related strategy in fund-raising is *cause-related marketing*, in which a business can promote its products or services and enhance its reputation while supporting a not-for-profit organization (Worth, 2009; Salamon, 2010). This approach presents great opportunities to not-for-profit human service organizations that may be able to develop partnerships with local or even national corporations for mutual benefit. In fact, all fund-raising tactics have the potential of not only bringing in needed resources but also fostering and furthering relationships with individuals and groups in the community.

RESOURCE DISPOSITION

The next major step in the financial management process is resource distribution, or disposition: allocating funds to areas identified in the budget and ensuring that funds are spent as planned and in a legal and ethical manner. This includes making adjustments during the fiscal year due to revenue cutbacks or unexpected expenses and managing all sources of funds in a coordinated manner.

We described earlier a process for designing a new human service program to meet identified community needs and then attaching predicted costs to it (the budget). Annual budgeting is also done for continuing programs. This annual updating is sometimes known as *incremental* budgeting (Mayers, 2004), when only minor changes are made in existing program budgets. We will begin this section by briefly discussing ongoing monitoring and controlling of a line item budget for a program. We will then discuss ways of making adjustments to program budgets.

MONITORING AND CONTROLLING FINANCIAL RESOURCES

Any human service organization should have well-developed financial management systems to keep track of income and expenditures. Such systems, including charts of accounts and cash and asset management procedures (Mayers, 2004), are beyond the scope of this book and will only be mentioned briefly. Human service agencies use accountants and other specialized staff to maintain these systems. It is the manager's responsibility to provide oversight and ensure that program operations and ethical behavior are maintained.

Operating budgets, on the other hand, should be monitored by managers on a regular basis. *Variance budgets* (Mayers, 2004) are used to keep track of differences between budgeted amounts and actual income and expenditures. Fiscal staff can provide managers with monthly statements that show actual income and expenditures for the current month and "year to date" compared with planned budgets. Variances then need to be addressed by moving funds from one line item to another, or by cutting expenses or increasing income.

UPDATING THE ANNUAL BUDGET FOR AN ONGOING PROGRAM

The continuation of an ongoing program includes the yearly submission of a proposed budget to the manager, board, funder, or governing body controlling resource allocation. The same type of routine tends to be followed whether the budget maker is a project director appealing for funds from a funding agency, a program manager vying with other departments for a share in an agency's total budget, a nonprofit agency executive presenting a proposal to the board of directors, or a public administrator seeking legislative appropriations of tax dollars.

The budget request is usually formulated in response to notification from the next higher authority that the document is to be developed by a particular deadline. The budget for the current year generally provides the basis for beginning analysis of needs for the following year. Usually, the final results of the current year, in terms of expenditures, need to be estimated. These estimations, along with reports of expenditures to date, help the budget developer determine projections for the coming year. The current year's budget is the building block on which analysis of the next year's need is based.

The decisions in question at this stage of the budgeting cycle tend to be oriented not toward the budget as a whole but toward the difference between the current and the proposed budget. This budgeting approach is termed "incremental" because it normally accepts the current funding level as a base from which to adjust, ideally upward if new funds are available. Applying the incremental approach to the budgeting process suggests that attention is directed to the changes that occur between the existing state and the proposed state. The marginal difference between what is and what is proposed is examined. This process accepts the existing base and examines in detail only the increments that extend the current budgeting program into the future.

Budget adjustments are made not only annually but also routinely during the fiscal year based on new developments. Such adjustments are made within parameters set by funders and the agency board. For example, a funding source may allow moving up to 10 percent of the nonpersonnel budget from one category to another (for example, from Supplies to Mileage) without prior approval, with larger changes requiring advanced approval from the funder. A program manager should be aware of all relevant time lines, parameters, and procedures to manage funds properly throughout the year.

We would like to believe that budgeting is a totally rational process, but in some agencies, particularly in government agencies, political processes may come into play in regard to these annual or midyear changes in resource allocation (Gummer, 1990). Competing programs, projects, and agencies, each with its own accepted base, must share limited resources. Preferences must be expressed, support bases sought, bargains struck, and agreements reached. Ideally, such discussions would be explicit, among program managers and executives, with advocacy for needed funds based on references to the agency's strategic plan, stated priorities, and organizational values.

Fortunately, there are some established budget planning mechanisms that can be of use when making difficult decisions regarding necessary changes in funding of programs. These processes include *performance-based budgeting, zero-based budgeting,* and *cutback management.*

PERFORMANCE-BASED BUDGETING

Performance-based budgeting (Kong, 2005) is a budget innovation in governmental organizations that became popular in the 1990s (Joyce, 2005). This method involves clearly showing relationships between inputs (i.e., funding) and results, and integrating budgeting with planning and ongoing program management.

A variation of performance-based budgeting, *budgeting for results,* (O'Looney, 1996, p. 202), attempts to make a direct connection between mission, goals, and objectives on the one hand and detailed revenue and expenditure estimates on the other. Budgeting for results (BFR) is based on three main principles (Cothran, 1993, cited in O'Looney 1996, p. 203): specification of goals from the top (for example, the strategic plan), choices on means of accomplishing goals and objectives determined at the program level, and accountability and incentives for results. The program model (intervention method or technology) chosen earlier based on its efficacy is now detailed by listing expenditures that will be necessary to accomplish results (objectives). BFR is based on several assumptions, which in reality are expectations that must be met for the model to work (O'Looney, 1996, pp. 206–211). First, there need to be clear and measurable objectives, and responsibility for their achievement needs to be clearly assigned to programs, units, or individuals.

More specifically, targets need to be established: the changes in client behavior or condition, numbers of clients or services to be delivered, and a time frame. Another important assumption is that "results are a function of organizational resources effectively used" (O'Looney, 1996, p. 208). This points to the importance of an appropriate program design: a model with a track record of being effective in the circumstances that are planned by the program. Next, managers and their staffs need to have the authority and responsibility to do what is needed to achieve objectives. This suggests a participative management philosophy in which lower-level staff members are entrusted to make decisions on how to accomplish objectives.

ZERO-BASED BUDGETING

Zero-based budgeting became popular during the Carter administration and was later used infrequently, but the technique has seen a resurgence lately, possibly due to the limited human service funding available in recent years. Zero-based budgeting provides an alternative to traditional procedures in that it emphasizes the need for each program to justify its very existence as part of the planning process. Instead of comparing a request for funds with the previous year's expenditures, decision makers compare and contrast every proposed program in terms of overall agency goals. Existing programs are, theoretically at least, in equal competition with untried innovations. Through analysis of comparative effectiveness, activities are prioritized so that decision makers can decrease expenditures on ineffective functions and reallocate these resources to programs identified as having higher priority. The process is zero based because each program must start from zero in justifying any commitment of resources.

Mayers (2004) explains the utility of zero-based budgeting in the following terms:

> While incremental budgeting starts with an established base of the previous year's operating levels and seeks to justify changes in the current year, zero-based budgeting (ZBB) attempts to provide some accountability by starting from a base of zero. In ZBB each proposed expenditure must be justified; this encourages the analysis of competing claims on resources, and it reduces the possibility of continuing obsolete, inefficient programs. (p. 46)

According to Ezell (2009, p. 395), "there are several situations in which ZBB (or 'quasi-ZBB') is recommended: (1) when major change (e.g., reorganization) occurs, (2) when a new CEO is hired to implement a new strategic plan, and (3) when competition for contracts is strong and bids are awarded on the basis of cost."

Zero-based budgeting is accomplished through describing a set of related activities (including objectives, methods, and performance measures) that lead to the accomplishment of a given goal or objectives. For instance, if a program objective involves placing 100 high school students in part-time jobs, decision makers can analyze and compare the costs and effects of eliminating the program altogether, increasing or decreasing the number of students placed, and using alternative methods (having the service provided by volunteers from the business community, paraprofessionals, or professional human service workers; using mail, telephone, or personal contacts; interviewing students in the schools or in centralized office settings). All of the choices, including program elimination and program expansion, would be analyzed, with priorities set on the basis of this analysis. The agency's entire budget would then be devised on the basis of rankings, under the assumption that resource allocation would then be tied closely to program goals.

CUTBACK MANAGEMENT

Resource scarcity brings with it the need for all stakeholders in human service programs to become involved in the search for program or administrative expenditures that may be cut or the development of more efficient administrative or service delivery processes. When resources decline, policy makers sometimes fall victim to the notion that indiscriminate slashing of funds can solve the problem. In reality, however, such approaches are oversimplifications of highly complex issues.

Since the term "cutback management" emerged in the literature during the 1980s, many successful strategies and tactics have been identified to address difficult financial and program decisions. In addition to making thoughtful cuts on budgets, cutback management can also involve creative programmatic strategies such as productivity improvement.

In a comprehensive review of cutback management strategies for nonprofits, Angelica and Hyman (1997) group strategies into three categories:

- *Financial strategies*, including cost cutting in areas such as purchasing, payables, facilities and infrastructure; staff or service reductions; and revenue increases through fees, fund-raising, service additions, and productivity
- *Structural strategies*, such as modifying the organization's mission, structure (e.g., creating one-stop shops, changing programs), or culture (e.g., eliminating bureaucracy, becoming more entrepreneurial)
- *Engagement strategies,* such as becoming more involved with community organizations

Brody (2005, pp. 243–248) offers a list of 50 cost-cutting ideas, ranging from outsourcing functions such as payroll to restructuring to eliminate non-income-producing positions.

A study of county health and human service organizations (Packard, Patti, Daly, Tucker-Tatlow, & Farrell, 2008) identifies several major themes in successful cutback management that have support in the literature:

- *Collaborative leadership:* use collaboration rather than competition both within and outside the agency, and compassion rather than judgmental attitudes
- *Adopt a "big picture" approach:* seek opportunities to shift and share employees across programs, leverage categorical funds in collaboratives to serve shared clients across departments, and pursue cross-agency collaborations
- *Maintain focus through strategic planning:* make budget decisions based on compatibility with the agency's mission-critical services or higher priority functions and eliminate low-value activities as necessary
- *Develop relationships with key constituencies:* spend time communicating with and working with community stakeholders and informing policy makers of the likely effects of cuts in particular programs

- *Communicate with staff:* devote extensive energy to keeping employees informed of the budget situation and actions that are being taken; use comprehensive communication strategies to build staff understanding, acceptance, and support of budget cuts, including sharing the "how and why" budget decisions were made to demystify the decision processes, counteract unfounded rumors, and show concern for staff and clients
- *Preserve staff capacity:* help workers transition to other jobs, hold recognition programs to minimize stress and contribute to a culture that values achievement, express concern for staff who were laid off, and model compassion toward surviving employees during budget crises
- *Decentralize decision making:* involve staff in creating solutions regarding program priorities and improving program efficiencies; decentralize decisions to develop their funding priorities
- *Use data to drive decisions:* use data to measure productivity and performance, streamline processes, and improve interagency collaboration

MANAGING MULTIPLE FUNDING SOURCES

Agencies should attempt to diversify their funding procedures so that the "drying up" of one funding source does not cause a fiscal crisis in the agency. According to Martin (2001, p. 57), the agency's largest funding source should account for no more than 50 percent of the total budget, and ideally less than that, because having multiple revenue sources will help prevent the agency from being too dependent on one source.

This diversity, however, will also demand paying greater attention to coordination and alignment among multiple funding sources. Once again, the agency's strategic plan can provide guidance. If the strategic plan is not adhered to, agency-wide coordination and long-range strategy implementation will be difficult to achieve. This factor also makes even the keeping of normally simple reports a complex endeavor. It is often difficult for agencies to consolidate information concerning a number of totally separate funding sources and projects, especially when time lines differ and reporting procedures vary among funding agencies.

Although having multiple sources of funding makes planning and reporting complex, it also prevents dependence on one source or one mechanism. Separate financial statements are needed for each earmarked fund; yet, in the interests of accountability and control, combined statements should also be available. We will now briefly review the use of financial reports as monitoring and reporting mechanisms.

RESOURCE REPORTING

FINANCIAL REPORTS

Financial reports can serve both monitoring and coordinating functions (Mayers, 2004). Financial statements help agencies monitor expenditures, and annual reports provide information about the agency's fiscal condition to funding sources, policy makers, and concerned citizens. Audits are periodic examinations of agency financial reports and their supporting documents, conducted by independent accountants not affiliated with the agency. Audits are done to determine whether financial statements were prepared in accordance with generally accepted accounting principles. Financial reports such as operating statements and balance sheets assist in coordination by providing an agency-wide picture of how programs are performing.

Program managers typically are required to develop, implement, and monitor budgets but will not be heavily involved with other financial reports. Agency executives will need to be more familiar with these systems, whereas program managers can rely on agency accountants for expertise. For managers wanting to become more knowledgeable about accounting and advanced financial management concepts and principles, many books (e.g., McLaughlin, 2009; Worth, 2009) are available. Nevertheless, because annual audits are such an important aspect of agency management, program managers should at least be aware of this process.

AUDITS

On completion of the audit, normally done annually, the accountant will submit to the agency's governing body an "opinion" or report as to whether the agency's financial statements fairly represent its financial position. Based on the auditor's report, the agency can then take whatever action is necessary, ranging from "Let's keep up the good work" to "We need to take corrective action." The periodic financial audit can be as anxiety provoking to fiscal managers as the program evaluation is to service providers, but if a system is well designed and properly used, major surprises can be prevented and opportunities for minor improvements or adjustments should emerge.

COST-BENEFIT ANALYSIS AND COST-EFFECTIVENESS ANALYSIS

Cost-benefit analysis and *cost effectiveness* analysis are analytical tools that are useful in planning a program's scope and its expenditures, making decisions when budget adjustments need to be made, and evaluating program results. They are included here because they relate directly to finances, and they will also be mentioned in the chapter on program evaluation because they relate costs to program outcomes. Analysis can begin with either a desired level of performance, which might be based on the expectations of a funding organization and allocating costs to reach this level, or with a specification of available resources and determination of the performance level that could be reached with a given amount of funding. In either instance, costs are related to measurable outputs or activities, which are, in turn, related to program outcomes or results.

In cost-benefit analysis, program outcomes must be stated in monetary terms so that programs are evaluated according to their economic benefits to the community or society. Packard, Delgado, Fellmeth, and McCready (2008) summarize applications of this method in areas including child welfare, interventions for juvenile offenders, and substance abuse treatment. Because outcomes in human service organizations are often difficult to state in financial terms, this technique is not often used for human service programs.

In contrast, cost-effectiveness analysis considers the relationship between costs and outcomes without translating results into monetary values. In the case of a program with one stated outcome, such as acquiring employment at a living wage for a youth leaving foster care, this computation may be as simple as dividing the program budget by the number of successful outcomes (e.g., youth who reached the desired level of employment). This technique is much more promising in the human services than is cost-benefit analysis, but huge challenges remain. Outcomes (effectiveness) in prevention terms are difficult to document, and in any case they may be evident only over a period of years. Direct services may be easier to document. For example, the cost-effectiveness of a program placing a youth in a job may be documented. This would involve allocating precise program costs to that objective distinct from other program objectives and dividing this number by the number of youth placed. Challenges here include, on the cost end, dividing worker, facilities, and other costs by program objective and, on the benefit end, having a clear definition of an outcome: Is it full-time employment? At a living wage? For how long?

Regardless of the challenges in doing cost-effectiveness analysis, this promises to be an increasingly important and useful technique in program planning and evaluation. Funding sources are increasingly expecting documentation of concrete results, with welfare-to-work programs being a vivid example. For budgeting purposes, this technique is useful in determining the best use of scarce resources as programs are designed or modified.

8.2	COST EFFECTIVENESS OF THE TEEN TRANSITION AND TREATMENT PROGRAM

In preparing their proposal for the county to obtain funding for their new Teen Transition and Treatment Program, GCC staff members had to compute the cost effectiveness of their program. Referring to the program objectives (see Chapter 3), they started with the requirement that they would serve 50 clients at a time, and that the program included a 14-week package of weekly individual counseling sessions and psychoeducational group therapy sessions. They decided that they could complete four cycles of the program during the fiscal year, which would involve occasional overlaps of two cycles of groups of clients going through the program. Therefore, they could serve 200 clients over the course of the year: 50 clients in each of four cycles.

Their outcome objectives indicated that they expected that 80 percent of the clients who completed the program would, upon program completion, achieve successful outcomes in the development of new skills, discontinued illicit drug use, and improved quality of life. A follow-up objective that 60 percent of clients would be clean of drugs as evidenced by a urine analysis conducted 6 months after completion of the program was not included in this cost effectiveness measure because the numbers are different than the numbers for the objectives at program completion. This illustrates the complexity and challenges in computing cost effectiveness when there are multiple objectives for the same group of clients in a program.

Combining figures from the program objectives and the budget, staff concluded that the cost effectiveness was $2,798 per successful outcome. This was computed by dividing the program budget of $447,634 by 160 clients (80 percent of the 200 clients in the program). This figure could be one of several indicators of program accomplishment. We will discuss in the program evaluation chapter how this figure can be used in evaluation. Because these program outcomes could not be described in strictly financial terms, a cost-benefit analysis for this program is not possible.

The decision-making data generated through these methods are potentially helpful for balancing priorities and distinguishing between efficient and inefficient programs. In its ideal form, a rational planning/budgeting approach can reallocate scarce resources so that agency services improve. Innovations can be emphasized, and the end results of programs can receive more attention than they have been given in more traditional procedures. When resources diminish, these methodologies can provide guidelines for change.

Some human service workers may be put off by trying to state program benefits in terms of cost, and by the increasingly common use of terms such as "value added" and "return on investment." But the reality is that part of being a good steward of public resources is making decisions in favor of the most effective programs that are most likely to have the greatest positive impact on clients and the community while recognizing that there will never be enough funding to fully meet all identified needs.

SUMMARY

The ability to operationalize a program into fiscal terms with an appropriate and well-developed budget is an essential aspect of human service management. Furthermore, the idea of openness in fiscal matters is one whose time has come. Agencies need to increase their openness in terms of both sharing financial information and seeking input from a variety of sources. This openness can begin to take place when human service professionals, managers, funding sources, and community members accept the fact that budgeting, far from being a mystical force only accountants understand, is merely a method for bringing plans to fruition. In the next chapter, we will turn to another aspect of demonstrating accountability: the use of information systems.

COMPETENCY-BUILDING ACTIVITY 8.1   BUDGETING

Now that you have developed a hypothetical program model, including staffing and job descriptions, and you know the basic principles for developing a line item budget, you can develop a budget for your program. Review the activities you identified as being required to implement your program. Identify staffing and other resource needs (e.g., facilities, supplies). For each component of the program, try to figure out what its costs might be. Take into account the timing of the activity, the personnel costs for workers who would be involved in carrying it out, any special consultant costs, and nonpersonnel costs such as supplies, equipment, and office space. Develop a line item budget to determine the funds needed to carry out this program for a year.

CASE ACTIVITY 8.1   THE BEST-LAID PLANS

Katherine Wilson, director of the Allenville Senior Center (ASC), was very much oriented toward planning. In fact, one of the first things she had done after her appointment as director was to set a planning project in motion. A committee made up of employees of the center, community leaders, consumers of the agency's services, and representatives of the American Association of Retired Persons and the

Gray Panthers had worked to develop a new strategic plan for the agency.

One of the first things the hardworking committee had done was to survey the center's members to assess their needs and interests. At the same time, an analysis of other human service programs in the community was also completed. A series of community meetings provided a transition from needs assessment to goal setting, and, as a result of all of these procedures, a new set of agency goals had been developed.

The ASC's mission was to bring Allenville's older citizens into the mainstream of community life. Toward this end, the center would provide services such as the following:

1. A foster grandparents program involving the center's members in helping care for young children in the community
2. A consultation project, through which retired members would provide consultation to young businesspeople
3. A placement program assisting retired people to share part-time, paying jobs
4. An educational program, in cooperation with the local college, providing credit courses that would allow members to work toward degrees

Many of the functions the planning committee identified could be carried out under current funding. Some, however, would work more effectively as specially funded projects. The central focus of the program was clear, and Wilson was ready to carry out her promise to the committee and her very supportive board of directors. She would try to obtain the funding needed to carry out community-based programs. In the meantime, some of the activities could begin through allocation of part of the time of currently employed staff members.

Wilson was occupied in completing a tentative budget plan based on the planned activities when she received a call from the chair of ASC's board of directors. With excitement in his voice, Jonas Pratt exclaimed that he had just been contacted by the Rodin Foundation. They were interested in funding a project to build a country retreat for senior citizens. Funding would be very generous, and they would welcome a proposal from ASC.

"Be sure to get on this right away, Katherine," Pratt bubbled. "He said he'd be interested in receiving our proposal, but you know we're not the only ones he called. The write-up had better be good. And be sure you come on strong with the needs assessment."

"But Mr. Pratt, what about the planning document we just did? That was approved by the board, and this project you're talking about doesn't sound as though it has any relationship to it. It sounds as if we'd be going in the opposite direction."

"Well, I know, but this idea is so new we just didn't think of it ourselves. The kind of funding they're talking about could keep us out of trouble for a long time."

"Mr. Pratt, it would also keep us from carrying out the plans for community involvement that we all agreed made sense," Wilson replied. "Our center members don't want to go to the woods on a retreat. They want to be involved in their own community. How can we show a needs assessment supporting a project like this when the needs assessment we really did pointed the other way? Do you think there might be any chance at all that the Rodin Foundation might be interested in funding one of our own projects?"

"Katherine, I just don't think so. They didn't sound as if they were just out shopping for proposals. They had something darned specific in mind. Listen, there's no point in our talking about whether we want this Rodin money when we don't even have the grant. We can always decide whether we want to accept it with the strings attached or not after we've gotten it. In the meantime, let's just put all our efforts into doing the proposal. If we don't get the funding, no problem. If we do, then we can decide."

1. If you were in Katherine Wilson's shoes, what steps would you take next? Would you write a proposal for a country retreat or try to convince the board to stay with the plan that had already been developed? What are the pros and cons of each course of action?
2. Choose one program idea—one of the four in the organizational plan or the retreat center—and develop goals and objectives for it. Then prepare a line item budget to accomplish the goals and objectives.
3. For your program idea, suggest ways in which funds could be acquired to implement it.

REFERENCES

Angelica, E., & Hyman, V. (1997). *Coping with cutbacks: The nonprofit guide to success when times are tight*. St. Paul, Minnesota: Amherst H. Wilder Foundation.

Benefield, E., & Edwards, R. (2006). Developing a sustainable fundraising program. In R. Edwards & J. Yankey (Eds.), *Effectively managing nonprofit organizations* (pp. 61–82). Washington, DC: NASW Press.

Bishop, N. (2009). Program Plan Paper. Unpublished manuscript, San Diego State University.

Brody, R. (2005). *Effectively managing human service organizations* (3rd ed.). Thousand Oaks, CA: Sage.

Browning, B. (2010). *Grant writing for dummies* (3rd ed.). San Francisco: Jossey-Bass.

Carlson, M. & Neal-McElrath, T. (2008). *Winning grants: Step by step* (3rd ed.). San Francisco: Jossey-Bass.

Coley, S. & Scheinberg, C. (2008). *Proposal writing: Effective grantsmanship* (3rd ed.). Thousand Oaks, CA: Sage Publications.

Ezell, M. (2009). Managing financial resources. In R. Patti (Ed.), *The handbook of human services management* (2nd ed., pp. 387–408). Thousand Oaks, CA: Sage Publications.

Fogal, R. (2010). Designing and managing the fundraising program. In D. Renz and Associates (Eds.), *The Jossey-Bass handbook of nonprofit leadership and management* (3rd ed., pp. 505–523). San Francisco: Jossey-Bass.

Gummer, B. (1990). *The politics of social administration*. Upper Saddle River, NJ: Prentice Hall.

Joyce, P. (2005). Linking performance and budgeting: Opportunities in the federal budgeting process. In J. Kamensky & A. Morales (Eds.), *Managing for Results 2005* (pp. 83–). Lanham, MD: Rowman & Littlefield Publishers.

Kettner, P., Moroney, R., & Martin, L. (2008). *Designing and managing programs* (3rd ed.). Thousand Oaks, CA: Sage.

Kong, D. (2005). Performance-Based Budgeting: The U.S. Experience. *Public Organization Review, 5*(2), 91–107.

Martin, L. (2001). *Financial management for human service administrators*. Boston: Allyn & Bacon.

Mayers, R. S. (2004). *Financial management for nonprofit human service agencies* (2nd ed.). Springfield, IL: Charles C. Thomas.

McLaughlin, T. (2009). *Streetsmart: Financial Basics for nonprofit managers*. New York: Wiley.

O'Looney, J. (1996). *Redesigning the work of human services*. Westport, CT: Quorum.

Packard, T., Delgado, M., Fellmeth, R., & McCready, K. (2008). A Cost-Benefit Analysis of Transitional Services For Emancipating Foster Youth. *Children and Youth Services Review, 30*, 1267–1278.

Packard, T., Patti, R., Daly, D., Tucker-Tatlow, J., & Farrell, C. (2008). Cutback Management Strategies: Experiences in Nine County Human Service Agencies. *Administration in Social Work, 32*(1), 55–75.

Salamon, L. (2010). The changing context of nonprofit leadership and management. In D. Renz and Associates (Eds.), *The Jossey-Bass handbook of nonprofit leadership and management* (3rd ed., pp. 77–100). San Francisco: Jossey-Bass.

Smith, S. (2010). Managing the challenges of government contracts. In D. Renz and Associates (Eds.), *The Jossey-Bass handbook of nonprofit leadership and management* (3rd ed., pp. 553–579). San Francisco: Jossey-Bass.

Taylor, K., & Shaver, M. (2010). Performance-based contracting: Aligning incentives with outcomes to produce results. In M. Testa & J. Poertner (Eds.), *Fostering accountability: Using evidence to guide and improve child welfare policy* (pp. 291–). New York: Oxford University Press.

Wang, X. (2010). *Financial Management in the Public Sector: Tools, Applications, and Cases* (2nd ed.). Armonk, NY: M. E. Sharpe.

Worth, M. (2009). *Nonprofit management: Principles and practice*. Thousand Oaks, CA: Sage Publications.

USEFUL WEB RESOURCES

Association of Fundraising Professionals. http://www.afpnet.org/index.cfm?

Children's Bureau Discretionary Grants Library. http://basis.caliber.com/cbgrants/ws/library/docs/cb_grants/GrantHome.

The Chronicle of Philanthropy. http://philanthropy.com/section/Home/172.

Idealist: Resources for Nonprofit Organizations. http://nonprofits.org/if/idealist/en/Home/default.

The Foundation Center. http://foundationcenter.org/.

Grants, etc.: University of Michigan School of Social Work. http://www.ssw.umich.edu/public/currentProjects/grantsetc/.

Grants.gov (federal grant resources). http://www.grants.gov/.

GrantStation. http://www.grantstation.com/.

Innovation Network. http://www.innonet.org/.

National Center on Nonprofit Enterprise. http://nationalcne.org/.

Nonprofit Finance Fund. http://nonprofitfinancefund.org/.

The Nonprofit Management Library: All About Financial Management in Nonprofits. http://www.managementhelp.org/finance/np_fnce/np_fnce.htm#anchor50325.

9

CHAPTER

DESIGNING AND USING INFORMATION SYSTEMS

Just as psychotherapist Fritz Perls defined responsibility as the ability to respond, accountability may be seen as the ability to account. We have already looked at several important accountabilities of human service organizations. Accountability to the community is addressed through needs assessments, strategic planning, and, in a most encompassing sense, a focus on the agency's mission. Accountability to clients, other service providers, and standards of professional organizations is reflected in the use of the most appropriate and effective service delivery models. Accountability to staff occurs through human resources policies and processes ensuring that staff members are well trained, supervised, and evaluated and that the high quality of working life is enhanced through factors such as fair and equitable treatment by the agency. We just reviewed how financial management systems can help ensure accountability to funders and the community at large, making it possible for agencies to demonstrate this accountability through financial reports and audits.

We will now look at another important way to account to the community, clients, board, and other stakeholders: by documenting the agency's activities and accomplishments. These processes, sometimes looked at by staff with as much annoyance as are references to the budget, are variously referred to as "data collection," "doing stats," "documentation," or the bane of bureaucracy: "paperwork." The most commonly used term is probably management information system (MIS), and it, too, requires some explanation: it is not a system for management to use for some mysterious purpose but for the management of information by all in the agency. Partly because of possible confusion or preconceptions regarding the term MIS, we will use a slightly broader term here: information systems (IS). This usage is intended to suggest that many types of information are useful and should be gathered, from units of service and client outcomes to staff turnover rates and assessments of employee job satisfaction. The term *information* as used here is within a continuum from *data* (usually numbers, such as age) to information, which attributes meanings to data (e.g., child abuse rates), to *knowledge*, which uses information to draw conclusions such as correlations among variables. The increasing attention to knowledge will be discussed later in this chapter in terms of the emerging field of *knowledge management* in organizations.

This discussion is based on three important assumptions. First, we assume that pressures for accountability and, more specifically, documentation of results will increase (Murray, 2010). Policy makers and the public can legitimately expect to be shown the results of the expenditure of governmental resources for any purpose, including child abuse prevention, mental health treatment, drug-smuggling interdiction, new weapons systems, or corporate welfare. We are concerned here, of course, about the stewardship of government, foundation, and other funds in the human services.

Second, we assume that all employees in human service organizations want to do well: they want to feel that their work is valued and that they are truly helping clients and addressing problems. The old axiom that "what gets measured gets done" is relevant here in the sense that what an organization measures is a reflection of what it thinks is important. Measurement is essential to understanding what is happening so staff can "keep up the good work," be rewarded and supported, and also identify opportunities for improvement.

Third, we assume that feedback on performance adds value in an organization. Receiving feedback on one's performance enhances performance (Poertner & Rapp,

2007) and, as noted regarding job design in Chapter 6, enriches the job for the employee. In this sense, feedback is an important component of motivation, with expectancy theory, McClelland's achievement motivation, and organizational behavior modification being vivid examples. Information systems, which document results and provide feedback to staff, can be immensely helpful in these areas.

We will begin with a review of the various purposes of information systems. We will then outline a process for designing, or redesigning, an agency's information system and look at common data collection methods and measures. The use of computers and the Internet will receive particular attention, followed by a discussion of other uses of information in areas including organizational culture, learning, and knowledge management.

One important conceptual distinction should be noted at the outset. When human service workers hear the term *management information systems* or *information systems*, their thoughts usually turn to computers. Computers will be an important or essential part of any modern information system, but it is important to note that for the foreseeable future IS will entail nonautomated aspects as well. More important, the system should first be designed conceptually without regard to data management procedures to keep the focus on organizational purpose and results. It is tempting to gather data that can easily be retrieved and presented using a computer, but although these data may be easy to collect they may be only marginally important. Many know the computer axiom "garbage in, garbage out," which represents this problem. Furthermore, it is a waste of time and resources to automate systems that are ineffective or inefficient—an endeavor that is sometimes referred to as "paving cow paths." Successful computerization depends on agency processes and procedures being in good shape before computerization. We will therefore address the design of the IS first and then review how computers can be used to maximum effect within the system.

PURPOSES OF INFORMATION SYSTEMS

According to Rapp and Poertner (1992, pp. 97–100), information systems can be categorized into three types, each with different purposes. Housekeeping systems are used for basic routine processing of information and are the most likely to be automated. These systems are used to "increase the efficiency and accuracy of 'getting out the checks' to clients, staff, and other agencies" (p. 97). In addition to handling finances (accounting, budgeting, personnel), housekeeping systems are used to maintain client records, provider agencies, and other databases. Decision support systems include Web searches for relevant databases, evidence-based practices and best practices, program evaluation results, and needs assessment or other demographic data. Performance guidance systems offer the most promise for human service organizations. The goal of a performance guidance system is "to instigate action" (Rapp & Poertner, 1992, p. 99). Based on organizational purpose, goals, and objectives, it provides data that staff can use to adjust their behavior, modify programs, or plan new activities.

This discussion will not address decision support systems, which, with the exception of Web searches, to date have not been common, or housekeeping systems, which are typically designed by the agency's accounting and human resources experts or consultants and often use specialized software programs. The focus here is on ways of tracking organizational performance so that program objectives can be accomplished and agency strategies can be effectively implemented and modified. The design or redesign of an information system is thus based on both a current strategic plan and a solid program design (theory of helping and clearly defined service activities) with well-written goals and objectives.

Regarding the notion of performance management, Behn (2003) has identified eight purposes for measuring performance:

1. *to evaluate*: find out how well the agency is doing
2. *to control*: ensure that staff are performing planned activities in the defined ways
3. *to budget*: using data to make funding allocation decisions
4. *to motivate*: rewarding staff for achieving identified goals and objectives
5. *to promote*: to show policy makers, funding organizations, and donors how well the agency is doing
6. *to celebrate*: agency rituals celebrating the accomplishment of key objectives such as reaching performance targets bind people together, validate their efforts, and energize staff
7. *to learn*: analysis of data can help show why things are or are not working, and what contributes to success
8. *to improve*: feedback can be used to identify opportunities for improving agency operations

Research and practice have revealed some other principles or characteristics of effective information systems. Perhaps most important, as Poertner and Rapp (2007) assert, "managers must know what constitutes performance" (p. 197). This knowledge is based on agency strategies and program objectives, but actual implementation requires serious thought and discussion on the part of the managers and in fact all employees. It is not enough to say "provide the best service possible to clients"; all staff must be clear on exactly what results are desired in terms of service outcomes and the way they use their time and focus their energy on a daily basis.

Organizations and staff need to be consciously purposeful, devoting scarce time and resources to service outcomes, responsible management of funds, a supportive organizational culture, and a high quality of working life. There need to be systems to track progress in all of these areas so that staff can celebrate accomplishments and be rewarded and so that adjustments can be made to ensure desired results.

Rapp and Poertner (1992) list these "principles for using information to enhance performance":

1. The role of information in an organization is to initiate action and influence behavior.
2. The act of collecting information (measurement) generates human energy around the activity being measured.
3. To increase the expenditure of energy for performance, the collection and feedback of information must be systematically linked to explicit goals, standards for performance, and rewards.
4. To insure that information directs human energy toward enhanced performance, data collection and feedback must be used to: (1) foster and reinforce desired

behaviors; (2) identify barriers to performance and problem-solve; and (3) set goals for future performance.

5. Feedback directs behavior toward performance when it provides "cues" to workers to identify clear methods for correction, and when it helps workers learn from their performance.

6. Feedback motivates behavior toward performance when it is used to create expectations for external and internal rewards, is linked to realistic standards for performance, and is directed toward the future versus used punitively to evaluate past performance. (p. 90)

The purposes and uses of an agency's information system should always be kept in mind by those designing or changing it. Every form, procedure, measure, data collection task, and data summary should be created in direct response to a particular need of the agency. These needs include expectations from funders for reports on accomplishments and the use of resources, but a system should not be driven by these external demands. Staff must know that all the agency's systems are designed by and used by the agency itself and that accountability to funders is only one purpose (albeit an essential one) of the system.

MEASURING PERFORMANCE

Because of the complexities of human service programs, the criteria of effective information systems just listed are, of course, not easy to apply. It is much easier for a car dealer, for example, to document results in terms of numbers of cars sold, gross income, or profit per car than it is for a human service manager to measure in a valid way the effects of services designed to reduce problems such as child abuse and neglect.

Until recent years, many funders did not demand precise documentation of success, perhaps understanding the complexity of isolating causal factors and measuring what activities made a difference, or at least concluding that the resources required to gather such data would be extensive and better used in simply delivering more services. Regardless of historical factors, pressure to document results and track organizational performance is likely to increase even further; and a proactive human service manager devotes considerable attention to this task, not only to answer the questions of funders and others but also to improve performance of the agency's programs to better serve clients. We will review some of these challenges and dilemmas, with the expectation that they can be met and that human service organizations can, in fact, document performance in valid, meaningful, and useful ways.

Partly in response to increasing accountability demands, the most important recent development in human service program information systems has been the growing interest in outcomes measurement (Magnabosco & Manderscheid, forthcoming). In the past, funders and agencies have focused primarily on outputs—numbers and types of clients, units of services provided—rather than ultimate outcomes. Even defining a unit of service can be problematic, particularly when trying to compare unit costs (Martin, 2001). Nevertheless, in recent years, the measurement of client outcomes has progressed significantly.

A powerful and influential analysis of this issue by Lisbeth Schorr of the Harvard University Project on Effective Interventions reviews where we are now and where we need to head. Schorr (1997) describes the trend this way: "What counts is no longer confined to whether rules are being complied with. Instead, accountability procedures are beginning to reflect common sense: what matters is whether public purposes are being accomplished" (p. 115). After outlining some of the things that this type of accountability can accomplish and some of the fears of program staff and their supporters, she lists some ways of "minimizing the dangers and maximizing the benefits of an outcomes focus" (p. 122). While focused on macro- or community-wide systems, some of these apply to the agency level as well:

- Choose the right outcomes: "get everyone who has a stake, including skeptics, to agree on a set of outcomes considered important, achievable, and measurable" (p. 122).
- Set ambitious goals for which measurable outcomes may be developed: a goal may be to have all children grow up safe and nurtured; outcomes may include items from increasingly popular "children's report cards" such as violent crime rates, family reunification, or poverty status.
- "Distinguish between outcomes and processes" to avoid "process creep" in which the focus shifts to means or activities rather than end results (p. 125).
- Place outcomes in "a broader accountability context" (p. 126) in which an agency is not held totally responsible for outcomes or conditions partly beyond its control (for example, lack of child care or transportation may affect parents' participation in an employment program).

To develop systems that provide the newer types of data that will be needed, Schorr suggests "human intervention mapping" (p. 130), referred to in Chapter 3 and later in this chapter as logic models that enable service providers and decision makers to document client conditions, service activities, and interim and ultimate outcomes and to show the links among them. This strategy presents opportunities not only to assess the effects of particular program interventions but also, on a macro level, to educate policy makers regarding the complexity of social and community problems and the activities necessary to address them adequately.

Another way both to educate policy makers and others and to design more comprehensive information systems is to note the multiple measures of effectiveness (or, more broadly, performance) in the human services. It is commonly acknowledged that performance in the human services is multidimensional and, in fact, socially constructed (Herman & Renz, 2004). Common approaches to measuring effectiveness (Balser & McClusky, 2005; Herman & Renz, 2004; Packard, 2010; Sowa, Selden, & Sandfort, 2004; and Rainey & Steinbauer, 1999) include:

- *Goal* approaches include setting measurable objectives in areas such as effectiveness and efficiency.
- *Internal process* approaches look at documented procedures and units of service—the most commonly used method in the past, now augmented by goal (outcomes) approaches but still relevant in terms of ensuring that funds are being spent according to programmatic guidelines.

- *Strategic constituencies* approaches are not part of a formal system but are important in assessing the extent to which an organization is responding effectively to the needs of key stakeholders.
- *Human resources* approaches measure job satisfaction and morale through employee attitude surveys, assessment of turnover, and absenteeism.
- *Systems resources* approaches assess the extent to which the organization can continue to bring in funding to grow and adapt to the environment.

Although the goal approaches will usually be the most important, a human service manager will benefit from assessing the ways in which any of the others may be relevant and require monitoring. The information system can then be designed to meet the multiple information needs of managers, staff, the board, and outside stakeholders such as funding sources.

An information system model that originated in the business sector and has now been applied in not-for-profit organizations and government is the *balanced scorecard* (Niven, 2008). This method is used for tracking multiple measures of factors that affect performance. The general model suggests that organizations gather and use information to answer four basic questions, each representing an important perspective from which to view the organization:

- *Customer*: What do our customers and other stakeholders expect of us, and how are we doing?
- *Internal process*: What key processes must we excel at?
- *Learning and growth*: How can we continue to improve, and to develop our staff?
- *Financial*: How are we managing our resources?

In a human service organization, both clients and other stakeholders can be considered as customers. For example, in a child protective services program, "customers" may include a child who is the victim of abuse or neglect, parents, and other family members, often with conflicting interests and expectations. Law enforcement and participants in the court system are other relevant stakeholders. Measures of customer satisfaction may include response time for initial investigations, actions taken by a social worker, and the quality of a court report. The important principle here is that an organization needs to define key goals, objectives, and criteria for a service and then create measures for them. Most of this defining, of course, is done at the program design stage. If the program design and methods and the original objectives are clear, developing useful measures will be easier.

Key internal processes that affect performance, quality, and efficiency should also be measured. Human services have been noted for measuring processes, such as units of services provided, but these are not often directly related to the accomplishment of objectives. Processes measured should be the key ones in getting results. Again, a solid program design based on empirically validated service delivery theories and methods will make it easier to identify key factors to measure. In the human services, staff skill and competence (for example, risk assessment in protective services), relationship building and assessment skills, and efficiency in conducting home visits and preparing reports may be relevant. Systems for maintaining an understanding of customer and community needs and adapting and innovating to respond are also internal processes. Processes from marketing (see Chapter 3) and fund-raising processes to improving quality and efficiency with techniques such as Total Quality Management (see Chapter 11) should be assessed here. In the human services, relevant variables to measure may include the number of new programs initiated, new funding acquired, employee ideas for program innovations, and cost savings related to increased efficiencies.

Organizations also need to monitor their own learning and development abilities. These range from human resources processed covered in Chapter 6 to maintaining an organizational culture that supports change and development of staff. An agency's activities related to becoming a learning organization or organizational change activities may be worth tracking. As much as possible, these activities (visioning, educational, or dialogue sessions with staff) should be measured in terms of relevant results, such as action plans for new programs or strategies, and connected as clearly as possible to actual desired organizational outcomes. Documenting the number of organizational visioning sessions will have little meaning or value unless these activities have effects on performance in the near or long term. Employees' views regarding human resources processes, morale, and levels of burnout can be measured through periodic employee surveys (see Chapter 12).

Financial goals are also important in human service organizations. Balanced budgets, increases in funds from various sources, and financial stability are legitimate measures and should be tracked, but not to the detriment of other goals such as customer satisfaction or program quality. In fact, a major point of the balanced scorecard is that measures in all areas should be assessed from a systems perspective so that improvements in one area do not happen at the expense of other areas.

Norton (2008, p. 231) suggests that there be a limited number of objectives (e.g., 10 to 15) in a balanced scorecard system. He adds that having an average of 1.5 measures per objective is a good guideline for developing performance measures, which we will cover next.

MEASURING INPUTS, OUTPUTS, AND OUTCOMES

Using the logic model framework from Chapter 3, and paying special attention to program objectives, we will briefly address ways of measuring the components of performance: inputs, throughputs, outputs, and outcomes (Kettner, Moroney, & Martin, 2008).

Inputs, essentially characteristics of clients, staff, and resources, can be documented through client demographics, history, problems, and strengths; relevant staff characteristics including degrees, licenses, and skills; and in some cases facilities requirements such as licensing standards in residential care. Staff and facilities characteristics are important measures of the *quality* of the input, and are often defined based on the evidence-based model being used.

Throughputs are the activities of program implementation: the processes in delivering services. In the information system, throughputs can actually be defined as *outputs*: the delivery of units of service. Outputs are commonly measured in human service programs and include intermediate outputs such as types and units of services provided. Units of service can be defined in several ways (Martin & Kettner, 2010). A unit can be an *episode* or *contact* such as a counseling session. A *material unit* is a tangible resource such as a home-delivered meal. It should be noted that such a unit does not automatically have a quality dimension. In this case, nutritional value and proper cooking and heating, and probably timely delivery, would be measures of quality. Quality can also be defined in terms of waiting time to receive a service. A service can also be defined as a *time unit* such as one hour for a counseling session, which may also be considered an aspect of quality. Measuring client satisfaction can be an assessment of the quality of a service output.

Final outputs are service completions and are not always defined in human service programs. Some evidence-based practices may have a standard, such as the number of sessions in an anger management course or a job training program, or the number days in a substance abuse treatment program. As with the case with units of service, there should be a quality dimension. For example, if a client misses two sessions of a twelve-session program, should that qualify as a service completion? Ideally, evidence-based practice standards would answer such questions.

Outcomes can be intermediate (client changes at the completion of service) or final (changes in client quality of life). Identification of outcomes is, of course, much easier if program objectives have been written in terms of outcomes rather than outputs. However, outcome objectives in the human services have been and in many cases still are difficult to develop. As human service technologies are refined and validated by research results, and to the extent that necessary resources are allocated to programs, outcomes will become easier to identify, achieve, and document. Examples of outcome measures are becoming more frequent in the literature in areas including behavioral health, child and family services, and health care (Magnabosco & Manderscheid, forthcoming). Several excellent Web-based resources regarding development outcome measures are listed at the end of this chapter.

Standardized instruments are available to serve diagnostic purposes as well as to enable tracking of change in a client over time (see Martin & Kettner, 2010, for examples). Agencies serving clients with varying problems can use measurements that are easily interpreted and that can assess clients' general levels of functioning. Such instruments can be used both to assist in working with individual clients and to evaluate the effectiveness of a program with entire groups of consumers. Standards can vary in terms of consumers' pretreatment functioning; so the objectives for one client group might differ in terms of realistically expected outcome from the objectives for another.

According to Poertner and Rapp (2007, pp. 235–244), outcomes may be assessed in several categories: affect, knowledge, behavior, status, or environment. Changes in affect (psychological status or attitude) are often measured in human service programs in areas from hopefulness and depression to satisfaction with services. Some, such as measures of decrease in depression, can be important outcome measures. Others, such as surveys of client satisfaction, may provide useful feedback to staff, but they do not necessarily correspond to desired end results.

Changes in knowledge can be useful as well (for example, regarding methods for birth control or safe sex) but again may not change ultimate behavior (practicing safe sex). Behavior changes can be seen in both skills and performance, with the latter usually being the most desirable end result.

Standardized instruments are available to measure many variables, from depression to client satisfaction. These include a set of structured questions to gather information about clients, and they usually have a set of uniform procedures for administration and scoring (Kettner, Moroney, & Martin, 2008, p. 88). Many such instruments will also have clinical cut points, which can be very useful in setting objectives for a program and tracking client progress and ultimate outcomes. Fischer and Corcoran (2007) offer an excellent resource on standardized measures. Program objectives could use data from these instruments to indicate, for example, the number of clients who entered a program at one level and later achieved a certain score on a standardized instrument.

Level of functioning (LOF) scales are "before-and-after assessment instruments, usually designed by agency or program staff for use with a particular target population, that attempt to capture important dimensions of client functioning" (Martin & Kettner, 2010, p. 100). A LOF scale may describe dimensions such as socialization or participation in a day care program with scales from very low to very high functioning to track before-and-after changes. Status changes are often highly desirable, such as when a client can move from a group home for the mentally ill to independent living.

Standardized instruments and LOF scales are particularly valuable for program evaluation. A wise manager will build these measures into the IS at the program design stage, anticipating an evaluation that may not occur until a program has been in operation for perhaps a year. Further information on such instruments is included in Chapter 10.

The final category Poertner and Rapp described is changes in the environment. This category is not commonly addressed. It can include assessment of the program environment, for example qualitative aspects of a day care setting.

After inputs, outputs, and outcomes have been defined, measurement systems to monitor actual implementation need to be developed. These typically begin with records, often in case files, which enable staff to document what took place with a client. Individual records are merged into *output tables* (Kettner, Moroney, & Martin, 2008) that summarize in numeric counts data from all clients. These are often used in periodic (e.g., monthly and annual) reports summarizing everything from client demographics to numbers of services and service completion and final outcomes. This process will be discussed in more detail in the following section, where the information system design process is described.

As a final consideration in the development of performance measures, it may help to use these criteria from Poertner and Rapp (2007, pp. 224–229):

- Measures need to be understandable when they are summarized in reports.
- Measures should be valid (for example, completion of a substance abuse program does not necessarily mean that a client is no longer using drugs).
- Measures should be reliable, or consistent: the definitions of a measure should be agreed to by all (for example, when placement stability is important in child welfare, it should be understood that temporarily transferring a foster youth for needed inpatient psychiatric treatment should not be seen as instability but rather as meeting a child's needs).
- Measures need to be susceptible to change within the period being reported.
- Measures need to be efficient (simple and easy to collect and report).

Once an organization has developed clear and viable program designs with measurable objectives and has articulated conceptually the various key success factors that it will need to monitor, designing an information system becomes much easier.

9.1   DATA FOR THE TEEN TRANSITION AND TREATMENT PROGRAM

After staff had developed the program model and objectives and the budget for the Teen Transition and Treatment Program, the next step was to develop the data elements and the information system that they could use to track program activities and document results.

The key inputs that they would need to document are client demographics. For their teen clients, this would include age, gender, race or ethnicity, living situation, and family members. They would also need to document the types, amounts, and frequencies of the clients' current use of illegal drugs. Data on staff inputs would document that staff members had required licenses and certifications. Also, staff members from other agencies including schools were included as inputs on the logic model. Contacts with outside agency staff would be documented as part of the throughputs.

The main throughputs (client activities) are scheduled weekly individual counseling sessions, group therapy sessions, and psycho-educational group therapy sessions. Outputs are the number of sessions held, and service completions are defined as completing 10 of the 12 sessions. The group sessions will cover topics including relapse prevention, life skills, self-esteem, family issues, recovery lifestyle, and recreation/leisure; so the information system would need to track sessions clients complete on each of those topics. A final output is the expectation that the program will maintain a minimum case load of 50 clients.

There are outcome objectives in four areas. The first area is a knowledge objective: skills competency on topics covered in group sessions will be documented by a score of 70 percent or higher on the skills competency post-test. The second and third areas are behavioral objectives. They focus on documenting the discontinued use of illicit drugs twice through urine analysis: upon completion of the program, 80 percent of clients will be drug-free (tested at 12 weeks); and 6 months after completion of the program, 60 percent of clients will still be clean of drugs.

The fourth and ultimate outcome is the expectation that 80 percent of clients will increase their quality of life, documented through decreased occurrence of internalizing and externalizing behaviors and increased social competence. This outcome will be measured by clients having a quality of life score at or above the midpoint of the Moderate functioning levels for the 3 components of the Child and Adolescent Measurement System (CAMS).

Now that staff knew what data elements they would need, they formed a task force to design the information system.

INFORMATION SYSTEM DESIGN GUIDELINES

After a program design has been chosen and goals and objectives have been written, the agency will need to design the information system to implement it. In the case of an existing agency, this may be more properly a *redesign* of an existing system. For a totally new program, design will start from scratch. In any case, thoughtful and detailed consideration will need to be paid to the task of ensuring that the information system can collect and compile all necessary data to monitor program implementation and document results.

Before reviewing the design process itself, we will look at some additional guidelines that will help make things go smoothly. First, those who initiate the design process should be aware of the dynamics of organizational culture and power in the agency. Staff may fear that a new information system will highlight inadequacies in their work or lead to more unnecessary paperwork. The idea of a new or improved information system should be introduced by executive leaders, but equally important is getting the commitment of workers at other levels of the organization. The best way to do this is to involve staff members in the process. Their knowledge and creativity will be invaluable in developing a good system, and their involvement will give them a stake in the outcome, broadening support for the initiative.

Related to this dimension is the issue of resources. Top management support needs to go beyond announcements and meetings to making in advance a sufficient commitment of resources to enable the system to be changed or implemented. Management should designate a key person to be responsible for this initiative. This will both demonstrate management support and help ensure that the process can proceed as planned.

Ideologically based issues may surface as well. Staff may see an information system as a bureaucratic method to control all staff and stifle worker autonomy and initiative. Staff will need to be shown what the purposes of the system will be and how data from the system will be used (for example, to improve services for clients and to demonstrate the value of the program to current and prospective funders). Concerns regarding confidentiality will also need to be addressed, such as controlling access to files and computerized databases. Staff members will also need to believe that a new system will not require a net increase in work on their part (for example, more paperwork or data entry). Through training it should be made clear how the system will actually be more efficient for workers and will provide valuable information. This does not involve "selling" staff: the system should be designed so that the benefits are real and evident to all.

Another implication of a well-designed information system is that decision making will become more data based and rational. This point may be seen as a threat to staff who are used to making decisions based on gut feelings, values, or impressions. It should be emphasized to staff members that no decision-making process is fully rational and that their impressions can in fact help guide decisions but that they should use all the data available to increase the likelihood that the decisions do lead to improved performance.

Finally, an effective way to deal with any resistance is to note the pressures for change. Funding sources are regularly increasing their expectations for accountability and results, and this point can be used to leverage both the organization's commitment in terms of resources and the staff members' interest in change: they must all see that a new system will have a concrete payoff for them. All of these dynamics should be taken into account during the development of plans for introducing an IS design process. The principles of organizational change in Chapter 11 may be helpful in such a design process.

THE DESIGN PROCESS

Recent experiences in the development of information systems and computerization have provided knowledge regarding the steps that should be taken to ensure that an IS is appropriate, effective, efficient, and valued by staff. The following steps are adapted from the process developed by Schoech (2000). This process may be used when updating, refining, or totally redesigning an existing IS or designing a system for a new program or agency. It will involve additions or changes to existing agency software or, in some cases, initial computerization. Specifics regarding computerization are discussed after the generic design process is covered.

STEP 1: PREPARATION AND COMMITTEE FORMATION

A decision to update or redesign an IS typically originates with a discussion among agency managers and perhaps other staff, and a good deal of dialogue should occur before making a commitment to proceed. Ideally there would be strategies or other elements in the agency's strategic plan, and perhaps even a strategy addressing this directly, suggesting that IS redesign and/or computerization is necessary. In any case, this idea should be announced to staff, outlining the intended purpose and objectives of the initiative. This announcement may also include a preliminary timetable and list of those involved.

9.2 INFORMATION SYSTEM DESIGN FOR GRANDVIEW COMMUNITY CENTER

When considering the design of the IS for the new program, agency director Leona Estrella realized that the information systems in other programs needed refinement as well. To address this situation, agency executive staff met with all program staff groups and announced plans for the formation of a steering committee to develop overall guidelines for a new IS for the agency. Volunteers were solicited for involvement in the steering committee and a design team for each program. Staff saw the need for this initiative, but to validate their informal impressions and to ensure that all staff could consider the issue, each design team assessed the needs for and the purposes of a new information system, developed proposed action plans and timetables, and prepared a feasibility report.

The steering committee consisted of Leona and directors of two of the program's three direct service staff, and the agency's director of administrative support. This committee was to prepare a plan for developing a comprehensive information system including a client database that could be used not only to demonstrate program effectiveness and efficiency to funding sources but also to provide information to aid in program planning and development.

Additionally, for the new Teen Transition and Treatment Program, a design team was formed to develop the information system for that program specifically. The design team would be coordinated with the efforts of the steering committee and design teams for other programs to develop the overall system and specific data collection tools for the new program. This design team included the new program director, a clinician, and a staff member from the agency's administrative support unit. Feasibility reports recommending a "go" were submitted to the executive team and the board of directors, and a decision was made to proceed.

To build employee involvement and commitment into the process from the beginning, a steering committee should be formed. In large, complex agencies, day-to-day work on the system design may be performed by one or more task forces or a design team, similar to the organization design process outlined in Chapter 5. Such a committee or team should include representatives from all major sectors of the agency: management; supervisors; line staff; office staff; IS staff, if any; and labor organizations, if any. Ideally the initial announcement would solicit volunteers from staff who would like to participate.

A preliminary estimate should be made of necessary resources, including time for staff to attend meetings and work on the project and perhaps costs for a computer consultant. Existing conditions such as staff skills, values, and ideologies; existing equipment and processes; and staff goals and visions should be assessed. The steering committee should comprehensively and honestly review the likely system impacts (such as a higher quality of data in more usable forms, inefficiencies during implementation and training, changes in the way work is done) and the likely effects on key stakeholders (particularly staff who will be using the system).

STEP 2: ANALYSIS OF THE EXISTING SYSTEM

If the agency decides to proceed, the next step is to analyze the existing system. The key to a system's effectiveness is the degree to which it meets the agency's unique planning, management, and evaluation needs. Agency personnel need to identify as specifically as possible the kinds of data needed, the source of these data, and the frequency with which they should be collected and distributed. Beyond this, planning for effective gathering and disseminating of information involves working out the type of system most appropriate for the agency's functions, size, and degree of complexity. The steering committee should bear in mind that the main purpose of an IS is to guide staff performance in accomplishing program objectives: to make a difference in the lives of clients and communities. This analysis should therefore begin by reviewing the program objectives and service delivery models.

An IS must enable staff and other stakeholders to track progress on objectives and provide other information useful to the program or required by any funding organizations. Information needs should be listed here: client demographics, staff tasks and units of service, intermediate and ultimate client outcomes, and so forth. The IS may also be needed to answer questions related to program evaluation or research. (An example would be, what effect does a particular job-training program have on the ultimate employment of selected welfare recipients?)

A program logic model and flowchart (see Chapter 3) may be helpful to document each step of the service process.

Activities occur at each stage that are based on the service delivery model and documented in case files and other records. Typically, at intake a face sheet is developed, containing basic demographic and other information. There may be a screening or assessment process during which client data are gathered, perhaps using forms or checklists. After problems are identified, a case plan, including objectives, is developed and documented in the client file. Activities at each stage of the service delivery process may be documented as well. Results are assessed at predetermined times, and eventually the case is terminated, ideally with follow-up planned. Designers of the IS can use this chart, program objectives, and other information needs of the staff and outside stakeholders to determine what data need to be collected in the new system.

	ANALYSIS OF INFORMATION NEEDS FOR THE
9.3	TEEN TRANSITION AND TREATMENT PROGRAM

The Support Club information system design team started by reviewing the program design outlined in the funding proposal. They concluded that it would be essential to develop measures for outcomes: the accomplishment of objectives listed in their original proposal. They also wanted to measure key outputs such as units of service so they would later be able to correlate amounts and types of services provided with ultimate outcomes. Finally, they wanted to document the characteristics of clients and staff to aid in making program refinements as needed. Given that this would be a new program, they could start from scratch in developing forms for case records and forms for data compilation and reports. They noted that in other programs in the agency, only outputs were measured, and they had no real way of knowing what the ultimate benefits to clients were. They wanted to avoid this situation in the Teen Transition and Treatment Program so that they would have some idea as to what activities really made a difference to clients. The design team prepared a flowchart describing what would happen to a client as she received services and what forms would be needed to capture data for both case management and later evaluation. They met with staff at programs that provided similar services and found only one program offering helpful guidance: a program with a computerized database for client records that kept track of demographic data and services provided. They concluded that they had a huge task in front of them but that they definitely should proceed so that they would be able to clearly show the program's accomplishments.

An assessment of the existing system and needs for a new system can point to the types of data needed and ways to collect them, ideally addressing ultimate and desired client outcomes. The design team or steering committee should summarize the results of this step. Measures for assessing outcomes will be reviewed in the next step.

STEP 3: DETAILED DESIGN

Once information requirements have been specified, agency personnel need to determine the appropriate sources for these data. Most agencies use forms that identify client characteristics and/or the nature of services delivered. Evaluation data requirements should be taken into account when such forms are designed.

This step involves answering questions about how the data will be used. The system should be easily usable by service delivery staff, of course; and program staff and administrators will use data summaries to track progress for the project as a whole, both as early intelligence regarding needed adjustments such as changing staffing configurations and as annual reviews or evaluations. Decisions can be made regarding which data will be automated and which will be maintained manually, and who will enter data into files and the computer. This approach will suggest the types of forms that will be needed in case files and for summaries to be used in monthly and annual reports. Evaluation needs such as correlations among variables should be anticipated so that required statistical manipulations will be easy to perform.

Other parameters such as the frequency of data entry, needs for links with other databases (such as those in other programs in the agency), and confidentiality should be taken into account here. If more than one option is under consideration, each can be evaluated with regard to the criteria chosen and the best design selected for detailing. At this point, software to meet the system needs can be selected, and new hardware can be chosen to match the software and provide necessary staff access and technology (printers and so forth). A very important decision will be selecting computer software for use with automated data. Lyons and Winter (2010) noted that an agency can consult other agencies and coalition or support organizations that are part of their services network to learn about systems similar agencies are using. In the case study they described, for example, the Alliance for Children and Families was a useful resource.

A method for handling evaluation data should be built into the routine agency operations, allowing the collection of evaluation data to become part of the agency's everyday operating procedures. Evaluators can determine what person or functional unit within an agency can most easily record needed information, to whom the information should be reported, and who should be responsible for analyzing the information.

Finally, the proposed design—including data that need to be collected, methods for collecting and storing data, data entry, forms for case files, and formats for data collation and analysis, as well as software and hardware needed—can then be prepared for review and decisions. If various design teams have been working on different aspects of the plan, their work is integrated and reviewed, typically by the steering committee and then by agency executive staff and other staff groups who will be using the system. After the design proposal is approved or modified, implementation can begin.

9.4	DETAILED DESIGN OF THE IS FOR THE TEEN TRANSITION AND TREATMENT PROGRAM

The Teen Transition and Treatment Program design team used the flowchart to note service activities at each step of the program and the data that would need to be gathered. They designed a face sheet for demographic data such as age, ethnicity, school performance, and current involvement with other service providers (for example, child protective services). This also would include pre-measures related to program objectives (drug use, skills competency, and quality of life). Another form would be used for the case plan, which would outline services to be provided, including attendance at counseling sessions and groups, and group session topics. The case plan would have individual case objectives written so that their accomplishment could be easily documented with a yes/no field or a behaviorally anchored rating scale. Demographics, pre-measures, and services received would be documented in the case file, using fields that could be used for entry into a computerized database. Each form was reviewed to ensure that data could be easily computerized and collated and that correlations and other statistical analyses would be possible. The design team coordinated their work with that of the other design teams and the steering committee to ensure maximum compatibility of formats.

STEP 4: SYSTEM TESTING AND AGENCY PREPARATION

After the design of a new system has been approved, adjustments to software and perhaps hardware will probably need to be made. This step often will require a lump-sum expenditure for hardware and software as well as initial training of staff. Regular maintenance and upgrading of hardware and software and training for new staff would then become ongoing budget items. The importance of the training of staff and other users of the system (data entry or IS staff) is often not fully appreciated or emphasized. In addition to learning how to use any new software and hardware, development of a new or significantly changed information system, automated or not, represents a significant cultural change for most organizations: staff will need to see and use information in a new way, as a more important component of their work in delivering services to clients and planning or modifying programs. Principles of organizational change, covered in Chapter 11, can be useful here.

In terms of the basic training, Zimmerman and Broughton (2006) offer some useful suggestions for training staff in computer usage, many of which are also useful guidelines for IS training not necessarily involving automation:

- Train in small groups....
- Train for short periods of time....
- Make sure workers have access to computers and software at their work site before training....
- Make sure workers train on the same software they have on their work computers....
- Do not interrupt training with other work....
- Have workers take classes appropriate for their level of competence....
- Give new computer users time to practice their new skills....
- Use the buddy system for training.... (pp. 336–337)

The new system also has to be built into the agency's policies and procedures. New staff positions, such as an information systems coordinator, may be created, and the job duties of others may change to include data entry. These changes need to be reflected in modified job descriptions, performance appraisal criteria, and perhaps as new criteria for particular staff positions.

During the testing of the new system, it may become clear that refinements in forms or procedures will be needed, and these changes can be made, with clearance through any relevant design teams or the steering committee to ensure that the overall system will still work.

STEP 5: IMPLEMENTATION, EVALUATION, AND MODIFICATION

At this point, the new system and its procedures can be implemented, perhaps in stages. Key factors now include ensuring that the new procedures are in fact followed (or changed as needed based on new experiences) and that mechanisms are in place for ongoing adaptation to new needs and conditions. As was noted in Step 4, principles of change management should be followed: someone should be responsible for ongoing monitoring and ensuring that the system is used as intended and continues to provide needed information. Questions to be asked have to do with the system's ease of use and the utility of its outputs: do staff use data in their daily work, and do managers use reports in monitoring and adjusting programs and activities?

The ultimate test of any organizational system, including an information system, is its performance in accomplishing stated objectives, from improvements in services to clients and increased responsiveness to stakeholders such as funders, to cost savings and increased quality of working life. All who have been involved with the design and implementation of the new system, including the steering committee, any design teams, and all staff who use the system, should have an opportunity to review the original goals, objectives, and expectations for the new system and compare actual results to these. Sometimes there is interest in assessing the effects of the new system on some aspect of performance, such as efficiency or cost savings. Assessing the views of staff through a survey or focus groups can identify accomplishments of the system and also emerging issues or potential problems and ideas for addressing them.

Any system will also need updating, notably regarding software but also in response to new programmatic needs. Provisions need to be made for not only the training of new staff on use of the system but also training for other staff whenever changes are made. The agency should have mechanisms such as periodic focus groups or discussions at staff meetings to monitor staff feelings about and use of the system so that it continues to be seen as valuable to them in their work. Presenting summaries of data gathered by the system can both provide a context for staff's daily data collection activities and show how their work helps lead to valued program outcomes. For example, if patterns or trends become evident regarding changes in client characteristics, amounts or types of services provided, or outcomes, these data can be fed back to staff for analysis and modification of program activity as needed. This is one aspect of program evaluation, a topic that will be addressed in the next chapter. At this point, we will review some current issues and developments regarding information systems.

9.5	IMPLEMENTATION OF THE NEW IS FOR THE AGENCY

Because the steering committee and design teams had representatives from a wide variety of staff, all employees had been informed on a regular basis about the status of the design and were able to offer suggestions. Because of the amount of staff involvement, there was little resistance to this major change; staff saw the value in it and had been able to provide input into the design of the system. Nevertheless, Leona and her staff made sure to allocate enough time for staff to test the new system, including the forms and the computer software, and to have training for all staff. A staff member from administrative support was assigned to write necessary policies and procedures to fully document the new system. Leona and her staff decided to reconvene the steering committee and design teams temporarily after 3 months to see how implementation was proceeding and to make any adjustments needed.

THE USE OF COMPUTERS AND OTHER ELECTRONIC MEDIA

As noted earlier, information systems are often equated with computers, and although they are not the same thing, they clearly overlap greatly in today's human service organizations. Computers and other forms of electronic media including smartphones and personal digital assistants are becoming increasingly prominent in the work life and personal life of human service staff and will become more so in the future. This development can be seen in trends in the literature, including Schoech (2009) and Zimmerman and Broughton (2006) and the *Journal of Technology in Human Services*. A recent book (Dunlop & Holosko, 2006, also published as a special issue of the *Journal of Evidence-Based Social Work* in 2006) addresses information technology and evidence-based practice. Here we will review briefly some of the common and emerging uses of computers in the human services.

Many agencies, particularly in the public sector, are now online, providing staff with access to email and the Internet. Zimmerman and Broughton (1998) note the increasing use of LANs (local area networks, in which computers within an agency are linked), which enable staff to share printers and use groupware for tasks such as sharing databases and doing group scheduling.

New uses of the Internet emerge regularly, from search engines, LISTSERVs discussion boards, and news groups to blogs, instant messaging and social network sites, which can be used for everything from communication and networking to research, fund-raising, and advocacy. Security and confidentiality will continue to require attention by agency administrators (Schoech, 2009).

This field is advancing so rapidly that readers of a book may find outdated information and will certainly have to consult journals, newsletters, newspapers, and, of course, online sources to remain up-to-date on computer and Internet developments.

ORGANIZATIONAL CULTURE AND LEARNING

We will end this discussion of information systems by putting "data" in a larger context. It is easy to get caught up in numbers, performing elaborate statistical manipulations and preparing impressive reports. As Poertner (2009) has noted, information can be an important factor in empowering staff and creating a culture that supports organizational learning. Staff may pay less attention to record keeping because they do not value the use of information highly (Carrilio, Packard, & Clapp, 2003). Organizational culture can be an important factor related to the use of information systems (Cronley & Patterson, 2010; Poertner & Rapp, 2007) and service effectiveness (Glisson, 2009). With specific reference to this current discussion of the use of data, part of the manager's job as a leader is to ensure that staff understand the importance of information and knowledge management in providing effective services to clients.

This chapter has focused primarily information—putting data in a context and providing meaning. Beyond information management is the emerging field of knowledge management: "the range of practices used to identify, create, represent, and distribute organizational knowledge for reuse and learning" (Leung, Chu, Chan, Lee, & Wong, 2010, p. 362). The focus in this chapter has been on using information and knowledge regarding service delivery, but information and knowledge are also essential to organizational learning, which will be addressed in Chapter 12.

The use of feedback is also a relevant consideration in staff quality of working life, in terms of job design and rewards, both of which add meaning to the work for an employee. In Chapter 6, job feedback was noted as a key component of the Job Characteristics Model of Hackman and Oldham, which if appropriately addressed can enhance both the quality of working life and staff performance. Feedback at a broader level is available through program evaluation, the subject of the next chapter. Such feedback can be a valuable tool to learn how the organization is performing and then make necessary improvements.

SUMMARY

A well-designed information system can enhance an organization's effectiveness and responsiveness and raise employees' sense of satisfaction and purpose. Managers should bear these points in mind to avoid having an IS designed only to meet external accountability and evaluation needs without being fully valued or supported by staff. An IS should be designed with careful attention to information needs (related to program outcomes, for example) and should include significant participation from staff who will be using the system. Such a system will probably involve computers, the potentials of which are increasing daily. An IS should meet both internal needs (for example, for feedback, program modification, and employee satisfaction) and external needs related to accountability and program evaluation, discussed in the next chapter.

COMPETENCY-BUILDING ACTIVITY 9.1 | INFORMATION SYSTEMS

Your hypothetical agency now has a logic model, goals and objectives, staff, and a budget. Now, you can use all of these elements to develop an information system that will enable you to document program implementation and the accomplishment of objectives, and to develop formats to document client demographics and to keep track of the types and numbers of all services provided and the numbers of clients served. Decide how you will measure the extent of accomplishment of all your objectives. Give particular attention to outcomes: how will you be able to show how the quality of life conditions changed for clients in the program?

CASE ACTIVITY 9.1 | EVALUATION EMERGENCY

Mario Rinaldi, director of the Developmental Disabilities Training Project, called an emergency meeting of the project staff.

"You've all been working really hard on the training manual," he said. "I hate to pull this on you right now, but I've got to tell you that I just had word. The feds are sending in their evaluator. He's going to be here next week, and we've got to be ready."

Amid the groans, Jane Carlin, a staff trainer, spoke up. "What's the big problem?" she asked. "We've been providing a training session every week. We've had workshops on developmental disabilities for the teachers, for citizens; we've had the TV show, now we've got a manual for parents. It seems to me we're in great shape. So what's the problem?"

"Well, I was kind of putting this part off," Rinaldi answered. "They sent along the new evaluation form so that we can complete the self-study before the evaluator gets here. That's the tough part. We're going to really have to dig to get the information ready."

"What kind of information do we need?" Carlin asked. "Remember, we did that pretest and posttest with all the people at the workshops. We've got a lot of data on the learning effects from the workshop. Of course, it's not that easy to do with the TV program."

"That's the least of our problems, Jane. Remember, this is a training project. What they want is information on all participants in any training workshop. They want the ages of trainees, their sex, their employment, their income—all the demographic stuff. I just didn't think about all that because the form we used last year didn't ask for it. You see, we're using the same kind of evaluation form as continuing education programs are. It doesn't make any sense, but I'll bet we can dig up that information somehow."

"Wait a minute!" George Steinberg called out. "I worked my tail off on that TV program, and there's no way in the world I'll ever be able to even guess who watched it. Does that mean the whole thing didn't happen? Does that mean I get a grade of zero? I flunk?"

"Now, George, you know it isn't like that. They just like to have the information so they can put it together with the data from all the other projects they funded. They've got to show results, just as we do."

"That's fine to say, John, but if they're going to evaluate us on how many men, women, and children show up at our sessions, we should do the kind of stuff that can lend itself to what they're looking for. I'm feeling as if my work just isn't going to make the grade."

"I'm starting to feel that way, too," Carlin said. "What's the point of doing one thing if they're evaluating something else?"

"Wait a minute, everybody," Rinaldi responded in frustration. "We're getting way off the track here. These people aren't here to tell us what we should and shouldn't do. They're not going to grade us on what we did. One of the things they ask us about in an open-ended question is the content of the program, the kinds of interventions we did. There's no problem there. The problem is just in putting together the data they want, the demographic characteristics and all that. Now, I've got most of it somewhere. All I need is for somebody to volunteer to help me dig through the files and see what we can find that might relate to some of the questions they're asking. We'll be able to get the sex of participants by looking at their names on those address cards we had them fill out. The ages will be hard. That, we'll have to guess at."

1. How might the agency have avoided this "emergency" situation?

2. How might the funding source have helped avoid the situation?

3. What data should the staff have been collecting for this program?

4. How should the staff deal with this immediate situation?

REFERENCES

Balser, D., & McClusky, J. (2005). Managing stakeholder relationships and nonprofit organization effectiveness. *Nonprofit Management and Leadership, 15*(3), 295–315.

Behn, R. (2003). Why measure performance? Different purposes require different measures. *Public Administration Review, 63*(5), 586–606.

Carrilio, T., Packard, T., & Clapp, J. (2003). Nothing in–nothing out: Barriers to the use of performance data in social service programs. *Administration in Social Work, 27*(4), 61–75.

Cronley, C., & Patterson, D. (2010). How well does it fit? An organizational culture approach to assessing technology use among homeless service providers. *Administration in social work, 34*(3), 286–303.

Dunlop, J., & Holosko, M. (Eds.). (2006). Information technology and evidence-based social work practice. New York: The Haworth Press.

Fischer, J., & Corcoran, K. (2007). *Measures for Clinical Practice and Research: A Sourcebook; Two-volume set.* New York: Oxford University Press.

Herman, R., & Renz, D. (2004). Doing things right: Effectiveness in local nonprofit organizations, a panel study. *Public Administration Review, 64*(6), 694–701.

Kettner, P., Moroney, R., & Martin, L. (2008). *Designing and managing programs: An effectiveness based approach* (3rd ed.). Thousand Oaks, CA: Sage.

Leung, Z., Chu, C., Chan, Y., Lee, W., & Wong, R. (2010). Assessing knowledge assets: Knowledge audit of a social service organization in Hong Kong. *Administration in social work, 34*(4), 361–383.

Lyons, P., & Winter, C. (2010). Data management system selection in a family service agency. *Families in Society, 91*(4), 440–446.

Magnabosco, J., & Manderscheid, R., Eds. (Forthcoming). *Outcomes measurement in the human services* (2nd ed.). Washington, DC: NASW Press.

Martin, L. (2001). *Financial management for human service administrators*. Boston: Allyn & Bacon.

Martin, L. & Kettner, P. (2010). *Measuring the performance of human service programs* (2nd ed.). Thousand Oaks, CA: Sage Publications.

Murray, V. (2010). Assessing nonprofit organization effectiveness. In D. Renz (Ed.), *The Jossey-Bass handbook of nonprofit leadership and management* (3rd ed., pp. 431–458). San Francisco: Jossey-Bass.

Niven, P. (2008). *Balanced scorecard step-by-step for government and nonprofit agencies* (2nd ed.). Hoboken, NJ: John Wiley & Sons.

Packard, T. (2010). Staff perceptions of variables affecting performance in human service organizations. *Nonprofit and Voluntary Sector Quarterly, 39*(6) 971–990.

Poertner, J. (2009). Managing for service outcomes: The critical role of information. In R. Patti (Ed.), *The handbook of human services management,* (2nd ed., pp. 165–181). Thousand Oaks, CA: Sage.

Poertner, J., & Rapp, C. (2007). *Textbook of social administration: The consumer-centered approach.* New York: The Haworth Press.

Rainey, H., & Steinbauer, P. (1999). Galloping elephants: Developing elements of a theory of effective government organizations. *Journal of Public Administration Research and Theory, 9*(1), 1–32.

Rapp, C., & Poertner, J. (1992). *Social administration: A client-centered approach.* New York: Longman.

Schoech, D. (2000). Managing information for decision making. In R. Patti (Ed.), *The handbook of social welfare management* (pp. 321–339). Thousand Oaks, CA: Sage.

Schoech, D. (2009). Developing information technology applications for performance-oriented management in a global environment. In R. Patti (Ed.), *The handbook of human services management* (pp. 183–205). Thousand Oaks, CA: Sage.

Schorr, L. (1997). *Common purpose.* New York: Anchor Books Doubleday.

Sowa, J., Selden, S., & Sandfort, J. (2004). No longer unmeasurable? A multidimensional integrated model of nonprofit organizational effectiveness. *Nonprofit and Voluntary Sector Quarterly, 33*(4), 711–728.

Zimmerman, L., & Broughton, A. (2006). Assessing, planning, and managing information technology. In R. Edwards & J. Yankey (Eds.), *Effectively managing nonprofit organizations* (pp. 327–344). Washington, DC: NASW Press.

USEFUL WEB RESOURCES

Free Management Library: Basic Guide to Outcomes-Based Evaluation for Nonprofit Organizations with Very Limited Resources. http://managementhelp.org/evaluatn/outcomes.htm.

Harvard Family Research Project: Results-Based Accountability. http://www.hfrp.org/publications-resources/browse-our-publications/overview-of-results-based-accountability-components-of-rba.

Urban Institute Outcome Indicators Project. www.urban.org/center/cnp/projects/outcomeindicators.cfm.

The Urban Institute: Developing Community-wide Outcome Indicators for Specific Services. www.urban.org/publications/310813.html.

National Resource Center-Outcome Measurements Articles: http://www.ccfbest.org/outcomemeasurements/.

10 CHAPTER | EVALUATING HUMAN SERVICE PROGRAMS

CHAPTER OUTLINE

In the context of current public policy debates about the value of human service programs and resource challenges in the human services field, program evaluation can be expected to become increasingly relevant (Carman & Fredericks, 2008). Ultimately, evaluation is needed to let us know whether services have taken place as expected and whether they have accomplished what they were meant to accomplish. This kind of information can provide the basis for making sensible decisions concerning current or projected programs.

Program evaluation can be defined as:

> The systematic collection of information about the activities, characteristics, and results of programs to make judgments about the program, improve or further develop program effectiveness, inform decisions about future programming, and/or increase understanding. (Patton, 2008, p. 39)

Patton, who is particularly interested in the *utilization* of evaluation findings, adds that "*utilization-focused program evaluation* (italics in original) is evaluation done for and with specific intended primary users for specific, intended uses" (2008, p. 39).

Human service evaluation, if it is to be of value, must be seen as an integral part of the management cycle and must be closely connected to ongoing management processes and daily activities. Its results must be disseminated to and understood by the people most concerned with program functioning, including community members, funding sources, and service providers, as well as administrators. It can be practical only if individuals who influence service planning and delivery see it as useful.

PURPOSES OF EVALUATION

Evaluators use research techniques, applying them to the needs and questions of specific agencies and stakeholders. Evaluation can be used to aid in administrative decision making, improve currently operating programs, provide for accountability, build increased support for effective programs, and add to the knowledge base of the human services.

ADMINISTRATIVE DECISION MAKING

Evaluation can provide information about activities being carried out by the agency as well as data describing the effects of these activities on clients. Information about current activities can help decision makers deal with immediate issues concerning resource allocations, staffing patterns, and provision of services to individual clients or target populations. At the same time, data concerning the outcomes of services can lead the way toward more rational decisions about continuation or expansion of effective programs and modification or elimination of less effective ones. Decisions concerning the development of new programs or the selection of alternate forms of service can also be made, not necessarily on the basis of evaluation alone but with evaluative data making a significant contribution.

IMPROVEMENT OF CURRENT PROGRAMS

An evaluation can be used to compare programs with the standards and criteria developed during the planning and program design stages. Evaluation can serve as a tool to improve program quality if it provides data that help contrast current operations or conditions with objectives and evidence-based standards. Activities performed as part of an agency's operations can be compared or contrasted with standardized norms, such as professional or legal mandates, or with the agency's own plans, policies, and guidelines. Evaluation of service outcomes means that results can be compared with identified community needs, leading to an assessment of the program's adequacy. Data collection technologies such as employee attitude surveys, management audits, quality audits, cultural competency assessments, and ethics audits can provide information that is very useful in improving program or agency operations. With systematically collected data on hand, agency personnel can make improvements either in the nature of the services or in the ways they are delivered. Although evaluation does not necessarily identify the direction an agency should take, its systematic application does point out discrepancies between current and planned situations. Without it, quality cannot be improved.

ACCOUNTABILITY

Most human service programs are required to submit yearly evaluation or monitoring reports for funding sources or public agencies, and many specially funded projects are required to spend set percentages of their budgets on evaluation. Agencies are accountable not only to funding organizations but also to the clients and communities they serve and even society as a whole. Since the 1990s an "accountability movement" in government and not-for-profit organizations has focused increased attention on adherence to laws and regulations and responsible stewardship of finances as well as effective and ethical implementation of programs. The latter concern, especially regarding the accomplishment of desired program outcomes, is addressed through evaluation.

According to Schorr (1997), in the past "outcomes accountability" and evaluation were separate activities, the former the province of administrators and auditors and the latter of social scientists. Now, however, "the accountability world is moving from monitoring processes to monitoring results. The evaluation world is being demystified, its techniques becoming more collaborative, its applicability broadened, and its data no longer closely held as if by a hostile foreign power" (p. 138). Dissemination of evaluation reports describing the agency's activities and their effects can help reinforce program accountability. People concerned with agency performance can gain knowledge about the results of services, and this information undoubtedly increases community members' influence on policies and programs.

BUILDING INCREASED SUPPORT

Evaluation can also enhance an agency's position by providing the means for demonstrating—even publicizing—an agency's effectiveness. One of the reasons that program evaluation is such an emotionally charged subject is that staff may realistically fear that evaluation results may show that a program has no effects or negative effects, an issue that is addressed later in this chapter. This is a legitimate concern, but a responsible agency administrator will welcome evaluation results that could help improve programs, as well as positive results that could showcase the accomplishments of programs.

Evaluation provides information that helps the agency gain political support and community involvement. Evaluative data and analyses can enhance the agency's well-being if they are disseminated to potential supporters and funding sources as well as to agency staff.

ACQUIRING KNOWLEDGE REGARDING SERVICE METHODS

Much of what is termed "program evaluation" has historically consisted of routine monitoring of agency activities. This approach is still common, but fortunately increasing attention is being paid to the assessment of program outcomes. Additionally, program evaluation methods can be used to develop knowledge about the relationships between interventions and desired outcomes. New knowledge regarding program effectiveness has historically been associated with experimental research—typically randomized control trials, which will be briefly mentioned later—testing the efficacy (done in a controlled setting such as a lab) and then effectiveness (done in a program setting).

Controlled experiments help determine whether clearly defined program technologies can lead to measurable client changes. Although such research-oriented studies rarely take place in small agencies with limited resources, they do play a major part in establishing the effectiveness of innovative approaches. Program designers need to be able to make judgments concerning the effects of specific services. Knowledge concerning such cause-and-effect relationships can be gained through reviewing research completed in other settings, carrying out ongoing internal evaluations, and utilizing the services of researchers to implement special studies of program innovations.

More feasible than controlled experiments, given limited resources for large-scale experimental designs, are recent developments in evidence-based practice and best practices benchmarking. Evidence-based practice and best practices benchmarking were discussed in Chapter 3 as important aspects of program design. They are mentioned here to emphasize the importance of explicit documentation of program operations to enable organizational learning and knowledge development.

PRODUCERS AND CONSUMERS OF EVALUATIONS

An elegantly designed evaluative research study is of little use if the people who have a stake in an agency's efforts do not recognize it as important. Evaluation efforts involve a number of groups, referred to here as stakeholders, including not only professional evaluators but also funding sources, administrators and policy makers, service providers, clients or consumers, and community members. These groups serve as both producers and consumers of evaluations, and they can have tremendous influence on the process if they see themselves as owning it. Patton's (2008) utilization-focused evaluation principles and methods have been shown to be very useful in designing and implementing evaluations so that the findings are actually used.

Historically, the various actors in the evaluation process—professional evaluators, funding sources, policy makers, administrators, and service providers—had separate roles and did not often collaborate, or even communicate, with each other. These role distinctions are blurring, however, as practitioners realize they need knowledge about their programs to make improvements and as policy makers and others realize that the complexity of the evaluation process requires broad-based involvement of all key stakeholders. Two evaluation approaches to be discussed later have addressed this issue: empowerment evaluation and participatory evaluation.

PROFESSIONAL EVALUATORS

A sizable proportion of the evaluation that takes place in human service organizations is performed by professional evaluators, researchers who use their skills either within the evaluation and research departments of large agencies or as external consultants offering specialized assistance. Whether evaluators are employed by the organization or contracted as consultants, they are expected to bring objectivity to the evaluation process. Their presence brings to the evaluation task a degree of rigor and technical excellence that could not be achieved by less research-oriented human service providers.

At the same time, evaluators need to fully engage in dialogue with the client agency and any other stakeholders to ensure that their approach is appropriate for the particular setting. At its worst, an evaluation can focus on the wrong variables, use inappropriate methods or measures, draw incorrect conclusions, or simply be irrelevant to ongoing agency work. Evaluators may produce reports that, although accurate, are too esoteric to be readily understood or used by the people who decide among programs or allocate resources. Evaluators who are overly detached from agency decision making often fail to affect services.

Another negative aspect of the use of external consultants as evaluators is agency workers' tendency to place evaluative responsibility totally in the consultants' hands. Evaluation can work effectively only if attention is paid to ongoing collaboration with and involvement of agency staff. If no one but the expert evaluator takes responsibility for assessment of progress toward goals, workers will see evaluation as unfamiliar, threatening, and potentially unpleasant.

Effective evaluators use their technical expertise not to impose evaluation on unwilling audiences but to work closely with others in developing feasible designs. Thomas (2010) suggests that the best approach is collaboration between outside evaluators and agency staff. The agency and the evaluator should have a clear agreement regarding the goals and methods of the evaluation and the specific roles to be played by the consultants and staff. If consultants work with internal evaluation committees, they can help administrators, service providers, and consumers clarify their goals, expectations, and questions so that the evaluation will meet identified needs. The external evaluator's objectivity and internal agency workers' active involvement bring the best of both worlds to the evaluation process.

FUNDING SOURCES

Funding sources, particularly organizations providing grants or contracts to human service agencies, can have a positive effect on evaluation. Human service agencies are often required to evaluate projects as part of their accountability to funding sources. Grant applications are expected to include discussions of evaluation designs, and these sections are carefully scrutinized before funding decisions are made.

Funding sources could have even more positive effects if attention were focused more on evaluation content rather than simply on form. Funders should not expect that the dollar amount spent on evaluation consultants necessarily coincides with the quality of the research, nor should they accept simple process monitoring as sufficient. Rather, funding sources should press for more effective evaluation of program effectiveness, for both direct consumers and communities.

POLICY MAKERS AND ADMINISTRATORS

Policy makers and administrators are among the primary users of evaluation because they make decisions concerning the fates of human service programs. Decision makers need evaluation data to inform them of alternatives, just as evaluators need decision makers to make their work meaningful.

Agency managers, as well as board members, can make evaluation work more effectively for them if they try to identify the real information needs of their agencies. Evaluations do not have to be fishing expeditions. They can be clear-cut attempts to answer the real questions decision makers pose. If administrators and objective evaluators work together to formulate research questions, the resulting answers can prove both readable and helpful.

HUMAN SERVICE PROVIDERS

A football coach in the 1960s (probably Darrell Royal of the University of Texas) said that his teams rarely passed the ball because "when you pass, three things can happen, and two of them are bad." In a similar way, there can be three outcomes of an evaluation, and two of them would be seen by staff as "bad": the evaluation could show that the program made no difference, made things worse for clients, or made desired improvements for clients. It is understandable that staff may feel threatened at the prospect of an evaluation. This is even more likely because providers of services have often been left out of the evaluation process. Involving staff and other stakeholders in the design and implementation of the evaluation can mitigate such concerns and will probably also result in a better evaluation process through the use of the program knowledge of these stakeholders.

Staff members may also feel victimized by evaluation. They are typically asked to keep accurate records and fill out numerous forms, but they are not involved in deciding what kinds of data are really needed. They are asked to cooperate with consultants making one-time visits to their agencies, but they are not told exactly what these consultants are evaluating. They are asked to make sudden, special efforts to pull together information for evaluators to use, but they are not encouraged to assess their progress toward goal attainment on a regular basis. Many human service workers feel that evaluation is a negative aspect of agency operations, serving only to point out shortcomings in their work, and they tend to provide information in such a way that their own programs are protected.

Human service providers could play a much more active and useful role in evaluation if they were involved in the design and implementation of the evaluation, using consultants primarily as technical assistants. Service providers are familiar with changing consumer needs, the relative effectiveness of varying approaches, and the agency itself. Through their involvement with an evaluation committee, they can ensure that the real goals of their programs, the objectives being evaluated, and the work actually being done are all properly addressed. As agencies move increasingly toward becoming learning organizations, as discussed in Chapter 9, staff are more likely to appreciate the value of evaluation in improving their operations and showing the outside work the value of their programs.

CONSUMERS AND COMMUNITY MEMBERS

Consumers and other community members need to be involved in planning and evaluating, from initial goal setting through developing evaluation designs and assessments of program effectiveness. Consumers are in a good position to be aware of the strengths and weaknesses of service delivery systems and the degree to which observed community needs are being met. Current principles of empowerment of staff, clients, and community members in the human services (Hardina et al., 2006) support involvement of these stakeholders in the process.

Regardless of the form their participation takes, citizens have a major role to play in deciding how, why, and for whom human services should be provided. Human service agencies are accountable to the communities they serve. Agency managers have a responsibility to ensure that their programs work to accomplish goals that both staff and consumers understand and value.

THE SCOPE OF HUMAN SERVICE EVALUATION

Human service evaluation can take many forms. The approach used in any one setting is likely to be a function of several variables, including (a) the resources and expertise available for use in evaluations, (b) the purposes for which evaluation results will be used, and (c) the orientations and philosophies guiding agency decision makers. Program evaluations may be categorized in two ways. An evaluation may be categorized based on its purpose: a *summative* evaluation looks at a program's accomplishments or results, typically at or near program completion; a *formative* evaluation occurs during program operation and is intended to provide feedback and information that staff can use immediately to make program changes and improvements. Evaluations may also be categorized as *process evaluations* or *outcome evaluations*. Using the systems approach to program design from Chapter 3, process evaluations focus on activities or outputs: the types and numbers of services that are provided. Outcome evaluations look at intermediate or final outcomes: how client conditions, skills, or knowledge have changed as a result of the program.

Human service programs vary tremendously in their approaches to evaluation, running the gamut from simple program monitoring to controlled experiments studying client outcomes. Regardless of their use of resources, depth, or concern for objectivity, however, evaluation efforts need to be reasonably comprehensive if they are to serve any of their stated purposes. Evaluation should provide, at a minimum, basic information concerning program processes and outcomes. Multiple data collection methods and measures (discussed later) will be needed on nearly any substantive evaluation.

TYPES OF EVALUATIONS

Essentially, program evaluation has four basic objectives:

1. To provide information about the achievement of the program goals and objectives (outcome evaluation)
2. To provide descriptive information about the type and quantity of program activities or inputs (process evaluation)
3. To provide information that will be useful in improving a program while it is in operation (a formative evaluation)
4. To provide information about program outcomes relative to program costs (cost effectiveness), costs per output (unit costs, or efficiency), or financial benefits (cost benefit)

We will first review these four types of evaluation and will then address evaluation methods, followed by a discussion of a process for conducting an evaluation.

OUTCOME EVALUATION

Both outcome and process evaluations depend on clearly specified objectives. In outcome evaluation, the objectives are stated in terms of expected results, whereas in process evaluations they are stated in terms of services delivered and program implementation activities. Grinnell, Unrau, and Gabor (2008) assert that "the essence of an outcome evaluation is captured by the familiar phrase 'begin with the end in mind'" (p. 431). This brings to mind discussions in Chapter 3 about the importance of having clearly defined outcome objectives when a program is designed.

Traditionally, funders focused more on learning about what types and amounts of services a program provided and the characteristics of clients served. Recently, however, funders and other stakeholders have become more interested in actual impacts on clients and communities. Outcome evaluations have therefore become increasingly popular in recent years.

According to Patton (2008, p. 243), six elements are needed to focus an evaluation on client outcomes:

- A specific participant or client target group
- The desired outcome(s) for that target group
- One or more indicators for each desired outcome
- Details of data collection
- How results will be used
- Performance targets

There are three general types of outcomes: individual, or client-focused, outcomes; program and system-level outcomes; and broader family or community outcomes (W. K. Kellogg Foundation, 2004). Individual client outcomes are the most common focus of a program and its evaluation. An individual client outcome such as having a former foster youth obtain independent living and a job adequate for self-support could also be part of a program with a system outcome of improving the quality of life for former foster youth. More broadly, family outcomes might include increased parent-child-school interactions or keeping children safe from abuse. A community outcome might be increased civic engagement in a low-income community.

Ultimately, then, at the program level the basic question underlying outcome evaluation must be, "To what degree have clients or the community changed as a result of the program's interventions?"

Client change can be evaluated in terms of level of functioning before and after receipt of services. Whether services are designed to affect clients' adjustment, skills, knowledge, or behaviors, some type of assessment tool must be used to determine whether change in the desired direction has taken place. Outcome evaluation requires the routine use of measures such as gauges of behavior change and standardized or specially designed instruments. If a program has been well designed (Chapter 3) and has a complete information system (Chapter 9), it will address all of the elements listed except a plan for use of results. This final point will be covered later, when a program evaluation process is presented.

PROCESS EVALUATION

Process evaluations can assess the extent to which a program is implemented as designed and provide a means for determining whether members of target populations were reached in the numbers projected and whether specified services were provided in the amounts required at the quality level expected. As in the case of an outcome evaluation, the program's logic model and objectives provide a valuable foundation for the process evaluation.

A specific type of process evaluation is a *formative evaluation*. As noted, formative evaluations occur during program implementation, whereas summative evaluations are done at the end of a program or a program cycle. A formative evaluation is intended to "adjust and enhance interventions ... [and] serve more to guide and direct programs—particularly new programs" (Royse, Thyer, & Padgett, 2010, p. 112).

Using qualitative methods such as interviews, a formative evaluation can also assess how the program implementation process is proceeding, suggesting possible changes in implementation. This type of process evaluation provides funders, the agency board, and any other stakeholders information on how the program is doing with reference to previously identified objectives and standards and also helps agency administrators make adjustments in either the means or the targets of service delivery. Feedback mechanisms must be built into the service delivery system to keep managers informed regarding whether the program is on course, both fiscally and quantitatively.

Process evaluations are usually ongoing; that is, they require the continual retrieval of program data. A process that funding organizations use to receive regular reports on program implementation is known as monitoring. Program monitoring, according to Rossi et al. (2004), is:

> the systematic documentation of aspects of program performance that are indicative of whether the program is functioning as intended or according to some appropriate standard. Monitoring generally involves program performance in the domain of program process, program outcomes, or both. (p. 64)

Program goals and objectives are used as the standards against which the evaluation is conducted. If, for example, Meals on Wheels states in its annual plan of operations that it will deliver 1 meal daily to each of 100 clients per program year, or an annual total of 36,500 meals, then it would be expected that approximately 3,042 meals will be provided per month. A process evaluation would entail the assessment of monthly efforts to provide the prorated number of meals, including whether they were provided to eligible clients (for example, the target population). This type of evaluation would also examine how the agency's human resources were used to provide the services.

A monitoring process typically includes a representative of the funding organization who is assigned to track implementation of the funded program as well as involvement from designated program staff, usually the program manager and a fiscal officer.

A final type of process evaluation is known as *quality assurance* (Royse et al., 2010, pp. 132–134). This answers the question "Are minimum and accepted standards of care being routinely and systematically provided to patients and clients?" (Patton, 2008, p. 304). This technique is most commonly associated with the assessment of medical or clinical records and other aspects of the operation of a program or facility that needs or desires accreditation. Governmental organizations such as Medicare and accrediting organizations such as the Joint Commission on Accreditation of Healthcare Organizations and the Council on Accreditation of Family and Children Services issue standards.

EFFICIENCY AND EFFECTIVENESS

The data gathered through outcome and process evaluations are sometimes used to measure efficiency and effectiveness. *Efficiency* is a measure of costs per output, often framed as *unit cost*. For example, a program that can deliver more hot meals to home-bound seniors for the same cost is seen as more efficient than a program with higher costs for providing the same number of meals. Effectiveness, on the other hand, measures cost per outcome, often described as cost effectiveness. Here, the measure is the cost per successful service outcome, such as gaining employment for an at-risk teenager. A program that arranges jobs of a defined quality for a certain number of youth for a certain cost per job is more cost effective than a similar program that gets jobs for fewer youth at the same cost or has higher costs to acquire jobs for the same number of youth.

The simplest efficiency evaluation involves the determination of unit cost. This figure is obtained by dividing the number of service outputs into the amount of dollars allocated (input) for that service. For example, an agency receiving $150,000 per project period to provide counseling services to 150 delinquent children per year could project a unit cost of $1,000 if the unit of service were defined as each unduplicated client (child) served. Of itself, the cost per unit of $1,000 is meaningless without accompanying process and outcome evaluations and without a comparison to at least one other, similar program whose services have also undergone process, outcome, and efficiency program evaluations. In this example, if the outcome is preventing recidivism for at least one year after the completion of the program, the cost of the program can be divided by the number of successful outcomes to determine cost effectiveness on that measure. This becomes more complicated if a program has more than one service and more than one outcome. Ideally, a program will have one overriding outcome and only one major service component, making this analysis manageable.

Royse et al. (2010, pp. 258–260) have listed the steps of a cost-effectiveness study. The first three steps should already have been done as part of good program design and implementation. Defining the program model and outcome indicators is the first step. The second step involves developing hypotheses or study questions. For example, a simple question would be, What were the program costs compared to the program results? The third step is computing costs, mostly accomplished through the development of the program budget. This step can be complicated if one program has multiple groups of clients and service packages, but eventually it should be possible to allocate all program costs (staff salaries and benefits, facilities, other nonpersonnel costs) so that they may be related to program outcomes. The fourth step, collecting outcome data, should already be occurring through the program's information system. Step five involves computing program outcomes, which would generally be the number of clients for whom there were successful outcomes (for example, no recidivism or rehospitalization, acquisition of self-sustaining employment or independent living status). Next, computing the cost-effectiveness ratio is done by dividing program cost by the number of successful outcomes. The final step, conducting a sensitivity analysis, involves looking at the assumptions about the relationships among program interventions, costs, and effects. For example, if some clients do not attend all assigned sessions, outcomes would not be expected to be as favorable as for clients who attend all sessions.

Less common and beyond the scope of the discussion here is *cost-benefit* analysis (Levin, 2005; Royse et al., 2010, pp. 262–265). This goes beyond cost effectiveness by attributing a financial value to the outcome, thus seen as a benefit to society.

A final aspect of effectiveness takes a much broader perspective. Although it is beyond the scope of this book, which focuses on programs, it should be noted that many human service programs are funded and implemented to have a broader effect on social conditions such as ending chronic homelessness or improving community well-being. National evaluations in areas such as welfare reform to increase self-sufficiency of poor families sometimes focus on this level. Such evaluations look at outcomes such as rates of homelessness, but another way to examine results at this level is to assess *adequacy* of services. For example, if a metropolitan area has 1,000 foster youth who emancipate each year by turning 18 and there are only programs to fund services for 250 youth, this becomes a social policy issue in terms of the adequacy of support to fully address an identified problem.

EVALUABILITY ASSESSMENT

Before reviewing the actual design and implementation of an evaluation, *evaluability assessment* will be presented here as a unique type of evaluation.

If a program has been thoroughly and thoughtfully designed and implemented, including the use of evidence-based practices, logic models, well-written goals and objectives, and a complete management information system, a program evaluation can be relatively easy. Although the human services field has made tremendous progress in recent decades regarding the design and implementation of programs, there are still many cases in which a program that has been in operation for some time is not configured in a way that makes evaluation easy. For this reason, a preliminary step in the program evaluation process may be to do an evaluability assessment: "a systematic process for describing the structure of a program and for analyzing the plausibility and feasibility of achieving objectives; their suitability for in-depth evaluation; and their acceptance to program managers, policy-makers, and program operators" (Smith, 2005, p. 136).

When evaluability assessment emerged in the 1970s, the purpose was "to assess the extent to which measurable objectives exist, whether these objectives are shared by key stakeholders, whether there is a reasonable program structure and sufficient resources to obtain the objectives, and whether program managers will use findings from evaluations of the program" (Trevisan, 2007, p. 290). Trevisan found common recommendations that pointed to weaknesses in program design and implementation in his review of the literature on evaluability assessment. These recommendations included "revised goals and objectives, the development of a mission statement, alteration of program components, and increased stakeholder understanding and awareness of the program" (2007, p. 295).

According to Chambers, Wedel, and Rodwell (1992), an evaluability assessment should begin by assessing the purpose and rationale of the evaluation. All key stakeholders (for example, agency staff, funders, representatives of policy makers, and community representatives) need to agree regarding expectations, questions, and goals for the evaluation. This typically happens through interviews by the evaluator with the stakeholders. Furthermore, the program should be assessed to see if it has a clear logic model, well-written goals and objectives, and data that can show the extent to which the program was implemented as designed. These elements can be assessed by reviewing documents such as relevant proposals or contracts and agency plans and information systems, and by meeting with stakeholders. If misunderstandings, disagreements, or a lack of clarity arises, these need to be addressed before the evaluation proceeds.

After staff members review the evaluability assessment findings, the model may be amended to ensure that it reflects the reality of program operations. It is also possible that, if discrepancies in program implementation are discovered, staff may change actual program processes to better reflect the model as designed. If a program has been well designed using a valid theoretical model, is appropriately staffed, and has a complete information system, it is likely to be evaluable without further modification. If not, appropriate program and information systems modifications can be made. At the conclusion of a thoughtful evaluability assessment, there should be a well-conceptualized and well-operationalized program that will be relatively easy to evaluate, in terms of both its processes and its outcomes.

ALTERNATIVE WAYS TO FOCUS EVALUATIONS

Before leaving this discussion of evaluation types, we should note some important concerns regarding an overemphasis on evaluability and goals in traditional terms. According to Schorr (1997), some funders may consider programs as evaluable only if they are

> standardized and uniform, ... sufficiently circumscribed that their activities can be studied and their effects discerned in isolation from other attempts to intervene and from changes in community circumstances, ... [and] sufficiently susceptible to outside direction so that a central authority is able to design and prescribe how participants are recruited and selected. (pp. 142–143)

Patton (2008, p. 273) frames this issue in terms of "problems with goal-based evaluation." These concerns can be mitigated by augmenting traditional evaluation methods with qualitative models such as case studies and methods including interviewing of clients or other key informants, participant observation, and analysis of documents that are more attentive to program complexities and unique characteristics.

Patton (2008, pp. 304–305) offers an extensive menu based on "focus or type" of evaluation that lists the types just discussed and several newer approaches. Two of these will be mentioned here as ways of implementing traditional methods that are augmented by newer ideas about the philosophy of an evaluation. These are necessarily brief summaries; and managers wanting to consider using these approaches should seek more detailed information on them.

PARTICIPATORY EVALUATION

Participatory evaluation "is generally used to describe situations where stakeholders are involved in evaluation decision making as well as share joint responsibility for the evaluation report with an external evaluator" (Turnbull, 1999, p. 131). A variation of this approach is *practical participatory evaluation* (Smits & Champagne, 2008).

Patton (2008, p. 175) has summarized principles of participatory evaluation:

- The evaluation process involves participants learning evaluation logic and skills ...
- Participants in the process *own* the evaluation. They make the major focus and design decisions.... Participation is real, not token.
- Participants focus the evaluation on processes and outcomes they consider important and to which they are committed.
- Participants work together as a group, and the evaluation facilitator supports group cohesion and collective inquiry.
- All aspects of the evaluation, including the data, are understandable and meaningful to participants....
- Internal, self-accountability is highly valued....
- The evaluator is a facilitator, collaborator, and learning resource; participants are decision makers and evaluators.
- Status differences between the evaluation facilitator and participants are minimized.

As this list suggests, participatory evaluations can only be viable in a receptive context, including evaluators being committed to a participatory process (Whitmore, 1998).

EMPOWERMENT EVALUATION

Empowerment evaluation (Fetterman & Wandersman, 2005; Fetterman, 2002) includes ten principles: improvement, community ownership, inclusion, democratic participation, social justice, community knowledge, evidence-based strategies, capacity building, organizational learning, and accountability. According to Patton (2008), "empowerment evaluation is most appropriate where the goals of the program include helping participants become more self-sufficient and personally effective" (p. 179).

EVALUATION DESIGN AND IMPLEMENTATION

Now that purposes and types of evaluations have been reviewed, we will present a process that can be used to design and implement the evaluation. This will be presented in linear steps, but the process is in fact more fluid: the sequence of activities may vary, activities will happen simultaneously, and steps may be repeated based on emerging developments. Ideally, much of this would be done at the program design stage, anticipating evaluation needs that will emerge later.

EVALUATION TEAM FORMATION

An evaluation depends on the active involvement, or at least support, of all workers in the program. Staff should not think of evaluation as a separate function that is performed by experts and unrelated to the work of the agency's programs. For a full, formal evaluation of a program, an evaluation team to design and oversee the process will help ensure that all in the program are aware of the evaluation and are committed to its successful implementation. Agency managers who are in charge of the evaluation should identify stakeholders inside and outside the agency who will bring relevant knowledge, expertise, and support to the process. Representatives from service delivery staff, supervisors, and administrative staff will ensure that internal program concerns are addressed. It may also be useful to invite outside stakeholders such as clients, community members, and, if appropriate, representatives of the funding agency for the program. If there will be outside evaluators designated by agency administration or the funding source of the program, they should be actively involved in working with the team.

Roles should be determined for each member to address tasks such as identifying data sources, gathering data, compiling and analyzing data, report preparation, and coordination functions such as scheduling meetings and managing the timeline for the evaluation. If a professional evaluator has not been hired, staff members may consider whether or not they will need outside expertise such as a professional evaluation consultant or qualified faculty member from a local university. Dowell, Haley, and Doino-Ingersoll (2006) have developed criteria for assessing evaluation consultants. In a large-scale evaluation, the formation of a community advisory board to review the process and provide input may be useful.

This would also be a good time to consider the use of participatory processes such as participatory or empowerment evaluation.

Staff should assess the resource needs for the evaluation, including staff time and any extra funds, such as for an evaluation consultant or purchase of measurement instruments, and ensure that these resources are made available.

ASSESS READINESS

There are two key aspects to being ready for an evaluation. Readiness in terms of program operations means having a clear logic model and goals and objectives, and an information system that gathers data to track implementation. The evaluability assessment discussed earlier is a way to see if the program is easily evaluable. If this assessment shows limitations, it will be necessary to go through the program design, budgeting, and information systems processes to create conditions for a good evaluation.

The second aspect of readiness involves staff. As noted earlier, staff, especially service delivery staff, may be wary of an evaluation, especially if it is coming from an outside source such as a funding organization. Managers have an essential role in creating an organizational culture that is supportive of organizational learning (discussed in Chapter 11) and enables staff to feel comfortable about proceeding with an evaluation. Managers may need to spend extra time here meeting with staff to discuss the purpose of the evaluation, how it will be conducted, and how the results will be used. Including broad representation of staff on an evaluation team can be a great help in addressing staff concerns.

DETERMINE EVALUATION QUESTIONS AND THE FOCUS OF THE EVALUATION

At this stage, certain things should be presented for discussion and finalization: objectives of the evaluation; any expectations from stakeholders, for example, including requirements if a funding organization; and study hypotheses. It will also be important to clarify how the findings of the study will be used.

IDENTIFY ANY ADDITIONAL DATA NEEDED

As noted earlier, if a program has been well designed and well implemented, all or nearly all the data needed for the evaluation may already exist in the agency's information system. Data not yet in the system may include follow-up data or feedback from clients or other stakeholders. If an evaluation was planned for when the program was designed, any pretest data will have been anticipated. For example, standardized instruments may be used at intake, with a posttest done at program completion to assess changes in variables under consideration such as depression or other psychological or behavioral characteristics.

Sources of data should be considered here as well. The information system, ideally including data entered into computerized software that can compile individual client data into reports, and client case records will be key sources.

DETERMINE THE EVALUATION DESIGN AND METHODS

Several decisions to be made here go back to the earlier discussion of evaluation types. In most cases, both process and outcome methods would be used, with the process component focusing on the nature of program implementation and services delivered, and the outcome focus assessing impacts. Depending on the evaluation purposes and questions, monitoring or quality assurance techniques would be appropriate. Formative and summative options could be considered. Often a formative evaluation takes place during the project and the summative evaluation occurs at the end. If there are evaluation questions repeated to cost effectiveness, efficiency, or cost benefit, these methods would be needed.

In terms of actual data collection methods, distinctions are made between *quantitative methods* and *qualitative methods*. Recently, a combination of both known as *mixed methods* has become very common. Historically, quantitative methods have been seen, at least by many researchers, as "better" than qualitative methods. Patton describes this as the "paradigm war" between "quants" and "quals" (2008, p. 420). In recent years, there is growing agreement that it is not a matter of quantitative versus qualitative but rather a matter of choosing the best method or combination of methods to answer the evaluation questions. For many, including those using evidence-based practice, the "gold standard" in quantitative evaluation has been the randomized control trial, ideally replicated in different populations. Such designs are not common in regular agency operations for reasons including cost (e.g., for follow-up contacts) and ethical issues such as concerns about denying treatment to some subjects.

QUANTITATIVE METHODS Quantitative methods may be further categorized into *experimental, quasi-experimental,* or *preexperimental* designs. Because these are covered in detail in statistics courses, only brief mention of them will be made here.

Preexperimental designs are becoming more frequently used in human service agencies. These include the one-group posttest-only design, the posttest-only design with nonequivalent groups, and the one-group pretest-posttest design. Preexperimental designs cannot be considered rigorous by scientific standards but can effectively answer simple questions such as to what degree the status of clients has changed upon program completion. According to Royse et al. (2010), preexperimental designs "are well suited and very satisfactory to many agencies with few resources that need to demonstrate some type of an effectiveness evaluation annually or biannually to funders such as the local United Way" (pp. 212–213).

Studies that attempt to control as carefully as possible for a number of variables but that do not meet the stringent definition of experimental design are termed quasi-experimental. A common design involves the use of a nonequivalent control group, which does not require random sampling. These designs are sometimes possible in human service programs.

Experimental designs, with randomized control groups, are less common in human service programs. True experimental designs require random selection of experimental and control groups, carefully controlled interventions, and scrupulously examined outcome measures.

QUALITATIVE METHODS   Common qualitative methods include observation by evaluators, document review, interviews, and focus groups. Intensive interviews can also point the way toward instances in which services are not delivered in standard ways by different individuals within programs. These methods require thoughtfulness and precision in selecting data sources, sampling, and doing content analysis (Kapp & Anderson, 2010).

Data evaluators gather through direct observation are useful in terms of objectivity because evaluators are freed from the concern that information might be colored by the subjectivity of service providers or consumers. There is the danger, however, that observation might in itself bring about changes in the activities being carried out. Direct observation can prove useful if systematic methods are used, but it is more helpful in some situations than in others. For instance, unobtrusive observation can be more appropriate in the context of a public educational program than in the case of a private counseling session. An alternative to direct observation can be the use of audio or video recordings of selected service delivery episodes, with proper confidentiality clearances.

SINGLE-SYSTEM DESIGNS   An evaluation method that has become increasingly common in the human services in recent years is the single-system research design. Although these can be used for needs assessments, formative evaluations, quality assurance studies, and summative program evaluations (Royse et al., 2010), they are probably most commonly used in clinical practice. The key requirements of a single-system research design are reliable and valid measures of the identified problem or outcome and the repeated use of this measure over time.

Use of service records can be helpful for analyzing the nature of the consumer population as well as for examining the number and nature of service delivery units. Such records as monthly activity reports can provide program statistics concerning number of individuals served, types of services provided, or other aspects of program processes. Client data forms can also be used to determine the degree to which service consumers are members of the population originally targeted for services.

Accurate information concerning service delivery can also be obtained through contacts with service consumers. Sometimes samples of entire communities can be surveyed to determine whether information concerning the program is being disseminated adequately and to the targeted consumer group.

MEASURES OF CLIENT PERCEPTIONS   Most agencies also use measures of client satisfaction, asking consumers to evaluate the services they have received. Such techniques can be useful only if they are obtained on a regular basis from people who have dropped out of treatment programs as well as people who have completed them. Consumers may be asked to rate their overall satisfaction with services or to respond separately to individual aspects of program delivery. Normally, such measures are based on questionnaires using four- or five-point rating scales. Grinnell, Unrau, and Gabor (2008) note an increasing use of client satisfaction surveys in program evaluation.

Royse et al. (2010) offer the following suggestions regarding the use of client satisfaction surveys:

1. Use a scale that has good reliability and that has been used successfully in other studies....
2. Use the same instrument on repeated occasions, and develop a local baseline of data so that departures from the norm can be observed....
3. Employ at least one and possibly two open-ended questions so that the consumers of your services can alert you to any problems that you did not suspect and could not anticipate....
4. Use a "ballot box" approach where one week is set aside when every client entering the agency is given a brief questionnaire while waiting for his or her appointment....
5. Do not focus only on solving the problems of the dissatisfied consumers, assuming that you will be able to convert them into satisfied consumers....
6. If you conduct a mailed survey, do what you can to get a response rate over 50 percent....
7. Target specific dimensions [e.g., availability of services, competence of staff]....
8. Keep your expectations realistic.... Favorable data do not mean that your program is achieving the results it was planned to produce....
9. Look for behavioral indicators (i.e., attendance) to supplement the client satisfaction data (pp. 184–190).

Interviews with or questionnaires distributed to clients can help determine consumers' perceptions of services, especially if they differ from providers' notions of the same activities. Information about consumer satisfaction with services is normally collected on a routine basis, and these data, too, can prove important for the purposes of comprehensive evaluation.

Gather Data

The gathering of some data will be ongoing through regular data entry in the program's information system. Some data may be gathered only at certain times, such as the administration of pre- and post-surveys, customer satisfaction follow-up evaluations, and interviews and focus groups.

All data available to the evaluation team should be reviewed to verify accuracy. The accuracy of stored information can be ensured if staff members receive training in record-keeping skills and if samples of forms are routinely checked. Existing and specially gathered information can then form the basis for evaluative analysis.

Analyze Data

Data are eventually compiled and presented in report format. Kettner, Moroney, and Martin (2008) note the importance of having a strategy for data analysis. The original evaluation questions can provide guidance regarding how data can be summarized to answer the questions. Output tables can be used to summarize demographic characteristics, units of service, and even program outcomes, typically on a monthly and annual basis. Frequency distributions, cross-tabulations, charts, and graphs can be used to present data in a way that facilitates analysis. Some designs, such as pre-post tests, can use tests of statistical significance to note changes in clients.

OUTCOMES DATA   Analyzing outcomes data may be more complicated than would be apparent at first glance. With good objectives, a good information system, and complete data entry, it will be easy to see how many clients are at certain levels of functioning. However, meaning will need to be attributed to findings. Ideally, data will show where clients were before and after the program in terms of particular variables, such as the extent of change for each individual.

Poertner and Rapp (2007, pp. 253–257) use "movement tables" to show client progress in a vocational training program, for example. Client vocational status can be described (with definitions) as no activity, moderate activity, substantial activity, and competitive activity. A figure can state the number and percentage of clients at the competitive activity level (e.g., in a paid job for at least 30 hours per week), but this number by itself has little meaning. Analysis would be required to determine how this number is different for these clients before the program, and should be considered using evidence-based standards in that field. A success rate of 30 percent for clients with severe disabilities may be considered excellent, and a success rate of 80 percent of fully functioning clients may not be seen as worth the cost of the program, especially if 70 percent of them were at that level before the program. These criteria and standards should be defined and agreed to at the program design stage through dialogue including agency service delivery staff and managers and representatives from the program's funding source.

Cost effectiveness can add further substance to an outcome measure. If funders know that clients to be served have notable challenges (e.g., teens from dysfunctional families in poor communities with low education performance and high crime), it would be recognized that cost effectiveness will be high. It may cost up to $5,000 (again, evidence-based standards can guide this) to provide a youth with enough of the proper services for her or him to be job-ready. If this keeps a youth out of the criminal justice system, costs avoided would be much higher than the cost of the program. This point can be vividly made when comparing cost effectiveness with efficiency, or unit cost. A program may be very efficient with a low unit cost, but if clients served do not have a successful outcome, cost effectiveness would be much higher.

Whereas cost efficiency (e.g., unit cost) looks only at costs for providing particular services, cost effectiveness can show the impact that a program has on clients. This can aid decision making regarding whether the level of effort, or cost, of a program was appropriate given the results that were attained.

Efficiency evaluation does not always point toward possible cost cutting; it involves recognizing that alternate methods might differ in the amount of resources used to arrive at the same end. Because the focus of direct service workers is usually on the services delivered with little attention to cost, and while at the same time funders are holding agencies to higher standards for prudent use of resources, a manager may need to use positive and proactive leadership to create a culture in which issues of cost effectiveness and efficiency receive sufficient attention.

Efficiency is typically measured in terms of unit cost and answers questions regarding the amount of resources that are used to serve a client or provide a package of services.

OUTPUT DATA   The process evaluation can use a variety of data sources and analytical strategies. Its basic purpose is to determine what services were delivered, to whom, and whether they were performed in accordance with the schedule set as part of the planning process.

Regarding service utilization, data from the information system are used to answer questions such as these:

- How many persons are receiving services?
- Are those receiving services the intended targets?
- Are they receiving the proper amount, type, and quality of services? (Rossi et al., 2004, p. 171)

The result of this analysis should be a descriptive report that allows the reader to form an accurate picture of the agency and its activities as well as of community members and their use of services.

Quality assurance, as noted earlier in the section on evaluation types, assesses organizational processes and systems, which can be a useful component of a more comprehensive evaluation. It is important to note that this method typically looks at process, not outcomes. Quality assurance can not only demonstrate that accreditation standards have been met but also be used to identify problems in organizational processes that should be remedied. Chapter 11 will show how such organizational problems can be addressed.

A process analysis using a flowchart is another useful technique to assess how the program is operating. A flowchart such as the one suggested in the previous chapter, where it was used to design the information system, is constructed to outline all the steps of the service delivery process. Staff and the evaluator then assess the extent to which the intended process is being followed, also noting unnecessary steps that are discovered and other possible improvements.

COMPILE FINDINGS AND PREPARE REPORT

All necessary data will now need to be compiled and put into a report. During the evaluation planning process, decisions should have been made regarding the data and presentation formats, the components of the report, and responsibilities for writing and reviewing the report. The interests and questions from all key stakeholders should be considered and built into the report format.

UTILIZATION OF FINDINGS

In spite of possible staff fears regarding evaluations discussed above, managers and staff should be eager to review results and discuss their implications. This can lead to staff making program adjustments and perhaps updating the plans for continuing the evaluation if the program will be continuing. The agency's board, funders, and perhaps community stakeholders will probably also be interested in the findings. Management should be clear with all regarding how comments on the evaluation will be used. Finally, the evaluation team and advisory board, if any, should debrief the process, assessing what went well with the evaluation itself, what was learned, and how evaluations in the agency could be improved in the future.

10.1	DEVELOPING A PROGRAM EVALUATION SYSTEM AT GRANDVIEW COMMUNITY CENTER

When Leona Estrella assumed the role of Executive Director for Grandview Community Center and completed a review of agency documents, she concluded that the agency's information system gathered little data beyond client characteristics and services delivered. The new contract for the Teen Transition and Treatment Program (TTTP) required a program evaluation, and Leona seized this opportunity to not only design an evaluation for the new program but also develop an agency-wide system for ongoing program evaluation. Because the agency had a successful experience with the agency information systems steering committee and IS design teams for each program, she decided to replicate this process for the evaluation. Some of the members of those groups continued with the new evaluation steering committee and design teams to build on their effective working relationships. They arranged to have one client and one community member on each team and on the steering committee.

The evaluation team for the TTTP concluded that the program had a high level of readiness for the evaluation because there was a clear logic model, good objectives, and a good IS to be used for the evaluation. They kept their evaluation questions simple: What are the characteristics of the clients in the program? Was the program implemented as intended? What services, in what amounts, were provided to what clients? Did the program have the desired impact on clients' quality of life in terms of skills development, social competence, and drug use? How satisfied were the clients, and what feedback could they offer to improve the program? They concluded that their IS would give them most of the data they would need. They knew they would have to interview some staff and clients regarding program implementation, and they would have to administer a client satisfaction instrument. They also knew that they would need to do pretests and posttests using several measures in their IS. Therefore, the evaluation would use mixed methods: both quantitative and qualitative. Because of their resource limitations, they could not use a comparison or control group and had to settle instead for a preexperimental design: a one-group pretest-posttest.

Their structure of a steering committee and evaluation teams in each program ensured that the evaluation was participative and would reflect input from a broad range of perspectives. They would compile and summarize demographic data for every client and would prepare summary tables to show how many clients attended the required weekly individual counseling sessions, group therapy sessions, and psycho-educational group therapy sessions, and how many service completions (completing 10 of the 12 session) there were. These data, added to documentation of staff having the required licenses or credentials and interviews with staff, would constitute the process evaluation of program inputs, throughputs, and outputs.

To measure outcomes, they planned to have clients complete the skills competency instrument before their first session and one week after completing the last session.

(continued)

10.1   DEVELOPING A PROGRAM EVALUATION SYSTEM AT GRANDVIEW COMMUNITY CENTER (CONT'D)

Success would be defined as a score of 70 percent or higher. At those same times, the clients would also complete the Child and Adolescent Measurement System, with the expected outcome that 80 percent of clients would increase their quality of life, measured by clients having a quality of life scores at or above the midpoint of the Moderate functioning levels for the 3 components of the instrument. For both of these, they used the pretests so they could assess progress the clients actually made. Finally, they would measure discontinuance of the use of illicit drugs at two points in time: upon completion of the program and 6 months after completion of the program. The standards of success would be 80 percent of the clients being drug free at program completion and 60 percent of the clients being drug free after 6 months. They also planned to have the urine tests administered upon entry to the program as a pretest.

When the program budget was designed, staff created formulas to measure cost effectiveness and unit cost. The evaluation team planned to apply this formula to the actual numbers at completion of the program.

To measure customer satisfaction, they purchased a standardized client satisfaction instrument and planned to have four focus groups with clients within a month of program completion. They would pay a professor and student workers from the local university as consultants for this, so clients would feel comfortable sharing their true feelings with assurances of anonymity.

They decided that their reports would include tables showing all the process and outcomes data, and they would prepare tables with cross-tabulations to show relationships among demographic characteristics, services, outcomes. They would do statistical tests to see if pretest and posttest changes were significant. They hoped that they would use the client satisfaction in all agency programs and gather data regularly so they could identify trends and opportunities for improvement.

They shared the evaluation plan with all staff and with the agency's board of directors and community advisory group, who believed the report would give them the information they needed to answer their evaluation questions.

ISSUES IN HUMAN SERVICE EVALUATION

In response to the call for accountability, managers of human services are becoming more proactive regarding program evaluation (Grinnell, Unrau, & Gabor, 2008). As human service organizations have increased their involvement in program assessment, they have had to confront a number of issues surrounding the evaluation process. These issues have been alluded to in the preceding sections of this chapter but are more directly dealt with here to emphasize their present and future importance for human service managers. As competition for scarce resources increases, so will the challenge to managers to confront these issues.

Primary among these issues is the meaning and definition of organizational performance. Whereas there is general agreement that service effectiveness can be measured by the extent to which program goals are achieved, there is now common agreement among experts in the field that there is no "one best way" to measure organizational performance. While experimental designs may represent the "ideal type" of program evaluation, they may, at the same time, not be reflective of what is practical, affordable, or desirable as a means of demonstrating service effectiveness. Because of logistic, financial, and ethical considerations, some agencies may find themselves having to resort to quasi-experimental or preexperimental methods. Furthermore, other measures beyond goal attainment are seen as in some cases equally relevant (Sowa, Selden, & Sandfort, 2004). What level of credibility of service effectiveness is to be accorded those programs whose measurement criteria fall short of strict scientific research applications? A contingency approach will be needed that reflects perspectives beyond goal attainment, as noted earlier. One way of doing this is to combine both process and outcome evaluation strategies in the evaluation design, including variety of measures of program performance.

A related issue is the use of new technologies, including computer hardware and software (Grinnell, Unrau, & Gabor, 2008). Agencies whose managers proactively research for and acquire appropriate information management software will become much better equipped to conduct comprehensive evaluations.

A third issue has to do with evaluation inclusiveness, or the incorporation of diverse perspectives in the evaluation of service effectiveness. In other words, how inclusive can or should a program evaluation be to reflect all significant and relevant aspects of service effectiveness? In this regard, Murray (2010) encourages staff and evaluators to include all relevant stakeholders throughout the process and to work to create an atmosphere of openness and trust, built over time through ongoing interactions. The use of multiple perspectives and methods, including participative methods such as participatory and empowerment evaluation processes, were discussed earlier as ways of addressing this issue.

Cultural competency is of course a key issue in human service organizations, and this is relevant in evaluation as well. Program evaluation design and the involvement of relevant stakeholders should be adapted to relevant cultural and contextual factors (Patton, 2008, p. 83; Madison, 2007). Kapp and Anderson (2010) suggest that evaluators acquire attributes including awareness and acceptance of the diversity of staff and clients, self-awareness, understanding the dynamics of diversity, knowledge of individual cultures, and the ability to adapt evaluation methods based on diversity considerations.

Evaluations inherently have a political dimension, such as the effect they can have on funding or policy decisions, the impact of ideology, and even the ways in which data are categorized and analyzed (Patton, 2008, pp. 525–531). This may result in a misuse of findings. According to one axiom, "Some people use statistics like a drunk uses a lamppost—for support rather than illumination." Managers and evaluators should take care to ensure that findings are not misused by those wanting to either continue or end a program.

Patton (2008) has suggested transparency, including public access to evaluation findings, to ensure that the findings are credible and understandable. Patton also suggests following the other evaluation process guidelines regarding formation of an evaluation committee discussed above.

There are also ethics considerations in evaluation. Patton (2008) suggests that these "Program Evaluation Standards provide general ethical guidance: Evaluation agreements should be in writing; rights of human subjects should be protected; evaluators should respect human dignity; assessments should be complete and fair; findings should be openly and fully disclosed; conflicts of interest should be dealt with openly and honestly; and solid fiscal procedures should be followed" (p. 545).

Finally, Grinnell, Unrau, and Gabor (2008) see a trend of using program evaluation not only to assess outcomes but also to improve program operations. Feedback from formative evaluations and ongoing monitoring can point the way to program improvements, using organizational change methods discussed in the next chapter.

SUMMARY

Evaluations may have several purposes, from aiding in decision making and improving programs to building support and demonstrating accountability. Evaluations may look at processes, outcomes, or efficiency, with increasing interest in outcome evaluation. Ultimately, the best evaluation uses methods that are appropriate to specific research questions and program conditions. Such an evaluation is likely to address processes and outcomes, quantitative and qualitative aspects, and dynamics of program uniqueness and generalizability. The actual utilization of evaluation findings for program enhancement and the involvement of all significant actors in the evaluation process are other key considerations that human service managers must address in the quest for organizational excellence.

Our discussion of evaluation takes us full circle. In Chapter 2 we discussed the social problems in our environment that human services are intended to address, and then discussed agency planning and program design to respond to these needs. The design of the overall organization, effective human resources and supervision practices, and financial and information systems to monitor progress and accomplishments were presented as important success factors for goal attainment. Finally, evaluation is used to assess the extent of program accomplishments and to identify opportunities for continuing improvement.

COMPETENCY-BUILDING ACTIVITY 10.1 | EVALUATION

Imagine that your hypothetical program is nearing completion of its first year. Who would be interested in knowing what happened with it? What evaluation questions do you think they would have? Using the information system you have developed for your hypothetical program, and referring back to the original goals and objectives for the program, think about how you would evaluate the program to answer the evaluation questions, seeing if it has been implemented as designed, and what its results were. Will you use quantitative or qualitative methods or both? What methods will you use to evaluate each objective? Which will be process measures and which will be outcome measures? How will you show unit cost and cost effectiveness for the program? How would you present your findings in tables, graphs, or other formats? Would this evaluation give you and the funders of the program the information necessary to conclude that the program was a success and should be continued?

CASE ACTIVITY 10.1 | EVALUATING THE CONSULTATION AND EDUCATION DEPARTMENT

At the Greenby Community Mental Health Center, the Consultation and Education Department was about to go under. Although consultation and education are required for all community mental health centers, not all centers have fully staffed and active departments. Instead, they implement consultation and education as a percentage of each professional's work. That was what Henry McDonald, the executive director, was suggesting for Greenby.

"You have to understand my position," he exclaimed to a distraught consultation and education director. "Our funding has been cut back. We're more dependent than ever on fees for service and third-party payments. Consultation and education are luxuries we really can't afford. They don't bring in the funds we need, and we've got to put our resources into programs that carry their weight."

"But you know that C and E programs are a high priority. Every center has to have one to keep up its funding," Andy Cutler replied.

"Andy, let's not play games here. You know we don't have to have a C and E department with a full-time director. We only have to provide the service. The real issue is whether your program stays in operation the way it is now, and I'm saying it can't. Now, stop worrying. Your job isn't in jeopardy. You'll be able to move over to the clinical program."

"Henry, believe it or not, it's not my own job that I'm concerned about. No matter what kind of measurement you use, you have to see that the C and E department does pull its weight. We've developed liaisons with every major employer in the area, we've got preventive programs going in the schools, and our divorce and family workshops are attracting more people every time we put them on. Word is getting around in the community."

"Sure, the workshops attract people. At five dollars a head, why shouldn't they? The program is self-supporting, I'll grant you that, but it's not pulling in enough capital to pull its weight with the center as a whole. There's no way it can."

"But what you're not recognizing, Henry, is that this program is supporting the other programs. You've had an increase in the number of people referring themselves for alcohol and drug abuse programs. I'm telling you that this is because of the preventive programs we've been doing at the factory. You've had an increase in self-referrals for family therapy. I think they're coming from our workshops. The programs we offer help people recognize their problems, and when they recognize them, they start to come in for more help."

"That's very possible, Andy. But I've got a board of directors to deal with, and I don't know whether they're going to buy that line of reasoning. They're not professionals, you know, and they don't necessarily see those relationships that way. What they can see is the difference between what a person pays to participate in a workshop and what the same person would pay for one of the other programs. It's a good thought to say that you're feeding into the other services, but we don't really know that. We don't really know anything about the impact you're having. Give me something I can tell the board. Give me something I can tell the state. Just give me something."

1. What steps might you take if you were Andy Cutler, the consultation and education director?
2. How might a more effective evaluation program have helped the consultation and education program?
3. What methods might prove helpful in demonstrating the effectiveness of Cutler's preventive programs?

REFERENCES

Carman, J., & Fredericks, K., (Eds.). (2008). *Nonprofits and evaluation: New directions for evaluation 119.* San Francisco: Jossey-Bass.

Chambers, D., Wedel, K., & Rodwell, M. (1992). *Evaluating social programs.* Boston: Allyn & Bacon.

Dowell, K., Haley, J., & Doino-Ingersoll, J. (2006). *Evaluating the evaluator: Development, field testing, and implications of a client-based method for assessing* evaluator performance, *Independent consultant evaluation: New directions for evaluation 111* (pp. 95–108). San Francisco: Jossey-Bass.

Fetterman, D. (2002). Empowerment evaluation strikes a responsive chord. In S. Donaldson & M. Scriven (Eds.), *Evaluating social programs and problems: Visions for the new millennium.* Mahwah, NJ: Erlbaum.

Fetterman, D., & Wandersman, A. (Eds.) (2005). *Empowerment evaluation principles in practice.* New York: Guilford Press.

Grinnell, R., Unrau, Y., & Gabor, P. (2008). Program evaluation. In T. Mizrahi & L. Davis, (Eds.), *Encyclopedia of social work*, Vol. 3 (20th ed., pp. 429–434). New York: Oxford University Press.

Hardina, D., Middleton, J., Montana, S., & Simpson, R. (2006). *An empowering approach to managing social service organizations.* New York: Springer Publishing Company.

Kapp, S. & Anderson, G. (2010). *Agency-based program evaluation: Lessons from practice.* Thousand Oaks, CA: Sage.

Kettner, P., Moroney, R., & Martin, L. (2008). *Designing and managing programs* (3rd ed.). Thousand Oaks, CA: Sage.

Levin, H. (2005). Cost-benefit analysis. In S. Mathison (Ed.), *Encyclopedia of evaluation* (pp. 86–90). Thousand Oaks, CA: Sage.

Madison, A. (2007). Cultural issues and issues of significance to underrepresented groups. *New directions for evaluation, 114,* 107–113.

McNamara, C. (N.D.) *Basic guide to program evaluation (including outcomes evaluation), free management library.* Retrieved April 6, 2011, from http://www.managementhelp.org/evaluatn/fnl_eval.htm

Murray, V. (2010). Assessing nonprofit organization effectiveness. In D. Renz (Ed.). *The Jossey-Bass handbook of nonprofit leadership and management* (3rd ed., pp. 431–458). San Francisco: Jossey-Bass.

Office of Planning, Research and Evaluation, Administration for Children and Families. (2010). *The Program Manager's Guide to Evaluation* (2nd ed.). Retrieved April 6, 2011, from http://www.acf.hhs.gov/programs/opre/other_resrch/pm_guide_eval/reports/pmguide/program_managers_guide_to_eval2010.pdf

Patton, M. (2008). *Utilization-focused evaluation* (3rd ed.). Thousand Oaks, CA: Sage.

Poertner, J., & Rapp, C. (2007). *Textbook of social administration: The consumer-centered approach.* New York: The Haworth Press.

Royse, D., Thyer, B., & Padgett, D. (2010). *Program evaluation: An introduction* (10th ed.). Belmont, CA: Thomson/Brooks Cole.

Schorr, L. (1997). *Common purpose.* New York: Anchor Books Doubleday.

Smith, M. (2005). Evaluability assessment. In S. Mathison (Ed.), *Encyclopedia of evaluation* (pp. 136–139). Thousand Oaks, CA: Sage Publications.

Smits, P., & Champagne, F. (2008). An assessment of the theoretical underpinnings of practical participatory evaluation. *American journal of evaluation, 29(4),* 427–442.

Sowa, J., Selden, S., & Sandfort, J. (2004). No longer unmeasurable? A multidimensional integrated model of nonprofit organizational effectiveness. *Nonprofit and Voluntary Sector Quarterly,* 711–728.

Thomas, J. (2010). Outcome assessment and program evaluation. In D. Renz (Ed.), *The Jossey-Bass handbook of nonprofit leadership and management* (3rd ed., pp. 401–430). San Francisco: Jossey-Bass.

Turnbull, B. (1999). The mediating effects of participation efficacy on evaluation use. *Evaluation and Program Planning, 22,* 131–140.

Trevisan, M. (2007). Evaluability assessment from 1986 to 2006. *American journal of evaluation, 28(3),* 290–303.

W. K. Kellogg Foundation. (2004). *W. K. Kellogg Foundation evaluation handbook.* Retrieved April 6, 2011, from http://www.wkkf.org/knowledge-center/resources/2010/W-K-Kellogg-Foundation-Evaluation-Handbook.aspx

Whitmore, E. (Ed.). (1998). *Understanding and practicing participatory evaluation.* San Francisco: Jossey-Bass.

USEFUL WEB RESOURCES

Administration for Children and Families, Department of Health and Human Services, The Program Manager's Guide to Evaluation. http://www.acf.hhs.gov/programs/opre/other_resrch/pm_guide_eval/reports/pmguide/pmguide_toc.html.

American Evaluation Association. http://www.eval.org/.

Free Management Library: Evaluation Activities in Organizations. http://managementhelp.org/evaluatn/evaluatn.htm.

11 CHAPTER | LEADING AND CHANGING HUMAN SERVICE ORGANIZATIONS[1]

CHAPTER OUTLINE

---

[1]Portions of this chapter have been adapted from Packard, 2009.

We have now reviewed all of the core managerial functions, from planning and program and organization design, to human resources management and supervision, to financial management and monitoring and evaluation. Leadership will be presented in this chapter as the force holding these elements together, aligning them, and enabling the organization to function as an integrated system. Because human services must be constantly adapting, we will also look at common methods of organizational change that a manager or other staff member may use to improve organizational operations or responsiveness.

As a human service manager ascends the hierarchy in a human service organization, the expectations for leadership increase. Increased positional power and visibility attract greater attention to and reliance on the manager's leadership style. Although a great deal has been written about leadership, even in the government and not-for-profit sectors (e.g., Collins, 2005; Perry, 2010; Renz, 2010), the coverage here will be necessarily brief.

LEADERSHIP: DEFINITION AND CONTEXT

There are countless definitions of leadership. Northouse (2010) defines leadership as "a process whereby an individual influences a group of individuals to achieve common goals" (p. 3). The term *followers* will be used to describe those whom the leader is attempting to influence. The term *subordinates* is often used in organizational settings, but the term followers suggests that leaders can be in any role or position, and a bureaucratic hierarchy is not necessarily implied. Additionally, the concept of shared leadership contradicts the notion of "solo" or unilateral leadership. According to Gill (2006), shared leadership is characterized by the quality of interactions rather than hierarchical level; team problem solving; "conversation rather than instructions, shared values, and beliefs"; and "honesty and a desire for the common good" (p. 30).

Leadership is a key factor in coordinating and aligning organizational processes. As with any aspect of organizational functioning, it should focus on organizational performance, and most importantly, effectiveness in achieving desired outcomes.

Leadership can contribute to outcomes at different levels (e.g., dyad, group, team, program, agency, community, and society). In an agency setting, outcomes can range from the accomplishment of agency objectives and results of program evaluations to client outcomes. For example, at the individual or team level, outcome variables such as job satisfaction or commitment can be measured; at the organizational level, leadership can affect overall culture or climate.

Another important aspect of the leadership context in the human services is the growing emphasis on evidence-based practice. This plays out in two ways in a discussion of leadership. First, in its traditional usage, evidence-based methods should be used by leaders in the design and implementation of the programs of their agencies, now being called *evidence-based programming* (Briggs & McBeath, 2009). Second, evidence-based practice principles can be used in assessing the theories, models, and practice guidelines for leadership. The newly emerging field of evidence-based management is an example of this application (Pfeffer & Sutton, 2006). When discussing leadership models and principles in the next section, the relevant empirical literature will be cited wherever possible.

LEADERSHIP THEORIES AND MODELS

We will now review key theories and models of leadership. After that discussion, detailed coverage of a key leadership function—organizational change—will be presented. We will begin with the earliest research on leadership in the twentieth century, which focused on *traits*, originally seen as innate characteristics of leaders. This area of study broadened to include *skills* and *competencies* as well as the evolution of *leadership styles* and the notion that there is no one "best way" of leading (*contingency theory*). The section will end with a review of several current theories and a discussion of several issues in leadership, including diversity and ethics.

TRAITS

Recently, there has been renewed interest in the study of leadership trait theory, especially characteristics of effective leaders, despite the fact that this perspective is limited. Little is known about how combinations of traits may impact effectiveness, or how traits affect organizational outcomes (Northouse, 2010, p. 26), but researchers do agree that traits are important only to the extent that they are relevant to a particular leadership situation.

In light of these limitations, traits associated with effective leaders include intelligence, self-confidence, determination (e.g., desire to get the job done, including initiative, persistence, dominance, and drive), integrity, and sociability (Northouse, 2010, p. 19); a high energy level and tolerance for stress; an internal locus of control orientation; emotional stability and maturity; personal integrity; emotional and social intelligence (including curiosity, inquisitiveness, open-mindedness, learning orientation intelligence); surgency (e.g., extroversion, high energy level, and power orientation); conscientiousness; and agreeableness (Yukl, 2010). In addition to these traits, leadership effectiveness has recently been associated with being "authentic." Grounded in positive psychology, the authentic leader "[is] ... confident, hopeful, optimistic, resilient, moral/ethical, future-oriented, ... gives priority to developing associates to be leaders ... is true to him/herself ... [and] exhibits behavior [that] positively transforms or develops associates into leaders themselves" (Luthans & Avolio, 2003, p. 243).

SKILLS AND COMPETENCIES

Competencies are reflected in the style theories of leadership: the notion that certain behaviors, for example task, relationship, or change-oriented behaviors (Yukl, 2010), make leaders more effective, and that these behaviors or styles (e.g., participative or autocratic leadership) can by and large be learned and improved. Competencies are defined as "the combination of knowledge, skills, traits, and attributes that collectively enable someone to perform a given job" (Zenger & Folkman, 2002, p. 83).

Although the "competency movement" (Zenger & Folkman, 2002, p. 85) has not yet produced a strong evidence base to relate "lists" of competencies to leadership effectiveness in specific situations or challenge the assumption that all competen-cies are equal, the literature shows that certain competencies are mandatory (to a greater or lesser degree) for effective leadership. For example, Zenger and Folk-man (2002) found that business leaders with strengths in multiple competencies were most effective; and, significantly, that particular *combinations* of competen-cies seemed to be more powerful predictors of effectiveness. For example, being able to give feedback did not always correlate with effectiveness, whereas giving feedback while building trust did (Zenger & Folkman, 2002, p. 151). They also found that listening skills alone were not particularly valuable, but listening skills plus other interpersonal skills (e.g., being considerate and caring) did make a difference.

Current thinking uses a "strengths perspective," in which administrators work to build on their strengths and find situations that optimize them (Buckingham & Clifton, 2001). Zenger and Folkman (2002) agree that magnifying strengths is the best overall approach, but they add that "fatal flaws" must be fixed. For example, they found that an inability to learn from mistakes and a lack of core interpersonal skills were fatal flaws (pp. 157–162).

Yukl (2010) has noted that different skill mixes are needed at different managerial levels, with conceptual skills more important at higher levels and technical skills more important at lower levels. Some of each skill will be needed at every level, and interpersonal skills are equally important at every level of management.

In social work, a set of generic management competencies, ranging from advo-cacy to interpersonal skills, has been developed by the National Network for Social Work Managers (http://www.socialworkmanager.org/); they include many of the competencies mentioned in the research and others that are tailored to human ser-vices settings.

LEADERSHIP STYLES

Competencies are also reflected in the style theories of leadership: the notion that certain behaviors make leaders more effective and that these behaviors or styles (e.g., participative or autocratic leadership) can, by and large, be learned and improved. The earliest work in this area, at Ohio State University and the Univer-sity of Michigan, contrasted task behaviors, such as directing and providing struc-ture for the group and focusing on production, with relationship behaviors, which emphasized building trust, respect, good relations within the team, and an employee orientation. Examples of these behaviors and a newly developing cate-gory of change-oriented behaviors are provided in Table 11.1.

Although research in this area is still inconclusive, "the overall pattern of results suggests that effective leaders use a pattern of behavior that is appropriate for the situation and reflects a high concern for task objectives and a high concern for relationships" (Yukl, 2010, p. 81). Leadership research now more typically recognizes complexities, which cannot offer simple answers. These insights are reflected in style models, including the Leadership Grid and Situational Leadership theories, which were discussed in Chapter 7.

TABLE 11.1	EXAMPLES OF TASK-, RELATIONS-, AND CHANGE-ORIENTED BEHAVIORS

Task-Oriented Behaviors

Organize work activities to improve efficiency.

Plan short-term operations.

Assign work to groups or individuals.

Clarify what results are expected for a task.

Set specific goals and standards for task performance.

Explain rules, policies, and standard operating procedures.

Direct and coordinate work activities.

Monitor operations and performance.

Resolve immediate problems that would disrupt the work.

Relations-Oriented Behaviors

Provide support and encouragement to someone with a difficult task.

Express confidence that a person or group can perform a difficult task.

Socialize with people to build relationships.

Recognize contributions and accomplishments.

Provide coaching and mentoring when appropriate.

Consult with people on decisions affecting them.

Allow people to determine the best way to do a task.

Keep people informed about actions affecting them.

Help resolve conflicts in a constructive way.

Use symbols, ceremonies, rituals, and stories to build team identity.

Recruit competent new members for the team or organization.

Change-Oriented Behaviors

Monitor the external environment to detect threats and opportunities.

Interpret events to explain the urgent need for change.

Study competitors and outsiders to get ideas for improvements.

Envision exciting new possibilities for the organization.

Encourage people to view problems or opportunities in a different way.

Develop innovative new strategies linked to core competencies.

Encourage and facilitate innovation and entrepreneurship in the organization.

Encourage and facilitate collective learning in the team or organization.

Experiment with new approaches for achieving objectives.

Make symbolic changes that are consistent with a new vision or strategy.

Encourage and facilitate efforts to implement major change.

Announce and celebrate progress in implementing change.

Influence outsiders to support change and negotiate agreements with them.

From Yukl (2010)

CONTINGENCY THEORIES OF LEADERSHIP

Contingency theory suggests that there is no one best way to lead, that different behaviors are appropriate in different situations, and that the effectiveness of leadership styles depends to a great extent on the situation (Hersey, Blanchard, & Johnson, 2001). As is the case with several leadership theories, the complexity of contingency theories makes them difficult to precisely implement and test (Northouse, 2010, p. 133), with research having produced mixed results (Yukl, 2010, p. 232). Regardless, applying principles of contingency theories and models to leadership practice requires leaders to engage in an assessment process of various factors (e.g., the subordinates' skill and motivation levels) and subsequent selection of mixes of task and relationship behaviors and appropriate leadership approaches (e.g., transformational or participative) for the situation at hand.

CHARISMATIC LEADERSHIP

Charismatic leadership (Conger & Kanungo, 1998) will be briefly discussed here as a prelude to a full discussion of current well-developed models of leadership, some of which include elements of charismatic leadership. A charismatic leader is a strong role model who demonstrates competence and confidence and communicates high expectations. Charismatic leaders foster the development of trust and can inspire followers to a new vision through self-sacrifice, risk taking, and a concern for followers. It should also be noted that charismatic leadership is risky: power can be misused, and followers can become inappropriately dependent upon a charismatic leader (Yukl, 2010, Ch. 9).

Also, as Collins (2001) noted, effective leaders do not need to be strongly charismatic in the traditional sense of "larger than life heroes" such as Lee Iacocca at Chrysler (pp. 28–30). In fact, Collins's research found that leadership attributes included a "paradoxical blend" of humility and a fearless determination to succeed, concluding that, "Charisma can be as much a liability as an asset, as the strength of your leadership personality can deter people from bringing you the brutal facts" (p. 89). The challenge here seems to be to demonstrate the characteristics noted without displaying an oversized personal presence, which puts more emphasis on the person than the organization.

TRANSACTIONAL AND TRANSFORMATIONAL LEADERSHIP

Currently, one of the most popular and studied models of leadership contrasts two related approaches: transformational leadership and transactional leadership. Much of the current work on this model has been reported by Bass and associates (Bass & Avolio, 2006). In transactional leadership, the more common approach, an exchange process involves the leader and followers agreeing to do or provide things to accommodate each others' needs. In transformational leadership, the leader motivates followers to higher levels of commitment by focusing on shared goals.

Transactional leadership has two components. First, contingent rewards are valued rewards received for performing desired behaviors. A transactional leader identifies factors that motivate a worker and provides the support needed for effective performance. Second, management by exception assumes that under normal circumstances, little supervisory intervention will be necessary. When exceptions (variations from routine activities) occur, management by exception is used. A leader can use active or passive management by exception. In active management by exception, the leader "arranges to actively monitor deviances from standards, mistakes, and errors that occur and to take corrective action as necessary" (Bass, 1998, p. 7). In passive management by exception, the supervisor does not actively monitor but waits for deviances or mistakes to occur and then acts.

To effectively lead professional staff, transactional leadership will probably not be enough to achieve outstanding performance. Transactional leadership should be augmented by the use of transformational leadership, which includes idealized influence, inspirational motivation, intellectual stimulation, and individualized consideration.

IDEALIZED INFLUENCE Leaders who are admired as role models who display high moral and ethical standards, are trusted to do the right thing, and are emulated by followers are demonstrating idealized influence.

INSPIRATIONAL MOTIVATION A key component of inspirational motivation is vision. The overuse of this concept in the popular press and misapplications in organizations has led to cynicism on the part of some employees. Nevertheless, when properly executed, visionary leadership can be a powerful tool for focusing and energizing staff. Another important aspect of this element is setting high expectations for the work unit or program. The leader then uses enthusiasm and encouragement to pull the team toward the vision and achievement of expected results.

INTELLECTUAL STIMULATION Intellectual stimulation involves encouraging innovation and creativity, questioning assumptions, and trying new ways of doing things. This principle is particularly important in the early stages of assessing the need for change.

INDIVIDUALIZED CONSIDERATION Individualized consideration involves coaching and mentoring workers as individuals and having ongoing personalized interactions with staff. Individual consideration involves finding ways for followers to identify growth goals and providing opportunities for them to achieve them. This can take the form of an explicit discussion with a follower, simply asking what is important to them and how these things can be achieved in a work setting.

According to Avolio and Bass (2002, p. 5), the best leaders use more transformational leadership than transactional leadership, but both used together are optimally effective. They also note that transformational leadership can be confused with "pseudotransformational leadership," which focuses on personal power, manipulation, threat, and punishment (p. 8).

Yukl (2010) has offered several guidelines for the use of transformational leadership. Articulate a clear and appealing vision, and explain how it can be attained. Act confident and optimistic, and express confidence in followers. Support the vision through resource allocations and emphasizing key values, and lead by example.

Summarizing research over the past 20 years, Bass and Avolio (2006, p. 48) conclude that transformational leadership is positively related to performance in the business, military, educational, government, and not-for-profit sectors. One meta-analysis of Full-Range Leadership, which includes the use of both transactional and transformational leadership (Judge & Piccolo, 2004), found that both transformational leadership and contingent rewards had significant relationships with outcomes, including follower satisfaction and group or organizational performance. In a review of the literature, Tucker and Russell (2004) conclude that transformational leaders can have a major influence on organizational culture and change. Yukl (2010) concludes that, in spite of conceptual weaknesses in the theory, "the available evidence supports many of the key propositions of the major theories of charismatic and transformational leadership." Transformational leadership is compatible with human services values and principles regarding valuing and empowering individuals.

EXEMPLARY LEADERSHIP

Kouzes and Posner's (2002) work on leadership, unlike some of the popular literature, presents a model with an empirical base. Although they have not formally named their model, we will use here the title of their most comprehensive book on the subject: *exemplary leadership.* Their model is structured around 5 "practices" and 10 "commitments" of leadership. *Model the way* involves clarifying one's personal values and setting an example by aligning actions with values. *Inspire a shared vision* includes envisioning the future and enlisting others in a common vision.

Exemplary leaders *challenge the process* by finding opportunities to innovate, change, and grow and by experimenting and taking risks. These leaders *enable others to act* by fostering collaboration through trust and cooperative goals and sharing power and discretion. Finally, such leaders *encourage the heart* by showing appreciation for individual excellence and celebrating values and victories through a spirit of community. In their research, they found several characteristics that people look for and admire in a leader:

1. *Honest*: truthful, ethical, principled, worthy of trust
2. *Forward-looking*: articulating a vision and sense of direction for the organization; using strategic planning and forecasting
3. *Competent*: having a track record and the ability to get things done; understanding the fundamentals; having relevant experience
4. *Inspiring*: enthusiastic, energetic, positive about the future

Kouzes and Posner (2002) conclude that these four make up *source credibility*—people believe in and trust them; they do what they say they will do, represented by the acronym DWYSYWD. "Do what you say you will do" requires that a leader practices what he or she preaches, "walks the talk," and follows through.

VISIONARY LEADERSHIP

Vision has been mentioned in several contexts, including transformational leadership and exemplary leadership, and because it is mentioned so often in the leadership literature, it will be given special attention here. According to Nanus and

Dobbs (1999), a vision is "a realistic, credible, attractive, and inspiring future for the organization" (p. 78). The vision should be challenging, but staff members also need to see that, with time and enough of the right kind of work, it is attainable. A mission statement describes why an organization exists (its purpose) and what it does (its unique niche of programs or activities), whereas a vision statement represents where the organization wants to be, or its ideal future.

Articulating a clear and compelling vision is an important aspect of leadership and, as will be discussed later, of change leadership as well. This is important to provide meaning, focus, and clarity of purpose for staff on an ongoing basis, and it may be even more important when organizational change is needed. The organization as a whole typically has a vision statement, and individual programs may have their own vision statements as well. Individual employees come to an organization with their own visions for what they want to accomplish in their careers.

It is important for a leader to learn about his or her followers' aspirations, build these into the organization vision as possible, and help followers see how their individual visions can be realized through a common vision (Kouzes & Posner, 2002). Ultimately, all of these visions should be in alignment (Senge, 2006). An initial statement of vision typically comes from the organization's leader, but alignment can be facilitated by having employees involved in creating a final vision statement and then promulgating it throughout the organization. This can occur through a visioning process or, if necessary, through a larger process of culture change or organizational change, as described later.

SERVANT-LEADERSHIP

Servant-leadership, developed by retired AT&T executive Robert Greenleaf (2002), has received increasing attention in the popular literature in recent years. It is a nontraditional model for leadership in several respects. It was developed by a successful career executive; it is explicitly based in philosophical, ethical, and moral principles; and it presents the unorthodox idea that the leader should first serve followers.

Servant-leadership focuses on the leader-follower relationship and can be considered to be in the *style* category of leadership models because it focuses on leader behaviors. Spears (2005, pp. 33–36) has identified 10 characteristics of the servant-leader, many of which are clearly associated with social work and other human services professions: listening, empathy, healing "broken spirits" and "emotional hurts," general and self-awareness, using persuasion rather than positional authority, broad conceptual thinking and visioning, learning from the past and foreseeing future outcomes, stewardship ("holding their institutions in trust for the greater good of society"), commitment to the growth of people, and building community.

Until recent years, much of the writing on servant-leadership emphasized the description of desired behaviors and principles, but research on this model is expanding. A professional journal devoted to it, *The International Journal of Servant-Leadership,* was launched in 2005. Further systematic empirical work on this model should more fully illustrate its potential.

Before concluding the leadership section of this chapter, several issues related to leadership deserve attention. These include political aspects of leadership in organizations, ethics, and diversity issues. Then, the leader's role in shaping organizational culture will set the stage for a discussion of organizational change.

| **11.1** | **LEADERSHIP OF GRANDVIEW COMMUNITY CENTER (GCC)** |

Leona Estrella came to Grandview Community Center (GCC) as the new executive with very little formal training in leadership. One of her graduate school courses briefly covered theories of leadership, but beyond that Leona felt that she was leading based on her basic personality traits and insights she had acquired from observing leaders in her previous jobs. After getting settled in her new job, she took a course in leadership through continuing education at the local university. Fortunately, she learned that, based on her genetics, upbringing, and prior experiences, she had several traits that would help her as a leader. She had intelligence, self-confidence, a sense of drive and determination, integrity, a high energy level, and tolerance for stress, which had served her well in her career to date. After studying leadership theories and considering the characteristics of her management team members and current conditions in the agency, she thought that she could enhance her effectiveness if she consciously tried to apply, as far as it would fit with her basic personality, principles of exemplary leadership, including modeling the way and inspiring a shared vision, and transformational leadership, especially inspirational motivation and individualized consideration. She also recognized that given the change demands facing the agency, she would need to use a lot of change-oriented behaviors, such as explaining the urgent need for change, encouraging people to view problems or opportunities in a different way, encouraging innovation, and experimenting with new approaches to doing the work of the agency.

ISSUES IN LEADERSHIP

POLITICAL ASPECTS OF LEADERSHIP

An effective human services leader must at times consider the political aspects of a situation, whether it be the demands of conflicting stakeholders or power struggles within the agency. A manager must be able to identify and deal with issues of organizational power and politics (Gummer, 1990).

Internally, a human service manager can appropriately use power tactics in several ways. First, the manager can be alert to political dynamics in any context. This is usually most obvious in budgeting, where fighting among program managers for scarce resources can become not only blatant but also dysfunctional. Political aspects appear in other organizational processes as well: decisions such as who gets what functions in a restructuring, what the hiring criteria for staff are and who makes the decisions, and what data are collected for program evaluation. All of these are important decisions in which many have a stake. A manager who can become aware of possible power and political dimensions in any issue or process can then act on at least two levels: by thinking and behaving politically and by empowering others. These actions may be seen as contradictory, but an effective manager can and probably should do both.

According to Gummer (1990) and Gummer and Edwards (1995), "thinking politically" involves diagnosing the interests and power bases of various actors on a particular issue and then attempting to control the agenda (for example, who can attend a meeting, what questions are open for discussion) and the decision-making process (options, constraints, decision criteria, and staff involvement). "Behaving politically" includes assessing and effectively using the psychological and motivational profiles of oneself and others, building good working relationships with others, communicating effectively and sharing information strategically, and creating influence networks throughout the organization. This can involve framing requests or proposals in terms of how they will benefit the target of influence and building up "chits" by doing favors for others. If such behaviors seem distasteful to human service professionals socialized with values of support, openness, and cooperation, remember that the use of power can be, as described by McClelland in Chapter 7, personalized or socialized, with the former seen as inappropriate and the latter as a legitimate way to accomplish shared organizational goals.

Also, Gummer and Edwards (1995) suggest that effective and appropriate political behavior involves playing by the rules, performing useful functions for the organization, and managing impressions:

> Managers can increase the positive political consequences of their work by carefully adhering to organizational norms, particularly those concerning the proper exercise of power and authority; identifying tasks that their units can do which are considered important to the overall organizational mission; and seeing that their accomplishments and those of their units are accurately and fully conveyed to others within and outside the organization. (p. 145)

It is also legitimate to develop one's own personal sources of power, such as one's reputation and leadership traits such as self-confidence and determination. This process can include developing the power bases discussed in the context of motivation in Chapter 7, particularly referent power (having qualities that others admire) and expert power (having valued knowledge and skills). Research by Yukl (2010, p. 181) suggests that core influence tactics include rational persuasion (explaining why a proposal or request is important), inspirational appeals (as in transformational leadership), consulting with others, and supporting those who will need to implement the request.

Perhaps even more important for managers is their ability and willingness to develop the power in others, commonly known as empowerment. Of course, client empowerment is a commonly discussed principle in the human services, but our interest here is in the empowerment of workers in the conduct of their jobs. Cohen and Austin (1997) assert that empowerment of staff should be formally sanctioned by the organization and built into organizational processes and the worker's job role. Staff empowerment as a way of life can enhance the possibilities of organizational effectiveness and change by more fully using the creativity and resources of all staff.

Terms such as *participative decision making (PDM)* or *participative management* are often used to describe techniques of empowerment. PDM is often based on human resources theories such as those of Likert and McGregor discussed in earlier chapters. There is some evidence of the value of PDM or participative management

(Pine, Warsh, & Maluccio, 1998; Ramsdell, 1994), including its perceived effects on organizational performance (Packard, 1989) and service outcomes (Guterman & Bargal, 1996). Managerial strategies for increasing PDM are available at the micro level through supervision methods that use participative leadership styles (see Chapter 7) and at the macro level through employee involvement in organizational change, as discussed later.

DIVERSITY AND LEADERSHIP

Although diversity issues in organizations have received increasing attention over the past three decades, specifics regarding leadership aspects of diversity have not yet been as fully addressed. Thomas (2006) has suggested that current notions of diversity need to be broadened to focus on *diversity management*, or "making quality decisions in the midst of difference, similarities, and related tensions" (p. 50). He adds that leaders will need to acknowledge the challenges in making decisions in diverse organizations; "become more comfortable with tension and complexity"; and be more strategic in their thinking, considering diversity issues in the context of mission, vision, and strategy (p. 51).

After assessing the literature on diversity as related to leadership in organizations, Yukl (2010, p. 454) offers the following guidelines for managing diversity:

- Set an example in your own behavior of appreciation for diversity.
- Encourage respect for individual differences.
- Promote understanding of different values, beliefs, and traditions.
- Explain the benefits of diversity for the team or organization.
- Encourage and support others who promote tolerance of diversity.
- Discourage use of stereotypes to describe people.
- Identify biased beliefs and role expectations for women or minorities.
- Challenge people who make prejudiced comments.
- Speak out to protest against unfair treatment based on prejudice.
- Take disciplinary action to stop harassment of women or minorities.

ETHICS ISSUES IN LEADERSHIP

The importance of personal values as a component of leadership is part of several of the models of leadership discussed here. Values represent concepts or principles that are considered to be valuable or important, whereas ethics include behavioral guidelines for operationalizing values. The leader's role in developing and encouraging the use of shared values in the organization is worth special emphasis. According to Gill (2006), "creating a sense of shared core values that support the organization's vision, mission and strategies requires their integration into every policy, procedure and process concerning employees: recruitment and selection, performance and management appraisal, training and development, promotion and rewards" (p. 152). Organizational culture is a useful medium through which to share and disseminate organizational values. However, actually changing and institutionalizing organizational values, a deep aspect of culture, requires ongoing, concerted leadership over a period of years.

Manning (2003) says culture is the "context for ethics" in an organization (p. 197), and that leaders must develop an "ethical framework," which includes the agency's mission, values statement, and ethical code, to guide staff (p. 221). She sees leaders as "architects" of organizational structures and processes that "enhance and promote a moral vision and ethical action," concluding that "the essence of ethical leadership is enacting professional values through every decision and action—values that contribute to the common good" (p. 264). The articulation and promotion of organizational values and ethical standards is thus a core aspect of leadership. Leaders can use models of transformational, exemplary, and servant-leadership in their daily behavior and in the ongoing maintenance of an ethical organizational culture.

Jeavons (2010, pp. 194–198) offers the following as core values: integrity (behaving consistently with one's stated principles), openness, accountability (answering for behavior and performance to funders, the community and the public), modeling expected behavior, service (focusing on organizational mission rather than personal accomplishments), and charity (caring for people in need). In a similar vein, Northouse (2010) suggests five principles of ethical leadership. First, leaders respect others, valuing their work and their input, and treating them as individuals. Ethical leaders practice service and altruism, behaviors that are totally consistent with human service work. Leaders behave in a just way, showing a concern for fairness and avoiding special treatment or consideration except when appropriate (e.g., accommodating an employee with a disability). Of course, ethical leaders are expected to be honest, not only telling the truth but also "representing reality as fully and completely as possible" (p. 314). Finally, ethical leaders build community, focusing on common goals and values as in transformational leadership.

In addition to general principles for ethical leadership, managers who are in professions in the field of human services, by definition of such membership, commit themselves to the goal of service effectiveness. They also have, as members of their professions, codes of ethics that govern professional conduct.

Ethical issues tend to arise when they are least expected, and thinking through in advance key guiding principles may expedite the process of resolving an ethical issue when it emerges. Ethical dilemmas can sometimes be avoided or made easier to deal with if an organization has clearly articulated values that are used regularly to guide decision making, as discussed earlier. Another way in which values and ethical guidelines may be communicated, demonstrated, and put into effect is through the management of an organization's culture. In recent years, the articulation of values and organizational culture are increasingly seen as important functions of organizational leadership.

SHAPING ORGANIZATIONAL CULTURE

Organizational culture, briefly discussed in Chapter 5, represents shared beliefs, assumptions, norms, and expectations in an organization. Organizational culture is a key factor in organizational effectiveness. Leaders play an important role in "embedding" and transmitting (Schein, 2010) the culture that they believe will most enhance organizational functioning. Leaders articulate an organization's existing culture, and in the case of an organization whose culture has become outdated or dysfunctional, can help change an organization's culture to better adapt to new conditions in the environment.

Leaders give staff important clues based on the aspects of the organization to which they pay attention. For example, if leaders focus on agency outcome data and the functioning of teams, they are likely to get different results than if they focus on following procedures and power struggles for resources. If leaders allocate resources for diversity initiatives and allocate rewards based on improved client outcomes through evidence-based practices and collaboration, employees will get clues regarding what is important.

Changing an organization's culture typically takes years. Schein (2010) suggests that creating a new culture requires leaders who have vision, persistence, patience, flexibility and readiness regarding change, ability to perceive the problem, insight and self-awareness about his/her strengths and limitations, strong motivation for change, emotional strength to handle the inevitable anxiety and criticism, ability to bring to the surface and change existing culture assumptions, and the ability to involve others in the change process. The next section will address the use of principles of organizational change to help the organization adapt in any ways necessary, from moving to an outcomes-focused culture to implementing evidence-based programming or addressing funding cuts.

ORGANIZATIONAL CHANGE IN HUMAN SERVICE ORGANIZATIONS

Thus far, the discussion of leadership has generally focused on a leader's role in ongoing operations of an agency. An increasingly important role for a leader in an organization is that of a *change leader* (Kotter, 1996). We will now discuss specifics of change leadership, with particular emphasis on organizational change and on creating a high-performance organizational culture.

Needs and demands for organizational change, coming from the agency's environment, staff, clients, and often from its own leaders, are so widespread as to be considered a constant of human service administration. Welfare reform, managed care, results-based accountability, reinventing government, and change efforts such as reengineering are realities affecting managers in a wide range of agency settings. Factors within the organization such as low morale, burnout, inadequate management skills, and high turnover can also present change opportunities. Program redesign, agency restructuring, developing program evaluation systems, enhancing diversity, and changing an obsolete or dysfunctional organizational culture can all be done more effectively using planned change processes.

In recent years, organizational change has received increasing attention in the human service literature (Austin, 2004; Proehl, 2001). However, most agency administrators have received little or no training in organizational change processes and models.

Three overall methods of organizational change will be presented here: leaders as change agents who both lead and empower staff, staff-initiated organizational change used by lower-level employees, and various consultation models. These are based on a comprehensive framework for describing types of organizational change in human service organizations developed by Resnick and Patti (1980), who grouped change approaches into change from below (also known as staff-initiated organizational change), administrative change, and organization development. Organization development has been expanded here to incorporate other forms of consultation.

Resnick and Patti note that each approach has unique uses, strengths, and weaknesses. Over the years, the distinctions among these have become less prominent. For example, lower-level employees are often empowered as change agents through initiatives such as TQM or group problem solving in organization development. Furthermore, a middle manager in a large agency may end up using staff-initiated organizational change tactics with superiors in executive management if she or he is not sanctioned to initiate change as part of the managerial role.

After a brief discussion of these approaches to change, we will review a model for implementing organizational change. This model is designed for administrative change: a manager as change leader wanting to improve some aspect of the organization. It could easily involve the use of consultation technologies described later. We will begin with a process that lower-level staff can use to initiate change.

STAFF-INITIATED ORGANIZATIONAL CHANGE

Unfortunately, after their appearance in some publications more than 30 years ago, change strategies initiated by lower-level employees, typically referred to as "change from below" or "change from within," have been rarely discussed in the professional literature. Summarized by Holloway (1987) as *staff-initiated organizational change* (SIOC), Resnick (1978) originally defined this process as:

> a series of activities carried out by lower or middle-echelon staff in human service organizations to modify or alter organizational conditions, policy, program, or procedures for the ultimate improvement of service to clients. The activities engaged in are legitimized by professional purposes as well as by organizational norms. (p. 30)

The process is typically initiated by line workers and involves five steps. First, for the initial assessment, a problem is identified, an action system consisting of individuals who have a commonality of interests and concerns is formed, data are gathered, a change objective is set, and possible solutions are considered. The potential influence of change agents is assessed, as are the organizational context, risks and benefits to change agents, and driving and restraining forces, with particular attention to the interests and concerns of the organizational decision makers involved.

The next stage, preinitiation, involves workers assessing and developing their influence and credibility ("social capital") and inducing or augmenting stress so that the problem will be addressed.

At the initiation stage, the change goal is introduced, with consideration of how it will be seen as conforming to the interests of key decision makers. Homan (2011, p. 466) suggests creating awareness of the need for change through disseminating symptoms of the problems. Change agents develop alliances with and support from other key individuals and groups and prepare specific proposals that conform to interests and values of key actors. They select representatives to meet with decision makers and introduce the change goal and proposal. Another of Homan's (2011, p. 467) suggestions is similar to a tactic in the following change model: change agents should assess possible reasons that decision makers may resist the change, such as a lack of information or recent major turmoil or current issues causing distractions in the agency, and address these.

Assuming that the change goal is approved, the implementation stage includes gaining support and commitment of staff involved and managing resistance, ensuring that implementation expectations are understood.

Finally, institutionalization involves making any necessary adjustments to the plan and then developing standardized procedures for the proposal and linking it with other organizational elements (for example, human resource systems, information systems).

This summary may make the process seem too easy, and, in fact, Holloway also acknowledges the risks faced by lower-level employees proposing potentially controversial ideas.

Cohen and Austin (1997) suggest an additional critique of the assumptions on which this model is based. They suggest a new model in which worker participation in decision making should be formally sanctioned, with participation in organizational improvement built into social workers' jobs and with a commitment to individual and organizational learning throughout the change process. Their proposed strategies—encouraging dialogue, opportunities for "taking stock" and off-site retreats, line workers "looking at the data," and action research—are, in fact, elements of the administrative change model discussed next.

Frohman's (1997) study of innovation by lower-level units in large business organizations supports the notion of officially sanctioning worker input: success occurred when low-level employees were supported in going outside their job descriptions to suggest changes—a condition that may not be part of the culture of some human service organizations. He adds that change proposals were accepted when they directly addressed existing organizational objectives, a point that low-level change agents should remember when developing change ideas.

USE OF CONSULTANTS

In situations in which an administrator or the agency does not have the knowledge or skills to respond to a particular need for change, consultants can be an appropriate, effective, and efficient alternative. Just as experts in management information systems are used to aid in automation or fund-raising specialists assist with development of a fund-raising strategy, organizational change consultants provide expertise in specific organizational change methods.

Patti and Resnick's next change approach, organization development, will be broadened here to include other forms of consultation or organization-wide change processes that are discussed later. Organization development is typically more client driven, whereas most other forms use more specialized change technologies in which consultants play a more active role. However, this distinction is becoming increasingly blurred, with the agency as the client taking the dominant role in deciding what to do and consultants providing methods to accomplish jointly determined goals. After a review of generic consultation approaches, some of the most common of these methods will be reviewed. Those presented here are the ones most likely to be applied in human service organizations and are included so that an administrator in an agency who has brought in such consultants will know something of what to expect and how to deal with the particular process being used, and so that an administrator wanting to initiate change requiring outside expertise will have some ideas on where to begin.

TYPES OF CONSULTATION

Yankey and Willen (2006) describe two broad types of consultation. The *expert model* involves a content expert, such as a specialist in program evaluation, who applies specific expertise to address a goal the organization identifies. Organizational change typically involves the other type, a *process model*, in which the consultant is in more of a facilitator role, using expertise in change management processes but not giving expert advice on what an organization should do to solve its problem, except by suggesting change technologies to use.

Consultants and clients should thoughtfully consider the needs of the situation and arrange for the best approach. The expert model can be used, for example, if a program has identified a specialized need such as training on working with incest victims. The agency can then solicit consultants with this expertise. For complicated situations ranging from poor morale to funding crises, process skills will likely be needed because there will be no easy "right" answer. Ideally, a consultant would have both process skills and expertise in selected areas. For example, in a funding crisis, process skills would be needed to help the client organization sort things out, identify issues, and consider actions; expertise skills in areas such as strategic planning, budgeting, and fund development would be valuable as well. In any case, a consultant should keep the client's needs paramount and, if she or he lacks needed expertise, suggest the use of other consultants.

SELECTING AND USING CONSULTANTS

Yankey and Willen (2006) provide useful guidelines for selecting and using consultants as well as guidelines for making the consultation useful. To find a consultant, managers can ask managers in other agencies about consultants they have used or can contact relevant foundations, funding organizations, or professional organizations. Internet searches can be especially useful here. A consultant being considered based on such a search should be asked to provide references from former clients.

Yankey and Willen (2006, p. 414) suggest that consultant interviews should cover not only consultant expertise and prior work but also these characteristics:

- Honesty about his or her capabilities,
- Compatibility with the organization,
- Beliefs and values regarding organizational development,
- Personality fit,
- Motivations,
- Ethics, and
- Appreciation for confidentiality.

There should be clarity regarding the consultation itself, reflected both in the request for proposals, if one is used, and in the contract with the consultant chosen.

A contract should outline responsible parties and their roles, the problem and goal, individuals and/or units or programs to be involved, consultant "deliverables" (for example, a report, recommendations, services provided), ground rules, fees, and a schedule.

We will now look at some of the consultation approaches currently being used to enhance organizational performance. These are all probably used more frequently in for-profit businesses, which usually have greater resources available for consultation. However, many are becoming more common in human service organizations.

SOME COMMON CONSULTATION TECHNOLOGIES

ORGANIZATION DEVELOPMENT   Organization development (OD) has historically been one of the most common consultation methods in business and industry and is being increasingly used in human service organizations. In OD, the consultant and the client organization jointly assess an organization's change needs and develop an action plan for addressing them (French & Bell, 1999). Organization development represents Yankey and Willen's "process" model, although OD consultants often provide technical expertise in areas such as strategic planning, reengineering, and total quality management (TQM, covered later), which vary on the "process" to "expert" continuum.

To change the way an organization solves its problems, the OD consultant may use interventions including:

1. Group process interventions such as team building and role clarification sessions;
2. Intergroup process interventions, including conflict resolution strategies, intergroup confrontation meetings, and joint problem-solving sessions;
3. Training programs designed to enhance organizational skills and using innovative educational strategies such as simulations and structured experiences;
4. Survey feedback, or the gathering and sharing of diagnostic data about the organization and its current norms and processes (see Chapter 12);
5. Action research, which involves broad participation in the development of change strategies based on structured research and behavioral science technologies; and
6. Changes in the organizational structure based on group agreement about suggested alterations.

The key to defining an intervention as OD is not the specific strategy used but the involvement of a consultant and staff that might be affected by a change. This assumes that the organization and its members must have some control over the change process. Also, regardless of specific consultation activities, an effective OD consultant will follow clear procedures that include problem identification, contracting, assessment, planning, intervention, and evaluation.

In many situations, the diagnostic process leads not to training or group process interventions but to changes in organizational systems. If members of an organization are actively involved in the process, they are likely to be as actively involved in supporting the implementation of solutions.

Action research is a core technology of organization development. As its name implies, action research involves, first, gathering data on a problem (a research phase) and then action—the implementation of a change initiative. The next cycle of research involves gathering data on results, analyzing the data, and making adjustments or planning new activities. Continuing with new activities constitutes another cycle of action, followed by another research phase of data collection.

APPRECIATIVE INQUIRY A recent approach to organizational change that offers an option to traditional action research is appreciative inquiry. It involves "the discovery of what gives 'life' to a living system when it is most effective, alive, and constructively capable in ecological, economic, and human terms" (Cooperrider, Whitney, & Stavros, 2003, p. 3). This innovative approach emphasizes asking positive questions to reveal the positive elements of an organization in order to help achieve its ideal future.

BUSINESS PROCESS REENGINEERING (BPR) Consultants are used for business process reengineering and total quality management implementation. These approaches may use either expert or process models, whereas other forms of consultation discussed later, including management analysis, typically use the expert approach.

BPR, sometimes referred to as simply reengineering, reached fad status in the business and government sectors in the 1990s in spite of evidence that many such efforts fail (Hammer & Champy, 1993). It has been defined as "a fundamental rethinking and radical redesign of business processes to achieve dramatic improvements in critical contemporary measures of performance such as cost, quality service, and speed" (Hammer & Champy, 1993, p. 32).

Reengineering typically involves a thorough examination of the whole organization, focusing on structures and processes. According to Grobman (2008, p. 297), reengineering is "the zero-based budgeting of business processes, contending that, at least theoretically, the past should have no bearing on what is planned for the future." The current organization is assessed, and a new, ideal organization is proposed that eliminates all processes that do not add value for customers. Through the 1990s reengineering came to be seen as a euphemism for downsizing, but reengineering experts asserted that they are not equivalent processes, although a common result of reengineering is the elimination of management layers and positions. When positions are eliminated, an organization should do everything possible to retain employees in still-needed positions.

TOTAL QUALITY MANAGEMENT (TQM) TQM is an organization-wide philosophy and process of continuous improvements in quality by focusing on the control of variation to satisfy customer requirements, including top management support and employee participation and teamwork (Grobman, 2008, pp. 295–296; Gummer & McCallion, 1995). As contrasted with reengineering, TQM focuses on the line worker level rather than the larger administrative systems and structures. TQM uses structured problem-solving methods to analyze work processes, eliminate unnecessary steps, and improve quality.

MANAGEMENT ANALYSIS Management analysis is a generic term involving expert analysis and audits of management structures, goals and objectives, and processes including organization charts, staff utilization, coordination mechanisms, roles and responsibilities, and work methods to improve efficiency and reduce costs. Recommendations often include reorganization, consolidation, downsizing/rightsizing, and, in government settings, sometimes privatization.

This is a clear example of Yankey and Willen's "expert" model, although some management analysts attempt to include employees in analysis of findings and preparation of recommendations in order to have "buy-in."

ADMINISTRATIVE CHANGE THROUGH LEADERSHIP

In the turbulent environment of the human services, good leadership, outside consultants, and employee empowerment or participative management can be useful change tools. Ultimately, the role of the manager as a change leader will be a key factor in creating successful organizational change. Some current models of leadership previously discussed are explicitly focused on creating change, but we will now focus explicitly on a process for leaders facilitating change. The change model presented later will describe steps and tactics that managers as change leaders can use to create change.

To underline the importance of a formal change process, we will look briefly at why so many planned change efforts fail.

WHY ORGANIZATIONAL CHANGE EFFORTS OFTEN FAIL

Because substantive organizational change often confronts indifference or resistance and leads to discomfort or stress on the part of employees or larger units in the organization, it is not surprising that many change efforts fail. Change from below often cannot sufficiently move the existing power structure, and many top-down initiatives fail because they are introduced in an authoritarian way. Kotter (1996) has found several commonalities in failed change efforts:

1. Allowing too much complacency—Change agents need to establish a high level of urgency in others, to motivate them to want change.
2. Failing to create a sufficiently powerful guiding coalition—Key leaders need to support the change effort publicly.
3. Underestimating the power of vision—As in the case of visionary leadership, "vision plays a key role in producing useful change by helping to direct, align, and inspire actions on the part of large numbers of people" (p. 7).
4. Undercommunicating the vision by a factor of 10 (or 100 or even 1,000)—People need to clearly see that the benefits to them will outweigh the costs, and they need to see their leaders behaving consistently with their stated intentions and values.
5. Permitting obstacles to block the new vision—A change vision can be stalled by existing systems such as organizational structure and rewards systems that are not in alignment with the change.
6. Failing to create short-term wins—Staff need to see some quick successes to combat complacency or discouragement.
7. Declaring victory too soon—Large-scale change, usually involving culture change, takes years to accomplish fully.
8. Neglecting to anchor changes firmly in the corporate culture—The results of change need to be visibly connected to improved organizational performance, and new behaviors and systems need to be based on the new norms and values.

The change model described next is intended to address factors that may lead to failed efforts, and it is based on the key elements of successful change models covered in the literature.

PLANNED ORGANIZATIONAL CHANGE

Organizations and staffs change in small ways, such as developing new procedures, perhaps without even considering that change is occurring. Beyond daily changes, there are three levels of increasing intensity of change.

LEVELS OF ORGANIZATIONAL CHANGE

Costello (1994, cited in Proehl, 2001) identifies three levels of organizational change. *Developmental change* involves adjustments to existing operations or improving a skill, method, or process that does not currently meet the agency's standard. This level of change is the least threatening to employees and the easiest to manage. Examples include problem solving, training, and improving communications. *Transitional change* involves implementing something new and abandoning old ways of functioning. This move through a transitional period to a new future state requires patience and time. Examples include reorganizations, new technology systems, and implementing a new program. The most extreme form of change is *transformational change*, which requires major shifts in vision, strategy, structure, or systems. This might evolve out of necessity, for example, as a result of major policy changes such as welfare reform and managed care. The new state involves a new culture, new beliefs, and awareness of new possibilities. Examples include privatization and managed competition.

For larger-scale changes, in which radical changes in the agency's culture or systems are required, the use of the process discussed next should enhance the prospects of the agency reaching its desired new state. Consultants may also be brought into any change process as appropriate.

A MODEL OF ORGANIZATIONAL CHANGE

This model of organizational change is appropriate for transitional and transformational change. A leader may initiate an organizational change process to meet a particular need or goal, such as moving the agency from a process-oriented to an outcomes-oriented culture, implementing an evidence-based practice, or addressing significant funding cuts. The model presented here is adapted from other models, particularly those of Proehl (2001); Fernandez and Rainey (2006); and Palmer, Dunford, and Akin (2009).

Although the steps below are presented in a logical linear fashion, they may at times overlap or be addressed in a different sequence, based on specific agency conditions. Throughout the process, change leaders should be alert to human factors, including staff resistance and need to be informed of activities. Consistent with principles of participative management, involving staff in the process should have a significant effect on creating staff commitment, as well as leading to better ideas and outcomes.

1. Assess the Present   A change initiative typically starts with a change leader such as an agency executive and her or his management team, and perhaps other staff, who need to develop a clear understanding of the problem, the need for change (the current state), and the desired outcome (the future state). This may involve gathering and assessing available data to focus the change.

Next, the change leader or team can assess the scope of the change and determine the type of change needed. Transitional or transformational change would suggest the use of this change management process.

Change leaders should also determine the extent to which important preconditions for change are present. In a human service organization, a core level of management competence, clearly articulated humanistic values, and a participative management philosophy would be desirable preconditions. The organizational culture and the state of labor relations should also be considered. Substantive change will be less likely with ineffective or authoritarian management, an excessively bureaucratic or political culture, or heavily conflictual management-staff relations. If these conditions exist, they should be the first targets for change and will require outside help.

The leader should also engage in some self-assessment. According to Burke (2008, p. 248), a change leader should have a tolerance for ambiguity, accept not being able to control everything, understand how feelings affect behavior, and be open to shared decision making.

Other aspects of organizational readiness to consider are likely levels of support and enthusiasm for the change, the capabilities of staff (their skills and abilities) and possible resistance (who may resist, and why). A useful tool for this is a force field analysis (Brager & Holloway, 1992) to identify driving forces, which aid the change or make it more likely to occur, and restraining forces, which are points of resistance or things getting in the way of change. The change goal, or desired future state, is represented by a line down the middle of a piece of paper. To its left, a parallel line represents the current state of the organization. The change process involves moving from the current state to the ideal future state. To the left of the second line (the current state) are listed all driving forces (individuals, key groups, or conditions) that may assist in the implementation of the change. On the other side are listed restraining forces that will make the change more difficult to implement. An example is presented in Figure 11.1: a force field analysis of a change goal to implement a program evaluation system (Linn, 2000). Stakeholders may be listed here as well: managers, bureaucratically oriented staff, or others likely to prefer the status quo. Arrows from both sides touching the "current state" line represent the constellation of forces.

Each force is then assessed in two ways: its potency or strength and its amenability to change. More potent forces, especially restraining ones, will need greater attention. Those not amenable to change will have to be counteracted by driving forces. The analysis of the force field involves looking at which driving forces may be strengthened and which restraining forces may be eliminated, mitigated, or counteracted. The change plan would include tactics designed to move the relevant forces, with particular attention to strategies for addressing resistance (step four).

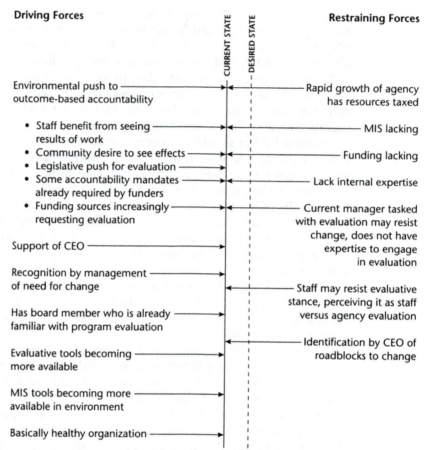

| Driving Forces | | CURRENT STATE | DESIRED STATE | | Restraining Forces |

FIGURE 11.1 | FORCE FIELD ANALYSIS: IMPLEMENTING A PROGRAM EVALUATION SYSTEM

Driving Forces:

Environmental push to outcome-based accountability

- Staff benefit from seeing results of work
- Community desire to see effects
- Legislative push for evaluation
- Some accountability mandates already required by funders
- Funding sources increasingly requesting evaluation

Support of CEO

Recognition by management of need for change

Has board member who is already familiar with program evaluation

Evaluative tools becoming more available

MIS tools becoming more available in environment

Basically healthy organization

Restraining Forces:

Rapid growth of agency has resources taxed

MIS lacking

Funding lacking

Lack internal expertise

Current manager tasked with evaluation may resist change, does not have expertise to engage in evaluation

Staff may resist evaluative stance, perceiving it as staff versus agency evaluation

Identification by CEO of roadblocks to change

2. CREATE A SENSE OF URGENCY The change leader will need to clearly and persuasively communicate the need, desire, and urgency for the change. Staff may be both comfortable and happy with the status quo and feel that they are overworked enough as it is; they may be disinclined to take on a significant change in the way they and their programs operate.

A change formula (Beer, cited in Proehl, 2001, p. 72) suggests that change can occur when (a) there is dissatisfaction with the current state, (b) staff have a clear vision of an ideal future state of the organization, (c) there is a clear and feasible process for reaching the desired state, and (d) these factors considered together outweigh the perceived costs of changing. From an employee's point of view, costs of change can include changes in employees' sense of competence, power or status, workplace relationships, rewards, and identity or roles. Therefore, the change leader can create conditions for change by creating dissatisfaction with the status quo, providing a clear and compelling vision for the new state, and establishing and using an effective and efficient process that minimizes the "costs" to participants.

The change leader can use data to show that if a change is not made, the organization and staff will suffer undesirable consequences, such as loss of clients, loss of funding, a decrease in service quality or productivity, or a serious morale problem. Problems can range from new government policies, funding cutbacks, or expectations for improved services to low staff morale, burnout, or inadequate management systems. As much as possible, existing data should be used to demonstrate the urgency for change.

3. CLARIFY THE CHANGE IMPERATIVE In addition to fully articulating the problem needing attention, the vision for success—outcomes for the change—need to be clearly communicated. In addition, there needs to be a clear and specific plan for how the change initiative will be implemented, including a basic strategy, who will be involved, and planned activities and persons accountable for them. The plan should also describe how any additional data will be collected and analyzed, and the use of task forces and other change processes. The timeframe for the project and available resources (especially staff time and any necessary financial support) should be noted.

4. ENSURE SUPPORT AND ADDRESS RESISTANCE Throughout the process, change leaders will need to continuously show support for the process and anticipate and address resistance. The force field analysis previously described can continue to be used for this. Top management, such as the agency's executive, and perhaps the agency's board should formally show support for the process.

Resistance will need to be thoughtfully addressed. As Proehl (2001) summarized, people resist for three possible reasons: not knowing about the change, not being able to change, or not being willing to change. Those who do not know about the change can be influenced by change leaders communicating the who, what, when, why, and how of the change, and by getting them involved in the process. Those who feel unable to change can be educated regarding the new knowledge and skills that will be needed during and after the change. This might involve training in problem-solving methods, new management skills, team building, or conflict management. A small number of staff may be unwilling to change. Their concerns should be recognized and addressed through feedback and coaching, showing how they may benefit. Rewards and performance management may be used as needed.

5. DEVELOP AN ACTION SYSTEM The executive or top management team cannot accomplish large-scale change alone. Building a broad-based action system with designated responsibility for implementing and overseeing the change initiative serves several functions. If many staff members are involved, multiple talents can be brought to bear to address the challenges and tasks ahead. Spreading the workload can help ensure that the additional demands of change do not significantly disrupt ongoing work. Additionally, getting staff members involved can increase their sense of ownership of the results.

A large-scale change initiative can be guided and overseen by a "change coalition" (Kotter, 1996) such as an organizational change steering committee that has representatives from all key stakeholder groups in the agency, including different levels of the hierarchy (from executives to line staff), different program and administrative areas, and labor organization representation if appropriate. Most members of the organization must consider this group legitimate.

Specific roles should be delineated. The CEO or other executive serves as a *sponsor*, who demonstrates organizational commitment to the process and ensures that necessary resources (especially including staff time) are allocated. The key staff person responsible for day-to-day operation of the initiative can serve as a *champion* who not only oversees implementation but also provides ongoing energy and focus for staff. There will probably be multiple change agents who are responsible for implementation at the unit or team level. They may be task force or problem-solving group chairs, facilitators, or external consultants.

Many other staff should be involved as task force or committee members or involved in data collection and analysis and the design and implementation of new systems or processes. Employees from various management and staff levels should be invited to participate based on their relevant knowledge and skills. People with credibility in the organization, formal or informal power, and particular interest in the problem should be especially considered. People who are directly affected by the problem are particularly important for inclusion.

Finally, organizational systems need to be set up to ensure effective functioning of the process. This includes structural arrangements, such as the reporting relationships of the various committees and task forces, and communication processes to ensure that all staff members are aware of what is happening. Newsletters, email bulletins, all-staff meetings, and reports at regular unit meetings should all be used on an ongoing basis. Communication systems for all the involved groups to coordinate with each other and several mechanisms for communicating progress on the initiative should be developed. Consultant and writer John Kotter has said that when it comes to organizational change, "you cannot overcommunicate." Messages about the need for change and what is being done need to be ongoing and frequent.

6. IMPLEMENT THE PLAN FOR CHANGE   After the situation is analyzed, people are involved, and change management processes are in place, strategies and processes can be initiated to implement the change. Problem-solving groups, going by various names such as task forces or action teams, are always needed in planned organizational change. Sometimes problem-solving groups use TQM techniques such as workflow or process analysis and cause and effect diagrams. Change efforts should usually include the analysis of existing organizational performance data to identify where quality, efficiency, and effectiveness improvements need to be made. Additional data may be gathered as needed. Employee attitude surveys (see Chapter 12) are a very useful way to develop a deeper understanding of employee concerns and needs, and perhaps to assess the current culture and climate of the organization. Survey results can provide guidance for issues to address and strategies for ensuring staff commitment to the process.

For organization-wide change, sometimes Business Process Reengineering is used to identify workflow and coordination improvements and eliminate processes that do not add value. Organization redesign, if necessary, should include not only traditional restructuring but also changes in decision-making and communication processes across organizational functions. Workshops using trained facilitators for team building, role clarification, conflict management, and other concerns can often augment the change effort.

An action planning system including tasks, persons responsible, and timelines should be used to track progress. Project activities should be revised as appropriate based on new information or changing conditions. Proehl (2001, p. 169) recommends "acting quickly and revising frequently," identifying opportunities for short-term successes so that staff can see tangible results from their efforts. When a new system is designed, procedures will need to be written and a staff training program developed. Proposals for change are commonly submitted to the steering committee and then forwarded to executive management for final approval.

It is important that adequate resources in terms of staff time and any necessary financial and technological support are made available. There should be widespread participation of staff in the change process, but staff should not feel "overtaxed."

7. EVALUATE, INSTITUTIONALIZE, AND CELEBRATE   Any changes made should be evaluated to ensure success, and they also need to be institutionalized. Staff will need to be retrained, and training for new staff should reflect the new system. Job descriptions and performance appraisal systems may need to be modified to support the new systems. Implementation of new systems should be monitored, with further adjustments made as needed. Changes and successes should be celebrated in ways consistent with the organization's culture. Special events can be held when major milestones are met, and smaller successes can be rewarded and celebrated in staff meetings and other arenas.

11.2   ORGANIZATIONAL CHANGE AT GCC

Early on, Leona Estrella recognized the huge challenges facing GCC, including expectations from its funding sources to better document the performance of its programs and a disorganized management team. She believed that having a team building session with her executive team would help unify them and begin to develop a shared sense of purpose, which would facilitate the agency doing a full strategic planning process. At the program level, she saw the need to develop a better information system and program evaluation process. She knew that in order to get staff invested in that kind of major change, and to develop systems that would really work for the agency, she should engage in a formal organizational change process.

After meetings with her executive team, she held an all-staff meeting to communicate the need for change, her vision for how the agency could be operating, and the urgency to begin moving on this. With some consulting assistance from a professor at the local university, she formed a steering committee to guide the agency-wide effort to develop an outcomes-oriented information system and evaluation process and an organizational culture that supported it. They then set up task forces in each program to develop new systems. Leona appointed Rick Levich, Director of Administrative Support, as the "champion" for the process. Rick was allocated staff time to facilitate training staff in analysis methods that would help them design the new information and evaluation systems. The teams in each program met regularly to update each other, and agency-wide communications through email and staff meetings kept everyone informed. Each

(continued)

11.2 ORGANIZATIONAL CHANGE AT GCC (*CONT'D*)

program developed a new system, and through coordination facilitated by Rick, the systems in each program were aligned. Leona held an all-staff meeting to share the results of the task forces and celebrate their accomplishments. Rick took the lead in rewriting agency policies and procedures to reflect these changes. They planned to monitor implementation with status reports every 3 months.

SUMMARY

Leadership plays a key role in tying together all organizational processes into a coordinated whole. Leadership behaviors are important factors in organizational effectiveness. In today's dynamic human service environment, change is a constant, and leaders play key roles as change agents in their organizations. In addition to leaders, other staff, even at the line level, can and should function as change agents. Occasionally consultants can provide valuable outside expertise

to aid change processes in which staff engage. On any changes beyond routine adjustments, a planned change process should help enhance the prospects for organizational improvement.

In our final chapter, we will review where we have been, with particular attention to the effectiveness of key organizational processes. Assuming that change will be constant, we will look at how a human service manager may remain competent through continuing development.

COMPETENCY-BUILDING ACTIVITY 11.1 | LEADERSHIP

Considering the characteristics of the hypothetical program that you have designed, what kind of a leader would be best to manage the program? What factors within the program, including the characteristics of its

staff, would give guidance as to the best leadership styles for that type of staff? What leadership traits, competencies, and theories would be appropriate for a leader of the program?

CASE ACTIVITY 11.1 | BUDGET CUT

The Women's Agency of Schaefer City offered a full range of services to women, including counseling, educational interventions, and career development programs. Services were offered by a combination of professionals, paraprofessionals, and volunteers, with self-help and peer counseling important components of most programs.

The one agency program that depended solely on professional service deliverers was the health center, located in a separate building but overseen by the

same board of directors and administration. The health center dealt with a variety of women's health needs and offered family planning and first-trimester abortions. Although medical service was provided by physicians and nurse practitioners, all counseling was provided by women with degrees in psychology, counseling, or social work.

For the abortion clinic, this approach worked very well. Each woman who came in for the abortion procedure talked first with a counselor, who took a medical history, answered any questions about the procedure, and explored the woman's readiness for taking this step. The process of exploration often led women to reconsider their options; certainly the decision-making process was enhanced.

This program was placed in jeopardy when severe cutbacks in funding for the total agency took place. There was no consideration of eliminating the abortion clinic itself; the cutbacks, however, were to affect the counseling aspect of the program. By cutting the number of professional counselors from nine to three, enough money could be saved that the number of women served could remain constant. The agency's administrator chose to limit the intake counseling interviews to 20 minutes each. In that time, medical information could be obtained and information about the procedure given.

The reaction to this cutback was immediate and strong. All of the professionals associated with the abortion clinic recognized that the suggested change in staffing patterns would be devastating, not just for the women losing their jobs but for the program itself.

From the patients' viewpoint, the problem involved the fact that they would be deprived of the opportunity to consider their decisions with assistance from skilled helpers. Although they would have factual information, many of them would regret their decisions, which could have lasting effects.

The change also seemed serious in terms of the well-being of the professionals still offering services. No longer would they have the opportunity to provide empathy and help to people in crisis. Instead, they would be spending their time with person after person, giving and getting information in an assembly-line approach. They would not be able to stay with patients through the medical procedure or provide emotional support later. Instead, they would stay in their offices, maintain business as usual, and quickly burn out.

1. Given the fact that the agency had to survive with fewer resources, how could financial cutbacks have been implemented more effectively?
2. What leadership behaviors may be appropriate at a time like this?
3. What principles or tactics of organizational change could have been used to reach a better outcome in terms of results and effects on staff?

REFERENCES

Austin, M. (Ed.). (2004). *Changing welfare services: Case studies of local welfare reform programs.* Now York: The Haworth Press.

Avolio, B., & Bass, B. (2002). *Developing potential across a full range of leadership: Cases on transactional and transformational leadership.* Mahwah, NJ: Lawrence Erlbaum Associates.

Bass, B. (1998). *Transformational leadership: Industrial, military, and educational impact.* Mahwah, NJ: Lawrence Erlbaum Associates.

Bass, B., & Avolio, B. (2006). *Transformational leadership* (2nd ed.). Mahwah, NJ: Lawrence Erlbaum Associates.

Brager, G., & Holloway, S. (1992). Assessing the prospects for organizational change: The uses of force field analysis. *Administration in Social Work, 16(3/4),* 15–28.

Briggs, H., & McBeath, B. (2009). Evidence-based management: Origins, challenges, and implications for social work administration. *Administration in Social Work, 33(3),* 242–261.

Buckingham, M., & Clifton, D. (2001). *Now, discover your strengths.* New York: The Free Press.

Cohen, B., & Austin, M. (1997). Transforming human services organizations through empowerment of staff. *Journal of Community Practice, 4(2),* 35–50.

Collins, J. (2005). *Good to great and the social sectors: A monograph to accompany good to great (why business thinking is not the answer).* Boulder, CO: Author.

Conger, J., & Kanungo, R. (1998). *Charismatic leadership in organizations.* Thousand Oaks, CA: Sage.

Cooperrider, D., Whitney, D., & Stavros, J., Eds. (2003). *Appreciative inquiry handbook: The first in a series of AI workbooks for leaders of change.* San Francisco: Berrett-Koehler Publishers.

Fernandez, S., & Rainey, H. (2006). Managing successful organizational change in the public sector: An agenda for research and practice. *Public Administration Review, 66(2),* 1–25.

French, W., & Bell, C. (1999). *Organization development: Behavioral science interventions for organization improvement* (6th ed.). Englewood Cliffs, NJ: Prentice-Hall.

Frohman, A. (1997). Igniting organizational change from below: The power of personal initiative. *Organizational Dynamics, 25(3),* 39–53.

Gill, R. (2006). *Theory and practice of leadership.* Thousand Oaks, CA: Sage.

Grobman, G. (2008). *The nonprofit handbook* (5th ed.). Harrisburg, PA: White Hat Communications.

Gummer, B. (1990). *The politics of social administration.* Upper Saddle River, NJ: Prentice Hall.

Gummer, B., & Edwards, R. (1995). The politics of human services administration. In L. Ginsberg & P. Keys (Eds.), *New management in human services* (2nd ed., pp. 57–71). Washington, DC: NASW Press.

Gummer, B., & McCallion, P. (Eds.). (1995). *Total quality management in the social services: Theory and practice.* Albany, NY: Rockefeller College Press.

Hammer, M., & Champy, J. (1993). *Reengineering the corporation.* New York: HarperBusiness.

Hersey, P., Blanchard, K., & Johnson, D. (2001). *Management of organizational behavior: Leading human resources* (8th ed.). Upper Saddle River, NJ: Prentice-Hall.

Holloway, S. (1987). Staff-initiated organizational change. In A. Minahan (Ed.), *Encyclopedia of social work* (18th ed., pp. 729–736). Washington, DC: NASW Press.

Homan, M. (2011). *Promoting Community Change* (5th ed.). Belmont, CA: Brooks/Cole.

Jeavons, T. (2010). Ethical nonprofit management. In D. Renz (Ed.), *The Jossey-Bass handbook of nonprofit leadership and management* (3rd ed., pp. 178–205). San Francisco: Jossey-Bass.

Kotter, J. (1996). *Leading change.* Boston: Harvard Business School Press.

Kouzes, J., & Posner, B. (2002). *The leadership challenge* (3rd ed.). San Francisco: Jossey-Bass.

Linn, S. (2000). *Agency change plan.* Unpublished manuscript, San Diego State University.

Luthans, F., & Avolio, B. J. (2003). Authentic leadership development. In K. S. Cameron, J. E. Dutton, & R. E. Quirm (Eds.), *Positive Organizational Scholarship* (pp. 241–261). San Francisco: Barrett-Koehler.

Manning, S. (2003). *Ethical leadership in human services: A multi-dimensional approach.* Boston: Allyn & Bacon.

Nanus, B., & Dobbs, S. (1999). *Leaders who make a difference.* San Francisco: Jossey-Bass.

Northouse, P. (2010). *Leadership theory and practice* (5th ed.). Thousand Oaks, CA: Sage.

Packard, T. (2009). Leadership and performance in human service organizations. In R. Patti (Ed.), *Handbook of Human Services Management* (2nd ed., pp. 143–164). Thousand Oaks, CA: Sage Publications.

Packard, T. (1989). Participation in decision making, performance, and job satisfaction in a social work bureaucracy. *Administration in Social Work, 13*(1), 59–73.

Palmer, I., Dunford, R. & Akin, G. (2009). *Managing organizational change: A multiple perspectives approach* (2nd ed.). Boston: McGraw-Hill Irwin.

Pfeffer, J., & Sutton, R. (2006). *Hard facts, dangerous half-truths and total nonsense: Profiting from evidence-based management.* Boston: Harvard Business School.

Pine, B., Warsh, R., & Maluccio, A. (1998). Participatory management in a public child welfare agency: A key to effective change. *Administration in Social Work, 22*(1), 19–32.

Proehl, R. (2001). *Organizational change in the human services.* Thousand Oaks, CA: Sage.

Ramsdell, P. (1994). Staff participation in organizational decision making: An empirical study. *Administration in Social Work, 18*(4), 51–71.

Renz, D. (Ed.) (2010). *The Jossey-Bass handbook of nonprofit leadership and management* (3rd ed.). San Francisco: Jossey-Bass.

Resnick, H. (1978). Tasks in changing the organization from within. *Administration in Social Work, 2*(1), 29–44.

Resnick, H., & Patti, R. (1980). *Change from within.* Philadelphia: Temple University Press.

Schein. E. (2010). *Organizational culture and leadership*, 4th ed. San Francisco: John Wiley & Sons, Inc.

Senge, P. (2006). *The fifth discipline: The art and practice of the learning organization* (Rev. ed.). New York: Doubleday Currency.

Yankey, J., & Willen, C. (2006). Consulting with nonprofit organizations. In R. Edwards & J. Yankey (Eds.), *Effectively managing nonprofit organizations* (pp. 407–428). Washington, DC: NASW Press.

Yukl, G. (2010). *Leadership in organizations* (7th ed.). Upper Saddle River, NJ: Prentice-Hall.

Zenger, J., & Folkman, J. (2002). *The extraordinary leader.* New York: McGraw-Hill.

USEFUL WEB RESOURCES

Appreciative Inquiry Commons. http://appreciativeinquiry.case.edu/.

Being First: World Leaders in Transformation. http://www.beingfirst.com/.

Center for Creative Leadership. http://www.ccl.org/leadership/index.aspx.

Free Management Library: All About Leadership. http://www.managementhelp.org/ldrship/ldrship.htm.

Free Management Library: Organizational Change and Development. http://www.managementhelp.org/org_chng/org_chng.htm.

Leader to Leader Institute. http://leadertoleader.org/.

The Leadership Challenge. http://www.leadershipchallenge.com/WileyCDA/.

National Network for Social Work Managers. https://socialworkmanager.org/.

Organization Development Network. http://www.odnetwork.org/.

ACHIEVING AND MAINTAINING ORGANIZATIONAL EXCELLENCE

CHAPTER OUTLINE

The purpose of this book has been to provide professionals in human service programs with an introduction to the field of management. Several assumptions underlie this purpose. One is that professionals in service delivery, although for the most part trained as direct practitioners, stand a good chance of moving into managerial positions relatively early in their careers and therefore should have at least a rudimentary exposure to the theory and practice of administration.

The second assumption is that the helping professions, as a result of the first assumption, are responding to the challenge of management facing their members by providing formal training in this method of practice. Some graduate programs in social work, public administration or public affairs, not-for-profit management, and business administration offer specializations in management education for human service workers. This book is intended to contribute to the managerial content of such programs from a human service perspective.

A third assumption is that HSO direct service staff with some management training and knowledge will be more aware of the context, system dynamics, and views of managers and other stakeholders of the organization. Such direct service workers, to the extent that they understand a managerial perspective and can incorporate this into their own worldview, will be more effective in influencing managers to make better decisions or to create or allow change to benefit clients and the community. These workers will also have deeper insight into the heretofore mysterious or inexplicable behavior of the managers in their organizations, which should help them both influence these managers and accept some organizational realities that cannot be changed, such as responding to accountability requirements of funding organizations.

We will now briefly review where we have been, starting with planning as a response to the complex human service environments and needs for service. We will look at how the design of organizations and programs should be based on chosen strategies, and we will consider the importance of other subsystems (human resources, information and evaluation, and financial systems). Finally, the need for constant organizational change and the essential role of leadership in pulling things together will be emphasized. Continuing in this vein, we will examine ways in which ongoing growth and renewal can occur at the individual, group, and organizational levels. After discussing the skills and education that human service managers will need in the years to come and how they can effectively make the transition to management, we will close with some observations on prospects in the future for human service administration.

HUMAN SERVICE MANAGEMENT FUNCTIONS: A SYSTEMS PERSPECTIVE

The most salient elements of the human service managerial process have now been covered in some detail. Together, these elements, or functions, constitute a managerial system. As part of a system, the managerial elements, or subsystems, comprise a set of interrelated and interdependent parts operating synergistically to produce efficient and effective organizational outputs and outcomes. All subsystems of the managerial process—planning, budgeting, designing, staffing, supervising, evaluating—are critical to the viability of the overall system. *Synergy* means that the effect of all the parts working together is greater than the sum of the effects of the subsystems taken independently: in other words, the whole is greater than the sum of its parts. At the same time, however, synergy implies that a system's strength is diminished by the weaknesses of its parts. Additionally, all the subsystems must be aligned with one another: they must be based on similar design principles and values and must be oriented toward the same goals.

The important implication of the systems approach for human service managers is that proficiency in all of the functions of the managerial process is essential for successful managerial performance. We will now take a final look at the human service management model presented in Chapter 1.

MANAGING THE ENVIRONMENT

A human service manager will need to monitor trends in the environment constantly, from the local and state levels to the federal and, sometimes, the global level. Political trends including devolution of formerly federal responsibilities, privatization of services, and increased accountability demands are likely to continue. Macroeconomic trends will always be relevant: in good times there may be increased funds for prevention, and in bad times less funding will be available when it is needed most. Social and organizational complexity will, if anything, increase, requiring managers to look clearly at wider aspects of society and anticipate change further into the future. Needs assessments, asset mapping, community collaboration, and advocacy will all help the manager and the agency deal with the environment.

PLANNING AND PROGRAM DESIGN

For the human service manager to survive and achieve in today's human service organizations, he or she must have knowledge and skills in the planning process, including assessment of the environment; the determination of strategy and goals, and their alignment with organizational mission and purpose; and the specification of program objectives, based on program goals, and their formulation in measurable terms. Strategic planning has emerged as an effective method for integrating the organization's mission and internal strengths and weaknesses with opportunities and threats in the environment. Thoughtful attention must be paid to the consideration and selection of program models and activities (including their possible social, economic, political, and legal consequences and the use of evidence-based practices) designed to meet program objectives and goals and to satisfy the organization's mission.

ORGANIZATIONAL THEORY

Organizational theories—from the traditional bureaucracy and scientific management approaches, through the human relations insights from the Hawthorne studies, to contemporary human resources approaches that maximize employee involvement—are all in evidence today. Systems theory and developments such as empowerment theory also offer useful perspectives for human service organizations. Contingency theory enables organization designers to select the most appropriate theories and models for a particular situation.

ORGANIZATION DESIGN

Organization design, as we pointed out earlier, is both a noun and a verb. As a noun, it describes the two components of an organization's design: structures, represented by organizational charts, and processes such as decision making and communication that cannot be seen on a chart. As a verb, organization design is the process for determining how the different parts will be organized and work together. Staff task forces can be formed to develop a design that proposes the best structures and processes for an organization at a given time.

HUMAN RESOURCE DEVELOPMENT

After the overall organization is designed to fit agency strategies and programs, individual jobs must be designed to fit the model chosen for a particular program. Jobs should be designed to accomplish program purposes and be fulfilling for staff. Then, criteria for jobs must be developed and staff must be hired. New staff members need to be oriented, and an ongoing program of staff training and development should be created. Staff should be evaluated annually, using behaviorally based formats. Striving for a diverse agency workforce is important. This will ensure compliance with relevant laws and executive orders and also increase the likelihood that the workforce will be able to respond to clients in culturally appropriate ways. The use of volunteers and employee assistance programs are other important aspects of human resource management.

SUPERVISION

Human resources are nurtured through the supervision process. An effective supervision relationship begins with the use of appropriate models of motivation and leadership. Contingency theory operates here: no two workers are motivated in the same way, and various styles of leadership may be appropriate depending on the situation. Staff members also need to be rewarded fairly and appropriately. Attention to all of these factors will contribute greatly to the effectiveness of a program's services by valuing and fully using staff—the agency's most important resource.

FINANCIAL MANAGEMENT

After the program model has been identified and the necessary staff selected, budgeting can begin, usually by estimating expenditures. An annual budget is created and may be updated during the year. Specialized techniques such as cutback management, zero-based budgeting, and cost-effectiveness analysis can at times be useful as aids to decision making. Fund-raising and writing proposals for grants or contracts are key management activities. Part of the accountability process is the preparation of periodic financial reports and the completion of an annual fiscal audit.

INFORMATION SYSTEMS

A well-designed information system can enhance an organization's effectiveness and responsiveness and raise an employee's sense of satisfaction and purpose. Managers should bear these points in mind to avoid having an information system designed only to meet external accountability and evaluation needs without being fully valued or supported by staff. An IS should be designed with careful attention to information needs (related to program outcomes, for example) and should include significant participation by staff who will be using the system. Such a system will probably involve the use of computers, the potential applications of which are increasing daily. The system should meet both internal needs (for feedback, program modification, and employee satisfaction) and external needs related to accountability and program evaluation.

PROGRAM EVALUATION

Evaluations may have several purposes, ranging from aiding in decision making and improving programs to building support and demonstrating accountability. Evaluations may look at processes or outcomes. There is increasing interest in outcome evaluation. Using evaluation findings for program enhancement, involving all significant actors in the evaluation process, and taking multiple approaches in the determination of service effectiveness are key considerations that today's human service manager must address in the quest for organizational achievement.

Evaluation takes us full circle. We began by assessing the social problems in our environment that human services are intended to address, and then discussed how agencies can respond to these needs through agency planning and program design. We then reviewed aspects of well-designed organizations, including effective human resources and supervision practices and financial and information systems to monitor progress and accomplishments. Ultimately, the implementation of these systems and their results are assessed by evaluation.

LEADERSHIP AND ORGANIZATIONAL CHANGE

Leaders can make essential contributions to organizational effectiveness. In today's dynamic human service environment, change is a constant, and leaders play key roles as change agents in their organizations. In addition to leaders, other staff, even at the line level, can and should function as change agents. Occasionally consultants can provide valuable outside expertise to aid change processes. Planned change processes can help keep the organization maximally effective and responsive to its environment.

We will now take a final look at the importance of leadership in human service management and then review some specific ways in which individuals, groups, and the organization as a whole can engage in ongoing change and development.

PUTTING IT ALL TOGETHER THROUGH LEADERSHIP

The human service managerial system of interdependent and interacting elements is depicted in model form in Figure 12.1. It should be clear that leadership, at the center, is the unifying force among all the organizational subsystems. A key challenge for the organization, and particularly for managers/leaders, is to achieve and maintain alignment among the functions. As we suggested in the previous chapter, top-level leadership is essential, but leadership throughout the organization, by many individuals, is equally essential. Leaders need to make sure that each subsystem is functioning well and that the subsystems are aligned, or functioning in harmony.

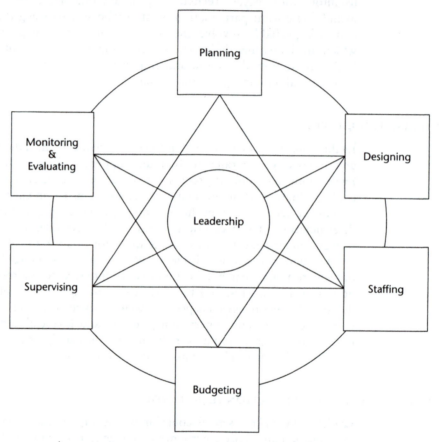

FIGURE 12.1 | A CONCEPTUAL FRAMEWORK FOR HUMAN SERVICE MANAGEMENT

For example, a well-conceived strategic plan will go nowhere unless there are well-designed programs to implement strategies. Well-designed programs cannot be monitored unless an outcome-based information system is in place to allow tracking of activities and results. If staff members are not trained to implement the service delivery models in use, good results are not likely. If funds are not allocated to high-priority activities, failure and cynicism may result. If teamwork is preached but staff members are rewarded only on the basis of individual performance, teamwork will not occur. If effective evaluation systems are not in use, managers and other staff members will not be able to answer questions regarding what has been accomplished: whether client and community problems have been solved and strategies have been successful. If there is a culture of attention to process rather than to results, or if going through the motions rather than innovating seems to be the norm, the organization will stagnate.

Leaders need to pay constant attention to all the subsystems and to organizational climate and the quality of working life to ensure that success will occur. This requires, first, good management and good management systems. Leadership to articulate organizational purpose, visions, and values and to manage constant change will be needed as well. We will now look at some of the ways that organizational excellence can be achieved and maintained at the individual, group, and organizational levels.

GROWTH AND RENEWAL FOR THE MANAGER

A human service worker intending to enter management should expect to develop skills in the areas outlined in this book. Additionally, some studies have been conducted about the particular skills needed on the part of human service managers. For example, Menefee (2009) reports that the social work manager's role is varied, requiring a multitude of technical and interpersonal skills. Some of the skills found to be important were communicating, supervising staff, boundary spanning, planning, organizing, team building, and advocating.

To be effective in the demanding arena of human services, managers clearly will need a good deal of education, development, and training. In addition to enrolling in a university program offering specialized management education for the human services, a manager can take advantage of workshops, continuing education, or certification programs locally or nationally. A large city may have capacity building organizations offering workshops on not-for-profit management subjects ranging from leadership and strategic planning to financial management and writing grant proposals. Nationally, professional organizations (some listed at the end of this chapter) are valuable resources. The Network for Social Work Managers has established the Academy of Certified Social Work Managers to help ensure the competence of social work managers.

Formal leadership development programs (Hernez-Broome & Hughes, 2004; Van Velsor, McCauley, & Ruderman, 2010) are available through specialized training organizations, in-house programs for a particular organization, and consortia in which similar organizations pool resources. In the human services field, a large-scale executive development program for county managers has operated in the San Francisco Bay area since 1994 (Austin, Weisner, Schrandt, Glezos-Bell, & Murtaza, 2006). A similar program has operated in Southern California since 2005 (Coloma, Gibson, & Packard, 2011). It should be noted that formal training programs are often considered to be only a minor part of leadership development (McCauley, 2008), with on-the-job experiences, challenges, setbacks, and learning from others seen as more important.

Leadership development can include several components, often including some combination of off-site training/development programs; multisource or 360-degree feedback; the use of instruments filled out by individual participants on their management styles or characteristics; executive coaching; mentoring; assessment centers; action learning such as real-world problem solving, which includes an explicit focus on what is being learned from the experience; and plans for applications of new knowledge and skills on the job.

Training programs are probably the most common leadership development activity. These often include presentations on leadership models, assessment instruments on styles, structured experiential learning, and group discussions. However, structured sessions alone are not adequate for substantive development of a leader. They need to be augmented by other activities.

360-degree feedback involves using standardized management style or behavior instruments that are filled out by the manager and his or her supervisor, subordinates, and peers (Richardson, 2010). Instruments used typically let raters describe managerial behaviors observed and provide an assessment of their perceived effectiveness. Results are collated by a consultant or training organization and fed back to the manager anonymously. The consultant providing the feedback then helps the manager process the results and decide on action steps to improve skills or adjust styles.

Instruments used in 360-degree feedback may describe a manager's behaviors (for example, his or her perceived effectiveness in delegating, assigning work, supervising, and working with others) or the manager's personal styles of interacting with others. One common instrument for the latter is the Myers-Briggs Type Indicator (MBTI) (Hirsh & Kummerow, 1998). The MBTI, based on the work of C. G. Jung, measures eight personality preferences on four bipolar scales. Results can be interpreted to identify strengths and preferences in the workplace, suggesting preferred work settings and opportunities for development.

Focusing only on identifying strengths, the StrengthsFinder (Buckingham & Clifton, 2001) identifies a manager's "themes," ranging from achiever and analytical to self-assurance and strategic. Based on an individual's profile, strategies can be developed to build on strengths in the work setting.

In any such instrument, profiles show characteristics that tend to work best under particular circumstances. The challenge is not to change to a "better" style but rather to become aware of strengths and cautions in one's preferred style and perhaps develop other styles, and then to use styles consciously, deliberately trying to meet the needs of a situation.

Other important leadership development activities are *coaching* and *mentoring*. Executive coaching is probably the fastest growing leadership development model (McCauley, 2008). Coaching involves a consultant working with a manager to help improve the manager's effectiveness. In contrast, mentoring involves a senior person in an organization working with a manager as mentee and focuses on career development, support, role modeling, and advising.

A final important component of leadership development is *action learning*. This involves a group of participants in a leadership development program being given responsibility for addressing assigned organizational problems and developing creative solutions. The process is later debriefed to identify individual and collective learning (McCauley, 2008).

In addition to activities such as these, McCauley (2008), after a study of the literature, reports five major categories of developmental events. One, coursework in training programs or advanced degree programs, was mentioned earlier. Others include challenging assignments, the influence of other people including bosses and role models, experiencing hardships such as downsizing or difficult subordinates, and personal life challenges.

McCauley adds that successful leadership development includes alignment of leadership development objectives with business strategies, top-level executive support, shared responsibility between line managers and HR staff, manager accountability for the development of subordinates, competency models, multiple development methods, and evaluation.

TEAM DEVELOPMENT

The importance of group dynamics has been acknowledged in organizations since at least the Hawthorne studies of the 1920s. More recently, it has become clear that in today's complex and dynamic organizations, teams are becoming an essential element of ensuring that the work of the organization is getting done. In organizations, many work groups hold meetings and perform activities involving communication and discussion. However, as any member of an organization can attest, not all work groups are teams. According to Johnson and Johnson (2009), in a work group,

> interdependence is low and accountability focuses on individual members, not the group as a whole. The product of a working group is the sum of all the work produced by its members. Members do not take responsibility for results other than their own. Members do not engage in tasks that require the combined work of two or more members. In meetings, members share information and make decisions that help each person do his or her job better, but the focus is always on individual performance (p. 527).

In contrast, Johnson and Johnson suggest that a team "is more than the sum of its parts" (p. 528) and that for a team,

> there must be a compelling team purpose that is distinctive and specific, and that require the joint efforts of two or more members as well as individual work products. Teams not only meet to share information and perspectives and make decisions, they produce discrete work products through members' joint efforts and contributions. (p. 528)

Of course, not every work group needs to be a team in this sense: many work units meet to exchange information, solve problems, and make decisions without needing to become a team in the pure sense. However, as organizational environments become more complex and staff members become more interdependent, the extra effort it takes to truly become and operate as a team may pay off in greater organizational effectiveness and efficiency, and perhaps an improved quality of working life for staff.

Teams can be intact work groups that do some amount of shared work (for example, staff in a residential program), interdisciplinary teams in which people from different professions work with common clients (such as in a mental health program), cross-functional teams that meet to coordinate functions across organizational boundaries (management teams consisting of different program managers in an agency, for example), problem-solving groups (ad hoc groups to solve particular problems), or permanent teams (for instance, quality improvement groups).

Johnson and Johnson offer several suggestions for forming teams:

1. Keep the size of teams small....
2. Select team members on the basis of their (a) expertise and skills and (b) potential for developing new expertise and skills, not on the basis of their position or personality....
3. Bring together the resources the team will need to function, such as space, materials, information, time-lines, support personnel, and so forth.

For structuring and nurturing the teams, they suggest the following:

1. Present the team with its mission, structure positive interdependence among group members....
2. Have frequent and regular meetings that provide opportunities for team members to interact face-to-face and promote each other's success....
3. Pay particular attention to first meetings....
4. Establish clear rules of conduct....
5. Ensure accountability by directly measuring the progress of the team in achieving its goals and plot it on a quality chart....
6. Show progress....
7. Expose the team to new facts and information that helps it redefine and enrich its understanding of its mission, purpose, and goals...
8. Provide training to enhance both taskwork and teamwork skills....
9. Have frequent team celebrations and seek opportunities to recognize members' contributions to team success....
10. Ensure frequent team-processing sessions. (p. 537)

Work groups wanting to move toward becoming teams may benefit from an organization development intervention known as team building (Dyer, 1995). In this context, team building consists of identifying team members, making a commitment to the process, gathering data from team members, feeding data back to the team, joint problem solving or visioning, and action planning. Team building is best accomplished in a workshop setting, away from the work site, for a one- to three-day block of time, and usually involves an organization development consultant. Such a workshop, if successful, can provide the foundation for team-work on an ongoing basis in the work setting. Team-building sessions can be used for existing work groups wanting to improve their functioning or a newly formed team.

Any work group or team operates within the context of the larger organization, which, depending on organizational culture and leadership, can enhance or stifle team behavior. A manager leading a team also functions as a boundary manager with other parts of the organization, which may at times involve negotiating on behalf of the team in furtherance of team goals. In an organization that is not supportive of team functioning, this role will, of course, be difficult to carry out, and this lack of support may need to be addressed through one of the organizational change activities discussed in the previous chapter. Fortunately, organizational cultures supportive of team behavior are increasingly seen as not only desirable but also essential to the accomplishment of the work of today's complex organizations.

ENSURING THE ONGOING GROWTH OF THE ORGANIZATION

ORGANIZATIONAL LIFE CYCLES

Theories of organizational life cycles suggest that organizations must be constantly alert to changes in their environments and internal conditions and must adapt effectively to survive and grow. Vinokur-Kaplan and Miller (2004) provide a useful model for describing the life cycle stages of a human service organization. At the *start up*, or *organizational infancy*, stage, the organization is entrepreneurial, with little structure, and uses informal managerial processes. The goal here is survival: creating and marketing programs.

In the *emerging growth*, or *organizational youth* stage, collective or pre-bureaucratic structures and systems emerge. Things remain mostly informal, with some procedures developed. The goal at this stage is growth, and leaders need to begin to delegate while retaining basic control.

At the next stage, *maturity* or *organizational adulthood*, formal and bureaucratic systems are developed, with clear hierarchies, divisions of labor, rules, procedures, and control systems. The organization now focuses on developing internal stability while expanding services. Finally, the organization reaches *revival*, or *organizational maturity*. If over-bureaucratization can be avoided, effective structures are developed, with teamwork and departmentation to ensure responsiveness to various client target populations.

As the growing organization moves into the maturity stage, it may risk taking a turn toward an overly bureaucratic stage, in which standardized procedures may stifle initiative, creativity, or responsiveness to change. If this happens, the organization enters a stage of decline or stagnation in which the status quo is protected. If this situation is not corrected, the organization may become irrelevant or ineffective, and go out of existence. The important point is that decline and stagnation can be prevented by revitalization, which can occur through quick and appropriate responses to environmental changes and a reexamination of the organization's mission, programs, and operations so that appropriate organizational changes may be made.

The mature organization needs to develop renewal capabilities including organizational learning systems, proactive management of the environment such as strategic management and client responsiveness, visionary leadership, and attention to managerial succession (developing lower-level staff as leaders of the future). This strategy will lead to new strategies and programs, with mergers or collaborations with other agencies becoming increasingly common. Employee empowerment and increased involvement with the community are additional activities that can contribute to renewal. In addition to performing environmental intelligence-gathering activities such as strategic planning, the manager also needs to monitor internal organizational conditions such as morale and productivity to be able to adapt effectively.

EMPLOYEE ATTITUDE SURVEYS

A popular method for assessing the internal climate of an organization is the employee survey, known as *survey feedback* (Burke, 2008). This is an organization development intervention with a rich history of usefulness. As is the case with other organization development activities such as team building, such a survey is best conducted with an experienced consultant's assistance. It should begin with a serious discussion within the organization, ideally at all levels, about the organization's need to learn about its functioning and level of commitment to making change. Top management support will be required (the "sponsors" of the process discussed in the previous chapter), and there will need to be "champions" in the form of staff assigned to fill leadership roles in the design and implementation of the survey. An organization-wide steering committee may be formed to provide overall policy direction and guidance, and a survey team is often responsible for the design of the survey and its implementation.

A qualified organization development consultant can assist an organization in defining goals of a survey, finding or creating an appropriate instrument, administering the survey, compiling results, and facilitating feedback sessions.

An employee survey may have questions that solicit employees' opinions on any aspect of an organization's functioning, including views on the mission, leadership behavior, processes such as hiring and promotions, facilities and equipment, supervisory styles, work group climate, and quality of working life factors ranging from pay to the job itself. Surveys are completed anonymously and returned to the consultant for data collation and analysis. Consistent with the action research process reviewed in the previous chapter, anonymous data are fed back to the organization for discussion and action planning. Data feedback begins with the executive management team, the steering committee, and the survey team. Data are then fed back to all work groups in the organization. Members of a work group normally receive data for the organization as a whole and for their own work group. The use of the survey in identifying opportunities for change is crucial: if no actions follow the survey, employees are likely to become disillusioned. Problem solving in the context of a change process should occur, and the survey should ideally be repeated after an appropriate interval—usually, 12 to 18 months—to assess changes. Some organizations conduct surveys on a regular basis to monitor organizational conditions.

THE MANAGEMENT AUDIT

Another way to assess how an organization is functioning is the management audit (Allison & Kaye, 2005; Packard, 2000). Traditionally, management audits are conducted by consultants who examine agency documents, observe agency processes, and interview staff. They then prepare a report for management outlining findings and recommendations. This is the "expert" consultation mode described by Yankey and Willen in the previous chapter. An alternative is to have a management audit done participatively, with staff involved with its design and implementation, much as an employee survey is conducted. The key factors are that the method used and the criteria being assessed need to be seen as valid and appropriate by members of the organization, so that the findings will be seen as relevant and legitimate.

A management audit format that has been used in human service organizations appears in the Appendix of this text. Such a form may be filled out by any members of the organization who have knowledge of the factors under consideration. As in the case of a survey, results can be collated by a consultant for feedback to staff. Of course, any staff members that have provided data for a management audit will expect to see the findings and will expect to see action taken. Problem-solving groups or task forces can be formed to address weak areas in the agency's management systems. For example, in one agency, a management audit revealed deficiencies in the agency's evaluation system, which gathered data only on client demographics and units of services. The executive director formed a task force to improve the evaluation system, and the agency implemented recommendations from the task force.

CULTURAL COMPETENCE ASSESSMENT

Another way in which the organization may evaluate its internal operations is a cultural competence assessment (see the National Center for Cultural Competence website at the end of this chapter). This may be implemented using the same procedures as those used in a management audit. Usually such an assessment looks at all aspects of cultural competence, from governance and policy to management and service delivery concerns. In one agency, an assessment of cultural competence made explicit what had been obvious but unacknowledged: the agency's staff members were almost all white women, and the agency's client population had become increasingly diverse. Highly committed to being responsive to the community, the agency formed a diversity committee, chaired by the agency executive, to develop strategies for making the agency more diverse and culturally competent.

THE LEARNING ORGANIZATION

The concept of the learning organization was mentioned in Chapter 9, which ended with a broadening of focus from data to the use of knowledge. Although the learning organization has been connected to information systems by Poertner and Rapp (2007), who assert that "a learning organization takes periodic readings on its performance and makes adjustments so that performance is improved" (p. 191), our focus here is being broadened beyond client information systems to examine how the organization as a whole can engage in ongoing learning to improve its operation and effectiveness. This is an important principle for managers, whose job it is to help staff and the organization remain intently focused on the organization's purpose and objectives and on getting and using feedback to improve performance, make adjustments, and reward employees.

The term learning organization was first popularized in Senge's (2006) *The Fifth Discipline*. A similar term, *organizational learning*, has recently become even more common (Austin & Hopkins, 2004). Definitions of these terms and the distinctions between them are still evolving. In the simplest terms, a learning organization "is an organization that is 'skilled at creating, acquiring, and transferring knowledge, and at modifying its behavior to reflect new knowledge and insights'" (Garvin, quoted in Austin & Hopkins, 2004, p. 11); and organizational learning is "the process of improving actions through better knowledge and understanding" (Fiol & Lyles, quoted in Austin & Hopkins, 2004, p. 12). More specifically, organizational learning, according to Argyris and Schon (1996), "refers broadly to an organization's acquisition of understandings, know-how, techniques, and practices of any kind and by whatever means" (p. xxi). They also make a distinction between single-loop and double-loop learning, with the former involving relatively simple adaptations and changes and the latter requiring an examination of the underlying theory in use that determines why the organization acts as it does. For example, discovering that 275 sign-offs are necessary to approve an innovation and changing this procedure would involve single-loop learning, whereas examining how people in the organization allowed this situation to develop would involve double-loop learning (p. 21).

Regarding organizational performance, Poertner and Rapp (2007, pp. 191–197) assert that this kind of organizational learning requires an organizational culture that supports learning, managers with skills and knowledge about performance management, and an information system to provide data on performance.

According to DiBella and Nevis (1998):

> there are three essential criteria of organizational learning: First, new skills, attitudes, values, and behaviors are created or acquired over time.... Second, what is learned becomes the property of some collective unit.... Third, what is learned remains within the organization or group even if individuals leave. (pp. 25–26)

They suggest that organizational learning involves 10 factors or steps. First, information is gathered about conditions outside the work unit, followed by an assessment of the identified gap between current and desired performance. Discussion about how key factors are defined and measured ensues, followed by discussion of creative new ideas. The organization must foster a climate of open communication and provide resources necessary for continuous education. Members must be open to the consideration of new and different ideas and methods, and leaders need to be personally and actively involved in maintaining the learning environment. Finally, a systems perspective (Senge, 2006) is necessary to recognize interdependence among units. Systems thinking and organizational learning are complicated concepts. Senge and his colleagues at the Society for Organizational Learning offer a range of resources and publications through their website, which is included at the end of this chapter.

There have been some applications of organizational learning principles in the human services, with Austin & Hopkins (2004) reporting several.

Learning organization applications are likely to become more common in human service organizations, and managers should become aware of these ideas so that they can make thoughtful choices about attempting to use them and avoid incomplete or inadequate applications of a complex process.

We have now reviewed growth and development concerns and strategies at the individual, group, and organizational levels. One final developmental process remains for our consideration: the transition that a human service worker makes from direct service to management.

TRANSITIONING TO MANAGEMENT

As direct service workers face the challenge of management and the need to broaden their managerial knowledge and skills, they concomitantly become increasingly aware of the complexity of their organization and its environment. Ascending the agency hierarchy often reveals issues and dimensions of organizational life previously obscured at the worker level. The move from service provider to manager brings an expanded awareness of the constraints and contingencies facing the organization. The higher the ascent, the broader the view; the broader the view, the greater the responsibility for dealing with the issues relevant to that level of the organization's hierarchy.

Moving from human service direct practitioner to manager entails a number of challenges. Not only must the neophyte manager learn to master a new technology—the technology of managing human service programs—but the manager-cum-clinician must also direct his or her attention to a new client system—an organizational unit or program. Promotion also means, in most cases, the acquisition of positional authority and responsibilities much greater than those that devolve to the direct practitioner. If the manager is to be effective, he or she must develop skill in the use of newly acquired authority and power. Moreover, the manager must be able to exert expert power; that is, he or she must demonstrate to subordinates mastery of the technologies they employ. In addition, the manager is expected to embrace the agency's mission and goals and to represent administration in the implementation of policy formulated at the top.

Perlmutter and Crook (2004) note the importance of role changes that a worker promoted to management experiences: the direct service worker focuses on individual clients or client groups, whereas the perspective of the administrator gets broader at each level up the hierarchy. An important implication here is that a manager may have a more difficult time setting priorities, but also he or she has staff members to whom tasks may be delegated.

Another factor that changes with a rise in the hierarchy is the orientation toward time. Whereas a line worker is more concerned with the present, a manager must look further into the future, anticipating strategy implementation and budget expenditures. Many clinicians are trained as facilitators or enablers; administrators are expected to be more decisive in providing leadership and vision.

In a related vein, line workers may be less comfortable with or accustomed to using power to accomplish tasks. As we noted in Chapter 7, there are different types of power, and a wise administrator will become comfortable with and skilled in the use of power to advance the organization's mission.

A new supervisor will be able to move more easily into a managerial role by being aware of these changes in role expectations and perspectives. Managers moving up in the hierarchy need a broader array of conceptual skills (for analyzing the environment, assessing connections among systems, and so forth) and less knowledge in technical areas such as service delivery methods. People skills, of course, remain essential at all levels.

Perlmutter and Crook (2004) offer additional guidelines for those moving up beyond supervision into middle management. Upper management can augment the effectiveness of middle managers with an agency-wide management philosophy of empowerment (Cohen & Austin, 1997; see also the discussion of empowerment in Chapter 11). In an article regarding mental health professionals becoming managers that was originally published in 1980 and republished in 1999 because of its continuing relevance, Feldman (1999) discusses the conflicted feelings that human service managers often have about the use of power and related issues of clinician autonomy versus allegiance to the organization. He suggests that managers strive for the optimum amount of employee participation in decision making, being sensitive to both employee and organizational concerns.

Middle managers can also be helped through ongoing formal and informal organizational communication. Perlmutter suggests that monthly meetings with executive management, a suggestion box system to keep upper management informed of staff concerns, and management development seminars can all make managers more effective. At the personal level, a new middle manager should take advantage of management development opportunities such as external workshops and training. Formation of a network of peers to allow discussion of problems and offer support can help enhance skills and prevent burnout.

Mentoring, mentioned earlier, and networking (Kelly & Post, 1995) can be immensely helpful for both new and experienced managers. A formal mentoring program must include matching mentors and protégés, creating time for mentoring, evaluating the process, and, most important, sanction by the organization (Kelly & Post, 1995). Networking in an organizational setting, according to Kelly and Post (1995), is "a relationship between one individual and another individual, group, or organization that provides a reciprocal benefit in terms of information, advice, knowledge, or collaboration" (p. 156).

Key elements of either a mentoring or networking program are clarity of goals (such as reducing turnover, improving communications); clear roles for mentors, protégés, and supervisors; and an evaluation design. In the case of a mentor program, mentors need to be carefully selected, ensuring that they are not in the chain of command of their protégé. Mentoring and networking are particularly valuable for managers who are women or people of color—still underrepresented in the management ranks (Mor Barak, 2009). These two strategies can be of great value to individual managers and to the organization as a whole, as those managers are able to add more value to the organization through their increasing abilities.

Professional advancement in organizations provides not only challenges but anxieties as well. The better prepared the clinician is to accept these challenges, the more manageable the anxieties. Direct service workers who enter the ranks of management bring with them essential professional values and ethics and important knowledge of the realities of human service work, from which the organization can benefit as these new managers develop managerial skills.

THE NEED FOR MANAGERIAL EXCELLENCE

Given the turbulent environments in which most of today's human service organizations find themselves—environments characterized by competition, ambiguity, and uncertainty—one of the issues revealed to the manager in the move up the managerial tiers is that of organizational survival. Mandates for accountability, demands to do more with less, and shifting political and economic priorities all constitute additional challenges to managers of contemporary human service organizations.

Managerial excellence requires not only technical mastery of the functions of planning, designing, developing human resources, budgeting, supervising, and evaluating but also the ability to address the social, cultural, and political dimensions of management. This includes knowledge of and attention to the values, beliefs, customs, and traditions of the organization and its environment, including the organization's client system. Managerial excellence, therefore, requires both technical and sociopolitical acumen.

Managerial excellence involves an expanded conceptualization of the human service enterprise. It involves being able to conceive of the organization—the agency and its various levels and programs—not only as a rational, technical instrument designed to carry out certain functions. Involved as well is the ability to see the human service organization as an evolving, adapting response to social needs, as an institution "infused with values" symbolic of societal aspirations. Managerial excellence thus includes both technical competence and leadership competence.

This capacity is often illustrated by contrasting management and leadership. Management functions include processes from program design to evaluation, and including information systems, financial management, and human resources. Leadership focuses on vision, strategy, inspiring and empowering staff, and organizational change. The functions can be contrasted as shown here (Roberts-DeGennaro & Packard, 2002):

Management
- program design
- financial management
- information systems
- human resource management
- program evaluation
- project management

Leadership
- visioning
- change management
- strategy development
- organization design
- culture management
- community collaboration

Both sets of skills are essential, but education of administrators, including those in the human services, has traditionally focused more on management than on leadership. For that reason alone, leadership warrants increased emphasis today. Furthermore, the challenges facing organizations in the twenty-first century are more complex than those of the past, when management skills were adequate. It is now more important than ever that traditional management thinking not override the need for leadership.

It should be clear by now that effective leadership and management are central to organizational viability. Whereas organizational efficiency is more a function of technical competence, organizational effectiveness is more a function of leadership competence. The combination of both usually translates into managerial excellence. Leadership competence, a more elusive goal, is built on technological expertise but usually depends, in addition, on a variety of other attributes, including personal style and values, acquired knowledge and skills, and on-the-job experience.

Another challenge facing the human service manager is that posed by the philosophy, values, and ethics of that person's profession. For human service managers—most of whom share a humanistic, client-oriented philosophy based on such concepts as social justice, self-determination, the right to privacy, and the dignity and worth of all individuals—the challenge is to align organizational values and behavior with professional values and ethical dictates. Fortunately, most human service organizations are founded on the same service philosophies and values human service providers share. Unfortunately, not all organizations that espouse humanistic, client-centered philosophies and values always translate them into action, in terms of the treatment of either their staff or their clients. It is the obligation of the professional manager to steer organizational behavior in the direction of humanistic values, standards, and goals at all levels of the organization, but most certainly at the line operations level, where the functions of the organization and the needs of its clients converge.

12.1   GROWTH AND RENEWAL AT GRANDVIEW COMMUNITY CENTER

Leona Estrella's first year as executive of Grandview Community Center was both challenging and fulfilling. The agency had made great progress in launching a major new program and fixing some long-standing problems in organizational operations. As Leona and her executive team reflected on the past year, they felt some pride and relief but also exhaustion. They wished that they and the agency could "coast" for a while, but they knew that the coming year would present new challenges. Therefore, they thought it would be important to take stock of their current situation and do what they could to create ongoing mechanisms for professional and organizational growth and development.

They were able to secure a small grant from a local foundation, which also provided a consultant to work with the agency on continued capacity building. The consultant arranged to facilitate a 360-degree feedback process for all of the executive team. Based on the results of the individual feedback sessions, the foundation would let the managers participate in an ongoing leadership development process offered to local community agencies.

After this leadership development process had been put in motion, they decided that they could do an agency-wide employee survey and have the consultant help them complete a management audit to identify new opportunities for growth. They expected that regardless of the findings from the survey and audit, they should develop their skills in creating ongoing organizational learning processes so the agency and staff members could continue to grow and thrive. They recognized that this would be extra work in the short run; but they believed that in the long run the agency would be even more successful, and would be a more fulfilling and satisfying place to work.

SUMMARY

Organizational excellence in the human services is more than a function of an efficient managerial technology; it is a function of several variables in synergistic interaction. One of those variables is the quality of the managerial leadership of the organization. Another is the nature of the organization itself—not just its structure and the sophistication of its direct service technology but also its culture and commitment to service effectiveness.

A third variable is the organization's environment and its legitimization and support of agency values and goals, as well as its provision of material resources that enable the organization to achieve service effectiveness. Although other variables influence organizational achievement, these are three of the most critical ones.

The administrator, the agency, and the environment constitute an interactive and interdependent triad. When they share the same values and aspire to the same goals, and when these values and goals center on the true needs of clients, the job of the managerial leader is facilitated and the results are gratifying. Disagreement and conflict over values and goals will create challenges that the administrator will need to address.

Managerial competence is a necessary but not sufficient condition for organizational survival and excellence. Without economic, social, and political support from the environment, the manager of a human service program, no matter how knowledgeable or skilled, will find it difficult to achieve organizational effectiveness. The human service manager's job must therefore include attention to these larger issues. In the political and economic climate of 2011 and for the near future, funding and policy challenges are likely to continue to be daunting, but human services administrators should continually advocate for changes in social policy to ensure high-quality services for all in need, particularly those disadvantaged by poverty, racism, or other forms of oppression.

The shift from direct practice to administration by professionals in the human services should be made in full awareness of the challenges and demands associated with the new role. Today's managerial leaders in the human services need not only the technical knowledge and skills related to managerial efficiency but also the sociopolitical talents associated with effective leadership. The responsibilities are great, and so are the rewards.

Pioneer social work administrator Mary Parker Follett described the challenge of integrating professional values, ethics, and standards with the expectations of the organization in these words, written in 1925:

> What I am emphasizing here is that in the profession it is recognized that one's professional honour demands that one shall make this integration.... When, therefore, I say that members of a profession feel a greater loyalty to their profession than to the company, I do not mean that their loyalty is to one group of persons rather than to another; but that their loyalty is to a body of principles, of ideals; that is, to a special body of knowledge of proved facts

> and the standards arising therefrom. What, then, are we loyal to? To the soul of our work. To that which is both in our work and which transcends our work. (cited in Graham, 1995, pp. 272–273)

Human service managers face profound challenges. First, we must do all we can to identify service delivery technologies with proven effectiveness and learn as much as we can about the organizational conditions under which staff can be effective in addressing the social problems and needs that shape our agencies' purposes. We must advocate for social policies that enable these methods to be effectively deployed, and we must effectively and efficiently operate our programs with managerial skill and leadership élan. We must remain true to our professional values and be responsible stewards of the resources entrusted to our agencies. We must make difficult decisions and always treat our staffs with respect.

We fervently hope that some of today's students and line workers as well as newly promoted managers will become excellent human service organization managers and leaders of the future. We hope that current managers will continue to enhance their skills and retain the professional commitments and passions that brought them into the human services. We hope that human service management educators will recognize the current and evolving realities of organizational life and continue to provide students with the cutting-edge knowledge and skills they will need to become managers and remain lifelong learners.

The challenges and opportunities ahead will continue to be massive and unprecedented, and it will take great talent, skill, and commitment to respond effectively. Managers will need simultaneously to enhance their own skills and quality of working life as well as those of their staffs and to both maintain and increase the effectiveness and responsiveness of their agencies. We hope that these skilled managers and leaders can maintain their visions, optimism, and energy under challenging circumstances, to lead fulfilling lives, and to help their staffs, clients, and communities do so as well.

| COMPETENCY-BUILDING ACTIVITY 12.1 | ORGANIZATIONAL EXCELLENCE |

Reflect once again on your hypothetical program. Assume that even though it is a new program that has now been operating for a few months, it is part of a much larger agency that has been in existence for 30 years. What challenges do you think this new program, and other programs and administration of the agency, may be facing in order to stay vibrant and current with changes in the environment and best practices in the field? Given your experiences with similar agencies, if this agency completed a management audit such as the one in the Appendix, what opportunities for improvement may become evident? What development, growth, or training activities may be helpful to the organization?

| CASE ACTIVITY 12.1 | DEINSTITUTIONALIZATION |

For several decades, an important force in mental health programs has been "deinstitutionalization." Many people who were formerly patients in large state hospitals have been transferred to smaller, community-based facilities.

Window on the World (WOW) is one of the new agencies that arose in response to deinstitutionalization efforts. It was designed to act as a halfway house for people recently released from the nearby state hospital. Although the funding for WOW comes from a number of sources, the primary source involves third-party payments from the state vocational rehabilitation agency and the state and local departments of social service. Essentially, these agencies pay room, board, and fees on behalf of the clients they place in the halfway house.

The WOW facility is clean and well kept. Staff members have real concern for the clients, and efforts are made to keep the surroundings comfortable. Yet some of the staff members have begun to question the treatment plans for individual patients.

In one such recent situation, John Billings, a staff member, asked to see Harmon Fisk, the executive director, about one of the patients.

"I'd like to talk to you about Gail Drew," he began. "I'm positive she's ready to get on her feet and start moving. If we could just cut back on her medication, I think we might really see an improvement in this case. She might even be ready to be placed in a part-time training program and come back here in the evenings. Maybe nothing really major at first, but if we could just give her a chance, just give it a try."

"Just what do you want me to do, John?"

"Well, I thought you might be able to check with Dr. Freund about whether he could change her medication. You know, the stuff she's taking now is keeping her kind of knocked out, and...."

"Look, John. Carl Freund has been the consulting psychiatrist here since the word go. You come in here with a fresh master's degree and want to tell him his business. Don't you think he knows what he's doing?"

"It's not that, Mr. Fisk. Of course I think he knows what he's doing. I'm just saying that I'm seeing a subtle change in this one patient, and I think she's ready to move toward a less sheltered existence. We won't know that unless we cut down on her medication. We can always change it back again if it doesn't work out. What have we got to lose?"

"I'll tell you what we've got to lose. We've got Gail Drew's fees to lose. She's a Social Service patient. They pay her way. But they pay her way only when she's incapacitated. If she's on her feet and out there being trained, the fees are cut to a quarter of what they are now, and we can't support her on that. And if she's out there working, her fees are cut to nothing. She can't support herself on that. Now, what do you want me to do? Put this woman out there on her own in the cold? On your say-so?"

"Wait ... wait a minute, Mr. Fisk. We can't just keep someone doped up because that's the only way we can make money off her."

"No, now just you wait a minute. For one thing, you sound plenty noble, but I don't see you turning down your paycheck on Fridays. Where do you think that money comes from?"

"I know, but...."

"I didn't make this system. If you don't like the way it works, talk to the government. The thing is, I don't like seeing a patient like that lying around all day any more than you do. But believe me, we wouldn't be doing her any favor cutting off her medication, getting her out there on the streets with her hopes up, and then having her lose the support that she's got. Face it. These people are chronic. They're not going anyplace. But at least here it's clean, it's comfortable. They've got a roof over their heads, and they're not piled one on top of another in an institution like they were monkeys in a cage."

"But Mr. Fisk, Gail Drew should have a chance...."

"Have a chance for what? To starve out there on her own? Look, we need fees to run this agency. If we don't get the fees, we don't get to exist. Then what

happens to Gail Drew and to the rest of the patients we've got in those beds upstairs? You think our going under is going to do them any good? Where do you think they'll go except back to State, where they came from?"

1. What ethical considerations exist in this case? How would you address them?
2. Are there ways that differing funding patterns might be developed to make deinstitutionalization work more effectively?
3. If you were John Billings, what would you do now?
4. If you were Harmon Fisk, the director, would you be able to come up with any better answers?
5. Are there insurmountable differences between human service professionals and managers?

CASE ACTIVITY 12.2 | COMMUNITY ACTION AND MENTAL HEALTH

The Community Action Coalition (C.A.C.) had occupied the same storefront setting for more than 10 years, but the times had changed. From a small group of neighbors, shop owners, and church groups that had joined to fight successfully against the potential encroachment of a superhighway through their neighborhood, the C.A.C. had grown into a major community organization. Block clubs and community interest groups still formed the backbone of the organization, but a variety of programs, services, and agencies had spun off from the original system. The C.A.C.'s attempts to enhance the lifestyle of community members had resulted in the development of programs to fight substandard housing and schools, encourage consumer awareness, provide recreational and training programs for youth, and bring thriving businesses into the area.

Throughout the years, however, the C.A.C. had maintained its little office in the heart of the neighborhood. And throughout the years, the same thing had happened again and again. When citizens of the community were faced with family problems, with concerns about their children, with crises in their own lives, the C.A.C. was the only place that attracted them. Although a community mental health center

was based in a hospital in the immediate area, and although a branch of the Department of Social Services had been built just two blocks away, these institutions were underutilized as self-referral agencies. Going to the community mental health center meant that one was sick. Going to the C.A.C. meant simply that one was having a problem in everyday living.

The staff of the coalition's storefront office welcomed the chance to try to have some effect on their neighbors' personal lives. Sometimes troubled individuals just needed someone to listen; sometimes they needed the kind of advocacy or linkage with sources of help that the organization was best at. There were times, however, when staff members felt inadequate to deal with the problems they were facing, times when they felt that at least one professional mental health worker should be present to provide training and supervision as well as direct therapy. The need for this kind of program became so obvious that the staff members decided to apply for a grant for seed money to get their new program started. They simply needed a way to begin to implement a more organized approach to mental health, one that would involve keeping the office open through the evening hours, with volunteers providing help under the supervision of professional mental health personnel. The funds would provide for training, for a portion of the salaries of the trainer/supervisors, and for materials needed for the immediate future. Later, they felt, the organization would be able to support the new program on its own.

They did make a good case for the need and for the concept. The foundation to which they applied for funding agreed to visit the community to learn more about the proposed program and about the community itself. The organization, accustomed to this kind of site visit, geared up by preparing materials, planning a presentation, and inviting a number of community members to present their views on the day of the visit.

The day arrived and the presentation began as scheduled. The staff members who had written the grant proposal felt increasingly optimistic about their chances for funding as more and more citizens rose to express their support. Suddenly, however, a man none of them knew rose to speak.

"I've come to represent the community mental health center that serves this catchment area," he said. "As much as we have appreciated the fine organizing work of the C.A.C. over the years, we reluctantly have to tell you that the service they are suggesting would be inappropriate for such a nonprofessional agency. It certainly would be a duplication of the services we are presently offering with the highest level of professional staff."

"Yes," answered the foundation representative. "We did get the letter of protest from your board of directors. It does seem as though some kind of liaison needs to take place here."

After a moment of stunned silence, pandemonium broke out in the room, as the anger of community members who disapproved of the mental health center's approach rose to the surface. Amid the shouts, one thing became clear. The Community Action Coalition would not be receiving funding to meet the mental health needs of its members.

1. How could this confrontation have been avoided?
2. What could C.A.C.'s leaders have done to prepare a better plan for mental health services?
3. What could staff of the community mental health center have done to represent their views on service needs in a more collaborative way?
4. The two agencies involved in the situation seem to have differing views concerning local needs. Does this mean that their assessments were inaccurate, or is there some other possible explanation?
5. If you were a member of the staff of the Community Action Coalition, what steps might you take now to salvage the planning and implementation process?

REFERENCES

Allison, M., & Kaye, J. (2005). *Strategic planning for non-profit organizations* (2nd ed.). New York: Wiley.

Argyris, C., & Schon, D. (1996). *Organizational learning II: Theory, method, and practice.* Reading, MA: Addison-Wesley.

Austin, M., & Hopkins, K. (2004). Defining the learning organization. In M. Austin & K. Hopkins (Eds.), *Supervision as collaboration in the human services: Building a learning culture.* Thousand Oaks, CA: Sage.

Buckingham, M., & Clifton, D. (2001). *Now, discover your strengths.* New York: Free Press.

Cohen, B., & Austin, M. (1997). Transforming human services organizations through empowerment of staff. *Journal of Community Practice, 4*(2), 35–50.

Coloma, J., Gibson, C., & Packard, T. (2011, in press) Participant outcomes of a leadership development initiative in eight human service organizations, *Administration in Social Work, 35*(5).

DiBella, A., & Nevis, E. (1998). *How organizations learn.* San Francisco: Jossey-Bass.

Dyer, W. (1995). *Team building.* Reading, MA: Addison-Wesley.

Graham, P. (Ed.). (1995). *Mary Parker Follett: Prophet of management.* Boston: Harvard Business School Press.

Hernez-Broome, G., & Hughes, R. (2004). Leadership development: Past, resent, and future, *Human Resource Planning, 27*(1), 24–32.

Hirsh, S., & Kummerow, J. (1998). *Introduction to type in organizations.* Mountain View, CA: CPP.

Johnson, D., & Johnson, F. (2009). *Joining together: Group theory and group skills* (10th ed.). Boston: Allyn & Bacon.

Kelly, M., & Post, K. (1995). Mentoring and networking in human services. In L. Ginsberg & P. Keys (Eds.), *New management in human services* (2nd ed., pp. 151–161). Washington, DC: NASW Press.

McCauley, C. (2008). Leader Development: A Review of Research. Retrieved September 11, 2009 from http://www.shrm.org/about/foundation/research/Documents/McCauley-%20Leader%20Dev%20Lit%20Review.doc

Menefee, D. (2009). What managers do and why they do it. In R. Patti (Ed.), *The handbook of human services management* (pp. 101–116). Thousand Oaks, CA: Sage.

Mor Barak, M. (2009). Social psychological perspectives of workforce diversity and inclusion in national and global contexts. In R. Patti (Ed.), *The handbook of human services management* (pp. 239–254). Thousand Oaks, CA: Sage.

National Center for Cultural Competence Self Assessments. http://www11.georgetown.edu/research/gucchd/nccc/resources/assessments.html

Packard, T. (2000). The management audit as a teaching tool in social work administration. *Journal of Social Work Education*, 36(1), 39–52.

Perlmutter, F., & Crook, W. (2004). *Changing hats while managing change: From social work practice to administration* (2nd ed.). Washington, DC: NASW Press.

Poertner, J., & Rapp, C. (2007). *Textbook of social administration: The consumer-centered approach.* New York: The Haworth Press.

Roberts-DeGennaro, M., & Packard, T. (2002). Framework for developing a social administration concentration. *Journal of Teaching in Social Work*, 22(1/2), 61–77.

Robertson, R. (2010). 360-degree feedback: Integrating business know-how with social work values, *Administration in social work*, 34(3), 259–274.

Senge, P. (2006). *The fifth discipline: The art and practice of the learning organization* (Rev. ed.). New York: Doubleday Currency.

Van Velsor, E., McCauley, C., & Ruderman, M. (Eds.). (2010). *The center for creative leadership handbook of leadership development* (3rd ed.). San Francisco: Jossey-Bass.

Vinokur-Kaplan, D., & Miller, P. (2004). When community mental health meets managed care. In D. Fauri, S. Wernet, & F. Netting (Eds.), *Cases in macro social work practice* (2nd ed., pp. 171–184). Boston: Pearson Education.

USEFUL WEB RESOURCES

Alliance for Nonprofit Management. http://www.allianceonline.org/.

Child Welfare League of America. http://www.cwla.org/.

Free Management Library. http://www.managementhelp.org/np_progs/org_dev.htm.

Leader to Leader Institute. http://leadertoleader.org/.

National Network for Social Work Managers. http://www.socialworkmanager.org/.

Society for Organizational Learning. http://www.solonline.org/.

MANAGEMENT AUDIT

Indicate the degree to which each factor is present in your organization. Use a rating of "4" if all aspects are fully present with positive effect; use a "1" when the factor is absent or not at all effective; use a "2" or "3" to reflect relative amounts of the factor being present/effective or problematic.

Planning

1. _____ The organization has a clearly defined mission that is well known, well understood, and well accepted by staff.

2. _____ The organization has and uses a current and relevant strategic plan.

3. _____ There is a written annual operational plan that includes timelines and identification of responsible persons for all outcomes and activities.

4. _____ The strategies, goals, and objectives of the organization are based on the mission.

5. _____ The goals and objectives are complete and clear.

6. _____ The objectives reflect measurable client benefits and other outcomes.

7. _____ The plans of the organization are used on a regular basis.

Management of the Environment

8. _____ The problems or needs the organization is intended to address are clearly identified and documented.

9. _____ The target populations (e.g., demographics, geographic boundaries) the organization is intended to serve are clearly identified and documented.

10. _____ Key stakeholders (funders, other agencies, regulators) are satisfied with the organization's programs and services.

Client Relations

11. _____ Clients' perceptions of their needs are clearly known by the organization.

12. _____ Clients are satisfied with the services as delivered by the organization.

13. _____ Policies and procedures regarding confidentiality and reporting requirements (e.g., abuse, dangers posed by clients) are compliant with laws and clear to clients and staff.

Program Design/Technology

14. _____ Service delivery technologies are appropriate to the achievement of the mission, strategies, and objectives.

15. _____ All services use explicit logic models of cause and effect, which are based on evidence-based practices.

16. _____ Each service is effective in accomplishing its stated goals and objectives.

17. _____ There are clear program standards that describe the quality and types of services delivered.

18. _____ The organization specifies objectives and outcomes for each client.

Structure and Design

19. _____ All staff members' roles and performance expectations are clear and agreed to.

20. _____ The organizational structure and reporting relationships are clear to all.

21. _____ The organization has clear, written policies and procedures that are consistent with the mission and goals and that drive expected behavior.

22. _____ The organization's structure is clearly aligned with strategy.

23. _____ The organization's structure is flexible and minimally bureaucratic.

24. _____ The organization's structure facilitates cross-function communication, coordination, collaboration, teamwork, and support.

25. _____ The organization has communication mechanisms to keep all staff informed about current and anticipated activities or developments.

26. _____ Decision-making processes support decision implementation and include clarity regarding who has input and who has responsibility for making decisions.

27. _____ Decision making is appropriately decentralized to lower-level staff.

Management Information Systems

28. _____ The organization has a computerized client data collection and processing system for demographic, services, and outcome data.

29. _____ The information system can identify and aggregate client outcome data (effectiveness).

30. _____ The information system can measure cost effectiveness.

31. _____ The information system has clearly defined units of service that can be used to measure the types and amounts of services provided and their unit costs (efficiency).

32. _____ There are clear performance standards for which aggregated client data are used in ongoing service monitoring and feedback.

Budget and Financial Management

33. _____ All programs and cost centers have clearly defined budgets, and administrative costs are an appropriate percentage of the overall budget.

34. _____ A budgeting process is in place that ensures the effective allocation of resources.

35. _____ A realistic short-term and long-term fund development or budget management program is in place.

36. _____ Financial reports provide managers with complete, accurate, and timely information.

37. _____ Expenditures consistently match program budgets and actual income.

38. _____ An external audit been conducted within the last year, results have been shared, and identified problems have been corrected.

39. _____ Administration and program budgets are clearly aligned with strategies and objectives.

Staffing and Human Resources Management

40. _____ All staff are fully trained and qualified to perform their duties.

41. _____ All staff are fully oriented upon hiring and are regularly supervised.

42. _____ There are appropriate and adequate staff development opportunities for staff.

43. _____ The organization recruits and selects staff whose professional ideology and training are compatible with the mission and values of the organization.

44. _____ The organization has a formal performance appraisal system that is appropriate and regularly used.

45. _____ There are appropriate rewards and recognition for all personnel.

46. _____ Comprehensive personnel policies and procedures are in compliance with relevant employment laws, regulations, and industry standards.

Leadership and Ethics

47. _____ Leaders help develop and articulate an inspiring and shared vision, purpose, and mission that drives strategy and programs for the organization.

48. _____ The organization has clearly defined values that are well known, well understood, and well accepted by staff.

49. _____ Leaders project a positive attitude (e.g., trust and respect) toward staff.

50. _____ Leaders in the organization use appropriate management styles that support and motivate staff to achieve high performance.

51. _____ Leaders clearly articulate high ethical standards and ensure that they are maintained.

52. _____ The organization has clearly identified standards and procedures for addressing key ethical issues including confidentiality, client self-determination, respect of clients' social and cultural norms, and protecting clients from harm.

Organizational Culture and Change

53. _____ Managers create an organizational culture conducive to organizational effectiveness.

54. _____ Managers pay attention to informal group and organizational processes that affect the organization's operations.

55. _____ People feel free to express unusual or unpopular views without fear of personal attack or criticism.

56. _____ There are opportunities for staff to discuss what changes should be made to improve organizational operations or processes.

57. _____ The organization's mechanisms and processes for organizational change are known by and used by staff.

58. _____ Staff feel empowered to take initiative, be creative, and solve problems.

59. _____ Team spirit within and among departments is encouraged and supported.

Program Evaluation

60. _____ The impact of programs compared to the need for programs (program adequacy) is evaluated.

61. _____ The organization gathers data from consumers to assess satisfaction and the long-term effects of the services.

62. _____ Each program is formally evaluated regarding effectiveness and efficiency on a regular basis.

63. _____ Data and the results of program evaluations are used to make changes.

64. _____ All relevant accreditation, licensing, or regulatory standards are met.

Quality of Working Life

65. _____ Salaries provide adequate and fair compensation.

66. _____ The organization provides safe and healthy working conditions.

67. _____ The organization provides adequate and appropriate work areas and necessary supplies and equipment for all staff.

68. _____ The organization allows for individual worker autonomy.

69. _____ Jobs permit the learning and exercise of a wide range of skills and abilities.

70. _____ Job assignments contribute to employees expanding their capabilities.

71. _____ The organization provides upward mobility.

72. _____ The work environment provides supportive groups.

73. _____ The organization possesses a sense of community that extends beyond face-to-face work groups.

74. _____ The organization allows for free speech and provides the right to personal privacy.

75. _____ The organization provides procedures for due process and access to appeals.

76. _____ The organization provides equitable treatment in all matters.

77. _____ The demands made by the organization allow for a balanced role of work that allows the worker to have leisure and family time on a regular basis.

Diversity and Cultural Competence

78. _____ Organizational environment: visual representations, policies, vision and mission statements, language training, and accessibility demonstrate the valuing of diversity.

79. _____ Community relations: Board membership, informational materials, special events, and community partnerships show that diversity is valued.

80. _____ Human resources: Diversity and cultural competence training is offered regularly, staff are culturally appropriate and competent to work with communities served, and policies (e.g., bilingual pay) are regularly assessed and revised for cultural competence.

81. _____ Service delivery: written materials are screened for cultural appropriateness, culture and other relevant variables are analyzed and used in services planning and design, and services are tailored to population groups served.

82. _____ Policies and procedures are fully compliant with all laws and regulations related to equal opportunities and disability issues, and staff are aware of these policies and procedures.

Risk Management

83. _____ The agency is fully compliant with laws, regulations, and industry standards regarding insurance and liability related to staff, clients, volunteers, and facilities.

84. _____ Records management procedures are compliant with relevant laws, regulations, and standards including confidentiality and backup capability.

85. _____ Policies and procedures are in effect to prevent and deal with workplace hazards including safety, crises such as client violence, OSHA criteria, and ergonomics.

86. _____ The organization has a disaster management plan that outlines staff and the organization's responses to disasters to ensure staff and client safety and services to the community; staff are aware of the plan and adequately trained to implement it.

Governance and Accountability

87. _____ The organization's governance structure (e.g., board) and systems are clearly defined and in compliance with relevant laws.

88. _____ The governance system provides appropriate oversight of the chief executive, finances, and operations.

89. _____ Organizational systems enable fulfillment of all of the organization's grant and contract requirements.

Items are adapted from:

Allison, M., & Kaye, J. (2005). *Strategic planning for nonprofit organizations* (2nd ed.). New York: John Wiley & Sons.

Daft, R. (2010). *Organization theory and design* (10th ed.). Mason, OH: South-Western Cengage Learning.

Jones, J. (1981). *Principles of organizational structure.* San Diego, CA.

Kettner, P., Moroney, R., & Martin, L. (2008). Designing *and managing programs* (3rd ed.). Thousand Oaks, CA: Sage.

Kurzman, P. (2006). Managing Risk in Nonprofit Settings. In R. Edwards & J. Yankey (Eds.), *Effectively managing nonprofit organizations* (pp. 275–290). Washington, DC: NASW Press.

La Frontera, Inc. (N.D.). *Building bridges: Tools for developing an organization's cultural competence.* Tucson: La Frontera, Inc.

Martin, L. (2001). *Financial management for human service administrators.* Boston: Allyn & Bacon.

Sugarman, B. (1988). The well-managed human service organization: Criteria for a management audit. *Administration in social work,* 12(4), 17–27.

Walton, R. (1975). Criteria for quality of working life. In L. Davis & A. Cherns (Eds.), *The quality of working life: Volume 1: Problems, prospects, and the state of the art* (pp. 91–118). New York: The Free Press.

Name Index

SUBJECT INDEX